T0308224

Also by Alistair Shearer

Effortless Being (photographs by Richard Lannoy) (Wildwood House)

The Upanishads (with Peter Russell; photographs by Richard Lannoy) (Wildwood House)

The Traveller's Key to Northern India (Alfred A. Knopf)

Thailand: The Lotus Kingdom (John Murray)

The Hindu Vision: Forms of the Formless (Thames & Hudson)

Buddha: The Intelligent Heart (Thames & Hudson)

Selections from the Upanishads (Bell Tower)

The Spirit of Asia (photographs by Michael Freeman) (Thames & Hudson)

India: Land of Living Traditions (photographs by Michael Freeman) (Periplus Editions)

The Yoga Sutras of Patanjali (Bell Tower)

Views from an Indian Bus (Trishula)

In the Light of the Self: Adi Shankara and the Yoga of Nondualism (White Crow)

THE STORY OF YOGA

ALISTAIR SHEARER

The Story of Yoga

From Ancient India to the Modern West

HURST & COMPANY, LONDON

First published in the United Kingdom in 2020 by
C. Hurst & Co. (Publishers) Ltd.,
41 Great Russell Street, London, WC1B 3PL
© Alistair Shearer, 2020
All rights reserved.

The right of Alistair Shearer to be identified as the author of
this publication is asserted by him in accordance with the
Copyright, Designs and Patents Act, 1988.

Distributed in the United States, Canada and Latin America by
Oxford University Press, 198 Madison Avenue, New York, NY 10016,
United States of America.

A Cataloguing-in-Publication data record for this book
is available from the British Library.

ISBN: 9781787381926

This book is printed using paper from registered sustainable
and managed sources.

www.hurstpublishers.com

Epigraph accreditations:
Yoga Sutra of Patanjali (1.13–1.16). Translation by Alistair Shearer 2019

'Bagpipe Music' by Louis MacNeice.
(© Estate of Louis MacNeice, reprinted by permission of David Higham)

Printed and bound in Great Britain by Bell & Bain Ltd, Glasgow

CONTENTS

CONTENTS

CHANGIN' TIMES

PART TWO: TODAY

PHYSICAL LIMITS

GOING WITHIN

CONTEMPORARY CAUTIONS

LOOKING AHEAD

The practice of yoga is the commitment to become established in the state of freedom. This practice will be firmly rooted when it is maintained consistently and with dedication over a long period of time. Freedom is that triumphant state of consciousness which resides beyond the influence of desire, when the mind ceases to thirst for anything it has seen or heard about, even what is promised in the scriptures. And supreme freedom is that complete liberation from the world of change which results from becoming the absolute Self.

From the Yoga Sutra of Patanjali (1.13–1.16)

'It's no go the Yogi-Man, it's no go Blavatsky,
All we want is a bank balance and a bit of skirt in a taxi.'

From 'Bagpipe Music' by Louis MacNeice

LIST OF ILLUSTRATIONS

1. Forest yogis, sandstone panel from Sanchi, first century BC. Author's collection.
2. Yogi with disciples and attendants; Lakshmana Temple, Khajuraho, tenth century. Author's collection.
3. Yoga pose from Achyutaraya temple, Hampi, fifteenth century. Sarah Welch via Wikimedia Commons, licensed under Creative Commons Attribution-Share Alike (CC BY-SA 4.0).
4. Indians performing yoga *asanas* under a Banyan tree in Seurat, 1688. Illustration from Jean-Baptiste Tavernier's *Collections of Travels Through Turkey into Persia and the East-Indies*. William Andrews Clark Memorial Library, UCLA, via Wikimedia Commons, public domain.
5. Shiva in eight yogic postures, with his trident, late eighteenth century. © Victoria and Albert Museum, London.
6. A prince and attendants visiting a noble *yogini* at an ashram, India, c. 1765. © Victoria and Albert Museum, London.
7. Lithograph showing three types of *pranayama*: *puraka*, *kumbhaka* and *rechaka*, 1851. Wikimedia Commons, public domain.
8. Lord Krishna instructs the warrior Arjuna in the *Bhagavad Gita*, c. 1820. Edwin Binney 3rd Collection, Accession Number: 1990.1251, via Wikimedia Commons, public domain.
9. Five *brahmin* priests, five kings and a deity, participate in a *yajna* fire offering to win the blessings of the gods. Gouache painting by an Indian artist, nineteenth century. Wellcome Collection, licensed under Creative Commons Attribution (CC BY 4.0).
10. An illustration of the *ankushasana*, the 'elephant goad' pose (now usually known as the *bhairavasana*, 'formidable' pose), from the mid-nineteenth-century *Shritattvanidhi*. Wikimedia Commons, public domain.
11. Raja Ram Mohan Roy, founder of the Brahmo Samaj and leading light of the Hindu Renaissance, in 1868. Wikimedia Commons, public domain.
12. Swami Vivekananda in September 1893. On the left, written in his own

LIST OF ILLUSTRATIONS

International Yoga Day in New Delhi, 21 June 2015. Government of India via Wikimedia Commons, licensed under the National Data Sharing and Accessibility Policy of Government of India.

ACKNOWLEDGEMENTS

Thanks are due to several friends. Firstly, my informal team of researchers, who keep their eyes open for snippets about India and things Indian I would otherwise miss: Suradeva Evenson, James Gibson, Jack McTigue, Tom Priestley and Alan Shrimpton. Thanks also to Frederick Smith of the University of Iowa, who made encouraging comments on an early draft of the book, and to Anne Clark, Bernadette Haley and Maidy Clark, who gave useful feedback on the text. Finally, many thanks to my old friend Toinette Lippe, writer, painter and publisher of wise books, who took the trouble to go through the manuscript at a time when she herself was under considerable pressure.

GLOSSARY

Advaita	'non-dualism', the perception of the world as a manifestation of the one, supreme Consciousness. *Advaitin* perspectives are found in many Hindu and Buddhist schools, but it is usually associated with the teachings of Adi Shankara, an eighth-century south Indian teacher and textual commentator. See *Vedanta* below.
Asana	'seat' or 'throne'; the general term for a posture in body-yoga. The third of Patanjali's 'Eight Limbs of Yoga'.
Bahiranga	the external aspects of yoga as contrasted to the *antaranga*, or internal, aspects of the practice.
Bandha	an 'energy lock' practised particularly in *hatha yoga*, to gain control over the flow of *prana* (qv). The three major *bandhas* are *mula* (contracting the pelvic floor), *uddiyana* (drawing in the abdomen) and *jalandhara* (blocking off the throat).
Brahmacharya	literally 'devotion to the Absolute', but usually taken to mean celibacy.
Chakra	a 'wheel', or 'node', of energy in the subtle body.
Darshan	(a) 'seeing', 'sighting': the experience of being in the presence of a saint or a great being; (b) 'perspective', 'point of view': used to describe a philosophical system, especially one of the six orthodox Hindu philosophies.
Dharana	focusing the attention in meditation. The sixth of Patanjali's 'Eight Limbs of Yoga'.
Dhyana	the moving inwards of the attention in meditation. The penultimate of Patanjali's 'Eight Limbs of Yoga'.
Durbar	a Persian-derived word, used in India, meaning a royal court or a formal meeting where the king held discussions on matters of state.
Dvaita	'dualism'; religious and philosophical systems, such as

GLOSSARY

	Jainism, Theravada Buddhism and Sankhya, that teach the eternal separation of spirit and matter.
Guna	'strand'. In Sankhya philosophy there are three of these which, in various combinations, make up the relative worlds of time, space and causation. They are: *rajas* (motion, energy), *tamas* (mass, inertia) and *sattva* (light, purity). The aim of yoga is to temper and balance the first two *gunas* and bring about the predominance of the third.
Hatha yoga	originally a rigorous system of purifying the gross and subtle bodies; nowadays often used as a general term for body-yoga.
Kaivalya	'aloneness'; the state of transcendence as the goal of Patanjali's *Yoga Sutra*.
Kali yuga	the fourth and last of the great cyclical ages of humanity (*yugas*); a time of ignorance and suffering that precedes the next Golden Age or Sat Yuga.
Kriya	'action'; a specific cleansing procedure in *hatha yoga*. Often grouped collectively as the *Shatkriyas* or *Shatkarmas*, i.e. 'the six (purifying) actions'.
Kundalini	'the coiled one'; the evolutionary energy latent in human beings, which is enlivened through yoga.
Linga (or sukshma) sharira	the 'subtle body', i.e. a second, or aerial, nervous system made of very fine matter which is imperceptible to science but can be enlivened and experienced subjectively. Purification of this body, which is intermediate between conventional concepts of body and mind, is the aim of yogic praxis.
Mudra	'seal' or 'mark', a symbolic gesture often practised with the hands and fingers, to direct the flow of *prana* (qv).
Parampara	the lineage of authoritative teaching passed down from master to disciple.
Prakriti	the 'primary nature', or causal energy of all matter, in contradistinction to *purusha* (qv). The term is also found in Jain and Buddhist teachings as well as yoga.
Prana	subtle life energy, similar to the ancient Greek concept of *pneuma* and the Chinese *qi*.
Pranayama	'the extension of the subtle life energy'; the general term for breathing exercises in body-yoga. The fourth of Patanjali's 'Eight Limbs of Yoga'.

GLOSSARY

Pratyahara	'towards/away from (*prati*) food (*ahara*)'; withdrawal of the attention from gross sensory impressions, allowing the awareness to move to more charming fields within. The fifth of Patanjali's 'Eight Limbs of Yoga'.
Purusha	'the Person' or transpersonal Self, as the ultimate principle, or unbounded spirit, eternally separate from the worlds of matter. The term is used from the Upanishads onwards, and, through *Sankhya* (qv) is essential to the philosophy of classical yoga.
Samadhi	'coming together' or 'coherence'; the general term for progressive levels of deep absorption in meditation. The last of Patanjali's 'Eight Limbs of Yoga'.
Sankhya	'enumeration', one of the six classical philosophical schools (*shad darshana*) in orthodox Hinduism. It forms the basis of yoga theory.
Sannyasin	a Hindu renunciate or religious mendicant.
Siddha	enlightened master.
Sthula sharira	the 'gross body', or quantifiable physical anatomy.
Tapas	literally 'heat'; a traditional word for spiritual austerities.
Turiya	'the fourth'; described in the Upanishads as being pure Being, beyond the changeable waking, dreaming and sleeping states of consciousness.
Upanishads	'a settling down near'; metaphysical portions of the Vedic scriptures, dating from about 600 BC.
Vairagya	the yogic virtue of dispassion.
Veda	'knowledge'; the root scriptures for orthodox Hindus.
Vedanta	the monistic 'fruition of the Veda', one of the six philosophical viewpoints in orthodox Hinduism.
Vinyasa	sequential movements in some systems of body-yoga.
Yamas and *niyamas*	regulations of behaviour. Respectively, the first and second of Patanjali's 'Eight Limbs of Yoga'.
Yoga	'union'; typically understood as the union of the individual awareness with the universal Consciousness.

INTRODUCTION

This is not a 'how to' book—there are already more than enough of those—but a 'how come?' one. How come a time-honoured road to enlightenment has turned into a $25 billion-a-year wellness industry? What were the historical twists and social turns on the winding path that led from the caves and forests of ancient India to the gyms, studios and village halls of the modern West? What have the original teachings of the sages lost, or perhaps gained, while being transplanted onto foreign soil? And how is it that there are so many very different forms of yoga, which between them seem to include everything from muscles to mindfulness, stress-busting to spiritual liberation? This book is in part an attempt to define what this thing we call 'yoga' really is.

Whatever the answer, yoga in some form is everywhere these days, taught and practised in almost every country in the world. The recent growth in the United States alone has been extraordinary. From a few hundred thousand engaging in some form of practice in the closing decades of the twentieth century, numbers rose to about 4 million in 2001 and then to over 37 million by 2016. That was twice as many as five years before, and the upward trend continues. According to surveys conducted by *Yoga Journal* another 80 million are 'very interested' in beginning some sort of practice.[1] This is not just clever industry promotion; the National Institutes of Health (NIH) backs these figures. In the United Kingdom the number of people doing yoga is less, of course, conservatively estimated at around 3 million, but that figure too is increasing rapidly. This enthusiasm looks set to continue as yoga becomes ever more firmly entrenched in our individual fitness routines and our communal education and remedial systems.

Body and Mind

In his influential book *Raja Yoga*, published in 1896, Swami Vivekananda, who, as we shall see in Chapter 11, was a prime mover in introducing the West to yoga, tells the story of a god and a demon who went to learn about the cosmic Self from a great sage:

1

They studied with him for a long time. At last the wise man told them, 'You yourselves are the Being you are seeking.' Both of them thought that their bodies were the Self. They went back to their people quite satisfied and said, 'We have learned everything that was to be learned; eat, drink, and be merry; we are the Self; there is nothing beyond us.' As the demon was by nature ignorant, he never inquired any further, and remained stuck in this materialist view. But the god was a purer being. Before long, seeing the disease, pain and mortality of bodies, he returned to the sage saying: 'Sir, did you teach me that this body was the Self? If so, I see all bodies die; but the real Self is immortal and cannot die.' The sage replied: 'As I told you, you are That. Find out what this really means.' And so, after much searching and investigation, the god at last had the realisation that he was the Self beyond all thought, the one without birth or death, whom the sword cannot pierce or the fire burn, whom the air cannot dry or the water melt, without beginning or end, the immovable, the intangible, the omniscient and omnipotent Being. He experienced in his own case that It was neither the body nor the mind, but beyond them all. So he was satisfied, fully enlightened; but the poor demon did not get the truth, owing to his undue fondness for the body.[2]

While we moderns may believe in neither gods nor demons, the good Swami's story is not without relevance. Behind the enthusiastic global adoption of yoga, there lurks a general confusion as to what its real aims might be. The relationship between body-culture and spiritual aspiration is as unclear now as it was in those distant days of Vivekananda's story.

The uncertainty is not helped by historical inconsistencies in yogic terminology. Many people who teach what has aptly been called 'modern postural yoga' (MPY)[3] use the traditional name *hatha yoga*—'The Yoga of Force'—to describe what they offer their students. However, as recent scholarship has shown, the oldest root texts of *hatha* pay very little attention to postures.[4] As we shall see in Chapters 5 and 10, such records are far less interested in the anatomy of the 'gross' (that is, sensible) body than in its invisible inner counterpart, the so-called 'subtle' body that acts as the conduit for the cosmic life-force.[5] By 'gross', I refer to the world as understood by our senses and limited to the laws of time and space; 'subtle', in contrast, refers to that which exists within/behind this reality, comprising forms of awareness outside of those confines and including perception of various discarnate beings such as spirits, demons and gods. The recommendations for the physical body are mainly confined to a rigorous regime of purification, utilising procedures collectively known as the *Shatkarma*, 'The Six Methods', the purpose of which is to purify and prepare the system, at both gross and subtle levels, to sustain expanded levels of consciousness. Such preparatory routines include cleansing the stomach by swallowing a long strip of cloth (*dhauti*), yogic enemas (*basti*) and cleaning the nasal passages by means of salty water or a waxed string (*nauli*). In addition, the whole discipline of *hatha yoga* is couched in a meta-physical framework that is largely inaccessible to the modern mindset. For example, it is said that when the gross and subtle bodies of a mature aspirant are suitably purified, deep meditation will yield him supernormal powers and, eventually, the total liberation from earthly constraints that is enlightenment.

Hardly surprisingly, most of this is lacking in today's typical postural class. Though they are clearly beneficial for health, fitness and a general sense of well-being, the programmes taught today under the name of *hatha yoga* typically bear little resemblance to the tradition whose name they use. Put simply, *hatha yoga* meant something quite different in fifteenth-century India, when the *Hatha Yoga Pradipika*, the classic text on *hatha*, was composed, to what it means in the twenty-first-century West.

Similar ambiguities hover around another common classification, *raja yoga*, 'The Royal Way'. Since Vivekananda's mission to the West, many, especially his followers, have taken *raja yoga* to mean the type of yoga in which meditation predominates. In fact, the ideas and practices historically grouped together under the kingly parasol of *raja yoga* have always comprised a highly variegated mix, which includes non-meditational practices and is presented with different emphases in different texts and at different times. The definition of styles becomes even more confused when we consider the astonishing variety of classical yoga, to say nothing of the modern scene. Not only is there no single system in Indian tradition called 'yoga', but one contemporary scholar/practitioner has identified no fewer than forty-two discrete approaches.[6]

Bearing this complexity in mind, in my overall approach to the subject I have settled for the simple categories of 'body-yoga' and 'mind-yoga' to serve as a general distinction. By 'body-yoga', I mean the physical routines of posture (*asana*), the *bandhas*, which are muscular contractions to close off the throat, contract and lift the abdomen or draw the pelvic floor inward, purification regimes (*kriyas*), and breathing exercises (*pranayama*).[7] On the other hand, what I call 'mind-yoga' comprises the practice of specific techniques of mental introversion, or meditation.

But even this simplification raises another point of confusion. The word 'meditation' is commonly used very loosely to cover a variety of different practices that are by no means congruent. Reflection and other kinds of discursive thinking, creative visualisation, affirmations, listening to mood music, mindfulness strategies, and guided imaginative journeys, as well as progressive relaxation techniques, are all often lumped together under the one catch-all term, and thereby given more or less equal status. In addition, many people claim that they 'meditate in their own way' whilst gardening, jogging or walking the dog. Activities such as these are certainly enjoyable and have beneficial effects, but when all is said and done, they are still activities, and so cannot rightfully be equated with the progressive physical and mental inactivity that characterises true meditation.

By 'meditation', then, I mean the process outlined by Patanjali in his *Yoga Sutra* (c. AD 250) and followed by many other authorities. In principle, this entails a silent and internalised journey that proceeds, independent of external input or guidance, through defined and progressive phases of relaxation, interiorisation and expansion. It begins with a withdrawal of the senses from their gross level of functioning (*pratyahara*), and proceeds through a focus (*dharana*) and a deepening movement of the attention inwards (*dhyana*) which results in successive levels of settled mental absorption (*samadhi*).[8]

An immediate caveat is necessary. Any division between body and mind is of course provisional, for, as science is now revealing at ever greater depth, body and mind influence each other intimately and continuously. From a biological point of view, the mental and emotional world we experience is largely the result of biochemical mechanisms shaped by millions of years of evolution; our perceived reality is always a psychosomatic affair, determined as much by chemicals as consciousness. Similarly, our mental setting creates changes in our biochemistry. It is more accurate to speak of the 'mind-body complex' than of separate categories. Yoga has known this for centuries, developing and practising both physical and mental techniques in order to create a subjective sense of well-being, whatever the outer circumstances. The neurological processes involved in such body-mind interaction may be complex, but they can be stimulated easily enough. Any holistic yoga teacher knows that performing a physical posture easily, and holding it without undue effort, calms the mind and inculcates a muscle-memory that, with the release of a dopamine-induced feeling of pleasure, motivates the desire to repeat the process. By the same token, every competent meditation teacher is aware that mental techniques bring about perceptible and enjoyable changes in the breathing and body. As the two complementary sides of one coin, then, body and mind can never really be separated. Nevertheless, as an approach to understanding the nuances of yogic praxis, the distinction between 'body-yoga' and 'mind-yoga' can serve as a convenient shorthand to describe practices that are discrete but overlapping, and always interconnected.

The distinctions made above may seem pedantic to some readers, but they are necessary to right an imbalance. Discussions of 'body-yoga' are generally

clear enough. The anatomical basis of postures, and their effects on the physiology, are being ever more thoroughly examined and catalogued, and the
latest research updates disseminated worldwide via a huge and growing number of papers, conferences, seminars and yoga festivals each year. But the
understanding of 'mind-yoga'—in the sense of the contemplative self-transcendence described above—is typically beset by imprecision. In fact, it has
been almost ignored as an integral part of modern practice, all too often
considered an optional extra that each person must discover on their own. As
a result, the mechanics of mind-yoga remain largely uncharted territory, in
which the traveller is left to meander without much guidance, finding their
way as best they can.

East Is East?

One recurring theme of this book is to explore what happens when ancient
teachings are uprooted and transplanted into modern soil. The confusions that
can arise in the transition from East to West, sacred to secular, are clearly
discernible in the three main branches of Indian wisdom that have been
exported from the Land of the Veda in the last century or so: postural yoga,
meditation and Ayurveda, or 'the knowledge of life'. This last, the traditional
Hindu system of medicine, is today closely linked with yoga, partly because
of the connection made between the two by various recent teachers, such as
Maharishi Mahesh Yogi, Sri Sri Ravi Shankar and Baba Ramdev.[9] As we shall
see, the process of transferring wisdom from one time and place to another
is by no means as straightforward an affair as is often assumed. Everything has
its own context; models of reality and vocabularies of understanding can dif-
fer widely from culture to culture, and from one era to another. At best, the
changes, adaptations and misunderstandings necessarily involved in such a
transition are insignificant and matter little, but in some cases the original
teachings can be eroded and even traduced. Some implications of this cultural
confusion as regards mind- and body-yoga are discussed in the second half of
this book.

Yoga Academica

Over the last twenty years, studies on yoga have largely focused on its
extraordinary rise in popularity. In response to this, there has also been a
recent explosion of more specialised academic interest, which seeks to
uncover yoga's sources, historical development and cultural contexts.[10]

Unlike earlier generations of scholars, many involved in this exploration are practitioners themselves. Exciting and long overdue this may be, but it is largely a separate phenomenon from yoga on the ground. Many who do yoga may wish to study the historical roots of their practice, but their attempts to do so can often become bogged down in a morass of academic jargon. The definitions of methodological choice and justifications of ideological positioning that render a study acceptable in the post-Derrida–Foucault halls of academia are not what yoga buffs are looking for; their understanding of yoga has not been formed up in the university library or out on an anthropological field-trip, but down on the mat. When seeking authority, they are more likely to turn to hands-on teachers who are considered advanced on the path than to fastidious academics squabbling over their respective perspectives.

Bearing this in mind, part of my purpose is to distil some of the most recent research and present it in a readable and accessible way, so that any teacher or practitioner of yoga, and, indeed, any general reader, can expand their knowledge and enjoyment. Mine is not a scholarly study (though the early chapters, which deal with early texts, are necessarily quite academic), but if it stimulates fresh thinking and debate, so much the better. For those who wish to take their exploration of specific topics deeper, well over a hundred and fifty sources, some academic, some more popular, are cited in the Notes as an encouragement to further study.

Translations

The major classical yoga texts are in Sanskrit, a language replete with poetic and imaginative nuance, multiple meanings, and sometimes oblique perspectives. Debates over translation—literal/academic versus poetic/yogic—can be highly charged, and etymologies are often contested and sometimes distorted. To me it seems that, to serve a yogic purpose, a translation should combine linguistic accuracy with an inspired sense of the possibilities that legitimately arise from the material. To this end, I have used a variety of translations. The early Vedic passages are taken from Jeanine Miller, a scholar-practitioner who had an interest in Theosophy. The verses drawn from Patanjali's *Yoga Sutra* are my own, reproduced from my published translation (Bell Tower, 2004); likewise, some of the Upanishadic passages are excerpted from my *Selections from the Upanishads* (Bell Tower, 2003). Others are taken from the best-selling version of *The Upanishads* (Nilgiri Press, 2007) by Eknath Easwaran, a professor of literature who was also the founder of The Blue Mountain Center of Meditation in Berkeley, California. Compared to other recent and lauded versions, such as those of Valerie Roebuck (Penguin, 2004) and Patrick Olivelle (Oxford University Press, 2008), Easwaran's are relatively free renderings, with, it must be said, occasional interpretative interpolations not warranted by the original. Nevertheless, they are always easily accessible, coherent and free-flowing, and unencumbered by excessive footnotes. It is these qualities that have made them so consistently popular among yoga students worldwide. Translations from the *Bhagavad Gita* are by Maharishi Mahesh Yogi (Penguin, 1968), while other translated passages, such as the esoteric medieval *hatha yoga* material, are credited as and when they occur.

In Sum

In attempting to explain the hybrid creature we call 'yoga', I have sought to shed some light on its very mixed parentage, the curious and sometimes convoluted circumstances that attended its birth, and the place it occupies in our modern world. As regards this last, given how deeply yogic praxis has become embedded in the fabric of contemporary life, it can no longer be divorced from other powerful movements currently shaping our society. Any in-depth study must consider some apparently diverse, yet interconnected, topics, including women's empowerment, the digital imperative, celebrity culture, the stress pandemic and the quest for an authentic identity in the face of unprecedented change. Such a broad cultural treatment has not been attempted before this book, which, as a result, offers generous, but I hope not promiscuous, accommodation to several unlikely bedfellows. These include scholarship and scandal, fads and philosophies, critique and credence, wisdom and waywardness. Welcome to the ongoing story of yoga.

PART ONE

YESTERDAY

BEGINNINGS

1

WAY BACK WHEN…?

It's a typical Friday evening in downtown America. A group of youthful practitioners, mostly women kitted out in fashionable sportswear and carrying
plastic water bottles, arrives at a large, well-lit gym. Tanned and toned, they
have come to relax after a hard day at the office, tighten up their abs and flabs,
reduce their blood pressure and cholesterol. During the session there is a lot
of talk of anatomical details amidst a pervasive atmosphere of 'no pain no
gain'; the stretching and relaxing may involve blocks, ropes and other appli-
ances, but there is a determined energy exerted in most of the postures.
Everything takes place in front of the wall-to-wall mirrors and the ethos is
one of goal-directed accomplishment. Everyone is getting somewhere, burning off fat and sweating out stress, improving themselves. At the end of the
session, recharged and clear-headed, people chat while quickly changing back
into street gear. Some are advocating the benefits of the latest detox programmes and high-energy diets, while almost all are checking their phones
and consulting their upcoming schedules.

Not far away on the other side of town, another group is meeting. Its members are older than the gym-goers but, again, almost exclusively female. Here
the lighting is dimmer, sitar music is playing softly in the background and the
scent of sandalwood wafts from an incense stick smouldering in front of an
image of the Dancing Shiva. The session, led by a Western teacher with an Indian
name who is just back from a three-month stay at an ashram in Rishikesh, begins
with mispronounced chanting from a sacred Hindu text, followed by some
mantras that the group repeats after her. Sanskrit terminology is used to describe
the postures, which are performed slowly and gently. The session is brought to
a gentle close with a guided meditation, and then, after some relaxed socialising
and prolonged hugging, people drift away into their various weekends.

* * *

The understanding of yoga typified by the first group above will be dealt with later in this book, but for the moment, let us focus on the second. As do millions of others, its members would see their practice as being in some way connected to the nourishing well-spring of Indian wisdom. However vaguely the connection may be articulated, practitioners and teachers take for granted that this yoga is the subcontinent's practical and perennial spiritual gift to the rest of the world. One of the most popular English translations of Patanjali's classic *Yoga Sutra* is *How to Know God*, a poetic collaboration between the California-based Indian guru Swami Prabhavananda and the English writer Christopher Isherwood. First published in 1953, this version is still the Vedanta Press' best-selling book, and has remained so respected over the years that until very recently the official governing body of yoga in the UK, The British Wheel of Yoga, chose it as the recommended text for its teacher training courses. In the opening paragraph of their introduction, the authors tell us: 'the yoga doctrine may be said to have been handed down from pre-historic times'. Such an impressive pedigree might perhaps be proved one day, but in fact there is currently no hard evidence to support such a claim, and certainly not as regards body-yoga. Much water has flowed under the scholastic bridge in the almost seventy years since this translation was first published, and such broad statements rarely go unchallenged today. Indeed, as we shall see, a great deal of what is practised as yoga in the twenty-first century actually has very little in common with what we now know of ancient India, in terms of both its socio-cultural norms and its spiritual aims.

Talking of timescales, it is often said on the yoga circuit that the practice dates from '5,000 years ago'. Now, as anyone familiar with India or Indians will know, when the tag '5,000 years' pops up in discussions on culture, it is not a precise figure but shorthand for 'an awfully long time ago, exactly how long no one really knows and anyway it doesn't matter because the subject at hand is a timeless truth'. Such an easy-going attitude is in part quite understandable, as early Indian history is notoriously vague on exact chronology and there are many lengthy periods when we know virtually nothing about what was going on in the subcontinent. Such inexactitude may well frustrate intellectuals, and their frustration is compounded by the fact that history and myth—to use the Western distinction—have always blended seamlessly into one another in India. One word in Sanskrit—*itihasa*: 'thus it happened'—covers both history and myth, thus conflating what, in Western eyes at least, is objectively 'true' with what is merely fanciful imagination. From the traditional Indian point of view, it is the exemplary value of events, rather than the details of their chronological order, that is important. From this perspective, the purpose of historical record is to educate and inspire people, both as individuals and as members of society. Current reassessment of history as a series of partial narratives, rather than an objective record, has not yet brought us to the traditional Indian view that the events of the *Mahabharata* are no less historically 'real' than the subcontinent's struggle for independence from the British Raj, though plenty of influential people in New Delhi are making this very claim. Given this, any attempt to locate the precise genesis of yoga, or accurately trace its early historical trajectory, is doomed to failure; in India reliable records are often just not there and we have only 'mythistory' in their place.

The paucity of written evidence is only partly because widespread literacy is a very recent phenomenon. In our time, literacy is seen as the yardstick of civilisation, so it is easy to forget that our ancient forebears did not share the respect we automatically grant the ability to read and write. Sacred knowledge was too precious to commit to writing, as written records are always susceptible to misappropriation and misinterpretation, and unschooled minds can all too easily destroy the purity of a teaching they do not fully comprehend. This explains the fact that when the written medium did first emerge in early cultures—such as Sumer and ancient China—it was used only to record commercial transactions, such as the payment of taxes, accumulation of debts and the ownership of property, but never to transmit philosophical or sacred knowledge. In fact, writing first arrived on the scene at just the same time and place—Sumer in around 3000 BC—as history's first known money, the 'currency' of barley, appeared.

Spiritual knowledge in India was always an aural tradition, passed on by word of mouth and made fast by personal praxis. Even the priestly custodians of sacred knowledge and ritual were not necessarily able to read or write, for what ensured the faultless transmission of their teachings was direct personal contact, mind to mind, heart to heart, hand to hand. Once it appeared on the Indian scene as a science of transformation, yoga was always a living body of practice transmitted in the context of the guru–disciple relationship and secured by the close monitoring of individual progress. This importance of a closed tradition also accounts for the exclusivity of the *brahmin* priestly caste throughout India's history. However much it may pain moderns, in traditional societies, important knowledge—and religion was the most important kind of knowledge—was always a highly specialised affair and not a democratic 'right'. Its purity was maintained through a functional hierarchy that was justified as being a microcosm of the divine order. This universal holism is known in Vedic India as *rita*, in later Hindu thought as *dharma*, and in the

Christian West as the Great Chain of Being first articulated by Plato. Such a view is the exact opposite of the post-modern relativism taught in our citadels of learning today, which sees hierarchy as an exploitative, and largely patriarchal, social construct to monopolise power, rather than enjoying such an elevated provenance. Of course, the ancients were swayed as much by mundane considerations as arcane theology. Implacable monsoon rains and floods, voracious ants and destructive military conflicts all threatened written records, whether these were made of bark, palm-leaf or, from about the eighth century onwards, paper.

Word of mouth accuracy was assured by the cultivation of an extraordinarily capacious memory, nurtured through a process of rote learning and continuous repetition, often synchronised with bodily movements that helped make it fast. In this way the student metabolised knowledge rather than merely accumulated it, and his expertise became part of his intrinsic identity. Literacy, which depends on external resources, tends to destroy our innate retentive faculty; as they say in India, 'the knowledge that is in the book stays in the book'. The prodigious feats of recall we know from classical orators in the West, and which can still (just) be found in India among professional balladeers and travelling bards, are well-nigh inconceivable to us highly literate yet often attention-deficient moderns.[1]

The '5,000 years' trope is an old romantic longing, projected onto an India imagined as a culture of timeless wisdom accumulated by saints and scholars over the millennia. It was already observable in some travellers' accounts in classical times. Around 320 BC, the Greek ambassador Megasthenes described India as 'this mystical and magical land', while almost three hundred years later the Pythagorean sage Apollonius of Tyana witnessed *brahmins* who worshipped their God by levitating two cubits in the air. The idea entered squarely into scholarly discourse in the late eighteenth-century Enlightenment.[2] The reservoir of this wisdom is often believed to lie in Vedic culture (see below) and its energetic child Hinduism, but the latter is itself a problematic concept. 'Hinduism' is a term that was coined by British missionaries, officials and, following them, scholars, during the late eighteenth and early nineteenth centuries. 'Hindu', a much older term, was originally used as a geographic or ethnic description of those people living around the River Indus; only later was it used as an umbrella adjective under which was lumped together the vast array of religious beliefs and practices found all over the subcontinent. Indians themselves did not naturally use the term. From the early nineteenth century onwards, we hear increasingly the epithet *Sanatana Dharma*, 'The Unchanging Law', being used by the orthodox to distinguish their old-time religion from what was then being taught by the various reform movements influenced by missionary Christianity. Today, *Sanatana Dharma* is often used by those who dislike the imported 'Hinduism' and see their inherited wisdom of living as being more than just one among the many other world religions. The word 'orthodox' is also important for us here, as several streams of Indic religious experience outside the fold of Vedic-Hindu orthodoxy—most notably Jainism and then Buddhism—have always practised some form of yoga. In fact, a good few of our earliest records of it come from these heterodox sources.

With all these caveats in mind, let us look at what we do know about the earliest strata of Indian civilisation and see what origins, if any, we can find there for what is now being practised so assiduously in the gyms, village halls and hospitals of the twenty-first century.

The Indus Valley Civilisation (c. 3000–1500 BC)

The Indus Valley Civilisation is the earliest evidence we have of an advanced and well-organised culture on Indian soil. Roughly contemporary with Middle Kingdom China and ancient Mesopotamia, the IVC's vast and well-organised urban culture extended over at least 500 separate settlements in a 1,000-mile arc stretching from southern Pakistan eastwards across to modern Delhi and south to Mumbai. Retrieved remains from these early times in the subcontinent are very thin on, or even under, the ground, but one artefact from this period was for many years advanced as early evidence of yoga, and it is still sometimes offered today as proof that postural practice goes back to the very beginnings. Excavated at one of the principal cities of the civilisation, Mohenjodharo (now in Pakistan), this is a small steatite seal measuring barely two inches square. It depicts an impressive seated figure that looks like a deity or a king or perhaps a high priest of some sort, sitting with legs crossed in what many have taken to be the *mulabandhasana*, a posture later to be much favoured by tantric yogis. Our figure sports an erect phallus and is seated on a low couch that resembles those still used for meditation in India today. He also wears a sizeable head-dress with protruding horns and is surrounded by wild animals—elephant, tiger, rhinoceros and bull—while in front of him sits what looks like a pair of deer.

All these details led Sir John Marshall, the British archaeologist who excavated the site in the early 1930s, to consider the figure as the prototype of the later Hindu god Shiva. One of Shiva's many forms is as *Mahayogi*, 'the Great Yogi', the archetypal adept and practitioner of austerities, while another is as *Dakshinamurti*, 'He who Faces South', i.e. the deity who sits in the high northern Himalaya looking down onto the subcontinent to impart sacred knowledge and protect those who follow it. Both these could be suggested by the figure's posture and evident authority. Another of Shiva's forms is as *Pashupati*, 'Lord of the Creatures', which fits with the entourage of animals. The symbolism could also be stretched to fit yoga, as in later Shaivite teaching the word *pashu*, which literally means 'the bound animal', designates the typical, unregenerate human being who stands in need of yogic transformation. For us worldly *pashus*, lost in bestial ignorance, Shiva as lord of yogic wisdom is our first resort and final liberator. He has other epithets too: 'Conqueror of Death' (*Mrityum jaya*) and 'Giver of Joy' (*Shankara*)—attributes that would later be ascribed to the accomplished yogi himself.

Marshall's theory that the seal's little figure was a 'proto-Shiva' advocating yoga was accepted uncritically for over half a century, but modern scholars have rejected it, some preferring to see the figure as a sort of a shaman rather than an original practitioner of postural yoga. At the dawn of civilisation shamanic seers were revered individuals, whose ability to move into exceptional states of mind rendered them essential to the group as its spiritual antennae yet simultaneously often ineffective in terms of day-to-day social function, for theirs was a higher calling than mundane work. The later yogis would also occupy this ambivalent status.

The shaman interpretation does seem to fit the sparse facts better. The IVC figure is clearly wearing the horns of some tutelary animal-deity, which could align him with the worldwide brotherhood of visionaries who derive their magical power from communing with the spirits of totemic animals. The buffalo of the American plains, the reindeer of the northern tundra, the yak and horse of the Mongolian steppes—all these were sacred to animistic tribes and all had their body parts used as part of the shaman's regalia, especially his headdress. Admittedly, shamanism is pre-eminently the religion of nomadic people and the IVC was a settled culture which built for permanence. That said, the origin of the IVC remains unknown.

Interestingly, the detail of this seal is not unique to India. A strikingly similar figure—sitting cross-legged on the ground, wearing some sort of antlers and surrounded by animals—is depicted on the Gundestrup cauldron, a richly decorated silver vessel dating from between 200 BC and AD 300 that was found in 1891 in a peat bog in Denmark, which is a long way from the Indus Valley. While we just don't know enough about the interconnectedness of ancient civilisations to say anything definite about this remarkable likeness, it does seem to favour the shaman-priest theory and cast further doubt on any connection with a subcontinental Shiva.

And then there is the 'yogic' pose. The figure's posture clearly denotes a degree of authority if not majesty, but sitting cross-legged has always been the natural way for Indians to sit, as it still is for many millions of non-Europeans. Perhaps more to the point, you don't usually do *asanas* wearing a large horned head-dress, or, if it comes to it, with a full erection. In addition, if yoga was such an important part of this early stage of Indian religious life, as some claim, would there not have been other IVC seals depicting other *asanas*, different postures? So, while our lordly figure certainly enjoyed some totemic status, little more can be said about him conclusively. Nor does the script imprinted on the seal help us here; tantalisingly, all IVC writing remains undeciphered to this day.

However, archaeology continues to shed more light on this question, albeit with painstaking slowness. A recent find at an IVC site at Balathal in Rajasthan revealed a skeleton dating back perhaps 2,700 years. The figure is sitting in the *samadhi* position: cross-legged, hands resting on his knees with thumb and index fingers touching in the yogic *jnanamudra*, symbolising spiritual insight. This is the posture that many yogis adopt for meditation and it is also assumed at the time of their burial, which has sometimes been known to take place while they are still alive.

The Vedic Era (c. 2500–500 BC)

This era, the next layer of early Indian history to be unpeeled in our search for the origins of yoga, is named after the Vedas, the scriptures that form the ever-erect backbone of orthodox Hinduism. There are four of these collections of hymns: *Rig Veda*, the knowledge of the divine Word; *Sama Veda*, the knowledge of the sacred songs; *Yajur Veda*, the knowledge of the sacrificial formulae; and *Atharva Veda*, the knowledge of the laws of nature. Appended to these works is a huge corpus of subsidiary texts known collectively as *Upavedas* and *Vedangas*. Taken together, this literature covers many different aspects of life in great detail: religion, sacred ritual, health and medicine, architecture, astrology, warfare, the arts. Nowhere in it, however, can there be found any specific mention of body-yoga.

The central religious rite of the Vedic people was the fire-sacrifice (*yajna*), a ritual performed by skilled priests with the purpose of soliciting the support of higher beings (*devatas*—literally 'the shining ones') that exist in the subtle strata of creation operating behind the scenes of daily life and controlling its outcomes. *Yajnas* were usually performed for communal, rather than individual, benefit, with the king often acting as the patron of the ceremony and representative of his people. One type of *yajna*, celebrated particularly in the ninth book (*mandala*) of the *Rig Veda*, involved the ritual preparation and ingestion of *soma*, a hallucinogenic plant that bestowed visions of the luminous subtle realms where the deities dwell, and that transported the priest into communication with these discarnate energies. Here at the dawn of its recorded history, Indic civilisation exhibits the instinct for ecstasy that has remained such an important feature of its variegated cultures ever since. Despite many theories over the years, *soma* has not yet been conclusively identified. Some scholars have speculated that it was ephedra or a type of magic mushroom.[3] 'Pressed out'—the etymological meaning of the word *soma*—filtered and mixed with cow's milk and other liquids, the distilled *soma* was poured into the sacred fire as an offering to the gods and also drunk by the sacrificial priests. It was credited with divine potency and the ability to remove sin and yield good health, longevity and the experience of immortality, as well as with bestowing paranormal powers. Significantly, all these boons would later be attributed to the practice of yoga.

When the word 'yoga' is used in these early texts, it appears to be with a meaning far removed from postural or even meditational exercise. The term is most often employed in the *Rig Veda* in the contexts of nomadism, warfare and death, and there are several descriptions of the dying warrior being 'hitched to his chariot (*yogayukta*) ascending to the celestial realms of the sun'. Interpretation of such metaphors is fraught with difficulty, as the succinct and synoptic nature of the Sanskrit language means images are typically packed with layers of meaning not immediately visible to the modern eye. This particular metaphor seems to bring together a military image with the common idea of the journey taken by the pious sacrificer who, through the sacrifice performed on his behalf by the *brahmin* priests, rises to the heavenly world of the gods. The same image is also used as a wonderfully evocative description of leaving the body at the time of death, with the dying person riding on an immaterial and 'self-fashioned' chariot loaded up with the harvest of his earthly deeds to present as his offering to Yama, the Lord of Death.[4] This sky journey could also be a metaphor for the inward ascent of contemplation, of course, when the mind 'dies' to the outside world and limited self, travels to distant psychic realms, and is then reborn with fresh vitality and insight.[5] All in all, the meaning of such esoteric passages remains unclear; most academics are unwilling to go out on a limb of speculation as they have reputations to preserve and livelihoods to earn.[6]

The Mahabharata (c. 300 BC–AD 300)

In this voluminous scripture, whose 200,000 verses took many centuries to finalise, we find the term 'yoga' mentioned no fewer than 900 times. Some of these citations refer to yoga in a philosophical sense, and rate it highly: 'There is no wisdom like Samkhya, no power like Yoga.'[7] Others continue the association of yoga with the Vedic warrior and his 'journey to the sun'. In that portion of the *Mahabharata* known as the *Bhagavad Gita*, the most popular of all Hindu scriptures, Lord Krishna, the supreme personality of the Godhead, is very clear that the most glorious fate of a *kshatriya* warrior is to die in battle. Such a self-sacrifice is his *dharmic* path to the celestial realms of the gods, offering him what Krishna calls 'an open door to heaven'.[8] Those undergoing this noble demise are also described by the word *yogayukta* as they ascend to heaven.

Significantly however, the *Mahabharata* also uses the word 'yoga' when describing arduous physical penances and austerities performed by holy men. In this context, there are many references to another, more localised, journey that takes place when the yogi leaves his own body and enters that of another. This skill of taking possession of another person (*parakayapravesh*) is mentioned by Patanjali[9] and is found later in standard lists of the supernormal powers (*siddhis*) attained by the proficient yogi. Even Adi Shankara, the eighth-century ultra-orthodox master of the doctrine of Advaita Vedanta, is accredited with this ability in all the popular accounts of his life. Indeed, it secured his victory in the crucial debate with a champion of Vedic ritual that established the superiority of his path of mind-yoga over the way of textual knowledge and priestly expertise.[10] These accounts are legendary hagiographies, mythistory par excellence, but nonetheless, they show that arcane yogic skills were very much part of the contemporary zeitgeist.

In time too, the sacrificial *soma* of Vedic ritual would be internalised and understood as a subtle physical substance generated in the yogi's body by his practice (especially his sexual continence) and the theme of mystical or astral ascent beyond the confines of the mortal body would become a metaphor for the yogic path of meditation that leads to the celestial Self. Yet the ritual use of hallucinogens would continue to be important. Perhaps fifteen hundred years later than the Vedic texts, Patanjali's *Yoga Sutra*, a relatively sober work, mentions herbs (*oshadi*) as one of the four means to promote paranormal powers in the yogi.[11]

21

Wandering Holy Men

In all the early texts, the yogis that are mentioned are not the clean-living, health-conscious and physically toned practitioners we would recognise by that word today. The holy itinerants who practised yoga, although generally known as *sadhus*, 'good men', seem to have been raggle-taggle gypsies who wandered the earth freely, unshackled by convention and in pursuit of spiritual ecstasy, which they would get wherever they could find it. Such wild *sadhu* groups, numbering millions of adherents, are still very much part of the richly varie-gated religio-social scene in India, though these days their preferred stimulant is hashish, or its decoction *bhang*, rather than the *soma* of Vedic times. They cast their influence over the latest wave of travellers seeking 'eternal India', the beats and hippies who made the overland trek to India in the '60s and '70s, many of whom, when they returned home, would be among the early adopters of postural yoga in the West.[12] Thanks to photographic studies and the glo-balised footage of the regular Kumbh Mela festival, where the *sadhus* gather in huge crowds, these wild-looking holy men are now familiar figures.

Wandering *sadhus* are also mentioned in Vedic texts, where they are described[13] as long-haired ascetics (*keshins*) who practise spiritual techniques and gain states of ecstasy. They seem to have formed groups that were outside conventional society and quite separate from the orthodox ritual priests who performed fire sacrifices for the king and the collective good. The *Atharva Veda*, which is somewhat later than the other three major compilations, con-tains many descriptions of one particular brotherhood it calls the Vratyas: 'those who have taken the vow'. This suggests membership of an initiatory brotherhood, but also alludes to one of their epithets: 'the honeybees', or *madhuvrata*, meaning 'those whose vow is to sweetness', because they roamed here and there in search of the nectar of bliss. As such, these sapient foragers, finely attuned to the rhythms of nature and their own bodies, constituted an evolutionary throwback to those unfettered times before mankind became tied to the fields he planted and trapped in the cities he built.

Travelling the northern areas of the subcontinent, especially the land to the east of modern Punjab, the Vratyas used carts drawn by horse and mule, and often moved in groups of thirty-three that were organised into a stratified, almost military social order. They must have been a colourful crew, distin-guished by black turbans worn in a rakish manner over long matted hair, a white blanket thrown across the shoulders with rounded silver earrings and heavy necklaces of jewels and beads. Their lower garments were deer-skins and they carried weapons—lance, bow and pointed goad—as many of today's wandering *sadhus* still do. Talented composers and singers, the Vratyas found they could sing a lot better, and probably hold the notes longer, if they practised what they called *pranayama*, a type of breath control. While some enjoyed sex with the women who accompanied the group, others were continent, employing their abstinence to generate spiritual energy. This is a strategy that, as we shall see in Chapter 5, was to play a central role in medieval *hatha yoga* and remain a concern of all subsequent yogic praxis.[14]

The Vratyas, so we are told, 'harnessed their minds and harnessed their visionary insights, to see the steady light they find within the hidden place of the heart, when they have sung their *mantras* which they fashion in their heart.'[15] This inner effulgence is beyond thought, being 'swifter than the mind': 'My ears, my eyes speed after this light lodged here within my heart.'[16]

The Vedic poets frequently link the ecstatic individual to the wider cosmos by equating his hidden inner light with the sun—'In the fourth degree of prayer the sage found the sun till then immersed in darkness'[17]—or by personifying this inner effulgence as Agni, the god of light and the flame of the sacrificial fire.

To join with the cosmic intelligence is not a matter of intellectual learning or ritual skill, but of a heartfelt receptivity: 'The lordly herdsman of the whole universe, the enlightened one, has entered into me, the simple one …'[18] Devotion, which would play such a role in medieval yoga, is also prefigured in such lines as: 'My songs-of-praise, high-aspiring, speed forth as messengers to Indra … uttered by my spirit to touch his heart';[19] and: 'May this song-of-praise be foremost in touching thy heart in blessedness.'[20]

The intoxicating sense of immortality, which would become a key concern of yoga, was also sought by these early seers, who tell us: 'I have known this mighty celestial man, refulgent as the sun beyond the darkness. Only by knowing him does one overcome death. No other way is there to go.'[21] And, in one passage: 'Desireless, wise, immortal, self-existent, contented with the essence, lacking nothing is He. One fears not death who has known him, the Self (*atman*), serene, ageless, ever youthful.'[22]

In the context of these proto-yogis, we also learn of an undying and omnipresent consciousness: 'the deathless flame in living beings without which nothing whatever can be done, that immortal essence whereby all is comprehended, that which is and that which will be hereafter.'[23]

These and similar refrains clearly prefigure teachings that are found perhaps a thousand years later in the *Upanishads*, and, from them in turn, not only the medieval texts but yogic philosophy up until today.

So much for early mind-yoga. But to return to our search for the origins of the postural sort, the important point here is that the route to these cov-

eted states of luminous introversion was clearly through ritual and meditation, probably aided by heady draughts of *soma* or its equivalent, rather than
hours spent assiduously on the exercise mat. Nowhere among these earliest
and varied uses of the term 'yoga' do we find reference to the *asanas* taught
today, nor even anything that can be recognised as the clear prototype of
modern posture work.[24] So to judge from the available evidence, the assumption often made by body-yoga enthusiasts that their routines were from the
very beginning a central pillar of ancient Indian culture just doesn't stand up.

2

THE LEGACY OF THE FOREST SAGES

While much of the Vedic period remains tantalisingly shrouded in the mists of time, we do have a flickering glimpse of what lay at its core. This, as we have seen, was the ritual of the *yajna* fire-sacrifice, which, accompanied by recitation of the spiritually empowered cadences of the scriptures, was a skilled and intricate procedure to infuse the human realm with divine influence.[1] The ritual was carried out by an hereditary priesthood, the *brahmins*, who were the living libraries of a corpus of sacred knowledge that had been passed down from father to son, generation to generation, since earliest times. However, from perhaps 800 BC onwards (roughly the time of the compilation of the Hebrew Old Testament) we begin to see the codification of spiritual disciplines that were practised by people who, like the Vratya brotherhoods before them, were not exclusively from priestly families. The demands made on the aspirants of this new way were no less stringent, however, for their goal was nothing less than a union (*yoga*) with the formless Absolute that lies within and behind all forms and phenomena. These aspirants undertook the supreme quest, aiming beyond even the heavenly realms of the deities invoked by the fire-offerings. Their concern was not merely to improve the conditions of everyday life, but to achieve complete liberation from its tedious insufficiencies and enervating limitations.

At this early stage of Indian history, then, there is evidence of a *yajna–yoga* split, a division between a concern with accruing worldly benefits in daily life through the 'outer fire' of sacrificial ritual and, on the other hand, the search for direct experience of a higher reality through ascetic *tapas*, the 'inner fire' of purification. The most celebrated of this new breed was the scion of a ruling family on the borders of modern Nepal, Prince Gautama Siddhartha, whom history knows simply as the Buddha: 'the one who has woken up'. There were other masters who also sat under sacred trees and attained the

25

coveted existential freedom. One, contemporary with the Buddha, was Mahavir, 'The Great Hero', last in the line of the twenty-four teachers of Jainism known as the *tirthankaras*: 'those who have crossed to the further shore'. These and others like them are the archetypal exemplars of mind-yoga, inspiring seekers after Truth right up until today.

Settling Down

As the Vratyas had already found, unmediated spiritual experience was encouraged by living close to nature, apart from householder society with all its time-consuming commitments. Gradually, itinerant spiritual wanderers coalesced into renunciate communities, which in time produced their own sacred literature, a subdivision of the Vedic corpus known as *Aranyakas*: 'the forest treatises'. And, distilled from these, came yet a further group of eso-teric teachings called the *Upanishads*. The word, derived from *upa* (near), *ni* (down) and *sad* (to sit, or settle), came to mean 'a sitting down near the teacher' to learn from him the hidden truth of life. The qualities quickened by such a spiritual apprenticeship are those that had been advocated centuries earlier in the *Rig Veda*: spiritual heroism, manliness, devotion, respect, con-tentment, generosity, self-control, dispassion and impartial friendliness. We shall meet all these again as ideal attributes in the later literature of yoga.

The early *Upanishads*, especially the two oldest, the *Brihadaranyaka* and *Chandogya*, reiterate some Vedic ritual themes, but now internalised through meditative practices as the ascending stages of mind-yoga. A favourite topic is the link between the inner and the outer worlds and the greater, all-inclusive reality that underpins both:

> What then is that which, dwelling within this little house, this lotus of the heart, is to be sought after, inquired about, realised? As large as the universe outside, even so large is the universe within the lotus of the heart. Within it are heaven and earth, the sun, the moon, the lightning and all the stars.[2]

This greater reality is the immaterial Absolute. All the universes inhere in this transcendental field of life, of which they are its temporary and non-binding modifications, and, for us humans, to realise the Absolute is the pur-pose of our life. The classical *Upanishads* seek to educate us in this fact: how to approach, understand and eventually unite with that One which is the source and essence of all. As the *Maitri Upanishad* tells us: 'He who is in the fire and He who is in the heart, and He who is yonder in the sun, He is One.'

Although itself unmanifest, the Absolute is richly imaged in various ways—poetic, symbolic, metaphorical—and the practice of mind-yoga is advanced

as the direct route to its realisation. To this end, a comfortable seated position, such as *padmasana*, is recommended to settle the body for meditation,
but nowhere amongst the mass of detailed and wide-ranging subjects dealt
with in the *Upanishads* is there a sustained or systematic treatment of the
many *asanas*, *kriyas* or *pranayamas* that constitute modern postural practice.
Instead, the *Maitri* advocates the means to inner union as 'the six-fold yoga',
explaining the term: 'Since one joins or unites (*yuj*) in many ways: the breath
and OM and the all, it is known as yoga. Since it is the oneness of breath and
mind and senses too, the renunciation of all becoming is called yoga.'[3]

The text stipulates the effects of the practice and its correct context:

> By the practice of yoga one achieves contentment, endurance of the pairs of
> opposites, and peacefulness. One should not make known this supreme secret
> to one who is not a son, not a student, or not at peace, so one should give it to
> one who is devoted to nothing else, who is endowed with all the virtues.[4]

It describes mind-yoga as an internalised sacrifice: 'The one who knows
this is a renouncer, a yogin and a sacrificer to the Self. Just as no one touches
amorous women if they have entered an empty house, the one who does not
touch sense-objects is a renouncer, a yogin and a sacrificer to the Self.'[5]

The *Maitri* is a relatively late *Upanishad*, but the third oldest, the *Taittiriya*
(c. 500 BC), also contains clear references to the ultimate Reality beyond the
mind that it calls *brahman*:

> Realising That from which all words turn back
> And thoughts can never reach, one knows
> The bliss of *brahman* and fears no more.[6]

The word *brahman*, 'the Totality', comes from the verbal root *brh* meaning
'to grow, swell, expand', a derivation that alludes to the creativity inherent in
the absolute source of all life. Several other passages in the *Taittiriya* describe
the blissful experience of this ultimate stratum, which is 'the inner Self which
is the source of abiding joy'.[7]

The *Taittiriya* also contains descriptions of inner cosmologies that reoccur
in medieval *hatha yoga* texts many centuries later, and of a five-fold hierarchy
of selves—constituted of food, life-breath, mind, understanding and bliss—
that, in later teachings, especially Vedanta, would become formalised as the
'sheaths' (*koshas*) that veil the luminescence of the inner Self.[8]

The purest exposition of the various modes of consciousness, a model that
became axiomatic in later yoga systems, is to be found in the *Mandukya
Upanishad*. With great clarity, this lucid work delineates the three varying

27

states of consciousness—waking, dreaming and sleeping—in contradistinction to their substratum, which it simply calls 'the fourth' (*turiya*). This 'fourth' lies beyond the volatile changeability of mind and matter and is by contrast forever serene, timeless and undisturbed. Other Upanishadic passages flesh out the contrast of the little ego-self, engaged in worldly experience and passing through its changes to this unattached fourth, the transpersonal Self, which does nothing but witness the play of life. This equanimity, which was to become a central leitmotif of yoga, is charmingly described:

> Two birds of lovely plumage, inseparable friends, dwell on the self-same tree. One eats the fruits of pleasure and pain; the other just looks on.[9]

Of all the classical *Upanishads*, it is perhaps the *Katha* that presents the fullest and most clearly realised account of mind-yoga. By this stage, the term *dhyana*, which had earlier appeared in the *Brahmana* and *Aranyaka* portions of the Vedas but with unclear meanings, has become accepted as the general term for introverted contemplation or meditation, and as such is recognised to be the key praxis of mind-yoga and the path to self-knowledge. In a teaching of great beauty and profundity, couched in the form of a dialogue between a young seeker and Yama the Lord of Death, the *Katha* exemplifies clearly the difference between the methodology of Indian wisdom systems and what is normally understood by the word 'philosophy'. Whereas the Western philosopher of modern times has been a professional thinker who employs discursive thought in search of the perfect and irrefutable conceptual model, the Indian sage is always oriented to that Truth which can only be found when the mind goes beyond its habitual activity of thinking. As the *Katha* says:

> Meditation enables them to go
> Deeper and deeper into consciousness,
> From the world of words to the worlds of thought,
> Then beyond thoughts to the wisdom that is the Self.[10]

This psychic expansion, visually conceived of as either an ascent or descent, relies on a model of the human personality that will become the basis of all subsequent schools of yoga. It divides the individual awareness into a hierarchy of functional levels of increasing subtlety:

> The senses derive from objects of sense-perception,
> Sense objects from the mind, mind from intellect,
> And intellect from ego, ego from undifferentiated
> Consciousness, and consciousness from *brahman*.[11]

This hierarchy is clearly set out in the orthodox Hindu school of thought known as Sankhya, 'The Enumeration', which is attributed to the Vedic sage Kapila, who lived around 600 BC, but virtually the same is found in contemporary Buddhist and Jain texts that lie outside the fold of orthodoxy, as well as in other *Upanishads*.[12] A later text, the *Bhagavad Gita*, is unequivocal about the connection between Kapila's theoretical model and the practical path of yoga: 'The ignorant and not the wise speak of *sankhya* and *yoga* as different ... he who sees *sankhya* and *yoga* to be one, verily he sees.'[13] And perhaps a hundred years after these words were written, it was Sankhya that would form the psychological underpinning of Patanjali's magisterial *Yoga Sutra*, as we shall see in the next chapter.

Among its many gems, the *Katha* provides a lucent definition of mind-yoga:

When the five senses are stilled, when the mind is stilled, when the intellect is stilled, that is called the highest state by the wise. They say *yoga* is this complete stillness in which one enters the unitive state, never to become separate again. If one is not established in this state, the sense of unity will come and go.[14]

The supremacy of this inner practice to outer ritual, which we have already heard about, is now, at times, stated in no uncertain terms:

But verily, these rituals are unsafe boats; they cannot reach the farthest shore. The Vedic sciences are but the lower knowledge. The ignorant, who take them as the higher, sink once more into old age and death. Though they think themselves wise and learned, they are fools lost in ignorance, a prey to suffering, wandering without direction, like the blind led by the blind. These ignorant children, bound by duality, think their journey is complete. Blinded by attachment, they fail to see the Truth.[15]

This disjunction became formalised in the doctrine of the two levels of knowledge: lower and higher, relative and absolute. That such trenchant criticisms of orthodoxy should themselves be welcomed into the scriptural canon and enjoy the highest respect therein, is a wonderful tribute to the open-minded nature of early Indian religious enquiry.

While other classical *Upanishads* contain discussions of the aforementioned 'subtle body' that will feature so prominently in texts such as the medieval *Hatha Yoga Pradipika*, there is virtually no mention of the *asanas*, *kriyas*, *bandhas* and *pranayamas* we know so well today. All the earliest yogic-philosophical material we have is interested only in the inner, or spiritual, aspects of the practice. To explain this lacuna, it has been argued that because physical yoga is such a hands-on discipline, requiring personal supervision between teacher and pupil, details of the postures would have been passed on orally and not committed to written texts. But while it is true that sacred knowledge was carefully guarded from casually inquisitive eyes, Indian authorities were always extraordinarily detailed classifiers of everything they considered important, from architecture and astrology to diet and sex. So, if there had been a generally recognised and authoritative body of body-postures at this early stage, they would surely have been listed somewhere, either in great detail or at least in the mnemonic form of the *sutra*, to be extrapolated by the teacher as living instruction when needed. Moreover, the inner realms of meditative awareness are certainly more finely nuanced than any manipulation of the body, and yet, as we have seen, the texts not only contain theoretical detail of these abstract states of awareness but provide at least general information on the techniques employed to access them. So why, then, is there nothing similar on body-work?

The Yoga Upanishads *(c. 100 BC–AD 400)*[16]

We have now to move forward perhaps a thousand years to find a secondary category of texts given the respectful name of *Upanishad*: the group of about twenty works known as the *Yoga Upanishads*. These later works mark a shift in concern from the abstract Absolute underlying all forms towards a preoccupation with psychic realms and the labyrinthine possibilities of introverted awareness. This, along with details of esoteric praxis, allies them to the early *hatha yoga* teachings we shall meet in Chapter 5. The most important of this collection are the five *bindu* ('seed') *Upanishads*, namely the *Amrita, Amrita Nada, Nada, Dhyana* and *Tejo*.

These texts do mention physical postures, although these are not covered in any great detail apart from the 'locks' (*bandhas*). This is perhaps the first time that physical postures, of varying complexity, are said to have their own specific benefits in a way we might recognise from today's practice. This signifies a change from the teachings of the classical *Upanishads*, the *Yoga Sutra* and the *Bhagavad Gita*, where the term *asana* refers only to seated postures whose value is confined to steadying the body for prolonged meditation. Such usage conformed to the sedentary character of the word itself, as the primary meaning of *asana*, being derived from the verbal root √*as*—'to sit, to be'—is 'seat' or 'throne'.

Kings and Saints

In hierarchical human societies, stasis often connotes status, the best example being the king, who sits happily on his throne while his courtiers and subjects scurry around energetically doing his bidding. In the Indian religious context, however, the acme of such social standing—or rather sitting—was the enlightened yogi, the spiritual monarch who, ruling through renunciation rather than possession, was fit to be addressed as *maharaj*, 'the great king'. Stationed serenely under his tree, such a sage was the unattached lord of all he surveyed, and more. Liberated from the tedium of gross physical action, he realised all his desires through the pellucid power of thought alone; doing nothing, he accomplished everything. As a living metaphor of his union with the unmoving Self of all, such a yogi often went nowhere, while the world came to him.[17]

A popular subject in Indian art, right from its beginnings in the carvings and frescoes of the Buddhist rock-cut sanctuaries (excavated circa 200 BC), is the king kneeling low before the yogi in his forest hermitage. The oldest *Upanishad*, the *Brihadaranyaka*, tells us the archetype of such a regal supplicant was Janaka—the ruler of Videha and father-in-law of Lord Rama—who studied with the famous holy man Yajnavalkya. A later text lauds Janaka for being prepared to give up his entire kingdom in exchange for the right to receive spiritual instruction from a yogi called Ashtavakra. The *Shrimad Bhagavatam*, the classic text of Krishna devotion and the first *purana* to be translated into a European language, was dictated by the sage Shukadeva to the king Pariskshit. The monarch was so fixed in his devotion to receive sacred knowledge that he is said to have sat unmoving for seven days, without food or water.[18]

The wisdom of stasis is evident in other contexts. In the classic work on statecraft, Kautilya's *Arthashastra* (c. AD 100), the word *asana* describes the strategy of biding one's time and making no move in any direction, 'sitting on the fence'. From the time of the later *Yoga Upanishads* onwards, however, there was a shift, and it became more common to use *asana* to describe a position adopted not only in yoga but also in more varied and dynamic contexts. These include wrestling, armed combat and sexual congress.

The earliest non-seated *asanas* are listed in assorted texts from the tenth century as the peacock (*mayurasana*), the cockerel (*kukkutasana*) and the tortoise (*kurmasana*). But even then, echoing the spiritual slant of earlier scriptures, the well-known *shavasana* or 'corpse pose' was still construed as a *samketa* or 'secret technique' of mind-yoga, rather than the simple physical relaxation taught in so many yoga sequences today. And significantly, nowhere

31

in any of these *Yoga Upanishads* is there a mention of the dynamic sequence that has become the signature favourite of much modern postural practice— the 'salute to the sun' (*surya namaskar*).

Overall, then, the seers of these early yoga scriptures were clearly far less interested in *asana* postures than in *mantra* meditation, breathing exercises (*pranayama*), and the 'subtle body' (*linga sharira*) with its conduits (*nadis*) of the life energy (*prana*) and energetic nodes (*chakras*). Much attention is paid to *kundalini*, the cosmic evolutionary force dormant in the individual nervous system and locked in at the base of the spine awaiting arousal. And finally, alongside the recondite descriptions of subtle physiology, there is also mention of the ultimate goal of yogic endeavour: prolonged experience of the mind's being settled in meditative absorption (*samadhi*), and its eventual immersion in the absolute Self. Every other practice, these texts maintain, be it outer or inner, is but a preparation for this ultimate state of introversion, and not an end in itself. Such, at least, was the stated ideal. In practice, though, as we shall see, this spiritual apotheosis appears to have remained a distant aspiration which gave way to a more seductive interest: the cultivation of supernormal powers that allow the yogi's awareness to play around in ways that transcend the mundane limitations of time and space.

All in all, the *Yoga Upanishads* demonstrate a rich, if inconsistent, amalgam of teachings that range from classical purity to baroque cosmologies, from worship of deities to Vedantic non-dualism. The typical academic view is that the coexistence of such divergent themes proves that ideas from different and often antagonistic philosophical schools were somehow lumped together any old how in texts so eclectic that their integrity becomes compromised by their contradictions. Some practitioners, however, take a different angle. They see such assorted topics as representing the various and successive stages of a long pilgrimage of transformation, stations in an ongoing and progressive journey of self-transcendence. As the mind moves beyond the limits of a self-hood defined by attachment to the body, travelling through the subtle and causal levels of the psyche to the transcendental source of all, it will experience many different perspectives, many variant realities. Each of them is a valid understanding, appropriate to the stage attained, but it is only provisional, as each petal of the lotus must unfurl before the blossoming of full enlightenment is possible. One authority who took this approach was the revered fifteenth-century textual commentator Vijnanabhikshu, to whom the perspectives of Sankhya, Yoga and Vedanta were sequential stages on the journey rather than irreconcilable destinations. Other seers, ancient and modern, have concurred, but Western scholarship, forever sharpening its Occam's razor, has tended to dismiss the idea.

3

THE GREAT PATANJALI PARADOX

If there is one text that almost everybody who practises yoga will have heard of, even if they have never read it, it is the *Yoga Sutra* of Maharishi Patanjali. Just who Patanjali was is open to question. Over the years tradition has connected the author of the *sutras* with several people bearing the same name—a great grammarian, a Vedic priest, a renowned teacher of Sankhya and a south Indian Shaivite guru among them. The question of attribution with Indian texts can be further complicated by the fact that an author would sometimes append his master's name to his own work if he felt he was transmitting the pure teaching he had inherited with no personal additions or interpretations. Preferring mythistorical origins, Indian yoga schools have often lauded Patanjali as no less than an incarnation of Shiva, who in his form as *Mahayogi* is the archetypal practitioner of yoga and patron deity of yogis, and when worshipped as *Dakshinamurti* is the root guru of yogic knowledge. Some even see Patanjali as a form of Adishesha, the cosmic serpent on whom the universe rests.

Questions of authorship aside, the *Yoga Sutra* was probably composed sometime before AD 350 and is the oldest text we know of that is dedicated solely to the subject. For many centuries it seems to have enjoyed considerable esteem; during the medieval era it was the most translated of the old Indian texts, rendered from Sanskrit into many Indian languages and even Old Javanese and Arabic. Then, after a mysterious fall from grace at the end of the first millennium AD and subsequent obscurity for nearly 700 years, the *sutras* received a renewed interest from Western scholars in the late eighteenth century. Finally, perhaps a hundred years later, they were first popularised through the writings of Swami Vivekananda, a key figure we shall meet in chapter 11.

Since that time, translations of the text into English alone have been legion, and they continue to be produced in numbers and widely studied in the inter-

national yoga community and beyond. Faithful translation is always an onerous enough task and a 'free translation' can veer a long way from the original.
Within the *Yoga Sutra* corpus, there are several versions produced by those
who, knowing no Sanskrit, have come up with their own by combining various existing translations and relying on their poetic empathy to connect with
what they deem to be the spirit of the original. Encouraged by the extreme
succinctness of the aphoristic *sutra* form, the imaginative interpreter can be
led to speculate on what a text might mean, or should mean, or is even meant
to mean. Whatever the value of these third-hand efforts, it cannot be denied
that, at the least, they evince some mysterious power of attraction inherent in
the original text.[1]

Vivekananda gave Patanjali's work the gold seal when he called it 'the highest authority and text book on *raja yoga*, the 'King of Yogas', by which he
meant meditation rather than postures. Curiously, though, even he succumbed to the temptation to elaborate on the original, producing what he
admitted was 'a rather free translation of the aphorisms (*sutras*) of Patanjali,
with a running commentary'.[2]

More recent authorities, including those focused solely on body-work,
have agreed with the Swami's estimation. Tirumalai Krishnamacharya, probably the most important single influence on modern postural practice, was
equally enthusiastic when he wrote: 'If it is not in the *Yoga Sutra*, it's not yoga.'
The distinguished American academic Wendy Doniger, who generally delights
in running counter to accepted opinion, concurs, stating that Patanjali's work
'is essential to anyone's understanding ... of the practice of yoga.'[3]

Similar support comes from more surprising sources. One such is Godfrey
Devereux, a prolific author and yoga-innovator who describes his brand of
Dynamic Yoga (an offshoot of the Vinayasa 'flow' method) as 'a fluid, lively
form of movement that is much less static than traditional yoga and which is
as effective a cardiovascular workout as a conventional exercise-to-music
class'. Despite the fact that, by his own admission, his workout system could
hardly be further removed from what Patanjali recommends, Devereux also
claims the text is indispensable, calling it 'the Bible of yoga'.[4] So, from various
angles—traditional, scholarly, innovative—the *Yoga Sutra* seems to be the one
essential work, the *vade mecum* for those who would travel the path of yoga.
No wonder then that so many training organisations place it top of their list
of required reading for students.

But wait a minute. There is one sharply dissenting voice in all this comfortable agreement, and since it belongs to the author of the most detailed biography of the text,[5] University of California scholar David Gordon White, we

might do well to heed it. White emphatically dissents from the general conflation of Patanjali with modern practice, as the opening paragraph of his introduction makes very clear: 'the *Yoga Sutra* is as relevant to yoga as it is taught
and practised today as understanding the workings of a combustion engine is
to driving a car'.

In view of the depth in which White has researched the topic, his voice
cannot just be ignored as a lone aberration. So, who is right here? Put another
way, what exactly is the relationship of modern yoga practice to the most
revered classical study of the subject?

Given their popularity, we might reasonably expect the *sutras* to be a catalogue of, or at least a seed-bed for, the multiple *asanas* taught in today's yoga
classes. But the first thing that strikes anyone who reads his little masterpiece
is that Patanjali devotes only three short verses out of a total of 196 to physical postures. It is worth reminding ourselves of this brief reference: 'The
physical postures should be steady and comfortable. They are mastered when
all effort is relaxed and the mind is absorbed in the infinite. Then we are no
longer upset by the play of opposites.'[6]

This sparse reference makes it quite clear that the criterion of mastery in
asana lies not in athletic flexibility, nor in its benefits on health and well-
being, but in the fact that it facilitates an effortless state of mental absorption. And this absorption is not simply a simple state of idle relaxation but
the profound mental equilibrium of 'the infinite' that lies 'beyond the play of
opposites'. (What a wealth of meaning is compacted into that last phrase:
everything from hot and cold to heaven and hell!) To compound his point
that the purpose of body-work is to refine the mind, Patanjali does not
bother to mention a single *asana* by name, let alone explain any in detail.
Instead, however, he does devote dozens of *sutras* to the various stages of
meditative interiority and their effects. In a text which delights in exploring
the nuances of a wholly psychological reality, the physicality of the body is
barely touched upon. Patanjali's whole orientation bears out the historical
lack of concern with postural work we have already encountered; it exemplifies the Upanishadic attitude that the body's prime utility is its role as the
perch of the mind.

At the very beginning of the text, Patanjali defines yoga as 'the settling of
the thought-waves in the mind'.[7] A couple of centuries later, his major commentator, the sage Vyasa, would reinforce this with an even more laconic definition: 'Yoga is the settled mind.'[8] This prioritising of mind over body is usually explained by following Vivekananda's assertion that Patanjali and his
school were exponents of *raja yoga*, the yoga of the mind, whereas today's

postural practice is the direct heir of traditional *hatha yoga*, the yoga of the body. That things are by no means this simple we have already discussed in our introduction, but even if for the moment we accept this inaccurate definition, the fact that modern postural yoga continues to look back to Patanjali as its guiding light remains curious to say the least.

Supernormal Powers

Things get worse. Patanjali goes on to develop his message in a direction that flatly contradicts those who seek to reduce yoga to a regime of physical fitness. It soon transpires that what largely, though not exclusively, interests him about meditation, if we are to judge from the fact he devotes over a quarter of his whole work to them, are the supernormal powers it bestows. *Vibhuti pada*, 'The Chapter on Expansion',[9] which is the third and longest section, details some forty of these 'perfections', the prime meaning of the word *siddhi*. The predominant characteristic of many of the *siddhis* is that they demonstrate the mind's ability to transcend the limits of the body and operate independently of its restrictive frame. As Patanjali says, 'perfect knowledge of the mind' comes only 'when attachment to the body is loosened'.[10] The revelatory power of such freedom from physicality is made clear: 'the operation of the mind beyond the confines of the body is known as "the great state beyond the body" (*mahavideha*). This destroys the veil that obscures the light of spiritual discernment.'[11]

In other words, the *siddhis* can be tools employed to destroy the final obstruction of ignorance—a kind of mental *asana* as it were—but, in themselves, are still limitations and not the final goal. This is because they are 'subordinate to the state of pure unboundedness', representing only 'the perfections of a mind still operating at the subtle level'.[12] To practise *siddhis* then is to employ the mind in the subtlest strata of life, at such a depth as to be able to bend the mundane laws of time and space operating on its surface. But all such activity is still activity, and as such, it is impelled by the desire of a limited individual mind. It is just this desiring that prevents the self from merging with the inactive plenitude of the absolute consciousness behind all our mental activity.

Patanjali also warns of the dangers of spiritual pride that may inflate the yogi if he becomes seduced by the allure of the psychic realms.[13] He frames *siddhis* in terms of *samyama*, a technique of refined mental focus that ultimately leads to complete self-transcendence, what he calls the state of 'aloneness' (*kaivalya*). While such a practice can be classed as a benevolent means to Self-knowledge, dozens of texts that were to become far more popular than the

Yoga Sutra did not always share such high aspirations. Despite the master's instructions, it seems that much yoga in the centuries following him was practised in order to obtain powers.

Some time after Vyasa, who lived in the fifth century AD, there appears to have been a major split between philosophers who studied the *Yoga Sutra* and practitioners who did not. Late in the first millennium AD, Patanjali's oeuvre completely disappeared from yogic praxis and it did not regain any prominence until well over a thousand years later with the beginning of European interest.

In its homeland, then, mind-yoga was valued as a means to gain powers, and from an early time. Some of these abilities were physical rather than psychic, such as longevity or increased physical strength and endurance. This fascination with extraordinary physical prowess was old magic. The *Arthashastra*, an important text on statecraft and economics that predates Patanjali, advises: 'By coating camel-skin shoes with the fat of an owl and a vulture and wrapping them with banyan leaves, a man is able to walk for fifty *Yojanas* [about 750 km] without getting tired.'[14] Other early texts include charms to transform a man's penis; similarity to that of an elephant, ass or horse was most desired.

Classical Hindu thought, excepting its many materialistic schools,[15] generally accepts the fact of paranormal abilities at face value. Non-orthodox yogic systems, such as early Buddhism and Jainism, may display less enthusiasm for *siddhis* but do not doubt their existence for a moment. Nor is it the case, as is sometimes claimed by those wishing to minimise its more baroque elements, that orthodox yoga dismisses all *siddhis* outright as being a deviation from the true goal of enlightenment. There is a group of them, known collectively as 'the Eight Powers' (*ashtasiddhi*), which, rather than constituting an impediment—or, as Patanjali teaches, a strategic means—to enlightenment, is said to arise spontaneously as the flowering of the liberated state. Vyasa lists these approvingly in his commentary on Patanjali[16] and in popular belief they are said to be enjoyed by the monkey-general Lord Hanuman, who bestows them on his favoured devotees. Nonetheless, as Patanjali reminds us, lack of attachment to these exalted gifts, even to the boon of omniscience, is the sign of a true yogi. It is this imperious dispassion alone which finally destroys 'the seeds of bondage' and ushers in the irrevocable liberation from the clenched fist of egotism.[17]

Patanjali's Message

Magical powers aside then, what is the essential teaching of the *Yoga Sutra*? Patanjali's perspective is based on the theoretical framework of the Sankhya philosophy. This delineates the various levels of existence, which is ultimately divided into two discrete principles. One—*prakriti*, 'the manifested'—is made up of twenty-four strata (*tattvas*) which constitute the entire *karma*-driven material cosmos, including the individual body-mind. The other principle, eternally distinct from *prakriti*, is a primordial ground of pure consciousness that is beyond not only the individual mind but all the restrictions of time, space and causation. This ground, known as *purusha*—'the Person'—is our real nature, our essential being. As Patanjali tells us in the opening verses of his work, the goal of yoga is to disentangle ourselves from the meshes of *prakriti* and consciously to realise our essential unity with *purusha*, our real Self. Correct yoga brings about the separation of the 'Seer' from the 'seen', destroying the metaphysical ignorance that is the cause of all human suffering. Once this separation is accomplished, we experience the totality of life, in both its objective and changing relative phases, and its subjective and unchanging absolute phase. Spirit is freed from the encumbrance of matter and life is lived in freedom, peace and an innate happiness beyond the changing pleasures provided by the senses. This liberation severs the fetters of *karma* binding us to the limited sense of isolated selfhood.

Sankhya, then, is a resolutely dualistic system, which aligns the *Yoga Sutra* with the teachings of Jainism and early Buddhism. The state of *kaivalya* ('aloneness; singularity') which is the goal of the *sutras*, can be seen as a subjective and internal unification with the ground of all being, but it has no bearing on the outside world and serves only to bring about a radical separation from it. However, interpretations of Patanjali's text often tend to overlook this, its core teaching. An example well known on the yoga scene is the ever-popular *How to Know God* by Swami Prabhavananda and Christopher Isherwood that we have already encountered at the beginning of Chapter 1. Towards the end of their introduction the authors say:

> Since yoga, prior to Patanjali, was originally grounded in Vedanta philosophy, we have interpreted the aphorisms, throughout, from a Vedantic viewpoint. In this we differ from Patanjali himself, who was a follower of the Sankhya philosophy. But these are merely technical differences, and it is best not to insist on them too strongly, lest the reader becomes confused.

However well-intentioned, to present and interpret a master from a position he himself clearly did not hold (there is no way Patanjali could be called a follower of Vedanta) and to do so under the guise of avoiding confusion, is, to put it charitably, disingenuous. The fundamentally differing positions of dualist Sankhya and non-dualist Vedanta cannot really be dismissed as 'mere technical differences'.

Integrated Growth

That today's yoga teachers have ignored the *siddhis* is hardly surprising. They are generally not affiliated to a lineage that would render such teachings, and the nuanced intricacies of meditation that Patanjali expounds, less opaque. Instead, modern yoga has focused attention on what has become the best-known part of his teaching: 'The Eight Limbs' (*ashtanga*). Indeed, for many people these 'limbs' *are* yoga. However, given that the limbs take up only thirty-one *sutras*,[18] this preference risks overlooking the remaining 80 per cent of his message. Many devotees of postural work take this selectivity one stage further, typically confining their interest to only half of the offered trajectory, i.e. just the first four limbs: *yama* and *niyama* (regulations of behaviour), *asana* (posture) and *pranayama* (breathing exercises). By overlooking the second quartet, the meditative stages of *pratyahara* (withdrawal of the senses), *dharana* (mental focus), *dhyana* (settling of the mind) and *samadhi* (mental absorption), they ignore what the master himself explicitly calls 'the heart of yoga, more intimate than the preceding limbs'.[19]

One common justification for disregarding this 'heart' is that the *ashtanga* represent a sequence of stages, and some degree of mastery in the earlier stages is necessary before the later ones can be attempted. Until quite recently this was the standard explanation being given in body-yoga classes worldwide. The trouble is that it blatantly ignores both the language and the logic of the text. A graduated progression implies that the first limb, *yama*, must initially be accomplished, or at least well developed, before the next is tackled. So, we must somehow become proficient in the five subdivisions of *yama*—the 'Laws of Life' characterised as non-violence, truthfulness, integrity, chastity and non-attachment—before we are fit to move on to the second limb, *niyama*, 'The Rules for Living', which comprise simplicity, contentment, and so on. And all this, by the same logic, must be achieved before we are ready to tackle the third limb: a basic set of *asanas*! Such reasoning is patently absurd. The very fact that nearly all yoga teachers will introduce their students to *asanas* at the very outset of practice violates any position they might hold that the *ashtanga* are meant to be taken as sequential steps on a progressive path.

The answer to this confusion is simple, as it lies in the terminology of the text. Patanjali deliberately chooses to use the term 'limbs' rather than any of the technical terms available that denote a stage or station on the way (e.g. *bhumi*, *jhana*, etc.). Why? Because the limbs of a body grow simultaneously, not one after another or in a linear sequence. Our left arm doesn't grow

before our right leg; the fingers don't have to lengthen before the toes grow
or the ankles thicken. A body grows as an organic whole and the development
of each of its separate limbs is perfectly synchronised to co-ordinate with all
the others for the good of that whole. In this way the entire structure naturally develops as a harmoniously functioning entity, with each of its component parts balancing and reinforcing the others. Similarly, the practitioner
grows in yoga through a simultaneous, complementary and mutually reinforcing development of each of the 'limbs', rather than trying to cultivate one
after another in the hope of eventually achieving the distant goal of the eighth
limb, the absorption that is *samadhi*.

The Primacy of Samadhi

In fact, far from being a distant terminus, *samadhi* is integral to the journey
from its very beginning. It is no coincidence that the first, and not the last, of
the four sections of the text is entitled *Samadhi Pada*, 'The Chapter on the
Settled Mind'. This opening section explains *samadhi* in considerable detail
and is followed successively by the three others: 'Treading the Path',
'Expansion' and 'Liberation'. From this sequence alone it can be inferred that
the state of *samadhi* is not achieved after much time and effort spent traversing
the preceding stages. The truth is quite the opposite. Some experience of
settling the mind comes from the outset, and is a prerequisite for 'treading
the path'. Otherwise, if *samadhi* were indeed the distant end-point of yogic
praxis, surely the *Samadhi Pada* would be the culmination of the whole work,
appropriately placed as the final, triumphant chapter, the crowning glory of
all the hard work that had preceded it?

The reason that *samadhi* is the beginning, not the end, of yoga is that, as
Patanjali makes very clear throughout the opening chapter, *samadhi* is a general term that covers many nuanced stages and subtle gradations of mental
quietude. Each has its own name and characteristic and can be brought about
by various means. *Samadhi*, then, is not one specific state, nor is it only the
final goal of total quiescence. By overlooking this too many people doing yoga
settle for a black-and-white version of possibility when, following the text's
advice to look a little deeper and explore a little further, they might well
discover a vista that is wondrously coloured. This is a lack of responsible
teaching. To claim, as some yoga teachers do, that their students are 'not yet
ready for meditation' is to betray their own ignorance of the subject and to
misinterpret Patanjali into the bargain.

The Tradition of Commentary

When dealing with a classic such as Patanjali's, we must also consider all the authoritative commentaries that have been appended to it over the centuries. The importance of such commentaries stems partly from the extreme succinctness of the *sutra* form. Patanjali's work contains nearly 200 of these axioms, but only six verbs between them! Each *sutra* ('thread; string'—we get our English word 'suture' from the same root) serves as an *aide-memoire* for the teacher, a densely compacted phrase from which various levels of meaning are first teased out, then spun and woven into a tapestry of instruction. In the place of a living teacher, this explanatory function is served by commentary. Over time, other commentaries are added to the first one and then other commentaries appended to them in turn, each contributing to the growing body of extrapolation. In traditions of exegesis, this means that to study a body of *sutras* is to study all its reputed commentaries as well.

Thus in our search for the origins of body-yoga, it is significant that Patanjali's major commentator, Vyasa, mentions just five *asanas* in his commentary. Some 400 years later, perhaps India's most influential philosopher-saint and commentator on major sacred texts, Adi Shankara, is similarly unconcerned with the physical side of yoga. His Vedantic perspective, *pace* Prabhavananda and Isherwood, does not rate *asanas* highly. In his own commentary on Patanjali, Shankara describes thirteeen of them, then follows Vyasa in adding 'and others' at the end of his list.[20] He concludes by explaining Vyasa's use of the word 'others': 'The word "others" (*adi*) in the commentary indicates that there may be variations prescribed by a teacher.' Whatever these 'others' were, it seems they did not constitute properly different poses, being merely 'variations', and as such did not merit any further discussion.

In fact, the master of non-dualism displays a diminishing interest in detailed description of postures the further down the list he gets.[21] When once asked which he considered to be the best *asana*, Shankara humorously replied it is *nididhyasana*, a level of mental expansion that transcends thinking and leads to an immediate experience of the real Self beyond the mind.[22] He also adds that 'painful breathing exercises are for the ignorant'. Nonetheless, his overall conclusion is that body-yoga is useful in the spiritual quest, as it 'kindles the fire of true knowledge'.[23] A similar disregard of physical detail is noticeable in other authorities who elaborated on Patanjali throughout the ages. Amongst these were some of India's greatest minds: the philosophical genius Vachaspati Mishra (tenth century), his follower King Bhoja (eleventh century), and the enlightened scholar Vijnanabhikshu (fifteenth century).

41

As a final a nod to the limitations of body-yoga, it is well to remember here that the great traditions of Indian spirituality always and everywhere agree with the doctrine—taught alike by many *Upanishads*, the Buddhists and the Jains—that human suffering is the consequence of egotism, which they define as a deluded sense of self stemming from an erroneous identification with the body. This attachment is only finally defeated by the self-transcendence that is liberation. Shankara himself often mocks contemporary materialist philosophers for espousing what he calls 'the body is the Self' philosophy.[24] In the same vein, Patanjali opens his work by describing our 'true nature'[25] as an unlocalised and universal awareness unclouded by the workings of the individual body-mind and concludes, in the very last *sutra* of the text, with the triumphant transcendence of the entire material realm of time, space and causation.[26] Set against this lofty metaphysical goal, the exclusive bodily focus of so much contemporary postural yoga can hardly be claimed to concur with the author of the *Yoga Sutra* and the many sages who followed him. None of these authorities saw the practice of yoga as a means to perfect the human frame itself, but as the way to transcend its irksome limitations altogether. All in all, the *Yoga Sutra* has gained its popularity partly by default, as there is just such a dearth of early texts that can be comfortably related to modern yoga practice.

4

GITA YOGA

How on earth is the serious student of yoga to approach the *Bhagavad Gita*? And approach it she must, sooner or later, as the text is universally agreed to be a celebration of the ancient teaching and a symphony of its many themes. In fact, in addition to yoga—a word they mention perhaps a hundred times—the 700 verses of the *Bhagavad Gita*, 'the Song of God', deal with subjects that cover almost every aspect of the Indian philosophical and religious spectrum. The vast range of topics discussed includes differing philosophical systems such as dualistic Sankhya and monist Vedanta; devotion to God (*bhakti*) and discriminative metaphysical insight (*jnana*); practical advice on how best to handle our daily activity (*karma*), how to deal with the process of dying and what happens with reincarnation. Then there is analysis of the human mind, its levels and psychology, together with instruction in the technique of meditation, that sit alongside advice on morality, warfare, the humanising effects of love and the self-transcendence of surrender. There is also plenty of high-octane theology. In discussions on the nature of the Divine, God is shown to be both immanent and transcendent, personal and yet also impersonal, while the whole narrative is coloured by the irresistible charm of the supreme personality of the Godhead, Lord Krishna. We are also introduced to abstract theories of time, conceived of as endless cycles of the creation, preservation and dissolution of the universe, as well as more mundane discussions on the ideals of social organisation and the importance of family and cultural traditions.

Given such a wealth of perspectives, it is little wonder that there is hardly an Indian teacher, whatever their affiliation, who has not at some time drawn on the *Gita*. Social reformers have done so as well. Mahatma Gandhi frequently declared the *Gita* to be his favourite scripture because, despite its daunting theological and philosophical range, he saw it as a practical guide-

43

book for living. Gandhi's closest disciple, the land-reform activist Vinobha Bhave, was of the same mind, once commenting: 'In the *Bhagavad Gita* there is no long discussion, nothing elaborate. The main reason for this is that everything stated in the *Gita* is meant to be tested in the life of every man; it is intended to be verified in practice.'[1]

Woven unbroken throughout the richly variegated tapestry of the Song of God is one singular thread: spiritual liberation allows us to live the Divine consciously in the midst of all the inevitable ups and downs of day-to-day existence. The secret is to gain unity with That which transcends the world of change. This teaching is the unifying core of the *Gita's* multiplicity.

The *Bhagavad Gita* comprises part of the sixth chapter of India's greatest epic, the *Mahabharata*, which, running to 100,000 stanzas, is the world's longest literary work by far: longer than the Odyssey and Iliad combined, and four times the length of the Bible. Finalised in the first or second century AD, the *Mahabharata* talks quite a lot about yoga—the word occurs almost 900 times in the text—and contains what is probably the oldest systematised treatment of the subject.[2] It also deals extensively with yoga's philosophical sister Sankhya, the dualistic philosophy discussed in the last chapter, and nowhere are these two topics more cogently presented for the relative newcomer than in the early chapters of the *Gita*.

The *Mahabharata* tells the story of the cataclysmic Great War, fought over eighteen days between two related clans, the Pandavas and the Kauravas, to decide which of them should rule the Kingdom of Bharat (Upper India). Thirteen years previously the rightful sovereigns, the Pandavas, had been tricked into losing their throne by a game of loaded dice, and retired into forest exile. Now, they have returned to stake their claim. One of the Pandava clan, Arjuna, is the greatest archer of his time, but although right is on his side, he is consumed with doubt. While his duty as a soldier, his *Kshatriya dharma*, is to fight to support his elder brother's legitimate bid to regain the throne, the opposing Kaurava forces are also family: cousins, some of his own former teachers and many friends are among their ranks. So Arjuna is caught on the horns of a dilemma: whatever he does will incur the loss and suffering of loved ones. Fortunately, he has as his advisor another cousin, Lord Krishna, who, as the incarnation of the god Vishnu, is in a position to offer guidance from a perspective elevated far above the anthill scurry of human partialities. The *Gita*, then, is essentially the dialogue between the warrior Arjuna and his divine mentor Krishna.

Seen in a wider context, Arjuna is an everyman figure whose predicament symbolises the human condition. We live in a world of myriad conflicting interests and making the right choice about which course of action to follow is often a difficult and contradictory affair. In response to this common dilemma, the *Gita* presents yoga initially not as a means of theological salvation, but as a practical method of bringing a broader perspective (and ultimately a higher wisdom) to bear on human agency. It offers a way to act with dispassion and potency in the everyday world, for as the Lord himself states very early in the text, 'Yoga is skill in action'. These three words alone—*yogah karmasu kaushalam*[3]—are in themselves a masterly double-edged teaching. Not only does the Lord make it clear that the unifying power of yoga is a means of handling the world of activity with adroitness, but he simultaneously implies that the most 'skilful' action of all is in fact that which leads to 'yoga', union with the Divine.

By yoga, Krishna is not referring to postural practice. In what is by now a familiar pattern, the *Gita* advocates only mind-yoga and pays no attention to *asana*. There is the brief, customary, reference to the desirability of a firm seat and sitting upright in a collected manner, but this, as in the *Yoga Sutra*, is included as an explicit instruction for meditation and presented in the context of uniting the little self—the individual body/mind, the egoic 'me'—with the cosmic Self—the transpersonal, infinite Consciousness that lies behind all human limitations.[4] Indeed, Krishna clearly has no time for the tough physical disciplines practised by some contemporary Buddhist and Jain ascetics. He dismisses such asceticism not only because it is unsanctioned by Hindu orthodoxy, but because it is all too often employed just to show off, by 'Those persons who, given to ostentation and pride, and possessed of passion, attachment and strength, undertake severe austerities not sanctioned in the scriptures.'[5]

What he offers instead of such extreme strategies is the practical recipe for a successful and rewarding life, both material and divine. For his devotees, Krishna is the Divine made manifest; when we become familiar with his story, we can begin to grasp our own.

In two crucial early verses the Lord counsels Arjuna that if he wishes to find the truth, without which his life will be like a dried-up leaf at the mercy of every passing breeze, his mind must travel beyond the entire range of the material world and find its unchanging essence deep within. Later, yoga will be presented as the supreme means to God-realisation, but Krishna is nothing if not pragmatic: first things first. Employing the terminology of Sankhya and its analysis of the three qualities or *gunas* that in various combinations make up the unstable world of change,[6] he advises: 'Be without the three *gunas*, O Arjuna, freed from duality, ever firm in purity, independent of possessions, possessed of the Self.'[7]

45

So, according to the Lord, the prerequisite to successful action is conscious inaction; all worthwhile 'doing' depends on establishing a prior state of 'being'. The means to this settled state of awareness is meditation, which takes the mind beyond mutable duality and into a stable, centred and unencumbered space that exists independent of outer possessions and devoid of physical or mental disturbance. Indeed, this inner fullness of pure potential is our only real possession, the true Self that can never be taken from us. Established on this unwavering platform we can think and act with calmness, power and non-attachment, for these are the inherent qualities of the ground of our own being.

While regular contact and eventual union with the absolute Self is clearly of practical benefit, Krishna goes on to point out that it is also the essential prerequisite for any valid experience of the Divine. As such, Self-knowledge is superior to what is commonly practised in the name of religion, and in this the *Gita* echoes the view, expressed 500 years or more earlier, of the Upanishadic sages we have already heard from. They tell us that the yardstick of the true *brahmin* is not inherited social position with its priestly expertise, but direct perception of the Absolute behind all forms: 'Looking on those worlds won by ritual, the true *brahmin* arrives at dispassion. For that which is not made comes not from what is done.'[8]

Now Lord Krishna goes even further, by adopting the radical position that even the Vedas themselves, the most sacred of all scriptures and the eternal fountain-head of nourishment for the orthodox, are inferior to the experience of freedom in the absolute Self: 'The Vedas' concern is with the three *gunas*. ... To the enlightened *brahmin* all the Vedas are of no more use than is a small well in a place flooded with water on every side.'[9] This is a quite extraordinary statement to find embedded deep within such an orthodox text, but mark well the word 'enlightened'. Krishna's inclusion of the word *brahmin* is also significant here. A person unschooled in priestly skills might well fail to recognise the Vedas as supreme wisdom, but the Lord's point is that even a knowledgeable and respected *brahmin*, who has gone through all the training and is fully conversant with the benefits rituals bring, must come to realise that the omnipresent Truth lies beyond anything obtainable through learning or ritual expertise. Such a realisation is the fruit of his enlightenment.

This state of elevated awareness is then equated with yoga: 'Established in yoga, O winner of wealth, perform actions having abandoned attachment and having become balanced in success and failure, for balance of mind is yoga.'[10]

Here again, yoga is described explicitly in terms of 'mind'. When the fully developed mind has transcended its limited individual status, it is freed from emotional reactivity and egoic attachment because it now enjoys conscious union with the transcendental divine Self. This state is the true 'wealth' and the greatest gain. In this verse, the state of yoga is presented as the freedom from attachment to outcomes. While we can easily see the benefit of feeling untouched by what we may judge to be 'failure', Krishna takes dispassion a step further by pointing out that what the fickle world calls 'success' also fails to overshadow the yogi's inner contentment. Fluctuations of fortune are inevitable, but they only impinge on us to the extent we derive our sense of self from them.

Krishna's phrase 'winner of wealth' has an additional connotation. The *Gita*'s lasting popularity stems largely from the fact it has always been taken as a guide for householders, those with jobs, commitments and families to support. Unlike the renunciate, living on the fringes of society, the typical householder seeks happiness and security through the accruing of material benefit and the enjoyment of human relationships, but in this verse Krishna subtly points out that the goal of all action—the subjective sense of fulfil-ment—has already been accomplished by the successful yogi. This supreme contentment is the result of the mind's union with the cosmic Self; the disin-terested sage is established in fulfilment no matter what is going on around him. This inner plenitude, an inherent happiness naturally maintained what-ever the outer circumstance, is the basis of a truly worthwhile life and brings us into proximity with the Divine.[11]

In the state of yoga, then, the entire realm of time, space and causation is seen to be quite separate from one's own inner ground of awareness. This is what, perhaps a couple of hundred years later, Patanjali would term *kai-valya*—'aloneness; solitude; independence'—the separation of the inner from the outer that marks the climax of the Sankhya-yoga system. United with the subjective principle of *purusha*, the real Self, the yogi enjoys eternal freedom from entanglement in the world of the *gunas*, and thereby liberation is irre-versibly established.[12]

Nishkama Karma

Yogic fulfilment is not a passive affair, but a mode of being that is energetically expressed in what the *Gita* calls *nishkama karma*: 'action (*karma*) performed without (*nish*) egotistic desire (*kama*)'. Such selfless activity is quite different from that generated by a limited ego-self, which is typically motivated by a sense of need, the 'lack' that is the original meaning of our word 'want'. Action attached to its outcome will create an emotional reaction—success bringing happiness, failure breeding sorrow—which will in turn engender further self-centred action. This is the cycle of *karma*, which can only be broken when the mind, fully expanded in the state of yoga, can consciously and continuously reflect the unalloyed consciousness that lies ever beyond action. In this state, there is no attachment to the mechanism of desire because the little sense of 'I' has expanded to become the Self which, as the highest happiness, is not dependent on any action whatsoever for its native and spontaneous contentment.

What then happens to the mechanism of desire? Desires may continue to arise for the yogi, but they have no binding force, as their goal of finding happiness has already been effortlessly achieved. Moreover, such desires will no longer serve a personal agenda, but exist rather for the benefit of the general good and the cosmic purpose. This is truly selfless action, free of bias and unmotivated by need, fear or lack. In a magnificent passage, the Lord describes the Self-realised being and his paradoxical relationship to activity:

> He is united, he has accomplished all action. He whose every undertaking is free from desire and the incentive thereof, whose action is burnt up in the fire of knowledge, him the knowers of Reality call wise. Having cast off attachment to the fruit of action, ever contented, depending on nothing, even though fully engaged in action, he does not act at all. Expecting nothing, his heart and mind disciplined, having relinquished all possessions, performing action by the body alone, he incurs no sin. Satisfied with whatever comes unasked, beyond the pairs of opposites, free from envy, balanced in success and failure, even acting he is not bound.[13]

In this freedom, the *jivanmukta*, 'the one who is liberated in life', draws his identity, spontaneously and at all times, from the universal Self. As a result, he dwells quite separate from the realm of action, unattached to any thoughts that may spontaneously arise in his mind or any actions performed by his own limited body. Indeed, he is unattached even to its inaction. This supreme disinterest is the experienced effect of the separation between essence and substance, spirit and matter, *purusha* and *prakriti*, Self and non-Self.

Whatever terms may be used, such an awareness bestows a completely new sense of identity and initiates a totally different relationship to the world. Krishna goes on to describe its effects as felt in everyday activity:

> One who is in union with the Divine and who knows the Truth will maintain, 'I do not act at all'. In seeing, hearing, touching, smelling, eating, walking, sleeping, breathing, speaking, letting go, seizing, and even in opening and closing the eyes, he holds simply that the senses act among the objects of sense.[14]

By using the word 'simply' Krishna implies that such a state of consciousness is not the result of a consciously maintained attempt to become 'detached'. To fight against the natural pull of the senses, or to attempt to cultivate a mood of serenity by denying the feelings that arise in the mind and heart, is not the way to freedom. What the Lord is talking about here is the spontaneous state of effortless being, free of artifice, expectation or motive; the yogi's lordly non-attachment is not the result of some continuously maintained strategy of renunciation, denial or control. Many centuries before the *Gita*, this inherent separation of the experiencing ego and the witnessing Self was first imaged as two birds, inseparable companions on the same tree, with one eating the bitter and sweet fruit and the other just looking on, unattached and free.[15]

The natural non-attachment of such *nishkama karma* is described by many other seers the world over. The influential Neoplatonic philosopher Plotinus, writing around the time the *Gita* was being finalised, tells us:

We may treat of the Soul as in the body—whether it be set above it or actually within it—since the association of the two constitutes the one thing called the living organism, the Animate. From the Soul using the body as an instrument, it does not follow that the Soul must share the body's experiences: a man does not himself feel all the experiences of the tools with which he is working.[16]

Over a thousand years later, the Dominican friar and metaphysician Meister Eckhart uses theological language to explain the spontaneous state of liberation from limiting self-interest: 'Whoever has God in mind, simply and solely God, in all things, such a man carries God with him into all his works and into all places, and God alone does all his works.'[17]

The experience of this radical disinterest may occur in any context and its salient characteristic is the sense of activity's being effortless. And effortless activity is a joy; it is play, not work. Top athletes and sportspeople speak of the state of 'being in the zone' to describe the experience of acting free of the shackles of strain, the body moving perfectly of and by itself, as it were, while they just look on. At the highest level, this is also the state of Krishna himself, by whose disinterested 'play' (*lila*) the entire drama of the universe is enacted, orchestrated and enjoyed.

The Highest Unity

The heterogenous nature of the *Gita*'s message is no doubt what has ensured its popularity with all sorts of different readers. Whatever your viewpoint, somewhere in the text you will find consolation, nourishment and inspira-

49

tion. But is there a way to unify the disparate teachings into a greater whole? One way, as was mentioned in the previous chapter, is to see them as progressive stages on a single journey. Indian philosophical systems are traditionally called *darshana*, which literally means 'a seeing; a perspective; a point of view', a term that implies they are partial and provisional.

As the early chapters of the *Gita* teach, the aim of Sankhya-yoga is to explain and establish the unwavering separation of 'the Seer' and 'the seen'. But as the supreme object of devotion, Krishna has deeper levels of teaching to unveil as his song develops, for this radical separation of spirit and matter, Self and non-Self, is not the final yoga; yoga means 'union' after all. Certainly, a type of union with the inmost self, the Alone (*kaivalya*), has been established with the culmination of Sankhya, but what about the outside world? The separation of subjective Self from objective non-Self, spirit from matter, must eventually be healed and reconciled into the higher and all-encompassing unity that is the Lord himself. To accomplish this we have to pass beyond the oppositional perspective of Sankhya and enter into the kingdom of oneness known as 'the culmination of knowledge' (*Vedanta*).

To the Vedantic non-dualist, the entire of time, space and causation is but a passing and non-binding phase of its absolute essence. Just how this quantum sleight of hand—this *maya*—is accomplished is a topic that will occupy the best metaphysical minds India ever produced, but for Krishna it is simply his own ecstatic cosmic play, unfathomable. Dwelling in the heart of everyone, he orchestrates the revolving *mandala* of the universe, and yet, untouched by the magic show of matter he has conjured up, he remains invisible, behind the scenes. As the Lord explains, he transcends time and so resides ever beyond birth and decay, but beings who are blinded by duality fail to perceive him.[18]

To fathom the mystery of the Lord's *lila*, or play, both a mature devotion (*bhakti*) to the divine principle and direct spiritual insight (*jnana*) into the ultimate status of all forms and phenomena are needed. Only then will the yogi be able to experience the highest truth, that the world is his own Self made manifest, and that all sense of separation is an illusion based on ignorance of reality. In this radical transformation of the subject–object relationship, objects are no longer seen to be material entities separated out in space, but non-binding transformations of Consciousness itself, and he is that Consciousness. To the fully enlightened, there is no 'other', only the omnipresent Divine, which is my Self. As Krishna explains: 'He whose self is established in yoga, whose vision everywhere is even, sees the Self in all beings and all beings in the Self. He who sees Me everywhere, and sees everything in Me, I am not lost to him, nor is he lost to Me.'[19]

Different Types of Yoga?

Back down on the ground, it is usually taught that the *Gita* presents different types of yoga—*hatha*, *karma*, *bhakti*, *jnana*—for different types of people. From another perspective, and one that relates to the practicalities of our daily life, the various yogas can also be seen as related aspects of an integrated process of growth, rather than separate paths. As such, they mimic Patanjali's 'eight limbs' of yoga, which, as we saw in the last chapter, have for too long been misunderstood as discrete and sequential stages. After all, none of us is exclusively a doer, or a feeler, or a thinker; we are all of these in various ways and at different times, and a balanced life would include them all in correct proportion. To develop, we must at least have a healthy relationship to our own bodies (*hatha yoga*), a praxis that includes diet, exercise, overall lifestyle and the problematic question of self-image. There is also the participation in, and understanding of, the world of activity (*karma yoga*) and the gradual realisation of our innate separation from it. The development of wholesome relationships leads to a heartfelt openness (*bhakti yoga*) and the dawning of the highest knowledge (*jnana yoga*), the realisation of the divine unity within and behind all apparent diversity.

This is not just dry philosophy, but living experience, the true scope of yoga. Traditionally, it is quickened through the dynamics of the *guru–shishya*, 'teacher–disciple', relationship, which is why the *Gita* is cast in the form of a dialogue. Krishna's instruction of Arjuna is the archetype of the transformative interplay of question and answer that serves to remove obscurations to truth, as the wind removes clouds from the sun. The sublime vision Krishna holds out is the unity of all life; he will teach the details in due course, when his pupil's level of understanding has risen sufficiently. For the moment though, the practical logic of the Lord's instruction is clear: First of all, realise your Self. For if we do not first know who we really are, then how can we truly evaluate the world?

A final word. It would be a mistake to think of the *Gita* as being only 'Indian wisdom'. Despite the distinctive cultural matrix of the text's setting, it is the universality of Krishna's message that has appealed to the many who have come under its influence over the centuries. They have seen the 'Lord's Song' as a masterly exposition of the metaphysical essence that unites all the great religions at their common core. From this point of view, it is the heritage of the whole human race. Aldous Huxley, following in the steps of the German polymath Gottfried Leibnitz, called that universal wisdom the Perennial Philosophy. On the *Gita*, he wrote: 'The *Bhagavad-Gita* is the most systematic statement of spiritual evolution of endowing value to mankind. It is one of the most clear and comprehensive summaries of perennial philosophy ever revealed; hence its enduring value is subject not only to India but to all of humanity.'[20] Many contemporary followers of yoga would heartily concur.

5

WILD MEN, DUBIOUS REPUTATIONS

The old Etonian and fifth baronet of Walthamstow is surely the only person mentioned in Burke's Peerage who likes to sport a loin cloth and wear his waist-length dreadlocks matted with sacred cow dung. This sartorial preference is not merely a personal whim, nor even a desperate bid to win attention among the extravagant hats at Ascot or the brightly striped blazers at Henley, but indicates his fully accredited membership of the Juna Akhara, probably the oldest and most respected brotherhoods of yogic *sadhus*.[1] Welcome to the many-hued world of Sir James 'Jim' Mallinson, the world's foremost scholar on the early history of *hatha yoga*, expert hang-glider, sometime ascetic, sometime family-man but at all times the latest in the long and noble line of eccentric British Orientalists.[2]

After gaining his doctorate from Oxford with work on the *Khecharividya*, a root text of *hatha* that dates from about the thirteenth century AD, Mallinson has spent the last twenty years studying relevant manuscripts and undertaking participatory fieldwork with Hindi-speaking *sadhus* in northern India. He currently heads an international project into the origins of *hatha* based at the School of Oriental and African Studies (SOAS), University of London.[3] It is largely thanks to his pioneering efforts and those of his collaborative team that the mists that long obscured the early history of yoga seem finally to be clearing. The growth of scholarly effort that has gone into this field in recent years has no doubt been spurred in part by a desire to give some context to the meteoric uptake of body-yoga in the commercial marketplace. Understanding the social and doctrinal roots of yoga, it is hoped, will in turn cast some light on the true nature of modern postural practice.[4]

A quick historical recap. As we have seen, schools of mind-yoga that taught union with the inner Self had flourished since at least the time of the *Upanishads*. These communities existed on the edges of conventional society in isolated forest retreats and their divergence from the official culture of the Vedic sacrificial religion is pointed up in many texts. In the *Chandogya Upanishad*, the arrogant young pupil Shvetaketu, puffed up with his newly acquired sacerdotal expertise, returns home thinking he knows everything. He is sharply brought down to earth by his father, who teaches him that the direct experience of the divine Self within is more valuable than all the priestly knowledge, no matter how recondite. The opposing approaches of the boy and his father would later become known respectively as the 'lower knowledge'—the ritual and expertise that lead to worldly gain and a desirable after death—and the 'higher knowledge' that bestows spiritual enlightenment.[5] The latter was inclusive and non-sectarian; one early text describes the 'imperishable Absolute' as lying deep within, 'without family, without caste'.[6]

We know that throughout the first millennium AD, as Indian society became increasingly urban, stratified and monetised, the culture of these sylvan forest retreats that studied and practised Upanishadic wisdom became ever more a romantic symbol of a time when life was less constrained and more natural. Any visitor to the early rock-cut shrines of Hindu, Buddhist and Jain anchorites that are found all over North India—the masterpieces of Ajanta and Ellora being the most famous—will notice that they are very frequently adorned with motifs that nostalgically mimic the wood, bamboo and thatch structures of an earlier era. The practice continued even in the architecturally sophisticated free-standing temples those religions went on to build in such profusion. Wooden beams and joists are now replicated in stone or marble; carved or painted, floral and vegetal motifs writhe across ceilings and walls and around pillars. This decoration serves no structural purpose; its value is purely as a symbolic reminder of a lost paradise, a purer simpler time, a golden age when spiritual knowledge was lively and human beings lived in harmony with the Natural Law that orders all life. And peopling these oneiric Edens you will also see many yogic sages, sitting beneath their sacred trees and easily identified by their long hair, beards and beads. This nostalgic view of yoga has never quite departed from the Indian psyche. As we shall see later, it was resurrected to great effect when the Indian nationalist movement rediscovered the practice at the end of the nineteenth century.

Other more dramatic changes were in the air too. The ninth and tenth centuries witnessed the start of the age of invasions when much of the subcontinent was overrun by a dynamic force of change: Islam. Energetic and often intolerant, the religion of the Prophet brought not only new beliefs and practices, but also a different social structure that had little understanding of the ways of Hindu India, and no time for its elaborate temple rituals, complex caste rules and dietary restrictions. The widespread social disruption these incomers caused must have pushed the reclusive schools of mind-yoga to become even more marginalised in their jungle and mountain retreats.

As Mallinson has shown, it is around this time that we see the first appearance of some sort of a sustained teaching of body-yoga. This begins to formalise the inchoate traditions of rigorous asceticism that had been part of the Indian scene since the Vedic times. Lists of *asanas* occur in texts belonging to the Pancharatra yoga schools, the earliest of which is the tenth-century *Vimanarchanakalpa*. These groups worshipped Vishnu, which hints at a broader appeal of early yoga than had previously been assumed, as it is usually Shiva who is considered the lord of all things yogic.[7] It is also at this time that other physical techniques associated with body-yoga, the *mudras* or 'seals'—physical ways of manipulating the subtle vital energies—were being taught. Such exercises are nothing new, and their forerunners can be found a thousand years earlier in early Buddhist and Jain texts, though in those teachings they are presented as being very much second best to the more highly valued techniques of mental introversion.

In the fourth century BC, the Greek general Alexander the Great came across a group of what his people called *gymnosophists*—'naked ascetics'—on the banks of the river Indus. These *sadhus* impressed him with their ardour, but they were unsuccessful in their attempts to convert the philosophers who always travelled with his army. The theoretical debates were lively, but when the holy men insisted that the Greeks take up ascetic practices to progress further in their understanding, the latter declined. In his voluminous *Indica*, the earliest first-hand account of India in Western literature, the contemporary historian Megasthenes was impressed by the effects of penances undertaken by Indian *sadhus*, assuring his readers that there were men without mouths who could survive on nothing but the smell of roasted meat and the scent of fruit and flowers.

Dating from around this time, the *Mahabharata* and *Ramayana* also describe ascetics adopting arduous postures and undergoing penances, grouped under the general term *tapas*, meaning 'heat', that sometimes lasted years: sitting, squatting, remaining standing on one leg, holding the arms in the air, sitting by blazing fires in the full heat of the summer sun or immersed in freezing water in the winter cold. Such mortification of the flesh has not entirely disappeared from the indigenous yogic scene and it is distantly echoed in the very name *hatha yoga*, where *hatha* means 'force', a point often overlooked by modern advocates of body-yoga who employ the term.

According to the early medieval yoga texts, successful *tapas* grants not only the everyday skill of blessing and cursing with great potency, but the more rarified ability—and here we do have a nod in the direction of the ancient forest sages—to win liberation from the onerous cycle of death and rebirth altogether. In other words, we see a continuation, albeit in a more baroque form, of the soteriological concerns that had motivated Patanjali a thousand years earlier. Moreover, the first text containing a coherent *hatha yoga* teaching, the *Dattatatreya yogashastra*, even contains an 'eight-limbed yoga', though it is attributed to the Upanishadic sage Yajnavalkya rather than the author of the *Yoga Sutra*. But in general, the overriding interest of these early practitioners was not progressive mental absorption, let alone final liberation, but rather semen. Or, to be more accurate, its rigorous preservation and sublimation, in order to benefit from its vital energy.

The Power of the Seed

Early Indian thinkers were fascinated by the latent power contained in the seed, the densely compacted intelligence of life itself, everywhere observable in nature. The fact that the mighty banyan tree emerges from a small seed, and one that is hollow at its centre, was a favoured teaching device to explain the mysterious emergence of the cosmos from the no-thing of pure spirit.[8] In human terms, the puissance of the male seed (*bindu*, literally 'dot' or 'point') was considered sacramental. According to yogic physiology, the life energy is produced in subtle centres of the brain, from where it drips down to be burnt up in the digestive fire or shed from the body as semen. Loss of semen is thus a debilitating waste of both physical energy and spiritual vitality, hastening ill health, old age and death. On the other hand, the retention and preservation of semen creates a subtle energy—*ojas*—that allows the yogi to transcend the processes of change and attain, if not immortality, at least youthfulness, excellent health and extreme longevity. Thus, against the whole evolutionary thrust of natural selection, the alpha males of the world of yoga—rather like Catholic priests or Chinese eunuch bureaucrats—turned their back on the biological imperative of sexual reproduction, preferring to direct the sex energy inwards and upwards to realise a more universal goal.[9] It is this esoteric physiological concern, rather than any moral considerations, that explains the importance that Indic tradition has always placed on sexual continence for those on the spiritual path and, especially, the way of yoga.[10]

The *Dattatatreya yogashastra* introduces ten physical techniques that in later works came to be classed as *mudras*; several of these were developed to bring about the retention of semen in the head. One such is the *khecharimudra*, in which the tongue is curled back into the roof of the palate. Other *asanas* popular today were originally means to the same esoteric end. The badge of honour of many a modern student, the headstand (*shirshasana*), was originally a prolonged inversion practised to defy gravity and prevent the downward descent of the vital force. Breath-control techniques served the same purpose. The *Amritasiddhi*, a twelfth-century text from the Vajrayana Buddhist perspective, teaches the equation of breath, semen and mind that was already axiomatic in the era of the classical *Upanishads*.

Central to this preservation of vital energy in the early *hatha* texts is a technique known as *vajroli mudra*. This, so it was claimed, allowed the yogi, should he inadvertently ejaculate—whether through sex, wet dreams or the arousal of *kundalini*—to create a vacuum in his abdomen and draw the spilled seed back up into his body through his penis. In the ritual acts of yogic sex practised by tantric schools, proficiency in *vajroli* could also enable him to draw in the sexual fluids of his partner and energise himself by circulating the combined elixirs around his own subtle body. Whether such a practice is physically possible is open to question. If so, it would require extraordinary control, lengthy practise and, more mundanely, the use of catheters. Certainly, modern practitioners do use such aids, and Mallinson's latest research, drawing on fieldwork with *vajroli*-yogis and current medical understanding, suggests that the prime purpose of the repeated insertion of these catheters may have been to desensitise the ejaculatory mechanism altogether, and thus prevent any loss of vital energy during normal, or even greatly prolonged, sexual activity.

If this theory is correct, it would imply that the early *hatha* texts, from the eleventh to the fifteenth centuries, were instrumental in bringing these recondite ascetic techniques, which had never previously been codified, to a wider audience, which presumably included householders as well as recluses. Henceforward, then, if a man was so minded and determined enough, he could be both a *bhogi*—'an enjoyer of sensual delights'—as well as a yogi. By the eighteenth century we find one text, the *Vajroliyoga*, that begins by paying 'Homage to the guru, glorious Krishna!'—who is the god of love—and goes on to recommend that such a yogi should perfect the art of *vajroli* semen-retention by regularly releasing, and then drawing back his urine into the bladder. 'He who does this every day in the manner taught by his guru gains mastery of *bindu*, which bestows all powers. By practising this for six months *bindu* should not fall even when sex is had with one hundred women.'[11]

Whatever the facts, one thing is certain: the concern to preserve the life-force is as old as Indian gnosis. The first known mention of attempted *vajroli*, albeit practised as a means to contraception, goes back to the oldest of the *Upanishads*, the *Brihadaranyaka*, which dates from at least the sixth century BC.[12]

Above all, supervision of a competent guru was necessary. The *vajroli* technique had its equivalent for women, called *sahajoli*, the purpose of which was to reabsorb their own generative fluid as well as their partner's semen, but although it does get a mention in the texts we know of, very little attention is paid to it. That such a male concern appears as the core belief and central practice of the *hatha yoga* from which much modern postural practice claims descent is an irony that will not have escaped the informed amongst the twenty-first-century yoga community, 90 per cent of which is female. Vedic literature mentions the odd female sage, most notably the formidable philosopher Gargi Vachaknavi who intensely questions the sage Yajnyavalkya in a famous debate recorded in the *Brihadaranyaka Upanishad*, and India has always had a powerful tradition of female saints in more recent times.[13] The fact remains, however, that early *hatha yoga*, drawing on its severely ascetic antecedents, seems to have been very much a male affair.

More widely, the belief in the seminal fluid as the elixir of life, and the consequent vital importance of retaining it wherever possible, persists in modern yoga practice under the rubric of *brahmacharya*, a word usually translated as 'celibacy', by which is meant sexual continence rather than remaining unmarried. The Sanskrit term is partly a historical hangover from the time when orthodox *brahmin* boys underwent a chaste period of religious study, called *brahmacharya*, before they adopted the married householder life. The word itself, however, does not carry the primary meaning of sexual continence at all—a more accurate translation would be something like 'devoting oneself to the Absolute'. Nonetheless it is ubiquitously used to mean chastity and, in general, the debilitating effects of loss of semen have remained widely accepted in Indian society.[14]

The Nath Yogis

Vajroli was a speciality of one group of yogis: the *Siddha Naths*, 'Lords of the Power', also known as the *Kanphata*, 'the split-eared', as their members wore various types of large earrings to denote the degree of adeptship attained. These Nath yogis, the standard bearers of a gnostic movement that blossomed from the eighth to the fifteenth centuries AD, came from a background of Tantra; their early texts do not use the word *hatha* to describe their routines. Their concern was not only to prevent the descent and waste of the vital *bindu* force but the allied project of arousing the *kundalini*, the individual spiritual force in the subtle body that was typically symbolised as the Great Goddess slumbering at the base of the spine, waiting to be awakened by yogic praxis. The Nath scriptures are classic and authoritative manuals on this secondary and energetic nervous system, giving much detail on its *chakras*, *nadis*, *sushumna*, *ida*, *pingala*, and so on. They specialised in crafting a vocabulary that many yoga students today will at least recognise, if not fully understand from their own experience.

Once the dormant *kundalini* force is aroused, she rises irresistibly, piercing the six *chakras*, 'vortices of energy in the subtle body', and releasing various 'knots' (*granthis*) of stress blocking the free flow of the inner life energy known as *prana*. This release causes a celestial ambrosia (*amrit*), known as the 'nectar of immortality', to flow. When circulated around the conduits (*nadis*) of the subtle physiology, this flow produces intense bliss and engenders occult powers such as communion with discarnate spirits, enjoyment of control over nature and extraordinary longevity, *siddhis* long described by classical authorities on yoga but typically cautioned against. The Nath lineage claims its descent from nine principle gurus, the first of which was Adinath, 'The First Nath', who is often identified with Shiva and they also revere an initiatory line of eighty-four miracle-working *siddhas*. While their path originally included yogic sexual rites with female partners, by the time the first *hatha yoga* texts were being compiled, the brotherhood seems to have turned more towards an ascetically celibate lifestyle, in which sexual techniques were wholly internalised and employed in the sublimation and transmutation of the precious energy. Thus the thirteenth-century *Gorakshashataka*, a key Nath text, ends with the following inversion of the classical tantric *panchamakaras*:[15]

> We drink the dripping liquid called *bindu*, 'the drop', not wine; we eat the rejection of the objects of the five senses, not meat; we do not embrace a sweetheart, but the *sushumna nadi*, her body curved like the *kusha* grass; if we have sexual intercourse it takes place in a mind dissolved in the Void, not in some vagina.

The ideal yogi was now the *urdhva-retas*: 'one whose semen flows upwards'.

The Hatha Yoga Pradipika

Such deep waters may be navigated by only the most intrepid, but one Nath text will be familiar to almost all practitioners of postural yoga: the *Hatha Yoga Pradipika* (HYP). The name of this fifteenth-century treatise, 'The Bright

Little Lamp of Hatha Yoga', proclaims its intention to shed some much-needed light on what it calls 'the darkness of a multitude of doctrines' and points to a general degree of confusion in yoga circles at that time. Its reputed author, Swatmarama, was the indirect disciple of the great Nath master Gorakhnath, and the HYP has, up until recently, been held up as the major source book of *hatha yoga*, second only to Patanjali's *Yoga Sutra* on today's recommended reading lists. In fact, despite its pedigree status, the work is more of a mongrel; Mallinson has shown it is a compendium of perhaps twenty other works of varying perspectives. The fact that most of these share a philosophical background of non-dualism (*advaita*) does little to unify Swatmarama's own text, because *hatha* teachings tend to focus on the details of physical practice and frequently pay little attention to the over-arching metaphysical context. As a result, amidst the 'multitude of doctrines' the HYP addresses, there are several conflicting teachings sitting happily side by side between its covers. For example, two quite different versions of the aforementioned *khecharimudra* are included.

As to postures, the text tells us: 'Eighty-four *asanas* were taught by Shiva. Of those, I shall describe the essential four.'[16] For the supposed authority on body-yoga to confine its interest to a bare 5 per cent of its source material is certainly curious. The attribution to Shiva is also noteworthy. While such a divine source is obviously intended to evoke respect, it was always the custom of a genuine spiritual lineage to attribute its genesis to an actual teacher (or at least a mythistorical one) and then to go on to name other historical preceptors in the succession of transmission, known as the *guruparamapara*. There is no such attribution in the HYP, or indeed anywhere we know of, to establish the provenance of physical *asanas*. Their only attribution is wholly mythical or divine.

Another important and roughly contemporary text, the *Shiva Samhita*, takes a more resolutely non-dualist direction; a trend which can be seen to increase in yoga texts as time passes. Its unknown author wastes no time in letting his readers know where he is coming from, with opening lines that read:

> Spiritual knowledge alone is eternal; it is without beginning or end; there exists no other real substance; all diversities which we see in the world are the results of mere sense-conditions. When these cease, only the knowledge of the Spirit remains.[17]

Later, the text shows its obvious debt to the *Hatha Yoga Pradipika* by saying: 'There are eighty-four postures, of various modes. Out of them, four ought to be adopted, which I mention below.'[18]

The poses meriting a detailed description are: the Accomplished (*siddhasana*); the Lotus (*padmasana*); the Cross (*svastikasana*); and the Ferocious (*ugrasana*). The first three are seated and to be used as an aid to meditative absorption. As in the HYP, although all the *asanas* are said to be divine gifts from the great god Shiva, and therefore presumably of more or less equal status, the other eighty postures are virtually ignored. The text does go on to name fifteen of them, but gives no details. From all of this, then, it appears that although by this time many *asanas* were known, only a few were listed, and an even smaller proportion of them were being recommended. If this was indeed the case, how many were being practised?

As well as the postures mentioned above, the HYP deals with other physical exercises—*bandhas*, *mudras* and various *pranayamas*—as well as physical purification and the necessity for a correct diet, but in conformity with Nath preference, Swatmarama seems much more interested in the subtle body, enthusiastically expounding topics such as *kundalini*, *prana*, and the different levels of *samadhi* that eventually lead to enlightenment. One decidedly physical instruction, however, is the technique of severing the tendon connecting the tongue to the bottom of the mouth and lengthening it so that it can touch the forehead. Many verses discuss the methods of *vajroli*. If the women who make up the majority of yoga practitioners find this a sticking point, they may also baulk at some of the master's other recommendations, such as 'fire, women and long pilgrimages should be avoided. Therefore, Guru Gorakhnath says: "Bad company and mixing with women … should be avoided"';[19] and his matter-of-fact observation that 'there are two things that are hard to obtain: one is milk, the other is finding a woman who will act according to your will'.[20]

All in all, Swatmarama's text is a rich stew of esoteric knowledge and complex technique, and it can only be due to the dearth of other more easily digestible early material that it has ended up on the reading lists of so many postural courses. One wonders what those earnest health and safety authorities who increasingly regulate 'official' yoga must make of it all.

Magico-sexual practices would continue to cause embarrassment. When Srisa Chandra Vasu, a respected scholar and prolific translator of *hatha yoga* texts into English from the 1880s onwards, produced his own version of the *Hatha Yoga Pradipika* in 1915, he left out any reference to *vajroli*, because 'it is an obscene practice indulged in by low class Tantrists'. Such bowdlerisation was the price of making yoga acceptable to a modern and mainstream audience, and it has continued up to the present. More than half a century after Vasu, a German translation, the English version of which was approved by B. K. S. Iyengar, continued the trend. The translator explained:

In leaving out these passages, we merely bypass the description of a few obscure and repugnant practices that are followed by only those yogis who

61

lack the will power to reach their goal otherwise. In these twenty *slokas*, (i.e. verses) we encounter a yoga that has nothing but its name in common with the yoga of a Patanjali or a Ramakrishna.[21]

That second sentence is certainly true, but the yoga presented by those two exemplary masters was not the only one on offer; there was always a more extensive menu than that. Nonetheless, Swatmarama's unexpurgated text is easily available today and the most popular version is published by the widely respected Bihar School of Yoga. It sells well on Amazon, but in something of a plain wrapper, being listed under the innocuous subsection of: Health, Family & Lifestyle > Fitness & Exercise > Aerobics.

The Exercise of Power

Another important early text, the *Khecharividya* (c. AD 1400), a critical edition of which comprised Mallinson's doctoral thesis from Oxford,[22] goes even further in its claims than the HYP. Explicitly promising a superhuman physique and ultimately, immortality, its author tells us that the accomplished yogi, 'with a body as incorruptible as diamond, lives for one hundred thousand years. With the strength of ten thousand elephants … he has long-distance sight and hearing.' He adds: 'One becomes ageless and undying in this world, all obstacles are destroyed, the gods are pleased and, without doubt, wrinkles and grey hair will disappear.'

This last promise is something of a come-down from quasi-immortality but does at least foreshadow some key concerns of twenty-first-century postural practice. In the same vein, other contemporary texts promise the yogi the power of sexual attraction. We later learn that the successful adept will gain the power to enter hidden subterranean realms guarded by fabulous serpents—the *naga* kings and queens—and find the treasures that are buried there. He will also master alchemy. Whether these powers are meant to be taken literally or are descriptions of an inner psychic journey couched in a Jungian type of imaginative symbolism is not clear. Perhaps it doesn't matter. The rational barriers between inner and outer, myth and fact, have always been blurred in a cultural milieu whose most respected sages have consistently critiqued the normal understanding of reality as being ignorance, frequently likening it to a waking dream or a collective hallucination.

Scholars have generally followed the scientific community in dismissing outright the psychic abilities that populate these yogic scriptures, although absence of evidence is not evidence of absence.[23] Foreign travellers in the subcontinent were less sceptical. One of the earliest we know of was Abu

Zayd al Sirafi, an Arab merchant, who journeyed around India in the ninth century and came across many *sadhus*. He tells us:

> there are some among them who are naked, and others who stand upright all day facing the sun, naked too but for a scrap of tiger or leopard skin. I once saw one of these men, just as I have described; I went away and did not return until sixteen years later, and there I saw him, still in the same position.[24]

Another testimony is from Francois Bernier, an aristocratic French doctor who first came to India in 1658, traversed the north of the country and wrote one of the most valuable accounts of life at that time: *Travels in the Mughal Empire*. Usually a devout rationalist, he seems to have succumbed to the charms of 'certain *Fakires*' he met:

> They tell any person his thoughts, cause the branch of a tree to blossom and to bear fruit within an hour, hatch an egg in their bosom within fifteen minutes, producing whatever bird may be demanded, and make it fly around the room, and execute many other prodigies that need not be enumerated.[25]

Fecund blossoms and fluttering birds notwithstanding, there was also a steely pragmatism to some of the touted benefits of asceticism; Bernier's informants assured him the adept was able to exercise control over whoever he wished.

Grandiose though this claim may sound, there is some historical evidence for it. As early as the beginning of the sixteenth century, European travellers tell us of meeting *sadhus* who were 'skilled cut-throats' and professional killers. Ludovico di Varthema, a native of Bologna, writes in his diaries about warrior ascetics who 'carry certain iron diskes which cut all round like razors, and they throw these with a sling when they wish to injure any person'.[26] A hundred years later, similar groups were sighted by the French jewel-merchant Jean Baptiste Tavernier and described in his chronicles. He remarks on large bands of up to 10,000 *sadhus* on the march who were 'well armed, the majority with bows and arrows, some with muskets, and the remainder with short pikes'.[27] With their quasi-military organisation, such 'holy men' were in effect mercenaries, and throughout the seventeenth, eighteenth and early nineteenth centuries they served any willing paymaster.[28] While the ideal of Upanishadic mind-yoga may have remained a potent nostalgia, the perceived realities of yoga, with its mixture of magic and militarism, typically evoked fear and disgust rather than respect or deference.

In fact, such negative reactions were not new. As far back as the fourth century BC, an astute royal minister called Kautilya engineered the rise of the Mauryan dynasty which expelled Alexander the Great's successors from north-west India and unified the subcontinent for the first time under a single rule. He was the author of the *Arthashastra*, India's classic work on statecraft and the unsurpassed manifesto of realpolitik. As Max Weber commented: 'compared to it Machievelli's *The Prince* is harmless'.[29] What today's politicians call covert intelligence was Kautilya's speciality. One of his preferred means of fomenting discord, subverting enemy armies and weakening his master's opponents, was the use of *agents provocateurs*. These, he tells us, are best drawn from the ranks of the most mobile members of society: 'secret agents appearing as holy ascetics, wandering monks, cart-drivers, wandering minstrels, jugglers, tramps, and fortune–tellers'.[30] Kautilya's idea of yoga is nothing if not pragmatic. In Books Twelve and Thirteen of his text, he uses the word to mean a deceptive strategy, defining it as: 'the secret methods used to do away with undesirables, particularly the use of weapons, poisons, etc.',[31] and he dignifies the spy who cunningly uses the disguise of a wandering ascetic to work his mischief with the title of 'Master of yoga' (*yoga-purusha*). In Book Fourteen, the term *upanishad* connotes a magical or occult trick. This alliance of yoga and deception was set to continue, ensuring that reactions to the ancient science would always be ambivalent.[32]

By about 1800, the Nath yogis had assumed a position of considerable power and influence across northern India and assumed an important, if paradoxical, role in society. Contemporary accounts mention one in particular, a *sadhu* known as Mastnath, 'Lord of Intoxication', whose psychic muscle included the ability to call down plagues on those who did not provide enough alms, and to turn camel bones into gold. As the latter skill should logically have removed the need for the former, Mastnath was obviously someone who enjoyed exerting his powers gratuitously over lesser beings. He also had a shrewd sense of power politics. In 1803, he lent his aid to a Rajasthani prince named Man Singh, enabling the young man to ascend the throne of Marwar, a desert state centred on its capital Jodhpur. Mastnath produced a series of supposed miracles that culminated in the sudden death of Man Singh's main rival, Bhim Singh, a claimant the East India Company had been backing. Thanks to the Maharaja's unwavering support, Nath yoga became effectively a state-sponsored religion. The British Political Agent, James Tod, was certain Mastnath, who he calls by his other name Deonath, 'Divine Lord', had poisoned the Company's preferred candidate. He tells us:

> Lands in every district were conferred upon the Nat'h, until his estates, or rather those of the church of which he was the head, far exceeded in extent those of the proudest nobles of the land; his income amounting to tenth of the revenues of the state. During the years he held the keys of his master's con-

science, which were conveniently employed to unlock the treasury, he erected no less than eighty-four *mindurs*, or places of worship, with monasteries adjoining them, for his well-fed, lazy *chelas*, or disciples, who lived at free quarters on the labours of the industrious. Deonat'h ...exercised his hourly-increasing power to the disgust and alienation of all but the infatuated prince.[33]

Infatuated or not, Maharaja Man Singh remained a devoted disciple. Among the paintings belonging to the Jodhpur royal family are many fine miniatures which show the ruler and various of his ministers receiving, worshipping and being instructed by the sorcerer *sadhus*.[34] The wily yogi was not invincible however; he was eventually assassinated in 1815.

That a band of renegade holy men had outmanoeuvred the mighty John Company was extraordinary enough, but if truth were told, the British were also indebted to them. What ensured the East India Company's dominance in South Asia was its capture of Delhi at just about the time Mastnath was helping Man Singh grab the throne. This triumph would never have happened had not the Company's main rivals, the Marathas, already been defeated by a Shaivite yogi-warlord called Anupgiri, who led his long-haired troops into battle wielding both weapons and wizardry.

Their new power did nothing to domesticate the Naths. On the contrary, they promptly enlarged their influence by forcing recruits into the order, often seizing the new converts' property to boot. They kidnapped women and were accused of other terrible crimes: boosting their occult powers by child sacrifice and cannibalism.[35] Given their transgressive lifestyle, feral *sadhu* groups understandably evoked a generally negative reaction from both fellow Indians and British officials. Their numbers alone were a cause for alarm. Contemporary chroniclers speak of over two million yogi-*fakirs* by the end of the eighteenth century, a sizeable percentage of the then population. Some of them crowded out temples, pilgrimage sites and public markets with their freak 'yoga' shows, harassing spectators for money, while others worked the pilgrimage routes as con-men, hustlers and footpads. As time went by, they gradually became more domesticated, establishing livelihoods as moneylenders, traders and property owners in all the principal towns of the Gangetic plain. Joining conventional society did nothing to endear them to the locals, however, and their bad reputation lingered doggedly on. In his *Yoga Shastra*, a combined translation of the *Gheranda Samhita* and the *Shiva Samhita* published in 1915, the aforementioned scholar Chandra Vasu castigated many so-called yogis as: 'those hideous specimens of humanity who parade through our streets bedaubed with dirt and ash—frightening children and extorting money from timid and good-natured folk.'[36] It became a convention in contemporary literature to depict the evil character as 'the yogi', and this image stuck. Today, Bollywood villains are often portrayed as wicked *sadhus*, and north Indian villagers still threaten their naughty children that if they don't behave 'the yogi will come and take you away'. One way or another, the yogi-man had become a bogey-man.

THE AGE OF INVASIONS

6

THE CRESCENT AND THE LOTUS

If much yoga became a controversial and divisive force in Indian society, there is one, perhaps unexpected, area in which its practice served as a social salve and healer of discord: the meeting of Hindu and Muslim. Such a balm was sorely needed, as since the ninth century, waves of Islamic invasion had been flooding into northern India and creating chaos. Strictly speaking, the incomers were not so much God-fearing followers of the Holy Prophet as voracious warlords and ruthless free-booters lured by India's reputation as a land of fabulous riches that offered the age-old promise of 'the three z's': *zan, zar, zamin* ('women, gold and land'). The destructive zeal of the incomers fell equally on all the indigenous religious structures. Successive conquerors drove Buddhism from the country of its birth, destroying its monasteries, razing its universities and decimating its communities, who fled south to sea-bound Sri Lanka or north to the protective remoteness of the Himalayas and beyond. Numerous Hindu and Jain temples were destroyed, along with their libraries, communal kitchens and almshouses. When the first mosque in north India, the aptly named 'Might of Islam', was speedily erected in 1192 just south of Delhi, it was built, according to an inscription over its eastern entrance, from the remnants of many local temples that had been smashed up to provide the stone.[1] The builder of the 'Might of Islam', Qutubuddin Aiback, established what is known as the Delhi Sultanate, and in the *Tajul-Ma'asir*, its first official history, he is praised for sacking Varanasi, the holiest Hindu city in North India, in 1194, destroying many temples and building mosques in their place. Perhaps paradoxically, the energetic iconoclast did leave a stable empire in his wake, that was to reign for over three hundred years, stretch through five dynasties and rule a large part of the subcontinent. It lasted until 1526, when Babur, a warlord from Turkmenistan who was descended from both Tamburlane and Genghis Khan, ascended the throne of

Delhi to inaugurate the Mughal dynasty. With only a short break, his family was to rule India until its last emperor, the dreamy eighty-two-year-old poet Bahadur Shah, was exiled to Rangoon by the British Crown when it took over governance of the subcontinent in the wake of the 1857 'Sepoy Mutiny'.

The official language of the Delhi Sultanate was Persian, a preference the Mughals continued, and the language retained its pre-eminence until replaced by English under the Raj. Inevitably, Sanskrit, the hallowed medium of *brahmin* high culture and yogic literature was sidelined and although the new rulers did allow many centres of Sanskritic learning to continue in operation, the fate of Hindu cultural institutions, like their religious buildings, was always precarious, dependent on the whim of the incumbent Emperor and his local representatives. While the Mughals left their adopted homeland an extraordinary legacy of cultural creativity and artistic patronage, these gifts often came at a high cost. For example, the seventeenth-century Emperor Shah Jahan is renowned for building the iconic Taj Mahal, long since the very symbol of India. Few know he also continued the pattern initiated by Qutubuddin of razing temples in Varanasi, as did his son and successor Aurangzeb. However, it seems such desecration was often as much for political reasons—to subdue a rebellious faction or publicly punish the disloyalty of a local king—as for strictly religious ones.[2]

When Islam surged through the Khyber Pass into Hindusthan, the desert confronted the jungle. The two cultures could hardly have been more different. The newcomer was a young, dynamic faith, bent on conversion and highly mobile. Carried by the nomad's horse and sword, its followers worshipped a single and totally transcendent God who could hardly be approached, let alone imaged. It came up against an ancient and static way of living that accepted no converts but was extraordinarily diverse and generally tolerant. Hindus sought mystical unity with a supreme being that expressed itself through dozens of deities depicted in variegated, sensuous images and richly imaginative myths. And while the custodians of their ritual and learning were priests who presided at the head of a highly-stratified caste system that regulated the details of daily life, Islam, by contrast, was relatively free of religious hierarchy or social distinction based on sacerdotal status. Even the food was different: many Hindus were vegetarians who revered the cow whereas all Muslims were ritual animal-slaughterers and daily meat eaters.

Despite all these differences, conversions to Islam were strongly encouraged and at least in north India, not uncommon. This was not so much due to piety but pragmatism: the desire to escape the *jizya* tax and other restrictions routinely imposed against non-Muslims. And for those with special talents, adopting the new religion could become the way to gain lucrative employment at the Mughal courts. This strategy explains, for example, why so many of today's most celebrated families of classical musicians in north India are Muslim.

The Role of Sufism

As the armies of the Prophet travelled north from the Arabian peninsula to spread the message of the One True Faith, they came across communities of hermits and ascetics scattered all over the Levant that had been practising spiritual disciplines in isolated retreats since the early days of Christianity more than five hundred years earlier. Many of these converted and joined the mystical brotherhoods of Islam, who were collectively known as *Sufis*, 'those who wear simple wool'. Over time, these contemplative orders were to provide a softer, more feminine side to the austere new religion. They were also more tolerant, and wherever the message of the Prophet went, Sufism went with it, absorbing and transmuting elements of local belief and practice in a way orthodox Islam could never allow itself to do.

The meeting of Sufism with indigenous Hindu devotional and yogic sects was to create an extraordinarily rich spiritual culture over much of north India; the experience of Turkish, Persian and Afghan traditions entered the Indian religious bloodstream as a benign and invigorating infusion. While some Muslim *fakirs*—a term derived from the Arabic for 'poverty'—emulated the tortured asceticism of the *sadhus* that had long been part of Indian culture, the more mainstream among them found a particularly conducive reception among the Hindu schools of *bhakti*—those who sought union with the Divine through the path of heartfelt devotion. Devotees of Lord Rama and worshippers of Krishna, the god of love, shared a self-transcending path of spiritual ecstasy with the incomers. Like them, they worshipped the formless Lord of all forms through music, dance, poetry, song and the visual arts. Both groups preached a unifying message of social egalitarianism, and contained many low caste members, but at the other end of the social scale there were also great ruling houses, such as Indore and Gwalior, where Sufi influence was welcomed and fostered. Not unlike the Nath yogis we saw in the last chapter, some sects rose to positions of considerable power. As the court poet Isami, who lived in fourteenth-century Delhi, tells us in his major work, *Futuh-us-Salatin* ('Gifts of the Sultans'): 'It is well known that it is only through the *fakir*'s blessing that a King or an Emir can come to power … when a Sufi leaves a country, that country suffers untold miseries. This is a proven fact.'[3]

71

Akbar the Great

The apogee of the Mughal firmament was the Emperor Akbar, the contemporary of another extraordinary monarch, Elizabeth I of England. Temperamentally more inclined to the tolerant Shia wing of his religion than the more rigidly orthodox Sunnis, Akbar had long been interested in the teachings of Sufism. Illiterate himself, he would have the royal library of many thousands of volumes loaded up to accompany him wherever he travelled, even on arduous battle campaigns. Among these were the works of Persian poet-mystics such as Rumi and Hafiz, which he particularly liked to have read to him. Before long, Akbar's religious tolerance was to take an eccentric deviation from orthodoxy. This was greatly encouraged by his spiritual mentor, one Sheikh Mubarak, who, in 1573, decided that his royal pupil should be declared the impeccable authority in matters of religion. The Emperor agreed with alacrity and an 'Infallibility Decree' was duly enacted, making Akbar supreme head of both Church and State. Emboldened by his new power, he immediately rejected formal Islam and founded a new faith, 'The Divine Religion', with himself enthroned firmly at its centre. Mubarak's son, Abu'l Fazl, became Akbar's right hand and was to remain his closest ally and confidant throughout the Emperor's long and eventful reign. While the new religion smiled benignly on the many non-Muslim faiths scattered throughout the subcontinent—Hindu, Jain, Zoroastrian, Christian, Jewish—it had little time for orthodox Sunnis who, of course, abhorred its blasphemous pretension.

Abu'l Fazl lost no time in creating an appropriate mythology for his master. Tracing his lineage back to Adam and claiming that he was in direct touch with the angel Gabriel (who, according to Muslim belief, had revealed the Quran to the Holy Prophet), he announced the Emperor to be a brighter spiritual beacon than even the renowned Sufi masters. Such acclaim drew Hindu *pandits* and holy men to the court as bees to nectar, and it fostered a new connection between the Hindu practitioners of yoga and their Sufi counterparts. As if to cement the alliance, Akbar had the *Yoga Sutra* and several other ancient Hindu texts on asceticism translated or summarised. Abu'l Fazl's royal hagiography, the *Akbar Nama*, shows its author was clearly impressed by the gymnastic Hindu body-yoga he encountered. He tells us: 'The ascetics of this country can so hold their breath that they will breathe once in twelve years,'[4] and that he had, 'gazed in astonishment, wondering how any human being could subject his muscles, tendons and bones in this manner to his will.'[5]

Yoga in Art

The Mughals were refined and enthusiastic patrons of miniature painting, a genre they saw as primarily a means to record the glories of their dynasty. The memoirs of Akbar's grandfather Babur, the *Babur Nama*, had been exquisitely illustrated in a hybrid Indo-Persian style, as had the *Akbar Nama* itself been, but then sometime around 1600 a talented young Hindu artist called Govardhan, working in the employ of the imperial atelier, turned his keen eye to a fresh subject. The conventional records of courtly life—scenes of battle and hunting, grand diplomatic receptions and elephant tournaments—began to be replaced by more domestic studies of contemporary life. These included vignettes of holy men performing yogic *asanas* or engaged in meditation. Influenced by European illustrations of the Gospels that had been brought to India by Jesuit missionaries, Govardhan's detailed portraits give us a delightful insight into the daily routine of these sages in their hermitages, as they followed the long and arduous path to spiritual liberation. Dignitaries visiting sages for instruction now became an artistic convention rather than just an historical record. This was probably attributable not so much to Akbar's patronage as to the rebelliousness of his son. To distance himself from the overbearing influence of his father, Crown Prince Salim had set up his own court in Allahabad, 'The City of God', as the ancient city of Prayag had been renamed. Sited at the confluence of the two most sacred rivers of the north, the Yamuna and the Ganga, the place had long been established as a site of pilgrimage and congregation for wandering holy men with their displays of yoga. By the seventeenth century the huge ascetic gathering of the Kumbh Mela was being celebrated there regularly, as it still is today.

The young Salim was as spiritually eclectic as his father, and exemplified a spirit of enquiry that stretched back as far as the eleventh century, when the Muslim scholar Alberuni had produced a Persian translation of the *Yoga Sutra* and a commentary. Two hundred years later, one of the most important Indian Sufis, Mu'in al-Din Chisti, wrote an encyclopedic work entitled *Treatise on the Nature of Yoga*, which emphasised the compatibility of Islamic and Hindu mysticism. Then, around 1550, a renowned Sufi sheikh of the Shattar school, *Sheikh* Muhammad Ghawth Gwaliyari, who had his disciples learn hatha yoga practices, translated from Persian a work later called *The Ocean of Life*. This is the earliest treatise we know of that contains a systematic series of illustrated images of yoga postures: twenty-two different *asanas* are discussed. Significantly, following the long-established preference we have already observed, they are almost all sitting poses designed to aid meditation. From now on, though, we will find textual descriptions of increasing numbers of *asanas* in a variety of yoga manuals.

It was not only physical contortion that fascinated the Muslim grandees. Akbar's great-grandson Dara Shikoh was also keenly interested in the spiritual traditions of Upanishadic mind-yoga. An accomplished scholar of Sufism, he appreciated yoga as universal wisdom and translated some major *Upanishads* into Persian. These went into Greek and from there entered the consciousness of Europe through versions in German and then English. Other yogic texts became influential in Persian culture, such as the monistic *Yoga Vasishtha*, which in the form of Nizam al-Din Panipati's late sixteenth-century translation, the *Jug-Basisht*, sat well with Sufi ideas on spirituality.

Like his great-grandfather, Dara Shikoh sought wisdom wherever he could find it. His discoveries were sometimes radical. He maintained, for example, that not only had the Prophet engaged in 'repeating the names of God' (a meditative practice that Muslims call *zikr* and the Hindus *japa*) but had done *asanas* and *pranayama* as well. Into the bargain, these yogic exercises had prepared him to receive the divine revelation of the Quran. Dara Shikoh also drew parallels between the 'centres of light' described by Sufi meditators and the *chakras* of the Hindu Tantric systems, and one of the most celebrated miniatures of the time, painted in 1630, depicts the clear-eyed young prince kneeling at the feet of a Muslim holy man or *dervish*. A charming detail is the cat—said to be the Prophet's favourite animal—lying curled in contentment on the sage's sumptuous carpet, no doubt engaged in its own meditation.

On the other hand, there was also a sub-genre of Mughal miniature painting that satirised the more dissolute Hindu *sadhus*, depicting them as wasted, apathetic figures, slumped in a haze of hashish and opium, busy only in preparing the next pipe. Another target is the hypocritical mendicant, bloated and misshapen by his excessive appetites, sometimes shown accompanied by dogs or under trees filled with monkeys. Not only were dogs regarded as ritually unclean in Islam, a dislike based on some of the *hadiths*—purported sayings of the Prophet—, but the less tolerant Muslim would immediately have recognised the veiled reference to Quranic passages popularly interpreted to describe the infidel followers of other religions as being descended from 'apes and pigs'.[6] In the context of Indian history, the presence of these dogs had perhaps an additional significance. As the first animals domesticated by man, many thousands of years before settled farming and compliant cattle, they recalled the affiliation of the itinerant *sadhu* with the asocial hunter-foragers who first populated the subcontinent. The freewheeling existence of such liminal figures challenged the settled, and often effete, life of the Mughal courts, which was, in truth, a degeneration of the true nomadic genius of Islam. The itinerant *sadhus* were atavistic Abels, whose very existence mocked the recently-civilised Cains.[7]

A satirical view of yoga was not new, however, nor was it confined to the Muslim conquerors. South of modern Chennai lies Mahabalipuram, once a capital of the mighty Pallavas, the maritime dynasty that took Hindu culture to south-east Asia. The little seaside town is now a laid-back tourist destination, but more than a thousand years before the Mughal paintings one of the superb stone-carved friezes here had depicted another cat, an animal Hindus generally distrust for what they see as its solitary cunning. This one, in ironic mimicry of a yogic pose, is shown standing on one leg in front of Shiva, the Lord of Yoga, squinting at the sun through its paws. In general, though, the images of sages and their life of yoga that lie scattered profusely through Indian art and architecture are adulatory, whatever the religious context. The portrayal of the yogi, serene in his luxuriant sylvan retreat, visited by kings and commoners, was a continuing theme of inspiration in the many schools of Hindu miniatures, particularly those of Rajasthan, that have come to represent Indian painting in the public awareness.

Yogic Art

Social scenes were not the only way of portraying yoga. From the eighteenth century onwards, a genre known as Yoga (or Tantric) Art arose. This included stylised, rather than figurative, studies of the yogi, showing his subtle body as a microcosmic map of psychic and cosmic realms that had been described from the *Upanishads* onwards. These remarkable depictions of the body which, mirror-like, contains far more than its outer form would suggest, anticipate Modernist attempts—Futurism, Expressionism, Dada—to portray expanded awareness and cosmic equivalences. Yogic art first became widely known in the late 1960s, as Flower Power India became fashionable, and interest peaked with an important exhibition—'Tantra, the Indian Cult of Ecstasy'—at London's Hayward Gallery in September 1971. This was curated by Philip Rawson, who ran the Gulbenkian Museum of Oriental Art and Archaeology at Durham University, and was an artist and author on tantric, and erotic, art.

Eroticism was, of course, a big part of it all. Tantra was perceived as the way to be spiritual but still enjoy sex, and lots of it. Given the prevailing lack of knowledge, art dealers in Delhi, London and New York did very well peddling erotic works of dubious provenance which purported to show acrobatic 'tantric' coupling. These usually came from Rajasthan, the one area of India

where, it just so happened, many artists still worked in the traditional miniature style. In fact, such pieces were taken, or more likely copied, from bed-
room manuals for the maharajas that, much in the manner of Japanese *shunga*,
were enjoyed by aristocrats as an aid to what the Indians call 'bed-pleasure'.
They had nothing to do with genuine tantric or yogic teachings.

Yoga art proper also includes geometric and schematic diagrams—square
yantras, circular *mandalas*—that are one-dimensional representations of the
universe, with its hierarchic levels of material reality depicted in regular
forms and symbolic colours. Recalling passages in the *Vedas* and *Upanishads*
that link the individual to the wider cosmos, they illustrate the fact that all
that exists in the universe lies within man himself. As a psychic portal to be
visualised and enlivened in tantric contemplation, the *mandala* or *yantra* is the
gateway to higher realms accessed within the yogi's mind. When utilised in
external rituals, these one-dimensional forms draw the psychic realms down
to earth. Charged with *mantras* and vivified with offerings, they serve as platforms on which the invoked deities descend, in a sacred performance art that
uses abstract images inspired by the ancient Vedic fire-pit.[8]

Changing Medium, Changing Message

As photography developed by the end of the nineteenth century, we can trace
a move away from conceptual paintings of the yogi and his inner states, towards
naturalistic representations of his impressive physical form. The photographic
image was an important part of the imperial project as an anthropological and
historical record. Along with its spin-offs, the topographic print and picture
postcard, it was also the means to show people back home what India looked
like. The change from depictions of the abstract, inner workings of introverted
awareness to concrete images of the yogi as a solid physical specimen reflected,
and encouraged, a general shift of interest away from mind-yoga as a means of
psychic exploration to postural work as the way to build up an admirable
physique. As noted by the researcher Mark Singleton (of whom we shall hear
more in Chapter 14), a seminal early work on mind-yoga, such as Vivekananda's
1896 *Raja Yoga*, had no need of illustrations, whereas a large part of the appeal
of what became the most influential study of body-yoga, B. K. S. Iyengar's
1966 *Light on Yoga*, was its 600-odd photographs.

This pedagogic use of the visual image has continued with the myriad
books on yoga available today and it inevitably plays a part in how many
practitioners see, or would like to see, themselves. With the internet and
social media, image importance has increased exponentially, of course. In this

context, it is significant that a very common venue for postural practice nowadays is the 'studio', a term that originated as the nineteenth-century workplace of artists, and later of filmmakers and musicians. As such, it has associations of a disciplined practice that leads to creative transformation and the production of something remarkable. In the context of yoga however, the work of art being fashioned is the practitioner themself. And, sure enough, excessive self-regard is easily observable at the more narcissistic end of the body-yoga spectrum, where it can verge on the autosexual.[9] In contrast, mind-yoga is to do with the Self, not the selfies.

Yoga's status in America, where it is now worth some $18 billion annually, was perhaps best signalled by an art exhibition. In October 2013, Washington's prestigious Smithsonian Institution hosted 'Yoga: The Art of Transformation', a magnificent show presenting the first-ever visual history of the subject. Exhibits ranged from statues of tenth-century *yogini* goddesses to a showing of the 1906 *Hindoo Fakir*, the first movie on yoga. The opening gala was chaired by Hollywood actor Alec Baldwin and his yoga-teacher wife, Hilaria Thomas, surrounded by photographers, well-heeled and toned habi-tuées of chic studios such as Yoga Shanti and Exhale Spa, and tables at $50,000 a pop. With celebrity glamour and monied muscle met together in such august surroundings, no single event has demonstrated more clearly yoga's acceptance into the comfortable club that is the American establishment.[10] We have come a very long way from those transgressive *sadhus* and their raggle-taggle magic.

7

AN IMPERIAL YOKE

On the very last day of 1600, a large and expectant group composed of landed gentry and wealthy merchants met together in the Freemason's Hall in the heart of the City of London. It was bitterly cold outside, and the atmosphere in the room was initially tense. But the unease turned to cheers of jubilation when the chairman of the meeting stood up to announce that her gracious Majesty Queen Elizabeth had at last agreed to grant a charter to 'The Governor and Company of Merchants of London trading into the East Indies'. This long-awaited permission ensured the newly-formed company would enjoy a fifteen-year monopoly to establish its share of the new, but already highly profitable, Indonesian spice trade. It was an exciting prospect, no doubt, but little did the two hundred-odd people present realise that their combined capital invest-ment of £60,000, now blessed by royal approval, had launched an enterprise that would in time account for half of the world's trade and be the foundation stone of the largest empire the world has ever seen.

The beginnings were not auspicious, though. The Dutch already had con-trol of the spice islands; their first twenty ships to Java had made a 2,500 per cent profit and Antwerp was established as the centre of the European exchange market and controller of prices. Nutmeg alone regularly gained a 600 per cent profit, many times the mark-up on cocaine today; in some places pepper became a substitute currency.[1] The Dutch had a well-trained and state-funded navy to defend their lucrative interests, and it did not take long for the ships of London's 'Honourable East India Company', as it was now called, to be chased ignominiously out of Indonesian waters. On the rebound, the Company turned its fledgling interest to India. Abundant spices, a navigable western coastline dotted with natural harbours and the fact that it was nearer to home, made the subcontinent appear an altogether easier and more rewarding prospect than those far-distant and well-defended islands. And so it proved to be. Throughout the early 1600s, (at just the time the artist Govardhan was busy painting his studies of yogis and Sufis), John Company's trade grew rapidly. Before long, what had begun as a solely commercial enterprise began to amass surreptitious political influence; trade was yielding not only profit but local influence and then territory. Gradually, almost casually, an extraordinary imperial dominance was being born.

By the eighteenth century, a small number of those departing Britain for India were not merchants at all, but intellectuals and scholars imbued with the intrepidly inquisitive spirit of the European Enlightenment. These people, sometimes called the Orientalists, had an insatiable scientific and anthropological curiosity to study the non-European world: its habitat, religions and customs. What they found in India fascinated them. Among the most notable was an Anglo-Welsh polymath called William Jones, who introduced the West to Sanskrit (thereby initiating the science of comparative linguistics) and pioneered the study of Indian botany. Another was James Prinsep, who deciphered ancient scripts and studied Indian numismatics and metallurgy. A third, particularly relevant to our story, was Henry Thomas Colebrooke. He studied Sanskrit and wrote canonical studies of Hindu law and the Vedas and then, back in England by the 1820s, he founded the Royal Asiatic Society. Colebrooke next turned his voracious attention to producing the first groundbreaking essay on the *Yoga Sutra* and its philosophical sister Sankhya. He was convinced that all civilisation had its origin in Asia, a theme that was to be taken up enthusiastically by the European Romantic movement, which, then reaching its peak, viewed ancient India as the perennial fountainhead of wisdom and spirituality. Such an exalted valuation still lies behind some presentations of yoga today.

The Orientalist view was not destined to prevail in India itself, however. During the early days of their presence there, the Europeans had generally enjoyed cordial relations with the local population. Intermarriage was not only common but encouraged; a third of Company employees had Indian wives and left them well provided for with land and property when they died. But as the nineteenth century approached, things began to change. The ruling Mughal dynasty had already begun its slide into spectacular decline and the East India Company, crowning a tripod resting on Calcutta in the north, Bombay in the west and Madras to the east, was poised to step ever more decisively into the power vacuum. This opportunity ushered in a new and far less tolerant colonial mission, that was partly fuelled by the need, both psychological and financial, to compensate for the recent disastrous loss of the American colonies. Lord Cornwallis, who had presided over the final humiliation of the British surrender at Yorktown in 1781, was moved halfway across the globe to make amends in his new role as Governor General and Commander-in-Chief in India.

The successful building of a new empire in the subcontinent was to be based on the imposition of English-medium education and the inculcation of the Western scientific attitude. A new breed of aggressive colonial administrators, the Anglicisers, was employed to erect such a structure. Their first duty was to oust the Orientalist sympathy for Indian civilisation. In so doing, they lost no time in perpetrating a withering scorn for native traditions of learning and culture that would come to have a devastatingly corrosive effect on Indian self-confidence. It is hardly possible for us today to credit the biliousness of some Angliciser prejudice. Witness the Marquis of Hastings[2] who began his tenure as Governor General of Bengal in 1813. Five years into the job he confides in his private journal:

> The Hindu appears a being nearly limited to mere animal functions and even in them indifferent. Their proficiency and skill in the several lines of occupation to which they are restricted, are little more than the dexterity with which any animal with similar conformation but with no higher intellect than a dog, an elephant or a monkey might be supposed to be capable of attaining. It is enough to see this in order to have full conviction that such a people can at no period have been more advanced in civil ability.

Such rabid bigotry was thankfully not the norm, but it clearly existed, and at the highest level.

A key plank in the attempted construction of the imperial edifice was the English Education Act, passed by the Council of India in 1835 under the direction of Lord William Bentinck, the then Governor General. Up until this time, the East India Company had been required by law to spend money supporting Hindu and Muslim traditions of education, and Sanskrit and Persian literature. Henceforward these funds were to be reallocated to establishments teaching a Western curriculum with English as the medium of instruction. This led to English becoming one of the languages of India, simultaneously dealing a blow to native Indian cultures. To gain support for the Act, the historian and politician Thomas Babington, Lord Macaulay, who had served for four years in India, circulated his notorious *Minute on Indian Education*, in which his disdain for non-European culture is evident:

> I certainly never met with any orientalist who ventured to maintain that the Arabic and Sanscrit poetry could be compared to that of the great European nations. But when we pass from works of imagination to works in which facts

are recorded and general principles investigated, the superiority of the Europeans becomes absolutely immeasurable. It is, I believe, no exaggeration to say that all the historical information which has been collected from all the books written in the Sanscrit language is less valuable than what may be found in the most paltry abridgements used at preparatory schools in England. In every branch of physical or moral philosophy the relative position of the two nations is nearly the same...

Macaulay's loathing of India's mythistorical tendencies convinced him that the corrective was the inculcation of the English language, for:

The claims of our own language it is hardly necessary to recapitulate... Whoever knows that language has ready access to all the vast intellectual wealth which all the wisest nations of the earth have created... we shall see the strongest reason to think that, of all foreign tongues, the English tongue is that which would be the most useful to our native subjects...[3]

The result of this policy, he would say a couple of years later, was an administrative group composed of those:

...who may be interpreters between us and the millions whom we govern, a class of persons Indian in blood and colour, but English in taste, in opinions, words and intellect.

In fact, the act was later repealed, but the intention behind it did not go away. India's frustration with the weight of the British colonial yoke finally erupted in the 'Sepoy Mutiny' of 1857—so-called by the British, now often referred to as the First Indian War of Independence—an event which, though localised in the subcontinent itself, traumatised Victorian England. Not only had the unquestioned right and might of Britannia been challenged, and with it an unthinking assumption of her racial and national superiority, but the atrocities perpetrated by the mutineers against both women and children struck a deep blow to the Victorian ideal of the sanctity of the family. This was a one-sided picture of course; brutality enacted by the British troops was either excused as being necessary and justified, or else just overlooked. And there was much brutality. A letter published after the fall of Delhi in the Bombay Telegraph, and subsequently reproduced in the British press, testified to the nature of the reprisals:

All the city's people found within the walls of the city of Delhi when our troops entered were bayoneted on the spot, and the number was considerable, as you may suppose, when I tell you that in some houses forty and fifty people were hiding. These were not mutineers [sic] but residents of the city, who trusted to our well-known mild rule for pardon. I am glad to say they were disappointed.[4]

Immediately after the Mutiny, and to safeguard its administration, the subcontinent was officially brought under the rule of the British Crown. Shortly afterwards, the East India Company was dissolved and nationalised. In India itself, a new policy was swiftly introduced to prevent any recurrence of such rebellion: educated Indians were henceforth to be groomed in the colonial model as loyal subjects, in an attempt to make them effectively non-Indian. The ideal for a native of the sub-continent was to be a 'Westernised Oriental Gentleman', an aspirational title that reinforced the idea that the properly educated Indian should have a hearty disdain for his own cultural roots and practices.

Macaulay's aspiration to anglicise the Indian elite was primarily a linguistic manoeuvre rather than a religious one. The role missionary Christianity played in the imperial project was much quieter, and more ambivalent, than is often assumed nowadays. In fact, British missionary activity was officially banned until 1813 and, after then, not openly encouraged. This was not so much a hangover of a benign Orientalism, but pragmatism; the more alert colonial officials were well aware that an open policy of Christian proselytising could cause dangerous unrest within the subaltern population. Nonetheless, for Macaulay, and most of his contemporaries, to speak English meant, if only in some approximate way, to *be* English, and to be English meant to be Christian. Given time, the right language would lead to the right liturgy. So, in 1836, he could write that, thanks to English education, within thirty years: 'there will not be a single idolator (i.e. Hindu) among the respectable classes in Bengal'.[5]

At root, this strategy was the logical conclusion of a stream of utopian thinking advanced by the European Enlightenment and most clearly expressed in the writings of its most prominent philosopher and ideologue, Immanuel Kant. As the spokesman of the emerging science of anthropology, Kant judged the white races to have all the attributes needed to progress towards human perfection, but believed Africans and Asians—the former uncultured and backward, the latter cultured but too static—to be, by their very natures, unsuited to share in this great destiny. Many influential thinkers of the time agreed. The political theorist James Mill, who was a member of the Examiner's Office of the East India Company from 1819 until his death in 1836, wrote his highly influential *The History of British India*, the single most important literary source of British Indophobia and hostility to Orientalism. His son John Stuart Mill, a champion of individual liberty and utilitarianism who spent thirty-five years as an administrator in the London headquarters of the EIC, was more tolerant. Yet he too believed that the inhabitants of the subcontinent could only achieve progress and happiness by abandoning much of their culture in favour of modern liberalism.[6] Even Karl Marx, for all his misgivings about capitalism as the malevolent engine of empire, defended colonial rule as a means of overcoming what he saw as the fatal torpor of native village life.[7]

On the other hand, not everyone involved in India was so unappreciative of its cultural treasures, even the more recondite ones. Late into the nine-teenth century, by which time the grand imperial project was very well advanced, there could still be found the odd—and decidedly odd to their colleagues, no doubt—British colonial official cast in the Orientalist mould. Central to the story of yoga and pre-eminent among such eccentrics was a man called Sir John Woodroffe. The son of the Advocate-General of Bengal, Woodroffe was called to the bar in Calcutta in 1890 and, as William Jones had done a hundred years before him, progressed to sit on the bench of the High Court there. Like Jones, he spent all his spare time mastering Sanskrit and avidly studying with *pandits*. Woodroffe's particular interest was esoteric yoga and Tantra and he produced several textual translations and commentaries that are still unsurpassed today.[8] Given the stiffly conservative milieu he moved in, it was perhaps understandable that Woodroffe chose to hide his considerable light under the bushel of a pseudonym, though he could not resist choosing one that had its own romantic and mythistorical echoes: Arthur Avalon. We shall hear more of him in Chapter 10.

Muscles Maketh Man

A particular focus of the Anglicisers' scorn was the comparatively slight phy-sique of the Indians, especially those who inhabited the Gangetic plain and Bengal, the main centres of colonial settlement and administration. Nineteenth-century chroniclers make many references to the fact that Indians were often small and physically refined, compared to the meat-eating and alcohol-drinking Europeans who governed them. The perceived gentleness of the native populations could also make some of their overlords uneasy; the most common adjective used in contemporary descriptions of the Hindus was 'effeminate'. In the eyes of the British missionaries, whose job it was to insert some moral backbone into the growing body of Empire, the remedy was fortunately at hand: 'Muscular Christianity'. Coined in 1857, the year of the Sepoy Mutiny, the term denoted the idea that true morality lay in the practice of Christian virtues combined with a vigorous and energetic masculinity. The connection was a venerable one, traceable back to St. Paul's encounter with Greek physical culture during his extensive travels and it was revived in the mid-eighteenth century in the writings of Jean-Jacques Rousseau, one of the most important Enlightenment thinkers.[9]

The doctrine of 'Muscular Christianity' was popularised by two English writers, Thomas Hughes and Charles Kingsley, who believed the Victorian middle-classes had become emasculated because their education did not include enough of the arduous challenges, and consequent stoic endurance, necessary to create a healthily robust individual and a properly virile society. Hughes had championed the connection between exercise and morality in his widely-read books about the fictional English schoolboy Tom Brown. In the twelfth chapter of *Tom Brown at Oxford*, he writes: 'The least of the muscular Christians has hold of the chivalrous and Christian belief that a man's body is given to him to be trained and brought into subjection, and then used for the protection of the weak and the advancement of all righteous causes.'

The doctrine was in many ways an adaptation of the medieval ideal of the chivalric knight, a theme the Victorians were particularly fond of. Queen Victoria's poet laureate Alfred Tennyson had initiated the fashion of medieval nostalgia with his *Idylls of the King*, a retelling of the legend of King Arthur, and it found visual expression through the lushly-hued paintings of Pre-Raphaelites such as Dante Gabriel Rossetti and Edward Burne Jones. In the context of the new imperial project, the young knight must now exchange his curly Camelot locks for a more manly short back and sides and moustache and, kitted out in khaki serge rather than ruffles and hose, transform into an officer and gentleman unswervingly devoted to loyal overseas service in honour of his fair lady, Britannia. And, just as the Crusades had emulated ancient Camelot in proving that a good knight could, indeed should, also be a good Christian, and that good Christians make the best knights, so now the time had come for the Raj to pick up the old standard to claim a new kingdom for a new time.

For his part, Kingsley, a social reformer and friend of Darwin, thought that no single ritual symbolised the philosophy of Muscular Christianity better than the cold bath, on which he waxed lyrical:

> That morning cold bath, which foreigners regard as young England's strangest superstition, has done as much to abolish drunkenness as any other cause whatsoever. With a clean skin in healthy action, and nerves and muscles braced by a sudden shock, men do not crave for artificial stimulants.

He summed up:

Everything which ministers to the CORPUS SANUM, will minister also to the MENTEM SANAM... and I cannot but see, that unless there be healthy bodies, it is impossible in the long run to have a generation of healthy souls.[10]

Cleanliness was clearly next to godliness, for as he remarked in one of his sermons: 'If you will only wash your bodies your souls will be all right'. Collectively, the best builder of character was the team game involving strong physical contact because: 'Games conduce not merely to physical but to moral health'.[11]

The Role of Sport

Sport as moral education first emerged as a solution to the endemic problems of the great English boarding schools. Mostly old charitable foundations, by the eighteenth and early nineteenth century these had become barbaric places in which the pupils endured miserable conditions and those in charge were self-serving and corrupt. A sensational article by the editor of the prestigious *Edinburgh Review* of 1861 exposed Eton College as a place where over the previous twenty years the Provost and Fellows had enriched themselves splendidly by syphoning off huge amounts of money from legacies and endowments, and by levying fines on their hapless pupils. As to the boys themselves, it was said that: 'the inmates of a workhouse or gaol are better fed and lodged than the scholars of Eton'.[12]

Largely under the influence of Thomas Arnold of Rugby School, a more benign educational vision began to emerge. Though Arnold himself was not a particular fan of physical culture—he advocated 'godliness and good learning' as the goals of proper schooling—the eponymous game of rugby football was invented at his school and came to serve as the model for manliness on the playing field. *Tom Brown at Rugby*, another of Hughes' books, published in 1857, spread the message of the redeeming power of team sport far and wide, and public schools across the land began to see its usefulness.[13]

Nowhere was this more needed than at Marlborough College under the headship of the clergyman George Cotton, who took over the school just months after the last of what were known as the 'Great Rebellions', outbursts of anarchic lawlessness that involved gunpowder and rioting that had raged for a full week. Such potentially dangerous adolescent energy had to henceforth be channelled into rigorous exercise on the playing fields, diverting the boys from their idle wanderings through the surrounding countryside in the long afternoons when morning lessons were done. In 1858, having successfully restored order to the bolshy schoolboys of Marlborough, Cotton was appointed Bishop of Calcutta. He immediately set sail for India, where his authoritative presence was no doubt welcomed in the shocked aftermath of another, far more serious revolt, the Sepoy Mutiny.

What worked in the English boarding school was rapidly applied to the 'white man's burden' being shouldered by so many of its alumni. Sport was to be the glue that held the Empire together, a way to inculcate British values and Christian morality. In India it soon became apparent that rather than rugby football, the slower and less physical game of cricket would be better suited to the physique, climate and temperament of the subcontinent. Into the bargain, its salient characteristics—a love of order, fair play and etiquette that spread the covers over a simmering passive aggression— matched the imperial project nicely. The game had already been introduced by Arthur Wellesley, the 'Iron' Duke of Wellington, in Thalaserry, John Company's main spice-exporting port on the coast of Malabar, and so was already well-estab-lished among resident British ex-patriots. Elite educational institutions mod-elled on the public school, such as Raj Kumar College and Mayo College, were soon playing cricket every day and the game found a wider audience thanks to men like Lord George Harris, governor of Bombay in the 1890s. A cricket fanatic, having played for his county, Kent, for forty years and cap-tained the English team, Harris was widely criticised during his tenure for his lack of attention to the city's many problems. But nobody could doubt his devotion to what he obviously considered a more important mission: to get India playing cricket.[14]

Such stiffening measures were deemed particularly necessary because, in the eyes of many Raj officials, the generic unmanliness of the Hindus went hand in hand with a moral flaccidity that was the fatal flaw of their religion. Mystical communion with gods and goddesses did not seem to serve the Indians that well in practicalities, nor save them from the fatalism inherent in their doctrine of *karma*. Even more useless was the emaciated yogi lying half-comatose on his bed of nails, a figure perfectly placed to become the stock image of this inherent turpitude. It was not only the self-mortification that horrified earnest Raj observers, it was the nakedness. However, those who protested seemed to have forgotten that the ancient Greeks they so admired also did their uplifting muscular exercise unclothed, but at least those ancients were *moving*, not just lying around doing nothing.[15] Cricket was now clearly part of God's purpose, a preparation for the ideal life of 'fighting the good fight' in the service of Christ, especially in the land of unbelievers.[16]

The popular Victorian writer J. G. Cotton Minchin graphically summed up the self-confidence of his age in his eulogy *Our Public Schools*, published in

1901: 'If asked what our Muscular Christianity has done, we point to the British Empire.' His definition of Muscular Christianity was equally forthright. To him it was: 'the Englishman going through the world with rifle in one hand and the Bible in the other'.[17] And had that intrepid Englishman been blessed with another pair of hands, like so many of those pagan Hindu deities, they would surely have been clasping a willow bat and red leather ball.

The YMCA Opens its Doors

If cricket was helping the educated Indian elite to overcome its congenital deficiencies, what about the boys in the street? How could the masses be toughened up? After all, however effective the colonial administration was, it would need the acquiescence of the youth in cities that were growing ever more crowded due to the rapid advance of industrialisation. The answer was again to be found in the English school system: gymnastics. If the smart schools were to spread the gospel of cricket for the governors, some sort of physical regime that, unlike cricket, did not demand space or equipment, must be found for the governed. Western gym routines were already tried and tested in the military context, but there was also the homegrown physical culture of yoga to consider. This had the distinct advantage of being familiar and acceptable to the locals, but whatever physical benefits body-yoga might have must be separated from all that religious superstition that so blighted its reputation. Cleverly managed, here was a meeting of East and West that would serve the imperial project and create a new breed of subject, sound in body, mind and spirit. The amalgam—innocuous *asanas*, western gymnastic techniques and the calisthenics that were part of British army training—was rolled out by an instructor who was usually a retired non-commissioned officer, typically a native *sepoy* who had served in the army and so knew the ropes. It was certainly not a prestigious or well-paid job, but it was a worthy and necessary one. And to house the project, where could be better than the Young Mens' Christian Association? Founded in Britain in 1844 to nurture those who had moved from the countryside to find work in industrial cities with all their temptations, the Association was ideal for the job. So it was that in 1857, amidst the smoke still drifting through the streets from the fires of the Mutiny, the first Indian branch of the YMCA opened in downtown Calcutta. Unlike those lethargic yogis lounging around on their beds of nails, Britannia's project to save India's soul by improving her body was now quite definitely up and running.

8

WE WANT TO BE FREE!

Even as the Calcutta YMCA was drilling its young charges into shape, a powerful yearning in quite the opposite direction—freedom from the yoke of empire—was growing apace. As the centre of imperial governance and a mighty port at the crossroads of East and West, Calcutta had always been a vibrantly cosmopolitan city and a cradle of intellectual and artistic endeavour. As the nineteenth century drew to its close, the place was beginning to buzz with many internationalist and revolutionary ideas, and the possibility of India's freedom from the British Raj was surely the most exciting of them all. Lord Macaulay's project of 'educating the natives' in Western ways had come full circle to yield a telling irony. Upper-class Indians, now fluent in English, encountered European intellectual perspectives, such as the ideologies of self-determination proposed by Rousseau and Marx, as never before. In claiming their liberty, Indian anti-colonialists adopted and adapted Western articulated philosophies of 'freedom' alongside their own and marshalled them against the Raj itself. Since the early nineteenth century, in small riverside parks, brocaded sitting rooms and dark, humid tea shops all over the metropolis, small groups of people had been meeting, talking, planning, dreaming. The search was on for a vital nationalist narrative: a vision of Indian greatness that could inspire her peoples to shake off centuries of foreign oppression and regain her rightful place in the pantheon of proud and free nations. The movement now known as the Hindu Renaissance was being born.

Under this general banner gathered several disparate reform movements that, despite their differences, shared the common desire to redefine 'Hinduism' to meet the changes and challenges of the modern world. As such, they addressed an educated elite and had very little impact on the vast swathe of village-dwelling Indians with their centuries-old beliefs and practices, but they did influence the social stratum that interacted with the wider world. The first of these movements, founded in 1828, was the Brahmo Samaj; its guiding light, often called the Father of the Hindu Renaissance, was a Bengali *brahmin* called Ram Mohan Roy. A highly educated man who knew Arabic, Persian, Greek and Latin, as well as Sanskrit, Roy had read the world's scriptures and concluded there was not much essential difference between them. Seeing pure Hinduism as stemming from the *Upanishads*, four of which he translated into English, he crusaded against what he called the 'superstitious practices' so often cited by British officials claiming moral superiority over his country. These included polygamy, child marriage and caste, as well as *suttee*—the immolation of widows on their husband's funeral pyre. It was partly due to Roy's passionate campaigning that the British banned the practice throughout Bengal in 1829, though it would not be until 1861 that the Queen Empress Victoria extended the prohibition across the country. Roy also worked for property inheritance rights for women, and educational reforms. Convinced that Indians should learn Western sciences, he wrote to the Governor General of India emphasising the need for schooling in: 'mathematics, natural philosophy, chemistry, anatomy and other useful sciences'. After some years of ill health, and in financial difficulties, Roy visited England in 1833 and stayed with some Unitarian friends near Bristol. He died suddenly of meningitis and is buried in the local Arnos Vale cemetery.

The Brahmo theology was clearly influenced by Christianity, and found fellow-spirits in the Unitarian movement and Transcendentalism, an American philosophical-religious movement which emphasised the necessity of personal religious experience over ritual and blind belief. Protestations of unity notwithstanding, the Brahmos soon splintered. One group, the breakaway Brahmo Samaj of India under Keshab Chandra Sen, was especially keen to create an accessible type of spirituality that foreswore the need for yogic renunciation and advocated instead a life of active engagement in the world. They ran outreach missions to uplift the lives of the poor, such as the Band of Hope, which tried to discourage Bengali youths from adopting the European vices of smoking and drinking alcohol. Sen, too, became increasingly attracted to Christianity, which alienated some of his followers, as did his rebuttal of the necessity for total independence from Britain. Matters reached a head in 1878, when most of the group abandoned him after it came to light that his own daughter had been married as a child, thus making a mockery of his vociferous campaign against the practice.

In 1875, another reform school, the Arya Samaj, was founded by a dedicated yogi, Sanskrit scholar and lifelong celibate from Gujarat named

Swami Dayanand Saraswati. Dayanand's primary interest was to purge Hinduism of its superstitions and ritualism, but unlike the Brahmos, he had no interest in submitting to Christian influence. Advocating a return to strict orthodoxy, Dayanand believed in the infallible authority of the Vedas and the doctrine of *karma* and reincarnation, though he lambasted popular astrology as a fraud and taught that idol worship was a later corruption of India's true spiritual message:

> All alchemists, magicians, sorcerers, wizards, spiritists, etc. are cheats and all their practices should be looked upon as nothing but downright fraud. Young people should be well counselled against all these frauds, in their very child-hood, so that they may not suffer through being duped by any unprincipled person.[1]

He was also an important political thinker, blending the idea of a radically reformed Hinduism with independence from the Raj. The ochre-robed figure first announced his vision of an 'India for Indians' in a public talk in 1876, when he introduced his concept of *Swaraj* or 'Democratic Self-rule'. The idea was soon to be taken up by Lokmanya Tilak, the first leader of the Indian Independence Movement who was also a keen supporter of physical culture, and later, most famously, by Mahatma Gandhi.

Dayanand himself practised a physical posture routine but was strongly critical of the tantrism he felt had infected yoga and tarnished its reputation. His disapproval was shared by the elite of Westernised Hindus, who, as we have seen, were embarrassed by the *Hatha Yoga Pradipika* with its decadent *vajroli* teachings. According to his autobiography, the Swami once pulled a corpse from the river Hooghly and dissected it to find the subtle body and *chakras* that feature so prominently in the HYP and other texts. Unable to do so, of course, he promptly threw his copy in the water and renounced its arcane message. Apocryphal or not, the story quickly entered the folklore and will surely have resulted in many of his contemporaries taking up the scalpel of scientific rationalism to cut at the heart of much traditional yogic belief and practice.

Despite Dayanand's down to earth version of yoga as a physical discipline for the body, magical legends soon accrued around his own practice, as if his supporters were keen to see some evidence of the legendary *siddha* in their beloved teacher. His yogic prowess is said to have saved him from several poisoning attempts. Another account tells how, while meditating by the Ganges, he was attacked by Muslims who were offended by his criticism of Islam; they threw him into the river, but his skill in *pranayama* allowed him to stay safely under the water until the attackers left the scene. He may have cheated death on several occasions, but a strange *karma* eventually caught up with poor Dayanand. He met his end in 1883, at the hands of a jealous dancing girl, who, furious at his attempts to persuade her patron, the Maharajah of Jodhpur, to give her up, spiked his milk with ground-up glass. After a month of agony, he died from internal bleeding.

The most important apostle of the Hindu Renaissance, a natural leader with the necessary charisma and drive, was soon to take the stage. This was a young man named Narendra Nath Datta, the favoured son of a well-to-do middle-class Calcutta family that belonged to a respectable *kshatriya* sub-caste of clerks and tax collectors. Narendra grew up to be a sceptical habitué of the sophisticated intellectual salons that flourished amidst the city's grandiose neo-Gothic buildings. His circle, chastened by chronic humiliation at the hands of the Raj and inspired by the practicality of Christian missionaries, was also keen to create a new national narrative. It had to be relevant to the brave new Westernised world order and free of the superstitions of the simple and uneducated, while at the same time staying true to India's spiritual genius. Above all, this new ethos should embody what was unique to Mother India, something that could be her real and lasting gift to the world rather than just the spices, cottons and teas that had attracted venal colonial powers.[2]

Narendra had originally been drawn to one of the Brahmo Samaj splinter groups, but his was always to be a unique vision and a very personal mission. The catalyst for it came one autumn day in 1881, when the young man—he was not yet twenty—reluctantly agreed to accompany some of his college friends to visit an old Kali temple in an overgrown garden on the banks of the river Hooghly, an hour's boat ride north of the city. The place was rapidly gaining notoriety due to the eccentricities of its presiding priest, an illiterate *brahmin* called Ramakrishna who didn't give a fig for social convention. Devoted to the fierce goddess as his divine mother, the man was undeniably in a continuous state of God-intoxication, frequently remaining in deepest *samadhi* and completely abstracted from the world for hours on end. Against all expectations, there was an instantaneous attraction of opposites. The suave young atheist surrendered to the unlettered godman and his life was transformed. To the astonishment of those who knew him, Narendra renounced his former sceptical self and was initiated as a monk. He was given the name Swami Vivekananda: 'the Bliss of Discernment'.

The young convert soon proved himself to be a dedicated spiritual aspirant, firmly committed to his other-worldly master. Following Ramakrishna's death in 1886, he continued his spiritual apprenticeship with his fellow dis-

ciples; together they rigorously practised yoga, meditated and devoted themselves to a life of service that involved travelling around India, meeting and
living alongside all sorts of people, taking the pulse of common humanity
and, little by little, feeling the way towards a cure for their ailments. As a
vehicle for the new vision, Vivekananda founded the Ramakrishna Mission,
which to this day carries out both social work and spiritual instruction
throughout the sub-continent and abroad. The Swami's dedication and organising abilities were augmented by his attractive personality, brilliance as an
orator and prolific talent as a writer. As we shall see in Chapter 11, he would
soon emerge into the limelight, proclaiming universal brotherhood and the
perennial oneness of all life. This was to be his yoga, beyond all barriers of
class, caste and creed an the world was ready and waiting...

9

MARTIAL YOGA

In the years leading up to Narendra's conversion there had been social changes taking place in India that would impact on the spread of yoga. The wild bands of itinerant *sadhus* we met in Chapter 5 were still plentiful in the mid-nineteenth century, a time of political flux and shifting power. These ascetics were organised into quasi-military orders known as *akharas*, a term that originally meant 'open-air gymnasium', and we have seen they were effective warriors. But were they really practising yoga, and if so, what sort? Certainly not a Patanjali brand, with its cardinal virtue of 'non-violence' (*ahimsa*). Did they rationalise their conduct by quoting Lord Krishna's teaching in the *Gita*, that the yogi who knows the imperishable and omnipresent Self, 'neither kills nor causes to be killed'?[1] Or was there a specifically military yoga, and did it, as some say, travel with proselytising Buddhist monks to China and Japan, seeding the martial arts there? The questions are intriguing; the picture far from clear. But research is slowly accumulating.[2]

The Yogi as Warriors

As we have already seen in Chapter 1, the tradition of warrior-ascetics was a very ancient one, harking back to the *Vratya sadhus* of Vedic times. More generally, those involved with the *yajna* fire sacrifice, whether priest or patron, were often described as exhibiting heroic virtues—forbearance, patience, strength and other similar qualities of the idealised warrior—that would later be celebrated as the fruits of yogic practice. Reciprocally, as early as the first *Upanishads*, the mind-yogi's control over the senses and wayward passions were cast as heroic achievements, likened to restraining the horses that pull the battle-chariot.[3] We also know of an early, pan-Indian, body of knowledge concerning military strategy and the art of warfare, called *Dhanur Veda*, literally: 'the Knowledge of the Bow'. Listed as one of the *upaveda* sciences, it covered the whole range of martial knowledge, but the symbolic pre-eminence of archery never diminished. As one eighteenth-century text tells us: 'If just one famous archer stays in a city, then the enemies will remain at a distance just as animals stay far away from the den of a lion'.[4]

The analogy between archery and the power of concentration was a commonplace in yoga texts. The archetypal example was the warrior-archer Arjuna, hero of the *Bhagavad Gita*, whose one-pointed concentration (*ekagrata*) was so great that, it was said, when he drew back his arrow and took aim, he 'saw only the eye of the sparrow'. The *Shrimad Bhagavatam*, the classic text of Krishna devotion which dates from about the eighth century AD, tells the story of a maker of arrows whose mind was so fixed on his work that he failed to notice the noise and show of a royal procession passing by his workshop.[5] And significantly, the word most commonly used for psychic ability—*siddhi*, which literally means 'perfection'—was originally an archery term, meaning to hit the target 'dead centre'.

In the *Mahabharata*, the great sage Yajnyavalkya instructs King Janaka:

> Just as a person of composed nature might ascend a staircase while holding a container full of oil, and yet, despite being alarmed upon being attacked by assailants armed with swords, does not spill a drop out of fear of them, so, in the same way, the mind of one who is absorbed in the supreme is fully concentrated.[6]

This combination of devotion and concentration is exemplified by the iconic guru of Indic body-culture, the monkey-general Hanuman, whose exploits are recounted in the *Ramayana*. The patron deity of body-builders and wrestlers, his strength is matched only by his resourcefulness. Able to carry a mountain covered with healing herbs in one hand while flying high across the ocean, inspired by his unswerving loyalty to Lord Rama, he defeats a whole range of wily demons. Like the realised yogi, Hanuman is majestically stationed far above and beyond the capricious instabilities of life, whose limitations he so effortlessly surmounts. Although the word 'yogi' itself is not found often in the *Ramayana*, by the time of the *Mahabharata*, a few centuries later, the yogic nature of the hero has become axiomatic, exemplified by such noble warriors as Rama, Parashuram, Krishna and, above all, Bhima, who by his own efforts slays all one hundred of the wicked Kaurava brothers in the Kurukshetra War. This is not to say that the yogi must literally be a warrior, but he is certainly a metaphorical one, who fights, and triumphs, on the battlefield of everyday life.

Apart from the generalised teachings of *Dhanur Veda*, India boasted various regional martial art forms. Some of these were revived in response to colonial aggression. Kalaripayattu, the martial art form of Kerala, which claims existence from the twelfth century AD enjoyed a revival in the 1600s when locals found their weapons ineffective against the fire-power of the Portuguese.[7] Following an armed revolt in Malabar in 1804, the British tried to ban the art, along with the possession of arms; those found guilty were condemned as traitors and faced deportation or the death penalty. The same thing happened five years later with another uprising further south, in Travancore. As a result, the few surviving gymnasia, or *kalaris*, retreated to isolated parts of the state and the tradition went deeply underground. By the time of Independence in 1947, it was barely still alive, though it flourishes once more today.

The Kalaripayattu gymnasium is a quasi-temple. Training sessions typically begin with a *puja* to the presiding deity (often a fierce form of the goddess) as well as meditation and the use of *mantras*. This prayer ritual purifies the atmosphere and the participants, and is ancient, said in the *Mahabharata* to have the power to summon up magical weapons. Acute mental focus is essential to learning the kicks and jumps. The knowledge of the subtle body that is essential to both yoga and Ayurveda is key to the herbalised oil massages that prepare, and restore the fighter, as well as identifying the location of meridian energy-points (*marma*) to target in his opponent.

It was the art of wrestling that seems to have had the most specific influence on the development of *asana*. A favourite exercise to build up the wrestler's physique was, and still is, the *dand*—a forward dive that lowers the chest to the ground and arches it back upwards. Performed in a rapid and repetitive sequence, the *dand* would become the 'downward dog', 'eight-limb pose' and 'upward dog'—postures well known in global yoga today. Wrestling routines made use of blocks, clubs and ropes which again are all very familiar in modern practice, especially Iyengar yoga. Moreover, the wrestler's lifestyle mimicked the yogi's. It included strict *brahmacharya*—facilitated and symbolised by the tight *langot* G-string he wore—and a *sattvic*, body-building diet high in milk and, especially, *ghee*, which was believed to increase the production of semen and potency of the life energy. Such religio-physical regimes continue today, and can be seen particularly in traditional centres of the sport, such as the sacred city of Varanasi.[8]

Then there is the seventeenth-century Maratha general, Shivaji. Famed for his armed revolt against the Mughals, and still a potent symbol of Indian nationalism, Shivaji studied physical development and wrestling routines under Samarth Ramdas, a holy strongman who had over 1,200 Hanuman temples built, with gyms attached. It seems likely that the *surya namaskar*, so well-known in modern postural routines and nowhere visible in early *hatha* texts, may well have originated in one of Ramdas' gyms.[9] By the early twentieth century, Bhavanrao, the Raja of Aundh, a prominent nationalist and follower of Gandhi, vociferously supported traditional Indian physical culture as a means of building up his country's strength and unity. He particularly advocated the practice of *surya namaskar*, writing: 'If our boys and girls, men and women will regularly practice *suryanamaskars* … there will shortly be produced a type of humanity that shall excel in body, mind, and soul more than any that the earth has yet brought forth…'[10] Leading Indian nationalists such as Motilal Nehru and Madan Malaviya advocated the physical and moral benefits of *akhara* culture, and Lokmanya Tilak, the first leader of the Indian Independence Movement—who the British colonial authorities dubbed 'the father of Indian unrest'—urged young Maratha men to follow in the footsteps of Shivaji and reputedly called on 'all students and youth to be devoted to strength and celibacy'.[11]

The Indian Club

Allied to wrestling was the art of body-building, and this became another ingredient in the *masala* being cooked up at this time. As we saw in the last chapter, since the 1860s the British had been promoting fitness regimes through the branches of the YMCA as part of their policy to install some moral and physical backbone into Indian youth. For years, British military officers stationed in India had been struck by the fitness of many of the native soldiers and policemen, derived from their systematic training with a variety of wooden clubs (*jori*) that had been used for centuries as both exercise prop and weapon. The army adapted these clubs, generally swung in pairs, into their own calesthenic routines; in time they were added to the YMCA drills. They are still in use today in traditional *akharas*, and the authority on Indian body-building, the anthropologist Joseph Alter, records that he witnessed a modern wrestler give a club-swinging demonstration using a *jori* weighing eighty kilos. Another traditional prop Alter saw in use was the *gada*, a club which consists of a heavy round stone, weighing anything between ten and sixty kilos, fixed to the end of a metre-long bamboo pole.[12] The divine prototype of all such implements was the mace carried by Hanumanji, a pedigree which added the aura of magical power. Thus, in the folklore of Kalaripayattu, where the club is known as an *otta*, it is said that: 'with expertise in *otta*, one can fight even during sleep'.

The person responsible for introducing the so-called 'Indian club' to Europe was Donald Walker, the author of *British Manly Exercises*, published in 1834. This was the nineteenth century's most influential book on exercise and it contained both sedate and vigorous club exercises performed by the British army. The next year he published *Exercises for Ladies Calculated to Preserve and Improve Beauty* that featured the 'Indian sceptre', i.e. smaller and more ornamental versions of the club, weighing about a kilo. But it was an American equipment manufacturer called S. D. Kehoe who really established the *jori* as a training prop in the West. Fascinated by seeing a gym instructor in London use what he called 'the mammoth war clubs', Kehoe vowed to introduce them back home. In 1862, he began manufacturing them in New York City and opened a shop there. After the publication of his keep-fit manual, *The Indian Club Exercises*, in 1866, the club really became popular, and was used in the training of both the US armed forces and the country's early baseball teams. A lighter version, called the 'swing club' figured prominently in the keep-fit sessions for women that were run by local churches across the nation. Each one was inscribed with an uplifting axiom of Muscular Christianity.

We have seen that the sense of Indian national identity, bolstered by physical fitness, developed especially in Bengal, the heartland of British colonial administration. The same year as Kehoe's book hit the stands in America, The Society for the Promotion of National Feeling was formed in Calcutta. Its 1867 prospectus states that its members:

> first of all use their best endeavours to revive the national gymnastic exercises … [that] the rising generation of Bengalees is not so strong and able bodied as the previous ones, is quite true. … The National Promotion Society shall publish tracts in Bengali on the importance of physical education with special reference to its prevalence in ancient times, quoting passages from Sanskrit books in proof of such prevalence and shall afford pecuniary aid to gymnasia established in the most important places in Bengal, where Hindu gymnastics will be taught'.[13]

The *akhara* was to be revived as an institution to develop physical fitness and moral character, and a year later the prominent Tagore family started a Hindu Mela which sponsored, among other things, wrestling tournaments and demonstrations of physical strength. By the first decade of the twentieth century, then, body-culture was locked arm in arm with protest against imperial authority. Members of these fitness clubs subscribed to strict rules of self-discipline, that, as we have seen, were yogic in character and provided an instinctively hallowed context for the growing political self-confidence.

Gama the Great

No one figure embodied this self-assuredness more than Gama the Great, the court wrestler of the Maharaja of Patiala. Although a low-born Muslim, his popular titles—the 'Krishna of the Kali Yuga' and 'the incarnation of Bhima'—were Hindu, and announced to the world that the new, united India reconciled even those habitual foes. When in 1910 the John Bull Society of London organised its 'world wrestling championships', Gama was set to fight with British champions in the very heart of imperial power. Arriving there, however, he was ignominiously judged too small to take part as he stood a mere five feet six inches tall and weighed only fourteen stone. Undaunted, Gama signed up with a local theatre and, for a salary of £25 per week, challenged all comers, offering £5 to anyone who could down him within five minutes. The first day, he beat three challengers; the second, ten. This earned him a bout with Stanley Zbyszko, the reigning world heavyweight champion, on 10 September 1910. He and the twenty-one-stone Pole spent most of their time together on the canvas, and the *The Times* gleefully reported the next morning: 'Gama rode gaily on Zbyszko's back and slapped him contemptuously…' Astonishingly, the three-hour contest was declared a draw, but as Zbyszko failed to turn up for the return bout, Gama strapped on the coveted John Bull belt and pocketed the £250 prize. His real victory, though, lay in promoting India's ancient *akhara* culture on the world stage. A national hero back in India, Gama was presented with a silver mace by the Prince of Wales on his 1922 state visit. An observer seeing him brandish it commented: 'it would appear the epic hero Bhima has been reincarnated'.[14]

While such prowess may not appear very yogic, we should bear in mind that, in Indian culture, participation in any skill or branch of learning was, in the broader sense of the term, a yoga. That is to say, it embodied a path of discipline that was framed in a general spiritual context, sanctified by a patron deity, transmitted through a venerable lineage and bolstered by a hoary mythology. Thus, for example, classical dance was historically associated with yoga. Breathing and stretching exercises enhanced the artist's stamina, flexibility and balance, while meditation increased mental focus. Such a routine, allied with herbalised oil massage from an early age and an avoidance of the unnatural strain that so characterises much of Western ballet training—often crippling dancers in later life—allowed Indian dancers to continue performing well into middle-age and even beyond. For their part, the practitioner must commit to honour their admittance to a specialised group, abide by its norms and faithfully transmit its knowledge to their own pupils when the time comes. In this sense, yoga represents a general understanding of the aims and purposes of human culture, rather than being just a specific set of physical or even mental practices. Such an attitude is not peculiar to India, but characteristic, in varying degrees, of all societies we can call traditional. It is clearly observable in the legacy of ancient Greece, for example.[15]

Circus Yoga

Gama was not the only Indian strongman who had to take to the boards to get by. Shocked by the Mutiny, and fearing future insurrections, the British authorities lost no time in rounding up and disbanding as many of the wandering groups of *sadhus* as they could. Some of the displaced ascetics did join the nationalist cause, but others went out on the road and took to begging or became itinerant carnival performers who displayed their more spectacular yoga postures to gawping onlookers. Such showmanship had been seen in the streets and circuses of the great European cities for many years. The turbaned performer, lithe as a python, would slide seamlessly from the lotus position into the headstand, or vigorously demonstrate the spectacular *nauli* technique—a *kriya* from *hatha yoga* that isolates the muscles of the abdomen and undulates them in a column, thereby massaging and cleansing the internal abdominal organs. In Britain, the trend of circus yoga was initiated by a savvy East India Company captain who in 1813 launched a travelling troupe of Indian jugglers with a show in London's West End, home to fashionable gentleman's clubs. *The Times* reported:

> The exhibition of the Indian Jugglers, at no. 87 Pall Mall, has been attended by nearly all the Families of distinction in town; and is becoming extremely popular. The swallowing of the sword, and the novelty of the other performances, have attracted the public attention beyond anything that has appeared in the metropolis for many years past.[16]

Regency England loved curiosities and extravaganza, and the combination of jugglery, acrobatics, yogic contortions and sleight of hand was an instant hit. Another troupe was soon giving displays in New Bond Street, and before long, fake *fakirs* from the English shires were donning mock-oriental costumes, blacking up and 'levitating' in theatres around the country. The genuine articles kept coming though, spicing up their performances with the type of austerities performed in their homeland. Contemporary accounts in *The European Magazine* and *London Review* describe performers 'holding the breath and meditating until there appears to be no respiration left in the corporeal frame'; 'immersing oneself in smoke from fire on all sides' or 'standing always on one foot'. Even Queen Victoria was entranced; she held a very English tea party for one troupe (most of whom were former *sadhu* mercenaries recruited from Jaipur jail), so that she could sketch them in their very un-English costumes.[17]

The thirst for Oriental exoticism meant novels such as Wilkie Collins' *The Moonstone* (1886), a heady draught of stolen jewels, opium and wily *brahmin* priests up to no good, went down very well. Popular interest in the contortions of fairground yoga received an erotic frisson following the publication of Richard Burton's translation of the *Kama Sutra* in 1883. Victorian England, already schizophrenically caught between public con-demnation and private fascination in matters sexual, began to experience the sort of ambivalence that yoga had long caused in its homeland. Ignorance of Indian culture and lurid assumptions about the rampant sexu-ality of non-white races slotted sex and yoga together in the popular imagi-nation as snugly as any *Kama Sutra* clinch.

As the growth of mass photography at the end of the nineteenth century emphasised the physicality of yoga, it also helped to eroticise it. In 1902 the cinematic inventor Thomas Edison made a film called *The Hindu Fakir* that became a staple in the saucy peepshow booths that travelled around the country. The mix of magic and sex was an enduring lure. Thirty years later, the star turn of the travelling Bertram Mills circus was billed as 'Koringa—the only female *fakir* in the world'. While touted as 'orphaned at age three' and 'raised by *fakirs* in Bikanir, India, where she learned the exotic arts of sorcery', Koringa was in fact, rather less glamorously, Renée Bernard from Bordeaux. Nonetheless, posters and programme inserts promised the crowds they would see for themselves that: 'she walks uncut over broken glass! ... dances barefoot on the edges of razor-sharp swords! ... walks over hypnotized wild crocodiles!'

The audiences were not disappointed. A striking figure with an afro hair-style, necklace of live snakes and troupe of four crocodiles (the largest of whom was called Churchill), Koringa exercised an apparently effortless com-mand over the laws of nature. She was the yogic version of the erotic female circus performers who had been strutting their stuff around the ring since P. T. Barnum's sell-out shows in the 1860s. Such circus strongwomen looked back at least to the 1830s, when Krakow-born Elise Luftmann had toured Europe juggling with cannonballs, while Athleta Van Huffelen, who was born in Belgium in 1868, waltzed around the stage of the Eden Alhambra theatre in Brussels with three grown men held above her head. Her three daughters followed in her footsteps, while her contemporary and great rival, Josephine Blatt, won her place in the Guiness Book of Records for lifting, in 1895, 'the greatest weight ever raised by a woman … 3,564 lb with a hip and harness'. This steamy mix of circus, sex and strength continues obliquely today, with those bikini-clad card carriers who sashay around the ring at many a boxing and wrestling bout.

Yogic showmanship persists in India, though it is almost always an all-male affair. Some have sat holding an arm aloft, or stood in one spot, for years on end. Ascetics emerge from seclusion at religious fairs, where a favourite crowd-puller is the emaciated *sadhu* who, exhibiting the virility of the celibate, lifts a heavy stone or a pile of bricks by a string attached to his penis. One contemporary world-conqueror is Lotan Baba, 'The Rolling Saint' from Madhya Pradesh, who, after spending seven years in his home village doing penance to the Mother Goddess by standing on one leg and eating only grass, has spent much of the last decade rolling along India's roads to promote world peace. Regularly featured on Indian news media, he travels up to eight miles a day and claims to have covered 20,000 miles in all. Figures like this capture the public imagination by exemplifying two historical faces of yoga—asceticism and showmanship—rolled, in this case literally, into one.

The YMCA Akhara

If the British authorities were largely successful in emasculating India's warrior-*sadhu* tradition, they had not given up on the ideal of infusing moral backbone into their subjects through physical exercise. As the twentieth century advanced, a crucial addition to the well-established YMCA gym-yoga routines was the series of exercises developed by a Danish gymnast called Niels Bukh. The trainer of the Danish team in the Stockholm Olympics of 1912, Bukh's system of 'Primitive Gymnastics' was itself inspired by a Swedish physiotherapist, Pehr Hendrik Ling, who had invented a sequence of exercises to cure his own poor health, then taught them widely and with great success, first in the military academies and medical centres of his homeland, then, from the mid-1800s onwards, throughout Europe. Favouring a more forceful approach, Bukh developed a tougher version of Ling's sequence as his own means to overcome turgid muscles and slovenly bodily habits. The British army adopted it in 1906 and Indian YMCAs and training colleges, which had already tried Ling's system and found it wanting, took to the Bukh method with gusto. It is an amusing irony that many young Indian men, keen to build up muscles and confidence for the freedom struggle that lay ahead, will have signed up enthusiastically for these YMCA courses under the nose of their unsuspecting colonial masters.

Bukh's system offered a complete course of exercise to stretch and strengthen. Graded into six progressive series, they were to be practised in what he called 'a vigorous rhythm', accompanied by deep breathing, with no pause between them. The names given to these postures were descriptive of their function, unlike classic yoga *asanas* which are often poetically named after animals, sages or deities. All these features remind us immediately of the Ashtanga Vinyasa yoga of Pattabhi Jois. Indeed, as our detective story unfolds, we shall see in Chapter 14 that Bukh's system was to have a crucial influence on Jois' guru, the man who is generally considered to be the founding father of modern postural yoga, T. M. Krishnamacharya of Mysore.

YOGA GOES WEST

10

YOGA THEOSOPHICA

As the nineteenth century drew to a close, conventional Christian belief was in tatters for many. The idea of Darwinian evolution, once a shocking new idea, was by now pervasive; age-old consolations could no longer suffice. Revolutionary political ideologies and economic changes were emerging to shake the existing order, and it would not be long before the carnage of the Great War dealt another blow to the comfortable idea of a loving parent-god watching protectively over his faithful children. As a result, several eclectic spiritual movements were stepping into the vacuum, and their leaders cast far and wide to find palatable doctrines for such uncertain times. The most powerful of these doctrines was to be Theosophy, a system founded by Helena Blavatsky, a Russian mediumistic visionary, working together with Henry Olcott, an American with a varied background in the army, the law and journalism, and William Q. Judge, an Anglo-Irish lawyer. Blavatsky was greatly influenced by Eliphas Levi, the nineteenth century French esotericist who coined the word 'occultism' and who, like many of the Westerners first drawn to yoga, was fascinated by the possibility of the magical powers it offered. He wrote about breath control and meditation as ways of developing these *siddhis*, though his definition of the 'true Magi' as 'Men-Gods, in virtue of their intimate union with the divine principle' chimes well with the higher aspirations of mind-yoga.[1]

Six months after Levi's death, the Theosophical Society was inaugurated in the aptly named Miracle Club in New York. According to the notes taken there on 17 November 1875, it was to dedicate itself to 'the study and elucidation of Occultism, the Cabala etc', and in their search for esoteric knowledge, the founders naturally became drawn to Eastern teachings. Under their direction, an energetic investigation of sources began, and Indian experts were commissioned to translate many of the more important works on yoga into English.[2]

The Theosophists were not so much interested in yoga itself, however; they were more concerned with what it could add to their ongoing occult project: the development and projection of an 'astral body'—an individual-ised entity distinct from the physical body, and capable of surviving death. This would be a 'body of light' able consciously to navigate the astral realms after the death of the physical shell that had housed it. To prolong life suffi-ciently to accomplish this aim, various methods were employed: temper-ance, fasting, sexual abstinence and meditation exercises. These echo yogic disciplines, of course, but Theosophy saw them as being linked more to a Western occult tradition that stretched from Pythagorean and Platonic teachings, through Renaissance occult and magical systems into the modern era. And, as in traditional Western esotericism, students of Theosophy ascended through degrees of adeptship in the occult sciences according to their level of progress on the path.

All this was to change in the early 1880s, not long after Blavatsky and Olcott arrived in India to further their research. Dramatically, the masters, Blavatsky's astral guides, instructed her that Westerners were not fit for prac-tical occult work. Henceforth, Theosophists must focus solely on the theory of occultism, rather than its practice, and devote themselves to establishing a sense of universal brotherhood. For those concerned, this was a momentous event. No more esoteric rituals, no more secret techniques, no more ascend-ing the ladder of initiation. As William Judge wrote: 'the Mahatmas, who started the Society, and stand behind it now, are distinctly opposed to making prominent these phenomenal leanings, this hunting after clairvoyance and astral bodies'.[3]

Whilst they were in India, it seems to have been politics, rather than yoga, that interested the founders of the Society. Blavatsky would stay with a fellow Theosophist, an ex-Bengal Civil Service officer and eccentric ornithologist called Allan Octavian Hume, at his capacious home Rothney Castle, in Simla. There she held mediumistic sessions which divided the mountain town; one of the unconvinced participants was Lockwood Kipling, Rudyard's father. At the Theosophical Society Convention in Madras in 1884, Olcott and Hume called for the founding of a political party to speak for the people of India, and the following year, organised by Hume, the Indian National Congress held its first meeting. It would rapidly become the prime mover for indepen-dence, and, as the Congress Party, has continued to shape the country's des-tiny right up to the present.

How much Blavatsky and Olcott came into contact with genuine yoga in India is a moot point. We know they met, and were impressed by, a *sannyasin* called Babu Surdass, who claimed to have sat in the lotus position for no less than fifty-two years. But Blavatsky was frequently critical of what she knew of *hatha yoga*. She shared the mistrust common at the time, calling yogic asceticism a type of 'hereditary illness' that exemplified 'a triply distilled SELFISHNESS'.[4] The 'true yoga', (i.e. Theosophy), derived from her own contact with the line of discarnate masters and associated celestial hierarchies, rather than from any embodied yoga practitioners, whatever their supple stamina. For his part, Olcott was far more interested in Buddhism and its revival, particularly in Sri Lanka, than in any yoga stemming from Hindu or Upanishadic traditions. His interest bore remarkable fruit: when he arrived on the island in 1880, there were only two Buddhist schools, with 246 students. By 1899, due to his efforts, there were a hundred and ninety-four, and some 15,490 students. Nonetheless, the organisation they founded was destined to play a crucial role in introducing knowledge of yoga to the West. With typical swagger, Blavatsky pronounced in 1881: 'neither modern Europe nor America had so much as heard (of yoga) until the Theosophists began to speak and write'.[5] In truth, for once her claim was not far wide of the mark.

The new direction decreed by the masters added to rifts already bubbling within the Society, and resulted in diminished interest in Theosophy throughout the subcontinent. By the time of Blavatsky's death in 1891, only twenty-nine out of the 135 lodges registered there were still active, but the search for knowledge continued. William Judge produced an influential 'interpretation' of the *Yoga Sutra* in 1889, by which time he had set up a breakaway group in America. A prolific author, he influenced many, including Alice Bailey, who was herself a committed Theosophist before becoming an important esoteric teacher in her own right. Judge's successor, a social worker called Kathleen Tingley, transferred the breakaway group's headquarters from New York to California, setting up a Theosophical-Yoga community called Lomaland, outside San Diego. This, surely one of the first ashrams on American soil, continued the pattern of blending East and West, with its 'Raja Yoga Academy' sitting happily alongside 'The School for the Revival of the Lost Mysteries of Antiquity'.

In 1907, with the death of Henry Olcott, the leadership of the mainstream Society passed to Annie Besant, a remarkable and energetic woman who was an early socialist, campaigner for women's rights and suffrage, and a supporter of both Irish and later, Indian, home-rule. The same year, at the Society's thirty-second anniversary in Banaras, she gave four lectures on Patanjali's yoga, which were published in a book that is still in print in several editions today.[6] Other Theosophists were to make important contributions to the already substantial corpus of yogic literature. One of these was Ernest Wood, a Sanskrit scholar who had moved to the Society's headquarters in Adyar, outside Madras, in 1910, and was part of the group who first saw the future 'world teacher', a dishevelled *brahmin* boy called Jiddu Krishnamurti, sitting on the beach there. Wood lived and worked in India for many years, earning great respect among his Indian colleagues, but he eventually became disillusioned with Theosophy, or at least the politics of the Society, and returned to his first love: yoga and the classic texts. He published over twenty works, including translations of the *Yoga Sutra*, the *Bhagavad Gita* and Shankara's *Vivekachudamani*. His most influential book, titled simply *Yoga*, was published in 1959 and so was right on hand for the yogic sub-culture emerging at the tail-end of the beat generation.

A Dangerous Path?

In Europe, the liveliest theosophical scene was to be found in the cultural melting-pot that was *fin de siècle* Vienna. The city had long been known for its intellectual brilliance, and influxes of refugees from the political upheavals of the late nineteenth century had created a diverse society with many different mind-sets. New ideas were bubbling up in the salons from all sorts of exciting thinkers—pioneers in physics, art, architecture and psychology—who were to play a significant role in shaping modernist culture. And, as always in turbulent and uncertain times, there was a keen interest in the occult. Vienna's occultists also adopted Indian esoteric knowledge, but in their case it was *hatha yoga* in general rather than textually derived tantric teachings.

The Viennese occult world was dominated by a talented trio of eccentrics.[7] The first of these was Friedrich Eckstein, a polymath, Freemason and writer, who, among other things, worked as private secretary to the composer Anton Bruckner. In 1886, Eckstein met Helena Blavatsky and was inspired to start a Theosophical Society lodge in Vienna, which soon became an active conduit for yoga. He was also a member of the Viennese Psychoanalytic Society that met each Wednesday in Sigmund Freud's flat, and this mixing with the early Freudians led him to write several contributions to the fledgling science. In fact, Eckstein was Freud's main informant on yoga, and, to judge from the master's assessment a quarter of a century later, was able to present the subject to him in a very acceptable way:

> Another friend of mine, whose insatiable craving for knowledge has led him
> to make the most unusual experiments and has ended by giving him encyclo-

paedic knowledge, has assured me that through the practices of Yoga, by with-drawing from the world, by fixing the attention on bodily functions and by peculiar methods of breathing, one can in fact evolve new sensations and coenaesthesias in oneself, which he regards as regressions to primordial states of mind which have long ago been overlaid. He sees in them a physiological basis, as it were, of much of the wisdom of mysticism.[8]

This last sentence was prescient, though Freud remained sceptical about the relevance of any altered states of mind yoga could induce. But he liked the psychoanalytic interpretation of them as regression and, as might be expected from his biological grounding, focused on the physicality of the praxis—breathing exercises, physiological functions and bodily sensations—rather than any 'higher' or spiritual insights it might yield.

The second key player on the esoteric stage was Carl Kellner, an electro-chemist who had made his fortune by inadvertently discovering a method for producing paper-pulp that revolutionised cellulose production and paper-manufacture. His real interest, however, was alchemy. He had a special back-room in his Viennese laboratory where he conducted experiments to find the elixir of life, and it was known he practised ritualised sex with his wife Marie Antoinette in attempts to generate the perfect balance of male and female essences considered crucial for the 'Great Work'. Kellner believed yoga would aid his alchemical endeavours, though he hoped it might also yield direct knowledge of his previous incarnations.

The third member of the trio was a physician called Franz Hartmann. He realised that a by-product of the cellulose manufactured in Kellner's factories could provide a treatment for tuberculosis and other respiratory ailments, and proposed the two join forces. So, in the early 1890s, Hartmann's know-how and Kellner's money produced a clinic they called an 'inhalatorium'. More importantly for our story, Hartmann was also a leading and longtime Theosophist. As a former close associate of Helena Blavatsky herself, he had served as chairman of the Board of Control of the Society's headquarters in Adyar, and, as one of the most important theosophical writers of his time, spread the word on yoga throughout Germany and Austria. In his study of the *Bhagavad Gita*, he defines yoga as a universal mystical method that lies at the heart of every religious system:

'Yoga' is derived from Yog = to join and means the union of the human soul with God. It therefore would be an equivalent to the term 'religion' if this word had not been misused like many similar ones and had not been identified with churchdom, so that it has almost lost its true meaning. Yoga is the art of

111

self-control through the divine spirit that awakes to consciousness within us. [...] Every religious practice, insofar as it is performed selflessly and without hidden agenda, is a Yoga exercise.[9]

This has a very modern ring to it, and, as we shall see in the next chapter, an Indian monk called Swami Vivekananda was galvanising American spiritual seekers with pretty much the same message at pretty much the same time.

Enter the Indian Masters

In his alchemical research, Kellner studied yoga with two Indian teachers. The first was Bheema Sena Pratapa, who arrived in Europe at the age of twenty-nine to begin giving public demonstrations of what he called 'yoga sleep', a state of mind in which he lost contact with the world around him, became insensitive to pain and could not be awakened except by specific hand gestures performed over his body. Pratapa explained his comatose state as one of blissful union with the divine spirit. In what must have been among the very first of such experiments, he drew crowds at the Millennial Exposition in Budapest in 1896, where he demonstrated yoga sleep each day for an entire week, while scientists measured his body temperature, pulse and respiration. The newspaper publicity brought him to the attention of the theosophical circle; Kellner and Hartmann examined his yogic powers and were convinced he could enter into deepest *samadhi* at will. Later that year, they accompanied him to a scientific conference in Munich, where he repeated the show, passing into yoga sleep throughout all three days of the conference, with no one able to disturb his otherworldly state.

Not long after this, Kellner became enthusiastic about another yogi, a Kashmiri *brahmin* called Sri Agamya Guru Paramahamsa. A Western-educated barrister by profession, Agamya advanced what was to become the very familiar claim of having spent several years in the remote Himalayas, meditating and mastering yoga. As a result, he could stop his pulse on command. He also stressed the importance of breath control in calming the mind, but unfortunately did not seem to practise this himself, as his outbursts of rage were so frequent that he became known as 'The Tiger Mahatma'. Before long he was judged a fraud, and in 1903, Kellner abruptly broke off relations with him. Agamya left for England, where the renowned occultist Aleister Crowley, Leamington Spa's very own Great Beast, was among those who attended his yoga retreats. The irascible yogi disappeared from the scene when he was imprisoned for molesting two of his female students.

Kellner may have been duped, but he was a tireless and intrepid explorer and had at least learned what he enigmatically called 'breathing exercises and other things' from his teacher. Their results, however, seem to have backfired, confirming fears, already voiced by the more conventional Theosophists, that such yoga could lead unwary aspirants to lose their way among the dark beings that inhabit the lower astral realms. In a letter to his friend Hartmann, written in April 1904, he explains:

> I am progressing favourably with my experiments. At the same time I have to contend continually with a very gruesome crowd.... for the preparation of the Elixir. However, I begin to get accustomed to that fight, as a trainer of wild animals gets familiar with ferocious beasts...

He later adds:

> I agree with you, that these arts as such are perhaps objectionable; but they are at least a new field of knowledge, and in so far they must be of some use. However, the dwellers of the threshold are to be dreaded; there are hosts of them guarding the door.[10]

The 'dwellers of the threshold' he refers to are malign discarnate entities, too impure to enter the higher spiritual realms and unwilling to let others do so. Such first-hand reports fuelled misgivings about *hatha yoga* shared by Theosophists, westernised Hindus, and many European scholars and psychologists. Kellner himself remained undeterred, echoing Hartmann's view that, despite all its possible pitfalls, yoga comprises the practical methodology of every religious system. As such, it is to be found somewhere in every holy book and within the practices and symbolism of esoteric societies. A booklet he published gets to the heart of things, describing yoga as 'certain exercises and a life style governed by certain rules that aim at dissolving the illusionary ego-consciousness (*Ahankara*) and reaching a union with the general world-consciousness (*Atma*)'.[11]

The little work earned a mention from no less an authority than the psychologist William James who, in his magisterial *Varieties of Religious Experience*, remarked that Kellner had reached the conclusion that yoga 'makes of its disciples good, healthy, and happy men'. As time went on, Kellner's interest focused more on the psycho-physiological aspect of the practice, a preference in tune with wider cultural changes taking place around him. In the esoteric world, many teachers, tired of the otherworldliness of much occultism, were experimenting with body-movements to culture a spirituality that was more fully grounded. One of these, J. B. Kerling, attracted Kellner by his insistence that the soul depended on the body. Most seekers ignore the physical in their

113

search for the spiritual, whereas what mattered was not escape from the body, but conscious grounding in it. A fellow leader of the Vienna circle, the writer Gustav Meyrink, agreed, using the recently-coined terminology of psychology to criticise astral projection as 'the worst kind of schizophrenia'.[12]

Altogether, the realisation was dawning in the heavily-chintzed drawing rooms of the Viennese haute bourgeoisie that the astral body must be fully integrated with its gross counterpart. Separation from the physical results in a disabling lack of co-ordination between the various levels of the personality; if yoga has any use, it is its physicality. This shift of emphasis was encouraged by the influx into mainland Europe of body-building and physical exercise systems from England and the USA. A healthy mind in a healthy body was the fashionable slogan and in Vienna, its chief advocate was the self-styled 'strongest man in town', Georg Jagendorfer, who ran a gym offering Indian club swinging, rhythmic gymnastics, wrestling and boxing. Kellner adopted the hybrid regime with gusto and hired Jagendorf to tutor his children. His new discipline obviously worked; a couple of years after his unnerving experiences of those 'dwellers of the threshold' he was writing confidently that: 'The Yogi needs a strong and in all of its parts totally healthy body. He has to possess perfect body control.' This comes not from traditional yogic *asanas* however, because, he tells us, they are too difficult for most Westerners and 'can only be performed by the so-called contortionists of our circuses and vaudevilles'.[13] Static *asana* may be useful as a posture for meditation, but dynamic body-building was the way forward for the well-balanced aspirant.

Kellner's personal trajectory exemplified yoga's Janus-headed position at the dawn of the twentieth century. One head looked back to the Nath traditions of medieval *hatha yoga* and their desire, initially shared by many Western occultists, to achieve psychic abilities, longevity and the elixir of life by a variety of means that included sexual magic and communication with discarnate realms. The other head, however, was turned flexibly in quite the opposite direction, looking beyond such murky concerns to locate yoga firmly in the context of an eclectic and quasi-scientific body-culture, informed and guided by the new insights of psychology. The benefits of this new discipline were not out-of-the-body adventurings, but a well-integrated life, grounded in the here and now.[14]

Helena Roerich

Following the Theosophist lead, other occultists investigated *hatha yoga*, and were to reach similar conclusions. One of these was Helena Roerich, a woman of great energy who had travelled widely in the Orient with her husband, the painter Nicholas Roerich, translated the works of her fellow Russian, Madame Blavatsky into English, written thirteen books under the title of the *Agni Yoga Series* and penned voluminous instructive letters to her worldwide followers. Like Theosophy, Roerich's richly imaginative teachings purportedly derived from a hierarchy of ascended spiritual masters, on whose advice she strongly cautioned her students against body-yoga, warning: 'Exercises in *hatha yoga* should not go beyond a slight and very careful *pranayama*, which strengthens health, as otherwise they might be dangerous and could lead to mediumship, obsession and insanity.'[15] In one of her letters she recounts the fate of several impatient disciples:

> whom we knew personally in India, went in for the practice of Hatha Yoga, notwithstanding our warnings. Of these, two developed consumption, one of whom died; others became almost idiotic; another committed suicide; and one developed into a regular Tantrika, a Black Magician, but his career, fortunately for himself, was cut short by death.[16]

The esoteric rationale behind such criticisms was spelled out by her astral guide, one Master Morya, a high-level initiate who was also in touch with Madame Blavatsky. He made it clear that *hatha yoga*, at least when practised in our current age—the *Kali Yuga* of ignorance and egoity—confines the practitioner to the lower astral realms, rather than facilitating any truly spiritual transcendence in the tradition of the *Upanishads* or Patanjali. Indeed, its practice may even inhibit spiritual growth and lead only to morbid fascinations. In another letter, Roerich continues in the same vein, drawing a very clear distinction between what she saw as the benefits of mind-yoga and the dangers of its sinister sister:

> One should not overestimate the achievements of Hatha Yoga and think that 'the adepts of Hatha Yoga are equal to those of Raja Yoga in ability to awaken the *kundalini* and to acquire various *siddhis*,' and that 'they reach bliss and liberation from matter.' It is not so! The degree of bliss reached by such adepts is very relative, and they never reach liberation from matter (in the sense which is meant by the Great Teachers) by means of Hatha Yoga. As it is said in the Teaching, 'We know of no one who reached the goal by way of Hatha Yoga'.[17]

In her withering conclusion, Roerich unwittingly foresees the future medicalisation of much modern postural practice: 'Quite correctly, the Hindu people of high spiritual development consider Hatha Yoga most undesirable, and they say that at best it is useful "for fat and ill people."'[18]

The 'Subtle Body'

The greatest lasting effect of Theosophy's interest in yoga was its role in pub-
licising the concepts of the subtle body and the *chakras* that would become
mainstream doctrine in global yoga and New Age teachings. This model of the
human being, found in various forms and in many cultures across the globe
from earliest times, envisages an inner structure made of imperceptibly fine
matter that acts as an energetic link between the immaterial mind and the
material body. This invisible intermediary between the abstract impulse of
thought and the physical vehicle acts as a subjective, or aerial, nervous system, bridging the Cartesian dualism of mind and matter that has dominated
the modern view of reality since the seventeenth century. As such, it fundamentally alters the understanding of the body-mind and greatly expands the
scope of human agency.

The earliest mention of such ideas occurs in the first *Upanishads*. In the
Brihadaranyaka, the great sage Yajnyavalkya teaches King Janaka about the
inner self 'that eats finer food than does this bodily self', while the *Chandogya*
tells us:

> There are a hundred and one channels of the heart,
> One of these passes up to the crown of the head.
> Moving up by it, one goes to immortality.[19]

By the time the great sage Adi Shankara formalised Advaita Vedanta in the
eighth century AD, the subtle body was established as one of three nested
structures that together comprise the individual: the observable anatomy of
the 'gross' body (*sthula sharira*), the intermediate 'subtle' body (*sukshma
sharira*, or sometimes *linga sharira*) and the deeply interior 'causal' body
(*karana sharira*). This last is the substratum of the localised and contingent
personality, beyond which lies the unbounded consciousness that is our real
Self.[20] A Chinese version of the subtle body is first recorded in Han dynasty
tombs from around 250 BC and, variously described, the model has remained
the basis of traditional Chinese, Indian and Tibetan understandings of the
human being. As such, it is central to the medical and spiritual systems of
these cultures and important in their martial arts traditions; albeit in simpli-
fied form, the idea is still current in Indian systems of midwifery. A similar
model, though less well-defined and with far less enduring cultural impact,
can also be found in Western esotericism since antiquity. It re-emerged, via
Renaissance occultism, in movements such as Freemasonry and Rosicru-
cianism, and is the basis of Mesmerism, an eighteenth-century doctrine of

animal magnetism that the original Theosophists were much drawn to as a useful tool in their search to develop the immortal astral body.

The subtle body took its definitive form in the medieval Indian tantric teachings we examined in Chapter 5. These describe the human organism, gross and subtle, as being animated by the universal life-force (*prana*) that moves through minute channels (*nadis*), traditionally said to number 72,000. The *nadis* are the hidden roots of the human tree, bearing the nourishing sap to all parts of the structure. Junction points drawing these conduits together are nerve complexes or vital centres known as *chakras*, 'wheels', or *padmas*, 'lotuses'. Six or seven major *chakras* (there are many minor ones) sit vertically aligned along the spinal axis. The *chakras* and *nadis* are closely linked to the concept of *kundalini*, 'the coiled one', a term denoting the female divine energy (*shakti*) that sleeps coiled like a serpent at the bottom of the spine. Once awakened by yogic endeavour, this energy ascends from one *chakra* to the next, purifying each, until she reaches the top of the head where she unites herself with Shiva, the masculine aspect of the Divine, and the yogi enjoys the blissful state of liberation (*moksha*) from all earthly constraints. From the point of view of Tantra, then, the serpent did not occasion our fall from Eden, but it does provide the way back in.

One of the more significant practical aspects of the subtle body is the way in which it connects the apparently separate individual to the world around him. Because it partakes of an energetic field not constrained by the limitations of the corporeal frame, this subjectivity can impact upon other people through their own subtle body complexes, and also upon the environment more widely. It is this connection to a field that transcends the boundaries operating at the normal, relatively gross level of perceived reality, that provides the rationale behind many of the yogic *siddhis*. By consciously entering deep into his own mind, the yogi can direct his awareness out beyond it, through the process Patanjali calls *sanyama*.[22] This psychic plasticity, which is central to the typically Indian view of the self, necessarily works both ways. As well as enabling the self to expand its territory of influence beyond its bodily limits, it also entails a porosity that renders the individual vulnerable to psychic invasion from outside. This can be a friendly merger or hostile takeover. Indeed, it was precisely the tantric yogi's expertise in handling the subtle body that enabled him to navigate the spirit worlds and practise magic, preoccupations that, as we have seen, gained him such a bad reputation.[23]

The Society had been introduced to classical Indian teachings on the subtle body by a Bengali scholar called Baradakanta Majumdar, who, as early as 1880, had written a couple of articles on the *chakras* entitled 'The Description of the Six Centres', in its magazine, *The Theosophist*. Well aware that Tantra was viewed askance by orthodox religionists, he sought to allay the Society's misgivings by calling as his main defence witness the *Mahanirvana Tantra*, an eighteenth-century Bengali text which described the subtle body within a context of monism, an acceptable 'spiritual' perspective, and downplayed any risqué magical elements. Another Indian Theosophist aiming to do the same was the Christian missionary-educated Sabhapati Swami, who, in his heavily illustrated 1880 book, *Om: a Treatise on Vedantic Raj Yoga and Philosophy*, put forward a version of the subtle body that included twelve *chakras*, linked with assorted higher planes of reality that fitted nicely with Theosophist ideas. In Sabhapati's view, the aspirant's attitude to the subtle body should be a kind of inner warfare waged against his lower nature; he should enter into dialogue with the various *chakras* and convince them that they were only material emanations and not the pure spirit. In this way, their influence was to be nullified, and if need be, they should even be cursed not to appear before the practitioner any longer, thereby ending up 'absorbed in the Infinite Spirit'. This curious blend of Christianised asceticism and *chakra* meditation was quite different from any authentically tantric teaching of course, but it became acceptable to the Society as an unobjectionable treatment of a foreign doctrine.

Not infrequently, the Theosophists preferred to employ their own interpretations of the original Sanskrit terminology. Even so, Blavatsky herself remained ambivalent on the whole subject. She sought to reconcile her doubts by proposing both a benign and a benighted Tantra, writing:

> As there are both magic (pure psychic science) and sorcery (its impure counterpart) so there are what are known as the 'White' and 'Black' Tantras. The one is an exposition, very clear and exceedingly valuable, of occultism in its noblest features, the other a devil's chap-book of wicked instructions to the would-be wizard and sorcerer.[24]

The Serpent Uncoils

It was under Annie Besant's stewardship of the Society from 1907 onwards that the subtle body and the *chakras* became central to Theosophy. This was mainly due to the influence of her protégé, a charismatic clairvoyant called Charles Webster Leadbeater, whose account of his own excursions through the subtle dimensions of reality soon became accepted as official doctrine. Leadbeater's cognitions introduced the *chakras* to not only Western and Indian Theosophists but a wider audience outside the confines of the Society. His main interest in this was to expand the classical model of the subtle physiology into a series of 'higher bodies'—astral, mental, causal and etheric—

deemed to co-exist with the physical and correspond to successive finer strata of materiality. Leadbeater's scheme was adopted and modified by other influential esoteric teachers who made their start in Theosophy, such as Rudolf Steiner, the founder of Anthroposophy, and Alice Bailey.

The most authoritative Western work on the subtle body, however, stayed closer to original sources. This was *The Serpent Power: The Secrets of Tantric and Shaktic Yoga*, published in 1918 by Sir John Woodroffe, a British judge in the High Court of Calcutta who we have already met briefly in Chapter 7. As the classic, and highly erudite, study on *kundalini yoga*, *The Serpent Power* is comprised of Woodroffe's translation and explication of two texts. One was the 'Description of the Six Centres' (*Satchakra Nirupana*) authored by a celebrated sixteenth-century Bengali tantric called Purnananda Swami, that Majumdar had already written about in *The Theosophist* magazine, while the other was the anonymous 'The Five-fold Footprint of the Guru' (*Paduka panchaka*). Woodroffe's book also included the Sanskrit originals, plus translation and explication of a Sanskrit commentary on the latter text, attributed to one Kalicharana.

During his time in India Woodroffe had become very familiar with Theosophy and worked on a number of translations with Majumdar. Significantly, though, he saw fit to devote over half of his introduction to *The Serpent Power* to examining the differences between Leadbeater's version of the subtle body and its description in his sources. Drawing on *The Inner Life*, which Leadbeater had written around 1910, Woodroffe notes many discrepancies between the two approaches. His more general criticism of the theosophical approach was that it had diverged from what he calls 'the true spiritual Yoga' whose aim is always, and only, to achieve unity with the Universal Consciousness. In his view, 'The Rt. Rev. Leadbeater' had become overly preoccupied with the forms and phenomena that populate lesser planes of being. However alluring these may be, they are merely the temporary and unbinding modifications of that absolute level of life sought by the genuine yogi, and, as such, they are a diversion from the true spiritual quest. This criticism echoed a familiar caution voiced by many classical teachers including Patanjali,[25] and Woodroffe concludes that his own book is something of a timely corrective, being: 'a first endeavour to supply, more particularly for those interested in occultism and mysticism, a fuller, more accurate and rational presentation of the subject'.[26]

In his emphasis on the need for a 'rational presentation', Woodroffe was keen to gain credibility for yogic models by linking the subtle physiology to ideas then current in science. This attempt to understand the esoteric in scientific terms was, as we shall see in future chapters, very much a theme of the time, and it was even evident among occultists. Indeed, way back in 1882, in a lecture delivered to local Theosophists in Madras, Olcott had made it clear that:

> We come not to pull down and destroy, but to rebuild the strong fabric of Asiatic religion. We ask you to help us to set it up again, not on the shifting and treacherous sands of blind faith, but on the rocky base of truth, and to cement its separate stones together with the strong cement of Modern Science. Hinduism proper has nothing whatever to fear from the research of Science.[27]

In 1926, a British-trained Indian physician called Vasant G. Rele presented a paper to the Bombay Medical Union titled *The Mysterious Kundalini: The Physical Basis of the Kundalini Yoga in Terms of Western Anatomy and Physiology*. Rele's own conflation of spirit and science was clear: 'I would define *kundalini yoga* as a science of physical and mental exercises of a particular form by which an individual establishes a conscious control over his autonomic nervous system so as to get in tune with the Infinite.'[28] His thesis went down so well it was published as a book the next year under the same title, with an introduction by Woodroffe, who emphasised the comprehensive possibilities of the subject: 'Kundalini Yoga is of great scientific, parapsychic, and meta-physical interest.'

Rele's work has remained one of the most important attempts to explain the subtle body by linking it to the observable anatomy; it associates each *chakra* with a gland of the endocrine system, with special attention paid to the pineal and pituitary glands. It was followed within twelve months by another study along similar lines: *The Divine Postures and Their Influence on the Endocrine Glands* by one Cajzoran Ali, one of several aliases adopted by Amber Steen from Iowa, who, surviving a disastrous marriage with a Trinidadian conman who claimed to be an 'Indian swami', ended up teaching tantric yoga on two continents.

The striking coloured images of the *chakras* in Woodroffe's *Serpent Power* were reproduced in many other works and they helped shape the modern iconography. The number and specific locations in the body were a matter of discussion, however. Over twenty years earlier Blavatsky had written that: 'no two authorities up to the present day agree as to the real location in the body of the Chakras', going on to mention seven 'principal plexuses in the body' in addition to: 'forty-two minor ones to which Physiology refuses that name'.[29] Woodroffe himself cites a tantric work that described a grand total of fifty-six *chakras*, each separately named. For his part, Leadbeater went on to write the highly influential *The Chakras* (1927), a considerably shorter and more readable study than what he calls Woodroffe's 'magnificent work', in which he included material from his previous work *The Inner Life*. He references earlier Western models of the subtle body, including a reproduction of an illustration from a nineteenth-century French version of *Theosophia Practica* (1701) by the German visionary Johann Georg Gichtel, showing both the body's physical organs and subtle centres to be linked with the planets, elements and some of the seven deadly sins. Leadbeater's book also includes colour plates of the *chakras*, which, he says in the Preface:

> so far as I am aware…are the first attempt to represent them as they actually appear to those who can see them. Indeed, it is chiefly in order to put before the public this fine series of drawings by my friend the Rev. Edward Warner that I write this book…

He continues his blend of Tantra and theosophical occultism, crucially increasing the number of major *chakras* from six to seven, defining them as: 'force centres … points of connection at which energy flows from one vehicle or body of a man to another' and synthesising them with the etheric bodies and human aura that his clairvoyance had revealed to him.

Wheels within Wheels

In their journey from Bengal to Bloomsbury, the *chakras* underwent such significant changes that we are justified in speaking of the development of a Western *chakra* system, quite different from its Indian origins. In the tantric texts, for example, each lotus is associated with a psychically-charged syllable, or seed-mantra that is understood to be the sound body of one of the deities that animate the subtle body. These intelligences can be invoked by correct mantric practice, and will bring the practitioner benefits from their clandestine assistance. A traditional Indian depiction of *chakras* had, in addition, its own colour and number of petals, an associated sacred animal, *yantra* and Sanskrit syllables associated with its particular seed-mantra.

Such arcane lore, crucial to traditional tantric praxis, proved too culturally specific to be easily transplanted in Western soil. Over time, it was increasingly replaced by more secular and psychological interpretations that are nowhere to be found in any original Sanskrit texts. In the latter, spiritual liberation from all material constraints was always the aim, whereas modern treatments of the *chakras* emphasise relatively mundane concerns of physical health, emotional well-being, and effective agency in the world. Very often, the purification of the self is construed as a healing release of trauma and emotional stress, an interpretation facilitated by the general acceptance of psychoanalytical theories that emphasise the primacy of unresolved psychic or emotional material in the formulation of existential dis-ease. In this way, what were once esoteric spiritual teachings were to become gradually aligned with a popular and, in time, highly commercialised 'wellness industry'. Sacred knowledge was becoming medicalised.

This transformation was facilitated by many contributing influences along the way.[30] Well-known psychics, such as Alice Bailey and Edgar Cayce helped popularise the *chakra* system in Western occult and healing circles, while the now commonly accepted rainbow spectrum correspondences of the subtle body were established by various colour therapists and healers from the 1930s onwards. Prominent among these were Roland Hunt, author of the standard work, *The Seven Keys to Color Healing* (1963), and Barbara Brennan, who wrote *Hands of Light, A Guide to Healing through the Human Energy Field* (1987) that has sold well over a million copies and been translated into twenty-two languages.

Academia also played its part, principally through two eminent German Indologists exiled from the land of their birth and working in America. One was the linguist and art historian Heinrich Zimmer, whose youthful brilliance had already established himself as the successor to Max Mueller in the vanguard of Indian studies. Zimmer taught at Columbia University, where his lectures were attended by Joseph Campbell, a literature professor interested in comparative mythology. Campbell's best-selling books and TV series 'The Power of Myth' were to introduce millions to the idea that ancient myths are stories of humanity's perennial quest for what his contemporary, the humanistic psychologist Abraham Maslow, was calling 'self-actualisation', the pinnacle of a hierarchy of human needs. Zimmer and Campbell became friends, and Zimmer encouraged the younger man to study the *chakras* in the context of the Indian saint Sri Ramakrishna, guru of the pioneering Swami Vivekananda. After Zimmer's tragically early death, Campbell edited his works, which included the classic *Myths and Symbols in Indian Art and Civilisation* and *Philosophies of India*.

Both these men were heavily influenced by the psychological interpretations of myth and symbol initiated by C. G. Jung, who thirty years earlier had written psychological commentaries on translations of eastern yogic texts such as *The Tibetan Book of the Great Liberation*, *The Tibetan Book of the Dead* and the Chinese *Secrets of the Golden Flower*. Such cross-cultural studies introduced the subtle body to non-specialist readers in Eastern religion as well as a wider psychotherapeutic audience of both practitioners and patients. Jung himself presented a seminar on *kundalini yoga* to the Psychological Club in Zurich in

1932, which is widely regarded as a milestone in the Western understanding of Eastern thought. To the Swiss psychologist, the subtle body was a conceptual model for the development of higher consciousness lacking in the Western syntax; he interpreted it in terms of what he called 'the process of individuation' which in his scheme constituted the true goal of human life.

The other influential scholar in our story was Frederic Spiegelberg, another talented linguist and something of a natural mystic, who taught courses in Indian civilisation at Stanford University. One of his students there was a young Californian called Michael Murphy who, on his tutor's advice, spent eighteen months at the Sri Aurobindo Ashram in South India after graduating. Another was Dick Price who, after leaving university, suffered a psychotic episode that gave him dramatic personal experience of altered states of consciousness. Recovered, he pursued his interests in Theravada Buddhism, Zen and Daoism by enrolling at the American Academy of Asian Studies in San Francisco, the first accredited US graduate school devoted exclusively to the study of Asiatic cultures. Here one of his his mentors was Haridas Chaudhuri, a Bengali philosopher and follower of Aurobindo who had been invited to the US to teach by Spiegelberg.

Price and Murphy met at the academy and the two went on to found Esalen, the world centre of The Human Potential Movement, in 1962. From its beautiful location overlooking the ocean in northern California's Big Sur, this was to prove the crucible in which many various influences would combine to create a major wave of change in collective consciousness. By the mid-'60s, the institute was drawing the best minds of the counter-culture and offering a wide and eclectic menu of teachings and techniques to develop human potential and self-discovery. These included Asian yogic and subtle body teachings (especially those of Sri Aurobindo), Western psychological theories and techniques, innovative body-energetic, group and dance therapies, assorted meditative and visualisation practices. Many of these themes would meet in the new formulation of the *chakras*. Another outcome was a revivial of the concept of a 'tantric sexuality' for moderns, popularised by such books as Omar Garrison's *Tantra: The Yoga of Sex* (1964) that attempted to marry sexual liberation and spiritual enlightenment.

In 1967, *Kundalini: The Evolutionary Energy in Man*, the autobiography of a Kashmiri social worker called Gopi Krishna, was published. With an introduction by Spiegelberg, the book created a stir with its vivid, and cautionary, account of the psychic turmoil unleashed by the spontaneous arousal of the *kundalini* energy. Krishna was an unprepared and unsupervised aspirant, and it took him the best part of twelve difficult years to stabilise and integrate the goddess' fiery benediction. One of her more benign gifts was a prodigious creativity, as he went on to write seventeen books on higher consciousness, accrediting them to inspiration from a higher source. His experience not only underlined the necessity for competent guidance that all genuine tantric teachings stress, but also marked a clear difference between a genuine and spontaneous arising of *kundalini* and the relatively anodyne 'visualisation' of the *chakras* that, over the succeeding decades, has come to pass for tantric praxis in many yoga classes.

Gopi Krishna's account also contributed significantly to the psychological interpretation of the *chakras*, as it was accompanied by a commentary from James Hillman, then the director of the C. G. Jung institute in Zurich. This in turn inspired the transpersonal psychologist Lee Sanella to set up the Kundalini Clinic in San Francisco in 1974; two years later, he published *Kundalini: Psychosis or Transcendence?*, another important contribution to the ongoing dialogue of Eastern and Western understandings on consciousness. Sanella's work was not merely in the interests of theory, however. It was in part precipitated by the need to deal with experiences unleashed by the teachings of popular meditation gurus—Amrit Desai, Yogi Bhajan, Swami Muktananda—who taught a neo-tantric praxis that attracted considerable numbers of ingénue followers.

The final ingredient in the confection of the Western *chakra* also came from sunny California. One of the Esalen therapists was Ken Dychtwald, who in his 1974 book *Bodymind: A Synthesis of Eastern and Western Approaches to Self-Awareness, Health, and Personal Growth* combined the colour healers' list of rainbow hues and endocrine glands with the idea that each *chakra* had specific qualities associated with it—survival, power, love, communication and so on. A month after publication, a synopsis of the book's themes appeared in *Yoga Journal*, and so the heavily freighted *chakra* became a crucial term in the growing lexicon of self-improvement.

If the picture was complete, all that was needed to launch it mainstream was the by-now mandatory celebrity endorsement. This took quite a time to come but when it did, it was in the personable form of the movie star Shirley MacLaine, who, by the end of the 1980s, had become well-known on the New Age scene for writing about reincarnation. Her public workshops on the *chakras* did for the subtle body what Jane Fonda had done so successfully for its gross counterpart a generation before (see Chapter 16). In 1990, MacLaine reached an audience of millions with her appearance on the primetime TV talk-show *Tonight*, where she enthusiastically pinned coloured circles representing the *chakras* onto its bemused host, Johnny

Carson. From now on the commercial promotion of the *chakras* would be unfettered. Amazon.com today lists no less than seventy-five pages of books on the subject, and therapeutic courses and services abound, alongside products ranging from roll-ons and oil to massage the *chakras*, to crystals and gadgets to stimulate them. At the theoretical level, attempts to explain these energy vortices in scientific terms continued the legacy of Woodroffe and Rele. Adventurous researchers such as the parapsychologist Hiroshi Motoyama, author of *Theories of the Chakras: Bridge to Higher Consciousness* (1988) and *Awakening of the Chakras and Emancipation* (2003), seek to connect *chakra* theory to a wide range of disciplines including physics, physiology and parapsychology and, by extension, to the general spiritual development of humankind.

11

THE SWAMI'S MISSION

On Christmas Eve 1892, six years to the day after he had taken his monastic vows, and after many months wandering the length and breadth of his home-land, Swami Vivekananda arrived at Cape Comorin, the southernmost tip of the subcontinent. He visited the great Kanyakumari temple, one of the seven most powerful goddess shrines scattered throughout the Land of the Veda, and took *darshan* of the virgin deity who is so regally enshrined there. Then, look-ing out to sea, he noticed a couple of small islands that, according to local legend, mark the place where the goddess first descended to earth. Moved to spend time at such a hallowed spot, the young *sannyasin* realised he had no money to pay for the boat, so he just waded into the sea and swam out to the nearest outcrop. He spent the night there, meditating on Mother India, and contemplating how her people could best be prepared to face the rising tide of modernity. As he later wrote to a fellow monk:

> My brother, in view of all this, specially of the poverty and ignorance, I had no sleep. At Cape Comorin sitting in Mother Kumari's temple, sitting on the last bit of Indian rock—I hit upon a plan: We are so many Sannyasins wandering about, and teaching the people metaphysics—it is all madness. Did not our Gurudeva use to say, 'An empty stomach is no good for religion'? That those poor people are leading the life of brutes is simply due to ignorance. We have for all ages been sucking their blood and trampling them underfoot...[1]

The next day he formulated his resolve to spread a doctrine of practical service to the poor and needy, a vision that blended the strengths of Indian spirituality shorn of its superstitions with a Western dedication to science, progress and social equality. Vivekananda will not have been unaware that his own mission was born on the day that celebrates another birth that changed the world. Like many fellow Bengali intellectuals, he had met and debated with Christian missionaries in Calcutta and been impressed by their work ethic and concern for social uplift. These practical virtues would combine well with India's perennial spiritual wisdom in his programme for global regeneration. And it is appropriate, if ironic, that the memorial temple erected on the island to commemorate his time there bears more than a touch of the neo-Gothic style that was so popular in late nineteenth-century Britain and also formed an ever-so-solid statement of her imperial power throughout the sub-continent.

The Chicago Conference

On 11 September 1893, ten months after making his vow to spread a doctrine of practical service to the poor that came to be known as 'the Kanyakumari Resolve', Vivekananda presented his message to a wider audience. The venue was the opening day of the World's Parliament of Religions, an international forum of faiths that took place in Chicago as part of the World's Fair being held there to commemorate the 400th anniversary of Columbus' arrival in the New World. When summoned to give his talk, the Swami was sitting on the stage with his eyes closed in meditation. After a pregnant pause, he rose majestically and began to speak. In a sonorous voice that immediately entranced his listeners, he began: 'Sisters and Brothers of America, it fills my heart with joy unspeakable...' At this, the previously sedate crowd of over 4,000 delegates suddenly rose to its feet and erupted in tumultuous applause. Vivekananda, who had never previously addressed anything like so large a gathering, was as shocked as they were. Flushed with emotion, he responded: 'I thank you in the name of the most ancient order of monks in the world, I thank you in the name of the mother of religions, and I thank you in the name of millions and millions of Hindu people of all classes and sects.'

While the other speakers had stressed the strength and uniqueness of their own particular brand, Vivekananda dismissed the pettiness of partiality and spoke on the overarching unity of all the diverse religions, emphasising how their perennial essence could be combined with modern scientific and social ideas to uplift all the people of the world. This idea that all faiths shared a common core was a theological bombshell. People were at first startled, but then delighted, by such a novel message, delivered with a calm assurance that needed no notes. Among the appreciative audience was Annie Besant, the British Theosophist who was to dedicate her life to bringing up the world-teacher Jiddu Krishnamurti, and then work tirelessly for Indian independence, acting as mentor to Jawaharlal Nehru, the country's first prime minister. These twin interests—the spiritual and the political—resonated powerfully with the message of the impressive young Swami on the stage, who she described as: 'a striking figure, clad in yellow and orange, shining like the sun of India in the midst of the heavy atmosphere of Chicago…a lion head, piercing eyes, mobile lips, movements swift and abrupt…' Besant saw him as 'a warrior-monk', adding: 'The Parliament was enraptured; the huge multitude hung upon his words. Not a syllable must be lost, not a cadence missed!'[2] At the end of the speech, the convocation rose again to give him an even more enthusiastic standing ovation. Another delegate described the scores of women scrambling over the benches to get near to the handsome young man, wittily commenting that: 'if Vivekananda can resist that onslaught, he is indeed a god!'

In fact, the whole affair did seem to have been orchestrated by divine providence. The Swami had first arrived in Chicago at the end of July, alone and virtually penniless, only to find the Parliament had been postponed until September. Unable to find accommodation he could afford, and the object of racial antagonism (he recalled that people took him for a 'negro'), he was walking in the street when a passer-by advised him that it would be cheaper to stay in Boston. While on the train there, he attracted the curiosity of a wealthy fellow passenger, Kate Sanborn, who offered to put him up in her home for some weeks. One of the people he met in her comfortable drawing room was a Harvard academic called J. H. Wright. Realising that the monk's innocent intention to speak at the convention was likely to be refused because he did not have the requisite academic qualifications, the professor provided him with a forceful letter of introduction that would ensure his right to appear on the platform. Fortunately, Vivekananda did not lose this letter, but he did mislay the address of the office in charge of the delegates, so when he returned to Chicago the day before the conference, he was again adrift. Coming across a railway yard, he spent the night on the floor of a wooden freight carriage there and was wandering the streets the next day when he caught the attention of another would-be benefactor with good connections, a Mrs Hale. She took him in, fed him and introduced him to the president of the Parliament. She and her husband were to become the young Swami's life-long supporters.

With his theme of the transcendent unity of all religion—the idea that all faiths were like spokes on a wheel leading to a common centre, no matter how far apart they may appear on the rim—Vivekananda had not only taken the Parliament by storm, he had introduced Indian spirituality (or at least his version of it) to the West. The empty hub of the wheel, the source and goal of all religion, was the all-inclusive perspective of Advaita Vedanta, of which, as we have seen in Chapter 4, mind-yoga is the first step. Those who heard him were captivated; so were those who just saw him. A report in *The Baltimore News* the following year captures the impact of this exotic figure from the East, with his 'gorgeous garb' and 'East Indian wit': 'Swami Vivekananda, High Priest of the Hindoos, walked into the lobby of the Hotel Rennert this forenoon attired in a flaming red cloak and a gaudy yellow turban that made him the centre of all eyes…' For some reason, the journalist was also fascinated by the fact that this strange apparition was able to whistle: 'and has enough music in his soul to start the tunes in class meeting as if he were Methodist instead of Hindoo'. Vivekananda obligingly whistled 'a couple of strains' for him, but as they were not recognisably American, the article concluded: 'they must have been some sort of a heathen Hindoo jingle'.[3]

Fortunately, it was not whistling, but lecturing, that was to occupy Vivekananda's attention for the next couple of years. He travelled and spoke all over the eastern and central United States, focusing on the cosmopolitan centres of Chicago, Detroit, Boston and New York. Each talk was a resounding success. His ecumenical message fell initially on the receptive ears of a small but elite group of well-to-do Americans, some of whom had already read translations of a few Sanskrit classics such as the *Bhagavad Gita*, while others were familiar with the German idealist philosophies that posited a higher Self free of the animal instincts. The most influential of such thinkers, Georg Wilhelm Friedrich Hegel, had been airily dismissive of Indian thought until his own encounter with the *Gita* four years before his death, which completely changed his opinion. Under its influence he began to rewrite his magnum opus, *Phenomenology of the Spirit*, but died before he could complete the task. Another important German philosopher, Arthur Schopenhauer, greatly admired the *Upanishads*, which he called 'the production of the highest human wisdom' adding that reading them 'has been the solace of my life and will be the solace of my death'.[4]

In June 1895, at the Thousand Island Park set in the St. Lawrence River, Vivekananda began a two-month course of private lectures to the dozen or so followers who were now his core group of disciples. An inner circle was being formed, and they would continue to support him, not least financially, though to judge from his letters over the years, his mission was often short of funds.

If spiritual seekers devoured his message, academia was next in line. Three years after Chicago, on the back of founding the Vedanta Society in New York, Vivekananda delivered another electrifying lecture, this time at Harvard's

Graduate Philosophical Club. Gertrude Stein, then a student at Radcliffe, was one who found it fascinating. As an indirect result of this talk, departments of Eastern Philosophy became established in the Ivy League curricula. That same year, 1896, saw the publication of the Swami's *Raja Yoga*, which was to become the key text in the West's education in mind-yoga. In it, the Swami equated what he called *raja yoga* with the teaching laid out in Patanjali's *Yoga Sutra*. This was a text few, if any, of his readers would have heard of, as, up until then, it had spent almost a thousand years in obscurity after enjoying a widespread influence throughout the first millennium. Ignoring the classical commentaries by authorities such as Vyasa and Shankara (a most unusual thing for any orthodox exegetist to do) Vivekananda was free to produce his own translation and commentary. What emerged was a mixture of the unified vision of Vedanta and the *Bhagavad Gita*, along with a rather Christianised concern for social improvement and a nod to the quasi-science of spiritualism that was then gaining popularity. The good Swami's eclectic mixture went down very smoothly with his thirsty audience.[5]

The soil for such potent seeds of knowledge had already been well pre-pared over the previous half century amongst the American intelligentsia. Especially receptive were those who belonged to the Transcendentalist movement based in New England. Ralph Waldo Emerson, the founder of the group and a renowned writer, had first come across the *Bhagavad Gita* back in the 1820s; its influence is particularly visible in his essays such as *The Over-Soul*. Emerson would die a decade before Vivekananda's Chicago speech, but his relative Sarah Ellen Waldo was to become a close devotee of the Swami, taking the name Sister Haridasi and cooking, cleaning and generally manag-ing for him and his visitors, as well as faithfully transcribing his dictated text of *Raja Yoga*.

Henry David Thoreau, a transcendentalist thinker who at various stages of his life lived with the Emerson family, had long seen a spiritual bond between the questing American spirit and the Orient as the matrix of civilisation, writing:

> There is an orientalism in the most restless pioneer, and the farthest west is but the farthest east. The great plain of India lies as in a cup between the Himmaleh and the ocean on the north and south, and the Brahmapootra and Indus, on the east and west, wherein the primeval race was received. We will not dispute the story.[6]

He decided to study Indian thought in his own version of an Upanishadic forest retreat, building a cabin in woodlands owned by Emerson near Walden

Pond, a lake in Concord, Massachusetts. He tells us: 'I went to the woods because I wished to live deliberately, to front only the essential facts of life, and see if I could not learn what it had to teach, and not, when I came to die, discover that I had not lived.'[7] He stayed alone there for two years, two months and two days, and the result was his book *Walden, or Life in the Woods*, published in 1854. It was not a great seller to begin with, but its ideas on justified civil disobedience would in time influence Mahatma Gandhi, and it has since become a minor classic of American literature. Then, in 1875, someone gave the poet Walt Whitman a copy of the *Bhagavad Gita* as a Christmas present; reading it opened the great American poet to the vision of India as a fountainhead of wisdom, what he called the 'soothing cradle of man'. For Whitman, the practical enterprise of pioneering America could tap the 'primal thought' of the ancients that was still lively in the East, and together they would work for the good of all mankind and create a world no longer 'dis-joined and diffused'. In his poem *Passage to India*, Whitman cele-brates the opening of the Suez canal as an achievement that exemplifies the innovative scientific spirit, but to him its real value lies in the fact it will grant easier access to hitherto distant spiritual riches, in India's 'flowing literatures, tremendous epics, religions, castes, old occult Brahma, inter-minably far back—the tender and junior Buddha...' Whitman shared Vivekananda's belief that a new era of world unity and peace might come of this joining of East and West. Sadly, the two never met, though the monk always had a high opinion of the poet, recognising him as a fellow spirit he called 'the Sannyasin of America'.[8]

In the following generation, leading intellectuals such as William James carried the torch of Vivekananda Vedanta. A Harvard psychologist who was perhaps the foremost American thinker of his time, James was the author of *The Varieties of Religious Experience*, the groundbreaking study of altered states of consciousness and the application of science to their understanding, adapted from lectures he had delivered at Edinburgh University. In it, he quotes at length from Vivekananda. In between writing and travelling, his younger brother, the novelist Henry, practised a bit of yoga; he particularly liked relaxing in the *shavasana*, 'corpse pose', to relieve chronic back pain his doctors could never identify. The brothers often met with the Swami socially and invited their academic colleagues along. One evening ended with the turbaned monk, 'dressed in rich dark red robes', receiving an offer to chair Harvard's new department of Eastern philosophy. Not to be outdone, another guest, a professor from Columbia University, promptly made his own offer of a position. Vivekananda deftly avoided the embarrassment of having to choose between two such prestigious institutions by declining both, citing his vows of renunciation. Not all were so generously disposed towards him. 'He has evidently swept Professor James off his feet', sniffed a Harvard colleague.

Many other progressive thinkers were drawn to Indian thought through their contact and friendship with the charming young monk from Calcutta. The novelist and social reformer Leo Tolstoy was particularly impressed by him, writing, 'He is the most brilliant wise man', after devouring *Raja Yoga* in a single sitting. Two years before his death he tells us he found it: 'most remarkable... [and] I have received much instruction. The precept of what the true "I" of a man is, is excellent... Yesterday, I read Vivekananda the whole day', adding later: 'It is doubtful another man has ever risen above this self-less, spiritual meditation.' Sarah Bernhardt, Gertrude Stein and John D. Rockefeller were also admirers, as well as powerful female funders such as Sara Bull in Cambridge, Josephine MacLeod in New York City and Margaret Noble in London. These women set up salons and avidly spread the word; some would follow him to India.

Another Bengali

Vivekananda's influence continued well into the twentieth century through the operations of the Ramakrishna Vedanta Centres throughout America and the Ramakrishna Mission in his homeland. Meanwhile, in Bengal, another charismatic figure emerged who, like Vivekananda himself, combined political awareness with a spiritual potency grounded in yogic practice. This was Aurobindo Ghose, also a native of Calcutta and member of the same sub-caste as Vivekananda, who, a year or so before the Swami set out on his US lecture tour in the wake of his Chicago triumph, was bidding farewell to the elegant quads of King's College, Cambridge. He had just passed the exam to become one of the elite cadre of a thousand souls that comprised the Indian Civil Service, but, failing to show up for the horse-riding exam, found himself in need of another job. Back in India, he soon found one on the staff of the Maharaja of Baroda, and became increasingly involved in the nationalist move-ment, particularly the wing that anticipated an armed revolt. In 1908 he was imprisoned in Alipore jail, undergoing a year's solitary confinement for his alleged part in a bomb attack in the town. While in prison he had a number of mystical experiences which led him, as soon as he was released with all charges dropped, to forsake the political for the spiritual. Retreating south of Madras to Pondicherry, a town then in the possession of the French, who had no extradition agreement with the British authorities, he set up the Aurobindo ashram and remained there, teaching and writing, until his death over forty years later. For all his youthful ardour, Aurobindo chose to follow the time-honoured path of renunciation and while his system of Integral Yoga never became a widely popular movement, it is a brilliant re-interpretation of the ancient way of mind-yoga. Fate decreed that Aurobindo would not be the political force he once promised, but his work is remarkable, not least for its blending of Western ideas of evolution with the age-old theme of the perfectibility of man. His magnum opus, *The Life Divine*, is surely one of the world's spiritual classics.[9]

Vedanta Spreads

Back in America, Vivekananda's more pragmatic message of a life of 'work and worship' based on the realisation of an inner divinity was perfectly in tune with a land growing increasingly tired of the punitive parent-deity of the Bible-thumpers. It particularly appealed to the sophisticated and intellectually curious who have always congregated on America's coasts, as if to distance themselves from the vortex of conservatism that is the country's heartland. The Vedanta Society of Southern California in Los Angeles, like the East Coast salons of the Transcendentalists almost a hundred years before, was an intellectually vibrant and open-minded place, whose power of attraction was ensured by its teaching of mind-yoga and Advaita philosophy under a succession of charismatic abbots. Perhaps the greatest was the energetic and jovial Swami Prabhavananda, yet another native of Calcutta, who had founded the society in 1930. His teachings appealed to many bright minds, including ex-patriot Brits such as Aldous Huxley, Alan Watts and Christopher Isherwood. Some of them lived briefly in the ashram. The story goes that Isherwood's friend Greta Garbo who, exceptionally among the Hollywood set, preferred yoga to tennis, asked if she too might move in. Told that a monastery accepts only men, the famously androgynous star exclaimed: 'That doesn't matter, I'll put on trousers!'

Igor Stravinsky, Laurence Olivier and his wife Vivien Leigh all came to Prabhavananda's talks to learn about the deeper levels of consciousness, as did W. Somerset Maugham. His successful novel *The Razor's Edge*, the story of a spiritual odyssey culminating in India that predated the Beat generation's interest in such things by more than a decade, got its title from a phrase describing the journey to enlightenment that he took from the *Upanishads*.[10] Maugham had visited the great sage Ramana Maharshi at his ashram in South India, and the book is full of allusions to Vedantic thought. The educator and prolific author Gerald Heard, who donated land for a Ramakrishna Mission monastery and retreat that still function today, went on to be a pioneer in the consciousness expansion movement, as did both Huxley and Watts. Huxley's account of a psychedelic mescaline trip, *The Doors of Perception* and Watts' *The Way of Zen* were to become required reading for many of the '60s generation. Huxley also wrote the introduction to the 1942 English-language edition of *The Gospel of Sri Ramakrishna*, a first-hand account of Vivekananda's master authored by a Bengali disciple, Mahendranath Gupta, and originally published in India almost half a century earlier. He described it as 'the most profound and subtle utterances about the nature of Ultimate Reality'.

Ten years later J. D. Salinger, whose iconic novel *Catcher in the Rye* was fast making him America's favourite living writer, exhorted his British publisher to pick up the English rights of *The Gospel*, calling it 'the religious book of the century'. Salinger's was an especially interesting case. At the peak of his fame in 1961, he delivered a warmly inscribed copy of his novel *Franny and Zooey* to his guru Swami Nikhilananda, the founder of the Ramakrishna-Vivekananda Center in Manhattan, who by then had formally initiated him as a devotee. Salinger confided to the monk that he had scattered a trail of spiritual clues through the book, and all his subsequent ones, hoping to entice readers to delve further. Soon to become a total recluse, whose later years were notoriously curmudgeonly, one thing that would tempt the author out of his self-imposed isolation were the personal retreats he took at the Vedanta Center in Thousand Island Park, where he would stay in the same cottage Vivekananda himself had occupied. In January 1963, at the New York celebration of Vivekananda's 100th birthday, presided over by the then secretary-general of the United Nations, U Thant, Salinger not only came out of his seclusion to attend, but even sat centre stage at the banquet table.

But it was a less celebrated, and English, writer who was to be the real force in spreading a much wider knowledge of Vedanta. This was Christopher Isherwood, a pacifist who, opting to leave the doomed playground of decadent excess that was Weimar Berlin, settled in the safer sunshine of California, partly to avoid wartime conscription. In addition to his translation/interpretations of three seminal mind-yoga texts in collaboration with Swami Prabhavananda,[11] Isherwood also authored a biography of Vivekananda and his master,[12] and many books and articles on Vedanta.[13] Reflecting on the Swami's Chicago speech half a century after the event, he surmised that a 'strange kind of subconscious telepathy' had infected the hall, so that: 'No doubt the vast majority of those present hardly knew why they had been so powerfully moved.'[14]

The resonance of that mood has sounded long and deep; Vivekananda's influence effortlessly crossed the boundaries of politics, psychology and lit-

erature. Mahatma Gandhi, the depth psychologist Carl Jung, poet and philosopher George Santayana, social reformer Jane Addams and mythology
scholar Joseph Campbell were amongst those touched by the Swami's colourful robe. There were some less likely recipients. In 1945, the hedonistic
Henry Miller, famous for his novels of a sex-fuelled Parisian bohemia, stated
that his most important discovery of recent years was 'two volumes on
Ramakrishna and Vivekananda'. Twenty years later he concluded that: 'Swami
Vivekananda remains for me one of the great influences in my life.' Pop culture felt his aura too. Once asked about the origins of his 1971 chart-topping
song *My Sweet Lord*, which was the top selling single in the UK that year,
George Harrison, the Beatle most interested in spirituality, replied that: 'the
song really came from Swami Vivekananda, who said, "If there is a God, we
must see him. And if there is a soul, we must perceive it."'

The echoes of the Swami's message are still being heard today, not least in
the more psychologically oriented yoga teachings. Other Indian gurus of the
'60s may have garnered greater numbers, but none of them matched the
extraordinary breadth of Vivekananda's appeal—his message reached from
the keenest intellects of the day to lauded artists, from cosmopolitan sophis-
ticates to unpretentious spiritual seekers.

A Fair Exchange

For his part, though, Vivekananda was always clear that his mission was as
much about embracing modern scientific rationality as offering ancient
Hindu wisdom. As he told a reporter from *The Baltimore News* on his first
trip in 1893:

> The main criticism I have to pass on to America is that you have too little
> religion here. In India they have too much. I think the world would be better
> if some of India's surplus of religion could be sent over here, while it would be
> to India's profit if its people could have some of America's industrial advance-
> ment and civilization.

In the Swami's eyes, then, Indian culture was apathetic, absorbed in unproductive spiritual byways and woefully lacking in practical motivation. What
was needed was to blend the new scientific rationality with a revival of the
'authentic' yoga, by which he meant a Vedantic teaching that harked back to
the culture of the *Upanishads*. Vivekananda's position on the relative merits of
body- and mind-yoga was to change over time, gradually abandoning the
former in favour of the latter, but for the moment, one thing was clear: the

first need was to obliterate the hazy hangover from the magical *hatha yoga* of those disreputable medieval *sadhus*. India had had enough of passive philosophies of 'being', what was needed was more 'doing'. If modern West and purified ancient East could be combined, nothing less than the possibility of a new dawn for humanity beckoned. This synchretism would be emulated by many later yoga teachers from India.

Aside from growing up in colonial Calcutta, where he was educated at the Scottish Church College, Vivekananda's espousal of the 'healthy mind rooted in a healthy body' doctrine was partly explained by his own history of almost constant ill-health.[15] Physical improvement must be the first plank in building the platform for moral and spiritual regeneration. As he explained in a discussion with a follower sometime around 1900:

Swami: First build up your physique. Then only you can get control over the mind. 'This Self is not to be attained by the weak' (*Katha Upanishad*, 1. ii. 23).

Disciple: But, sir, the commentator [i.e. Adi Shankara] has interpreted the word 'weak' to mean 'devoid of *brahmacharya* or sexual continence'.

Swami: Let him. I say, the physically weak are unfit for the realisation of the Self.

Disciple: But many dull-headed persons also have strong bodies.

Swami: If you can take the pains to give them good ideas once, they will be able to work them out sooner than physically unfit people. Don't you find in a weak physique it is difficult to control the sex-appetite or anger? Overly thin people are quickly incensed and are quickly overcome by the sex-instinct.

Disciple: But we find exceptions to the rule also.

Swami: Who denies it? Once a person gets control over the mind, it matters little whether the body remains strong or becomes emaciated. The gist of the thing is that unless one has a good physique one can never aspire to Self-realisation. Sri Ramakrishna used to say, 'One fails to attain realisation if there be but a slight defect in the body.'[16]

This mix of practicality and physical discipline is very much of the period; so too is the Victorian distaste for the debilitating effects of sex, an attitude that recalls the concerns of the *hatha yogis* a thousand years earlier. Later, Vivekananda was to reject body-yoga as being too difficult and lengthy a path. As time went by, he had serious doubts as to whether postural practice really led to any genuine spiritual growth, fearing it could even be dangerous. Like the Theosophists, he came to prefer European-style physical culture for the well-being of Indian youth, and once remarked to a sickly student that a good game of football would get a boy closer to God than reading the *Bhagavad Gita*. It was simply a case of priorities:

> First of all, our young men must be strong. Religion will come afterwards...
> You will understand the Gita better with your biceps, your muscles a little
> stronger. You will understand the mighty genius and the mighty strength of
> Krishna better with a little of strong blood in you. You will understand the
> Upanishads better and the glory of the Atman when your body stands firm
> upon your feet, and you feel yourselves as men.[17]

Vivekananda's Gita

The Swami acknowledged the perennial charm of the *Bhagavad Gita*, a scripture so multi-layered that almost any orthodox teaching can be elicited from its pages. Vivekananda certainly took what he needed from what it offered. Earlier teachers, such as the sixteenth-century saints Vallabhacharya and Chaitanya Mahaprabhu, had seen the Krishna of the *Gita* as the ecstatic God of Love, who unifies all differences and transcends all man-made barriers, and many devotional schools interpreted Krishna texts as a type of liberation theology that sought to overturn rigid caste discrimination and social disadvantage. Such reforming energy may bring chaos in its wake. After all, did not the *gopi* cowgirls lose all sense of propriety in their desire for the dark Lord, and married women leave food burning on the stove and children untended to follow his magnetic charge? Even their husbands let the ploughs fall in the fields, abandoning their work to follow the blue-skinned Pied Piper of love. The force of Krishna's transgressive allure is epitomised by the fact that his chief paramour, Radha, is a married woman.

This ecstatic Krishna, however, was not at all what Vivekananda drew from the *Gita*. He preferred another face of the omnipresent Lord: the wise and sometimes stern guide on the battlefield of life, the Krishna who was, in effect, the archetype of the no-nonsense martial leader needed by the emerging Nationalist Movement. He particularly liked the emphasis on right action—*karma yoga*—as the way to live out our born duty or *dharma*. When Arjuna, the Everyman hero of the text is vacillating on the battlefield, unable to commit himself to the conflict for fear of hurting or killing friends or relatives on the other side, Krishna has no time for such shrinking sensitivity. He robustly exhorts Arjuna to brace up and do his duty, telling him to 'stand up' and reject all *klaibyam*—a word variously meaning 'weakness, unmanliness, effeminacy, cowardice or timidity'.[18] Whichever interpretation you prefer, 'Muscular Hinduism' was the order of the day.

Yogic Christianity

Very well-educated and widely read, the Swami loved to discuss Christianity with his Western disciples, often pointing out its similarities to Vedic teachings. Alongside the *Gita*, the one book he always carried with him on his travels was Thomas à Kempis' *The Imitation of Christ*, of which he translated several chapters into Bengali. While he often seemed to present Christianity and Advaita as but different aspects of one universal teaching, he had no time for what most Christians made of practising their own faith and understanding their own Bible:

> Look where we may, a true Christian nowhere do we see. The ugly impression left on our mind by the ultra-luxurious, insolent, despotic, barouche-and-brougham driving Christians of the Protestant sects will be completely removed if we but once read this great book with the attention it deserves.[19]

The echo of the hurt caused by the snobbish arrogance of the Calcutta Raj is loud and clear. Nor did Vivekananda concur with Christianity's simplistic eternities of salvation or damnation. Applying the logic of *karma*, the cosmic law that consequences are always commensurate with their causes, he argued that a finite act, whether good or evil, could not result in anything infinite, be it reward in heaven or punishment in hell. He also disputed the historical uniqueness of the Christian saviour, preferring (as do most Hindus today) to see him as an incarnation of the Divine, an *avatar*, 'of which' he said 'there are hundreds'. In fact, in private at least, it seems he doubted Jesus' historical authenticity. As he once confided to his inner circle of followers whilst on retreat in Kashmir to avoid the summer heat of the plains:

> Almost all Christianity is Aryan (i.e. Vedic derived), I am inclined to think Christ never existed … Buddha and Mohammed alone amongst religious teachers stand out with historical distinctions… on the whole, I think old Rabbi Hillel is responsible for the teachings of Jesus and an obscure Jewish sect of Nazarenes—a sect of great antiquity—suddenly galvanised by St. Paul furnished the mythic personality as a centre of worship. The Resurrection is of course simply spring-cremation.[20]

To him, the real value of Jesus was as the cosmic archetype of the *sannyasin* so revered in Indian culture, the renouncer who turns his back on the workaday world and places his unflinching faith in the support of the Divine. To the extent that materialistic Christians fell short of the Galilean's example of complete abandon, they traduced his memory and teaching. A true Christian should: 'Better be ready to live in rags with Christ than to live in palaces without him.' However, when it came to world teachers, his ideal was clear:

But Buddha! Buddha! Surely he was the greatest man who ever lived! He never drew a breath for himself. Above all he never claimed worship. He said 'Buddha is not a man, but a state. I have found the door. Enter, all of you!'[21]

To elevate another teacher over one's own initiatory guru—in this case the charismatic Ramakrishna, who could hardly have been less like the Buddha—was certainly a break with Indian tradition. This, along with his choice of the most secular and rational of Indian masters, demonstrates the Swami's westernisation.

At the age of thirty-nine, exhausted from ceaseless work and untreated diabetes, Vivekananda returned to his homeland, taking up residency in the monastery he had founded outside Calcutta. He would not stay there long. One evening he excused himself from the assembled company, went into his room, meditated awhile and left the body. Earlier, he had remarked, 'I have given enough for fifteen hundred years.' Just what more this extraordinary man could have given we will never know. But even in such a short life, his role in bringing Eastern teachings to the West, and the galvanising part he plays in the story of yoga, are surely unequalled.[22]

12

ROGUEY YOGIS SET THE TREND

Vivekananda's vision of yoga as the path to an upright and productive life would resonate with many today. But although postural practice has become a highly respectable pastime for millions of respectable citizens worldwide, synonymous with physical fitness, organic good health and clean living, some of its earliest proponents in the West were decidedly less anodyne. One of them was Yogi Ramacharaka, an enigmatic figure not least because, like an astral illusion conjured up by some wily *siddha yogi*, he may never really have existed.

To begin with, some solid facts. We know that in 1884, an already successful businessman from Baltimore called William Walker Atkinson was admitted as an attorney to the Pennsylvania Bar. His law practice went well, but the stress of running two careers together took its toll and he eventually experienced a complete physical and mental breakdown, along with financial ruin. His search for healing led him to the New Thought movement, a universalist spiritual doctrine that influenced Christian Science and contributed to the New Age doctrine of the power of positive thought. The journey to recovery opened new vistas for Atkinson, and he soon became an avid student of the occult sciences.

The next chapter in his life began in Chicago, when he visited the 1893 World's Fair held there. It is not known whether he attended the Parliament of Religions but given his interests it is not hard to imagine him sitting spellbound in Vivekananda's audience and noting well the appreciative reception the young Indian monk received. Also attending the Fair, so the story would go, was another Indian spiritual teacher called Baba Bharata; he too gave talks and gathered a following, though there are no contemporary records corroborating his appearance there.[1] One of his admirers was Atkinson; the two hit it off and decided to collaborate on a series of books which, as a mark of

THE STORY OF YOGA

respect, they would attribute to the Baba's late guru, an accomplished yogi called Yogi Ramacharaka, who had died a couple of years previously. Again, this is mysterious, as no record exists of any Yogi Ramacharaka having lived and taught in India at that time, nor does the US immigration office have any mention of his disciple Baba Bharata's ever setting foot on American soil.

Whatever the truth about the Chicago meeting, as well as working as an editor and publisher for the New Thought movement, Atkinson began to strike out on his own, founding the Psychic Club and the Atkinson School of Mental Science. In 1900, what was probably his first book appeared. It was called *Thought-Force in Business and Everyday Life* and comprised a series of step-by-step lessons in developing personal magnetism, psychic influence and will-power by using concentration, visualisation and auto-suggestion. As time went by, Atkinson established himself at the centre of a web of publishing companies and affiliated businesses that all shared the same address, from which, like some *prana*-energised spider with each of its legs busily scribbling magazine articles, books and pamphlets, he produced an extraordinary amount of material by different authors, all of whom were probably pseudonyms for himself.

As part of this outpouring, starting in 1903, a full ten years after his supposed meeting with Baba Bharata, Atkinson revived the Ramacharaka connection. Articles attributed to the yogi appeared in one of his magazines, followed by a steady stream of books: a dozen titles in six years, published by his Yogi Publication Society. These covered Yoga and techniques of *pranayama* as well as studies of the *Gita* and the *Upanishads*, and they were hugely popular; some, such as *Advanced Course in Yoga Philosophy and Oriental Occultism* continue to sell well today. Among his many personae, Atkinson clearly preferred the Indian, as he went on to create three more of them: Swami Bhakta Vishita, Swami Panchadasi and O. Hashnu Hara. A further three dozen books on yoga, mind-control and mediumship came out under these names.

Atkinson was not alone in wrapping his esotericism in an exotic oriental robe. At this time not a few occultists were gaining acceptance by promoting fictional Hindu or Buddhist masters who vouchsafed special knowledge and secret techniques to their followers. But Atkinson was surely the most successful. Under his various pseudonyms he produced over 100 books, and all in the last thirty years of his life. Mystery followed him to the grave and even beyond. There was that certificate of copyright issued three years after his death in 1932 that clearly appears to have been signed by the author himself.

142

The Omnipotent Oom

Less phantasmagorical than these literary swamis was a larger-than-life character called Pierre Arnold Bernard. He was an accomplished mystic, scholar and businessman, but in his own time enjoyed more notoriety as a conman, seducer and high-living philanderer. Perhaps he was one of those notorious Naths from medieval India somehow reincarnated in the American century, cast adrift and trying to reconnect with his occult path? At any rate, although the initial effect of his teachings was to reinforce popular suspicion of the lost souls who chose to dabble in the murky waters of Oriental spirituality, history has judged Bernard more kindly as one of the more important players in the story of yoga's journey West.

And player he certainly was. A natural showman with a grand sense of style, he had made his first appearance in 1898 at an evening sponsored by an outfit named the San Francisco College of Suggestive Therapeutics. On stage he demonstrated what he called the *Kali mudra*, which he described as an ability to enter an almost 'death-like trance' that allowed him to have his upper lip sewn onto his nose without anaesthetic. This ghoulish trick was only the opening act of what was to be a glittering, if controversial, career.

Yoga Gets a Bad Press

We know little of Bernard's origins, though he is thought to have been born in 1876 as Perry Arnold Baker, the son of a barber in Leon, a town of some 1,200 souls in the middle of Iowa, a place itself considered by many to be in the middle of nowhere. He soon escaped, travelling, so he claimed, to the far reaches of Kashmir and Bengal, before returning to the West to set up the Tantrik Order of America in San Francisco in 1905. Not long afterwards came a chain of 'tantric clinics' in Cleveland, Philadelphia, Chicago and New York City, that traded on the persisting exotic fantasy that Tantra is all about mystical sex. Nonetheless, his use of the medical term 'clinic' reveals the beginnings of the continuing strategy to legitimise Indian spiritual teachings by presenting them in a quasi-scientific or medical context.

But Bernard was no fraud. He had been tutored for almost twenty years by a little-known tantric adept—half-Syrian, half-Indian—called Sylvais Hamati and he was also a scholar of recondite scriptures. Following the success of his clinics, he opened a more academic institution, the New York Sanskrit College, in 1910. This all sounded respectable enough and the future looked bright. But that very same year Bernard's trajectory began to falter. Two teen-

THE STORY OF YOGA

age girls claimed he had taken psychic control over their lives and had him charged with kidnapping. The papers dubbed him the 'the Omnipotent Oom, loving guru of the Tantrics' and were to accuse him of orchestrating orgies, performing abortions, hypnotising wealthy female benefactors and fleecing gullible followers of their hard-won savings. Their sales rocketed as they helped create one of the first twentieth-century examples of instant celebrity. Headlines such as: 'Police Break in on Weird Hindu Rites: Girls and Men Mystics Cease Strange Dance as "Priest" Is Arrested',[2] escalated in forty-eight hours to: 'Tantrik's Worship calls for Dead Bodies and Young Girls'.[3] The situation wasn't helped when it came out that Bernard did in fact encourage his most advanced students to become his 'nautch girls' and engage in certain tantric practices, including ritualised sex on a raised bed in a room with walls painted blood red. The Oom was duly arrested, and his trial was a five-day feast for reporters and readers alike:

> 'OMNIPOTENT OOM' HELD ON BIG BAIL High Priest of Tantrik Order Accused of Statutory Offense by Young Woman TELLS AN AMAZING STORY Before Becoming Dupe, Girl Punctured Hand and Wrote Name in Her Blood in Book ...

> 'Oom the Omnipotent', alias Peter Coon, alias Pierre Barnard, high priest of the Tantrik Order of Worship, was held in $15,000 bonds today for trial in the court of general sessions, on a statutory charge made by one of his dupes... This girl, 'Gertrude Leo' of Seattle, one of the two complainants, has been inveigled into a den of iniquity...the testimony showed the dangerous character of this man and his practices.[4]

One of the girls involved, Zelia Hopp, explained breathlessly to the waiting journalists:

> I cannot tell you how Bernard got his control over me or how he gets it over other people. He is the most wonderful man in the world. No women seem able to resist him... He had promised to marry me many times. But when he began the same thing with my little sister Mary, who is only sixteen, I decided I would expose the whole matter. If it had only been myself I wouldn't have done it for the whole world.

The New York Grand Jury returned indictments against Bernard for abduction and fraudulently impersonating a doctor, and he was sent to Manhattan's notorious Tombs prison for three months. However, Hopp and other witnesses soon relented and refused to testify further. The Omnipotent Oom was released on appeal and the charges against him evaporated.

However, the image of yoga—and anything that seemed to be cut from the same cloth—had been badly stained, and this would last for a long time. The next year, a Christian mystic named Evelyn Arthur See was arrested in Chicago and charged as a white slaver. As with the Bernard trial, lurid headlines titillated the public for weeks. Then, back in New York, a Dr William Latson who called himself an 'esoteric psychologist' and taught 'Indian dancing' to his female patients to free them from their inhibitions, committed suicide in his office pending an official investigation of impropriety.

Bernard, however, was not going to be put off by what he dismissed as uninformed prejudice and wasted no time in bouncing back, re-opening his Sanskrit college. Intrusive media attention continued to follow him, however, much as with Aleister Crowley, the almost contemporary esotericist who may have assumed the grandiose title Mahatma Guru Sri Paramahansa Shivaji for his book on yoga but was simply 'the wickedest man in the world' to *the Daily Mail* and its readers. Yoga began to be seen as a foreign pollutant entering the American bloodstream. A 1911 *Washington Post* headline lamented: 'This Soul-Destroying Poison of the East: The Tragic Flood of Broken Homes and Hearts, Disgrace and Suicide That Follows the Broadening Stream of Morbidly Alluring Oriental "Philosophies" into Our Country'. American womanhood was considered especially at risk. The *Los Angeles Times* was typical in its fears. Under the headline: 'A Hindu Apple for Modern Eve: The Cult of the Yogis Lures Women to Destruction', its readers were informed that:

> At first their way lay through the populous cities where the sun rises now on the gilded minarets of their mosques and pagodas. More recently they have reached the smaller towns and villages where have been formed branches and circles that are exerting a widely increasing influence… (yoga) is a dangerous knowledge to lure any but the best-balanced brain. In the pursuit of it, too often the listening devotee is offering her sacrifices even at the altar of her soul.

As further evidence for its hopelessly muddled accusations, the paper also alluded to women who had started to sunbathe nude or even 'abandoned home and husband and children to join the sun worshippers'.[5] There was no denying it, yoga and all things yogic had become Public Enemy Number 1.

Mother India

Christian moral outrage, sexual fantasy and barely disguised xenophobia were all combined in such attacks at just the time American popular opinion was being poisoned against India by a journalist called Kathleen Mayo. Her hugely

influential book, *Mother India*, was published in 1927 and remained a suppu-
rating source of prejudice right up until the 1960s. It was based on a three-
month visit she had made to a small area of northern India to gather ammunition against Indian demands for independence from the British. Though she
lambasted all aspects of Indian society, especially its idol-worshipping religion, caste system and treatment of women, Mayo singled out what she saw
as the rampant and fatally weakening sexuality of Indian men to be at the core
of the country's manifold problems. The racist ire of her criticisms is transpar-
ent today, but her tirade fuelled popular ignorance to create a picture of the
subcontinent as a potent mix of bad religion, hopeless lasciviousness and
cultural barbarism. Yoga, already linked to lurid scandal, was clearly just
another example of India's congenital degeneration.

Mayo's diatribe fed into a more general suspicion of Orientals that had
been around for some time. Chinese workers, who had flocked to join the
Gold Rush and stayed on to take low-paid work in the faltering economy that
followed the Civil War, had finally been prohibited from entering the country
in the 1880s, on the grounds they were driving down wages and taking scarce
jobs. Three years after the publication of Mayo's book, the ban was extended
to Indians, though on racial rather than economic grounds. One of the effects
of this was to eliminate the flow of subcontinental yoga teachers into the
country; Americans now had to make the long pilgrimage east if they wanted
to study the ancient teachings firsthand. That ban was not fully lifted until
1965, ten years after Bernard's death, resulting in the immediate arrival of
influential teachers on America's shores.

Yoga Moves Upstate

Though the police raided his yoga clubs on numerous occasions and the Feds
kept a file on him, 'The Omnipotent Oom' was not dispirited. Operating on
the principle that all publicity was good publicity, he gradually assumed a
place in the American pantheon of daring and flamboyant anti-heroes. In
time, his celebrity allowed him to become the recognised, and lucrative,
model for film villains, and even a cartoon character. His highly palatable
blend of yoga, philosophy and good living ensured he remained popular with
wealthy New York socialites throughout the 1920s and '30s, and his position
was cemented by marriage to the society hostess Blanche de Vries.[6]

With such good connections, The Oom soon went upmarket and upstate,
founding a yoga retreat in Nyack, a sleepy little place on the Hudson River
two hours' drive north of Manhattan. He gave it the innocuous name of the

146

Clarkstown Country Club, no doubt hoping to discard his, and yoga's, louche reputation. The project was funded by a student, Mrs Anne Vanderbilt who, as a member of America's richest family, was to funnel many useful friends into The Oom's band of followers. Over the years these would include the millionaire socialite Rebekah Harkness (who many years later was to invite B. K. S. Iyengar to America), the conductor Leopold Stokowski with his lover Greta Garbo, and Ida Rolf, founder of the Rolfing body-therapy. There were those who were yet to make their mark too, including the teenaged Pete Seeger, the future singer and archivist of America's folk music traditions. Another frequent visitor was Ora Ray Baker, The Oom's half-sister and cousin of Mary Baker Eddy who founded the Christian Science Church in the USA. She came with her husband, Sufi master and distinguished musician Hazrat Inayat Khan whose collected works remain perhaps the best introduction to the subtleties of Islamic mysticism.[7] All in all, such illustrious interest ensured that membership of the club grew apace and funds flowed in. The motives for joining were mixed. Some came for *hatha yoga* and the philosophy behind it, some for romance and fresh air away from the city grime. Some, having been abandoned by hospitals, psychiatrists and unsympathetic families, were keen to try what was called 'the Bernard Cure'; others were simply in retreat from the Roaring '20s, nursing lethal addictions and Great War nightmares.

Behind the walls of the 200-acre Clarkstown estate sat a million-dollar clubhouse, several English-style mansions, a zoo with a trained herd of elephants, a gym, a theatre and a brightly painted yacht. The entertainment was fun too; it included baseball games in drag and some circus-like acts that blended yoga, dance and body-building. In 1931, the same year that Jagannath G. Gune's landmark book *Asanas* was published, a future Pulitzer prize-winner called Joseph Mitchell was dispatched by *The New York World-Telegram* up to Nyack to see just what The Oom and his acolytes were getting up to. The wide-eyed journo reported back: 'It is a place of mystery. On summer afternoons townspeople crowd about the estate and look through hedges as the solemn students of Sanskrit go through their Oriental calisthenics. Small boys dare each other to go through the gates.'[8] By today's standards it may all sound rather tame but those were different times, at least for anyone unfortunate enough to have to work for a living.

The timing of Bernard's enterprise was also significant. Like modern body-yoga, it appealed predominantly to women, at a time economic and cultural changes were giving birth, at least amongst the relatively privileged, to the idea of the 'New Woman' whose financial independence was allowing her greater social, and sexual, autonomy. At the same time, in a crisis of masculinity largely precipitated by the fruitless sacrifice of life in the recent war and a dire economic situation, some men were searching for new forms of cultural expression to restore their sense of identity. Bernard managed to present physical yoga as both an antidote to the emasculating effects of contemporary conditions and as a way to help wealthy Americans in their search for new and more relevant forms of gender presentation. At the same time, his wife DeVries taught women a combination of yoga and sensual Orientalist dances that offered a form of empowerment through emphasising feminine embodiment. All these themes continued to be important in the Western understanding of yoga as offering a combination of athleticism, beauty and an enhanced sense of potency.[9]

The Omnipotent Oom was in some way a classic American success story of the Great Depression: a showman hero-cum-orientalist Gatsby, rambling over his landscaped acres in leisurely tweeds, hosting glamorous parties and, this being the USA, making money. Lots of it. At one point, he shifted his attention from his luxury ashram to investing, and sometimes losing, money in a variety of projects: baseball stadiums, dog-tracks, an airport and a bank. A fan of boxing, he was often to be seen at Madison Square Garden, whooping it up with the sozzled hacks at the ringside, chomping on a massive cigar. His life was a complex and enigmatic mix; as one Nyack local commented to a newspaper reporter: 'Nobody knows if he's got religion, but everybody knows he's got money.'[10]

Despite his multiple worldly interests, the Omnipotent Oom never neglected his yogic side. Some of the business proceeds went to build his library, which boasted 7,000 volumes on philosophy, ethics, psychology, education and metaphysics, as well as related material on physiology and medicine. It boasted the best Sanskrit collection in the country and scholars visited from all over the world to do research there. In his own inimitable style, Oom had put yoga well and truly on the map. More on the map than his native Iowa, probably.[11]

The Mission Continues

One of the regular and presumably more impressionable visitors to the Clarkstown Country Club was the founder's young nephew, Theos Casimir Hamati Bernard. Hamati was the name of his uncle's tantric guru, and the boy grew up to assume his uncle's esoteric mantle. While an undergraduate at Columbia University he became the first American to write a thesis on Tibetan Buddhism and in 1936, he toured India and Tibet with his wife Viola, studying *tantric yoga*. On his return to the States the following year he took to calling himself 'the first white *lama*' and his travel experiences were syndicated across the country's newspapers. Lectures and radio appearances followed; then came the books with catchy titles such as *Penthouse of the Gods*, *The Madman's Middle Way* and *Heaven Lies Within Us*. Under the guise of an autobiography, this last explored *hatha yoga*, particularly what he saw as the incomparable benefits of the headstand.

In 1939, Theos Bernard opened a twin-headed facility on Manhattan's fashionable Upper East Side, the American Institute of Yoga and the Pierre Health Studios, the latter named after his uncle. He taught yoga and its philosophy there and married one of his students, Ganna Walska, a wealthy Polish opera star. They moved to California and purchased a large estate they called Tibetland, with the idea of setting up a cultural institute to house his extensive library, provide accommodation for visiting *lamas* and generally further research into Tibetan studies. Before long, however, *karma* intervened, and their marriage exemplified the cardinal Buddhist teaching of universal impermanence. New directions beckoned, however; while Ganna proceeded to convert the property into a horticultural museum she renamed Lotusland, Theos busied himself producing a fourth book: *The Philosophical Foundations of India*, which remains a fine study of the subject. Then, in 1944, his *Hatha Yoga: The Report of a Personal Experience* was published. Based on his doctoral thesis submitted at Columbia the previous year, it was a major sourcebook for yoga throughout the 1950s and is still read today, more than half a century later. Nevertheless, something of the family showman genes were at play. Many of the experiences Theos describes in his books have recently been discovered to have been fabricated, based on the reported experiences of his uncle rather than his own.

Galvanised by a new wife and a new project, the restless scholar returned to India in 1947. The wife was called Helen, the project was to locate some rare manuscripts in the mountains of Spiti, near Ladakh. These, he had heard, would prove a theory long held by an ostracised Muslim sect called the Ahmadis, that was then gaining considerable mileage in esoteric circles: Jesus had survived the crucifixion, left the tomb empty and travelled to India to study yoga. He ended up spending the rest of his life in Kashmir and neighbouring Ladakh.[12] The remote Ki Monastery in Western Tibet was believed to hold manuscripts that would confirm the story. Theos set off there, travelling with a Tibetan *lama*. While in Lahoul, a river valley north of Kulu, the two became unwittingly embroiled in a local tribal feud; Theos was shot, the *lama* and the horses thrown off a cliff into the rapids below. Conflicting reports about their whereabouts circulated for several months while Helen waited expectantly for her husband in the sweltering heat of Calcutta. He never returned and his body was never found. There was belated justice of a sort, however. Two quite innocent men had been murdered and the local people began to feel that the gods had visited a curse on the whole area in punishment. Disgraced, the killers and their families were eventually hounded out of the valley. Years later, a memorial *stupa* (the typical Buddhist commemorative monument) was constructed on the bank of the river at the site of the murders in the hope of expiating the curse that many felt was still operating.

As flamboyant and energetic pioneers of what has since become culturally mainstream, the Bernard boys certainly lived out their destinies in zest and style. We shall see later where eccentricity has led some of their successors in more recent times.

13

STRONGMAN YOGA

A crucial, if unremembered, figure in the emergence of a modern postural yoga was the most celebrated Indian body-builder of the 1930s, KV Iyer of Bangalore. A consumate showman, he blended *asanas* and physical culture regimes to perfect the body in a praxis that was unconcerned with self-knowledge but promoted a cosmetic ideal of fitness. In this approach, in which the psychic defers to the somatic, lie the seeds of much body-yoga today. Iyer was, by his own confident admission at least, 'India's most perfectly developed man', possessing 'a body which Gods covet'.[1] He always credited his remarkable physique to traditional yoga, claiming that: 'Hatha-yoga, the ancient system of body-cult... had more to do in the making of me what I am today than all the bells, bars, steel-springs and strands I have used.'[2]

However, it is highly likely those rippling muscles did not result solely from the gnostic science of his forefathers. For one thing, Iyer was friends with, and often stated his admiration for, Eugen Sandow, the original circus strongman known as the father of 'body-building', a term he himself coined in one of his books. Iyer liked the fact that Sandow, who billed himself as 'The World's Most Perfect Man', was no shrinking violet, and the Prussian colossus served as his model. After launching his career in Britain, Sandow gave his first US performance at the 1893 World Fair in Chicago, where Vivekananda made his Western debut and William Atkinson first heard about the nebulous Yogi Ramacharaka. Pumped up by assorted gymnastic techniques, hs lifted impossible weights, broke iron chains across his fifty-two-inch chest, had three horses run over his arched body one after another and made women who had paid for a back-stage feel of his biceps faint with the power of his testosterone-soaked aura. It was not only women who fell for his charms. Like some Maharaja symbolising his power through the court wrestler by his throne, George V, the King Emperor of India, issued a royal proclamation which named the showbiz muscleman as his personal 'Professor of Scientific and Physical Culture'. Sandow's methods lived on in his Institutes of Physical Culture, which taught their students various methods of exercise, dietary habits and weight training.

Iyer was also in touch with another US strongman, Charles Atlas, the then 'Mr Universe'. Atlas had made his own start in the body-business working at a Coney Island sideshow where, like a latter-day yogi incongruously deposited amidst the day-trippers, hot-dog stands and ferris-wheels, he lay on a bed of nails and urged men from the audience to step up and stand on his unflinching stomach. Atlas' muscle-building method of 'Dynamic Tension' was to popularise body-building for a whole generation of insecure Clark Kents who longed magically to turn into Superman and stop the beach-bully kicking sand in their pimply faces.

Inspired by such examples, Iyer set up his own gym in Bangalore from where he ran classes, and a highly successful correspondence course, under the banner of the Hercules Gymnasium and Correspondence School of Physical Culture. His method, which he called 'blending of the two Systems'—body-building and yoga—was a combination that aimed to supplement outer strength with inner health: medical gymnastics, *asanas* and dumbbell workouts were yoked to assorted body-building techniques. An advertisement pictures him posing under a signboard that dramatically announces: 'Weakness is Sin, Disease is Death! Make health and strength your blood and shadow!'

The slogan may not have been wholly original—it was in fact adapted from another of Iyer's inspirations, Bernard Macfadden, who had succeeded Sandow as America's leading physical fitness guru—but the sentiment had a venerable provenance. Hughes and Kingsley, those Victorian champions of Muscular Christianity we met in Chapter 7, would surely have applauded its virile exhortation.

Iyer himself might not have relished such a direct connection. He was adamant that the spread of European gymnastics through organisations such as the YMCA had done nothing to improve his country's health and strength. He called for a nationwide boycott of them in India's educational institutions, while making an impassioned plea for his own system as a more indigenous path that could better contribute to the struggle for India's freedom: 'Will our women bring forth only healthful useful children to save our motherland from this degeneration, this slavery?'[3] Iyer also had the reputation of being a healer, a skill gained not by psychic power but an abdominal massage he had invented. This was to pay him huge personal dividends and opened the door to his part in the shaping of modern body-yoga. His name came to the ears of the Maharaja of Mysore, who had suffered a stroke. Iyer treated him and effected a recovery. In gratitude, the Maharaja financed the construction of the strongman's famous Vyayamshala gym in Bangalore in 1940 and, crucially for our story, also sponsored a branch of it in a wing of his own palace in Mysore. Run by Iyer's most trusted student, this was set up just a few yards down the corridor from the already well-established yoga studio of the man who is acknowledged to be the father of modern postural practice: Sri Tirumalai Krishnamacharya.

Modern Strongmen

The conflation of yoga with the strongman aesthetic was to remain an important, if not always visible, strand in the growing subculture. As postural work began to spread widely in America after the Second World War, a couple from Latin America gave it a big boost on the West Coast when they set up shop in San Francisco in the mid '50s. Walt Baptiste, who had won the 1948 Mr America title, opened a gym devoted to body-building and yoga in partnership with his wife, Magana. He had learned some yoga from the Paramahamsa Yogananda lineage, while she was a dancer in the movies who had been runner-up for the Miss USA crown five years earlier. Along the way, she had also studied body-yoga with Indra Devi, a pioneering Russian yoga teacher who had been an early disciple of Krishnamacharya in the Mysore Palace gym. Together the Baptistes got the San Francisco body-show on the road, offering yoga instruction for $5 a month alongside her Egyptian belly-dancing lessons and his dumbbell gymnastic classes. The yoga they taught was an energetic workout that was a long way from Patanjali, but it fitted very well into the Californian beach and body-beautiful ethos.

In 1971 the couple set up the Baptiste Health & Fitness Center, an innovative venue that drew several aspects of the workout subculture together under one roof, offering a yoga room, a gymnasium and a dance studio, along with a natural food store and restaurant. Once again, the Baptistes were ahead of the curve, creating what was to be the prototype of the type of health club that really mushroomed in the '80s. Everything a fitness enthusiast wanted became available in one place, with the added benefit of a chance to socialise with like-minded, and like-bodied, people. Such places would really take off as the baby-boomers came of age, the conventional family model collapsed and the freewheeling, yet health-conscious, singles culture emerged. The Baptiste lineage continued to flourish; their children, Sherri and Baron, both went on to be highly successful body-yoga teachers themselves.

The most flamboyant figure in the pantheon of strongman yoga, however, was part of the wave of Indian gurus that flooded the West in the late 1960s, following the suspension of American immigration controls. This was Sri Chinmoy, a truly exuberant character who did everything with gusto and on a grand scale, pushing his own limits, and inspiring others to do the same, in pursuit of his philosophy of self-transcendence. A writer, poet, musician, vegetarian, humanitarian and advocate of inter-faith harmony, he was also hailed as a spiritual teacher, the first to lead meditation sessions at the United Nations in New York. But, above all, Chinmoy was an extraordinary physical phenomenon. A decathlon champion in his youth, a runner in later life with twenty-two marathons and five ultra-marathons under his belt, he was also mentor to the Olympic gold-medal sprinter Carl Lewis. When a knee injury curtailed his own running career at the age of fifty-four, Chinmoy took up weightlifting. Over the next twenty years he gave public displays of hoisting cars, planes and elephants on platforms, but his speciality was holding people aloft with one arm. The total number was no less than eight thousand. In his eighty-third year he even lifted the then world heavyweight boxing champion Muhammad Ali and his wife overhead, together! When Chinmoy died in 2007 the Russian premier Mikhail Gorbachev called his passing 'a great loss for the world'. This was stuff that the materialist West could really relate to, a blend of body-strength, yoga, celebrity and a desire to do good in the world; it was strongman yoga at its glitziest. Chinmoy's enthusiasm was clearly infectious and spawned some bizarre imitation. One of his disciples celebrated the guru's birthday by pogo-sticking backwards across Manhattan in a type of 'reverse neo-*asana* with prop', for which he earned a place in the Guinness Book of World Records.

Chinmoy's all-round expertise and brio were unparalleled, but he was not to be the most influential of the strongman yogis. That destiny belonged to K. Pattabhi Jois, whose official biography contains ample hints of his future greatness for those minded to see them. Born in 1915, on the spiritually auspicious day of Guru Purnima—the July full moon—he was the son of a well-to-do *brahmin* astrologer and priest in Karnataka, who performed his hereditary duty by instructing his son in Sanskrit and sacred rituals from the age of five. When he was only twelve, the boy attended a lecture and yoga demonstration by the yoga master Krishnamacharya and was so impressed he arranged to become his student the very next day. Every morning for two years, without anyone knowing, the lad would sneak off before school to practise with his teacher. Not long afterwards, following a pattern much beloved of Indian spiritual biographies, he renounced his family, leaving home with only two rupees in his pocket, and set out to study Sanskrit full-time. After assorted wanderings, he eventually met up again with the charismatic Krishnamacharya, this time in Mysore, where the guru had set up a small *yogashala* in the city. Jois duly resumed his yoga apprenticeship.

The turning point for everyone concerned came not long after this when Krishnamacharya, as something of a last resort, was invited to treat the Maharaja of Mysore for a serious illness that none of his doctors had been able to cure. The yoga master did so, it was a success, and he was rewarded with royal patronage and premises for a yoga gymnasium set up in a wing of the rambling royal palace. This became known as the Mysore Palace school, and we shall examine its crucial role in the formation of modern body-yoga in more detail in the next chapter.

It was here in the Maharaja's ancestral home that Jois studied and taught for twenty-five years, perfecting his ability and honing his knowledge into a system he would launch upon the world as Ashtanga Vinyasa Yoga. While Jois' biographies contain the obligatory acknowledgement of his debt to classical texts we have already heard about—the ancient *Upanishads*, Patanjali's *Yoga Sutra* and the medieval *Hatha Yoga Pradipika* (none of which are traceable in his actual method, incidentally)—the main scripture he claimed as the source of his system was the 'five thousand-year-old' treatise *Yoga Kuruntha* which his teacher Krishnamacharya had discovered in a library in Calcutta and dictated verbatim to him. Significantly, Krishnamacharya makes no mention of the scripture in his own writings, and we shall never know what it contained, as despite its obvious rarity and importance—sanctity even—it was apparently not looked after well enough to save it from being eaten by ants. As a result, not a single copy of it can be found today; like some levitating Himalayan adept, the work hovers suspiciously on the edge of unreality.

It would be easy to dismiss the whole story as a fraud. In the West, where individuality and novelty are highly valued, inventions and modifications would be promoted as evidence of a teacher's unique creativity. In the Indian context, what mattered, ostensibly at any rate, was adherence to the tradition, and innovations might be disguised by reference to antiquity in the form of texts or gurus. One thing that is certain in this hazy story, is that Jois followed his teacher's preference of seeing yoga in a quasi-medical context. In 1948 he established the Ashtanga Yoga Research Institute with the stated aim of 'experimenting with the curative aspects of yoga'.

Jois taught yoga in Mysore until 1975 when he left for a four-month stay in California to establish his system in the US. He would return several times over the next twenty years, usually to the West Coast, where a body-culture had been flourishing since the early days of Hollywood. His system comprised a graded menu of various 'flow' sequences: several *surya namaskar*, 'salutes to the sun', followed by a series of demanding postures performed while practising the breathing exercises known as *ujjayi pranayama*, 'the conquering breath'. There were six of these sequences, unvarying and progressive, and they were to be practised daily, ideally at dawn. So demanding were they that most of his pupils never got beyond level three or four. In fact, there is considerable dispute amongst Jois' worldwide group of students as to the exact nature of the sequences; over the years several different versions have been presented as the master's authentic method.

One way that Jois' system departed from traditional yoga as described in textual sources, travellers' reports and modern field research amongst ascetic *sadhu* orders, was that it had no time for the custom of holding postures for relatively long periods. The fixed, rhythmical sequence of the Ashtanga style was also an innovation. Although he claimed to be teaching only what his guru taught him, in fact Jois concocted a highly individual and aerobically vigorous system that in turn would spawn its own imitators in gyms and studios throughout California,[4] many of which are grouped together as the sub-genre known as 'Power Yoga'.[5] Jois' arrival in the US coincided with another important milestone in yoga's journey westwards: the publication of the first issue of *Yoga Journal*. Its brief was wholeheartedly to promote better health and greater vitality through therapeutic physical exercise; almost no traces of transcendence were to be found loitering within its glossy pages.

Ashtanga soon gained the mandatory celebrity endorsements that were to become *de rigueur* for any new version of postural practice. Madonna, Sting and Gwyneth Paltrow sang its praises and before long it became the yoga of choice for many results-oriented urbanites, earning a reputation as the must-do yoga for type-A personalities. Its vigorous physicality appealed particularly to men who, then as now, were generally very much in the minority in the yoga culture, especially its softer forms. All in all, Ashtanga fitted well with dominant American values, offering a sweat-based path for a nation of self-actualising achievers. It was a no-pain, no-gain exercise regime with just enough of a hint of a higher, though always rather ill-defined, purpose.

The success of Jois' method also owed much to his own charisma. By the time he died in 2009, at the ripe old age of ninety-three, he was famous enough to merit obituaries in all the global mainstream media. But they were not all favourable. One critical assessment in *The Economist* doubted his adherence to the cardinal yogic virtue of non-violence, claiming that he had used undue physical force on many of his pupils: 'a good number of Mr Jois's students seemed constantly to be limping around with injured knees or backs because they had received his "adjustments", yanking them into Lotus, the splits or a backbend'.[6] Respected yoga scholars and experts had already criticised these trademark 'adjustments', one noting that, often accompanied by 'an impatient or irritable slap', they were 'overwhelming, producing fear and extreme discomfort in students as they are pushed beyond their physical and psychological comfort zones in often difficult, even dangerous *asana*'.[7]

The same *Economist* obituary also raised a more controversial question about Jois' adherence to the standards of traditional yoga: the principle of sexual continence that so often hovers uneasily somewhere around the mat. The piece voiced accusations, whispered around the yoga world for some time, that Jois' female students received rather different types of 'adjustment' from those offered to his male students, stretching the definition of 'hands-on yoga' beyond its legitimate limits. An article in the left-wing magazine *CounterPunch* went so far as to describe Jois as a 'reported sexual abuser of students'[8] and there were other published references to his 'sexually harassing' female pupils. One of the master's most successful followers, David Life, who taught his own version of Ashtanga in the highly fashionable Manhattan Jivamukti Yoga school, countered that for his part, Jois never claimed to be a monk or renunciate, and had a wife and three children to prove it. Such a defence rather begged the question of the correct teacher-pupil relationship, as critics lost no time in pointing out.[9] However, no formal accusations were ever levelled against Jois. This was not to be the case with other charismatic and successful yoga teachers. We have opened a can of worms here whose contents we shall have to examine in Chapter 27.

14

THE MYSORE PALACE MASALA

His Royal Highness Maharaja Krishnaraja Wodeyar IV of Mysore ascended the throne at the age of eleven in 1895 and ruled until his death in 1940. The kingdom he inherited was considered, after neighbouring Hyderabad, to be the most important of the princely states. Mysore's size, ancient lineage and the enormous wealth it generated, persuaded the British Raj to allow it, up until 1917, to be one of only three royal houses meriting a twenty-one-gun salute. This was an honour that put it at the pinnacle of the princely hierarchy, second only to the Viceroy, who got thirty-one guns. India's colonial rulers were always aware that the co-operation of the native princes was essential in their attempt to govern the vast and variegated landmass of the subcontinent, and they saw the house of Mysore as playing a crucial part in the enterprise. From his side, Wodeyar had no objections and he maintained a policy of non-confrontation with British rule, attending the royal *durbars* and entertaining the Viceroy and other Raj officials as required. More importantly, he contributed unstintingly to the war effort by raising and maintaining troops for active service and by donating money to various war funds. There was good reason for his loyal attitude, for Wodeyar was well aware of the debt his family owed the imperial rulers. Ousted from their throne back in the 1760s, they had had it restored to them by the Raj in 1799. And when they again lost power in the 1830s due to widespread peasant unrest, the British once again re-established them as legitimate rulers, though this time it took almost fifty years.

By any standards, Krishnaraja Wodeyar was an extraordinary man. He worked tirelessly to modernise the administration of his kingdom—and where Mysore led, others followed. Several young rulers of other states were sent to his court to learn the art of good governance; one of these was the Maharaja of Travancore, who would in time become the most forward-looking of all the native princes. Wodeyar was also a shrewd businessman. He maximised the

159

profitability of the sandalwood industry and made it famous around the world; he set up textile, paper and iron mills and implemented irrigation and hydro-electric schemes. Seeing the necessity of a dependable water system for the kingdom's agriculture, he sold his own ancestral jewellery to fund dams on the Kaveri river. Numerous social and educational programmes followed, particularly for women and historically disadvantaged groups, and it was under his patronage that Bangalore, now the country's IT hub, became in 1905 the first city in India to have its streets lit by electric power.

One of the things that endeared Wodeyar to the Raj was the fact that he was the first native prince to recognise that India needed greater contact with Western science. To facilitate this, he collaborated with the Parsi industrialist J. S. Tata to set up the Indian Institute of Science, still the premier facility of its type in India. He also valued Western medicine, travelling to Europe in 1936 for medical treatment he felt his native land could not provide. Yet alongside his openness to innovation, the Maharaja was also a stalwart believer in Indian culture and religious traditions. Scholars and artists were always welcomed at the Jagamohan Palace and he patronised music, dance and the visual arts as well as maintaining and archiving a library of ancient Sanskrit texts and miniature paintings. Mahatma Gandhi, who was not known for throwing compliments around, addressed him as *Raj Rishi*, a Sanskrit term that is the Vedic equivalent of Plato's 'philosopher king'.

One of Wodeyar's many interests was physical education, and under his energetic patronage Mysore became the hub of a physical culture revival. To advance this project he decided to set up a yoga school in the palace and in 1932 he hired T. M. Krishnamacharya to run it. He had chosen a man who was not only an expert yoga teacher but also a scholar trained in the foremost southern school of Vaishnavite theology and a Sanskritist of high reputation. The master's initial job was to teach the young princes of the royal family, but before long a keen group of students gathered around him. Crucially, amongst these pupils were two young men who were destined to become the principle proponents of body-yoga in the West: Krishnamacharya's young brother-in-law B. K. S. Iyengar, and the precocious K. Pattabhi Jois.

In India *hatha yogis* are renowned for their fierce tempers, and, for all his bookishness, Krishnamacharya was by all accounts a fearsome presence and a very hard task master. Iyengar would reminisce: 'He would hit us hard on our backs as if with iron rods. We were unable to forget the severity of his actions for a long time. My sister also was not spared from such blows.'[1] The effect of this domineering style would imprint itself on both his most successful pupils, as they recalled when they met at Jois' ninetieth birthday celebrations in

2005. This meeting came after a mutual estrangement, at times acrimonious, lasting sixty-five years. But time is a great healer and looking back amicably over their long illustrious careers, both men recalled how their master had shown them that true yoga was *tapas*, a Sanskrit term going back to Vedic texts that is usually translated as 'austerity', but literally means 'heat':

K.P.J.: We began to understand yoga the moment he made us stand in a stone courtyard burning in the sun for hours on end!

B.K.S.I.: Shall I add something more? You have to sweat 100 per cent, not only physically but intellectually. If you sweat 100 per cent intellectually then you know something of yoga. So, 100 per cent from the body, 100 per cent from the intelligence. You have to sweat, intelligence has to sweat.[2]

If Krishnamacharya was a fierce teacher, he was also something of an enigma. He left few personal records—a dozen pages jotted with autobiographical details a few years before he died—so what we know of him comes from four biographies, authored over twenty years by his son T. K. V. Desikachar and his grandson Kausthub. These are informative but almost equally confusing, as they contradict each other in several key points of the master's life. They are, however, in agreement on the fact that the guru's undoubted expertise was based on his unrivalled mastery of yoga philosophy and in particular Patanjali's *Yoga Sutra*, which his own father had introduced him to at the age of five as his initiation into the ancient discipline. As we have seen already, connecting oneself to this text is a virtually indispensable credential for those wishing to teach a serious yoga. It is curious then that in the four books he authored himself, spanning over fifty years, Krishnamacharya pays scant attention to Patanjali's work. When he does, it is only with a cursory treatment of the Eight Limbs, confining himself to the initial two: *yama* and *niyama*. In none of his writing does he say anything substantial on the inner, meditative practices that Patanjali himself describes as 'the heart of yoga, more intimate than the preceding limbs'.[3]

The most important of Krishnamacharya's books, *Yoga Makaranda* ('The Nectar of Yoga') is more concerned with the good effects that yoga has on health and physical well-being, though it does list other influences which conform with the mix of Tantra, *hatha yoga*, *Upanishads* and Vedanta we have already seen in much medieval yoga. But yoga-scholars who have interviewed a number of the master's pupils from the Mysore School concur that his teachings there made no mention of the philosophical or spiritual aspects of the practice, preferring to focus solely on the gymnastic.[4] Indeed, Anant Rao, who ran K. V. Iyer's body-building gym down the corridor from

Krishnamacharya's *yogashala*, is of the opinion that Krishnamacharya was merely 'teaching circus tricks and calling it yoga'.[5] One of Rao's students agrees, but sees it as a marketing ploy, a bait to attract students: 'In the thirties and forties when he felt that yoga and interest in it was at a low ebb, (Krishnamacharya) wanted to create some enthusiasm and some faith in people, and at that point in time he did a bit of that kind of circus work... to draw peoples' attention'.[6]

Krishnamacharya's son Desikachar, the third most celebrated exponent of the Mysore Academy lineage after Iyengar and Jois, credited his father with making great use of Patanjali, but for the sounding of the Sanskrit text rather than its philosophical import. Recitation is a venerable tradition going back to Vedic times; the sounds of the *mantras*, irrespective of any translated meaning they may have, are credited with embodying a potent resonance that purifies, heals and enlivens the physiology at various levels.[7] Krishnamacharya's innovation was to chant the *sutras* as an accompaniment to postural practice. This was a departure from orthodox tradition, as recitation was usually reserved for works that were considered divine revelation and fell into the category of *shruti*, 'that which was heard' (i.e. the four *Vedas* themselves), rather than for subsidiary texts authored by historical human beings such as Patanjali. The beauty and efficacy of Krishnamacharya's method is certainly not in question here, but it is not a practice sanctioned by the mythistorical 'five thousand years' of tradition as is sometimes claimed by its proponents.

The accounts of Krishnamacharya's early life are also somewhat confused. The youth's rapid progress seems to have been enhanced by his access to rare yogic knowledge vouchsafed in mysterious texts. At the age of sixteen he allegedly had a prolonged vision in which the 1200-year-old spirit of a great yogi and distant relative, one Nathamuni, dictated to him the entire text of a long-lost work called *Yoga Rahasya*, 'The Secret Teaching on Yoga'. Some sixty years later he taught this *Rahasya* text to his son Desikachar, though when interviewed on the subject, the latter was adamant that the verses, which contain mention of sixty-nine (mostly energetically vigorous) *asanas*, were composed by his father himself and had no mysterious astral origin. Scholars of literary style tend to agree, assessing the work to be a modern composition.

After studying at assorted colleges and yoga institutions, the sequence and nature of which vary depending which biography you read, Khrishnamacharya progressed to a spiritual apprenticeship with the great yogi Yogeshwara Ramamohana Brahmachari in a cave on the slopes of Mount Kailash in Western Tibet. As yogic credentials go, this would be rated a hardly surpassable five-star-plus. Kailash is not only the most sacred mountain in the world in both Hindu and Buddhist mythology, but constitutes its divine centre, the symbolic *axis mundi* that marks the junction of the celestial and mundane worlds, where the veil obscuring Reality is at its thinnest. The fact that, due to political reasons, Kailash was virtually inaccessible at this time (unless, of course, one was using astral travel) adds to the mystery. The venerable Yogeshwara apparently knew no less than 7,000 *asanas*, of which he instructed his pupil in 700, with a special emphasis on those who were effective 'for people with sickness'. Leaving aside the question of whether 7,000 *asanas* could really exist, each one sufficiently different from all the rest to merit its own name, form and function, this emphasis on the medical application of yoga would prove very significant for Khrishnamacharya's own teaching and the system he inaugurated. As we shall see, the curative aspect of yoga is particularly evident in the mission of B. K. S. Iyengar, and it is significant that Krishnamacharya's son Desikachar practised for years as a medical doctor before he devoted himself to yoga.

Although, according to all his biographies, the master was a spiritual healer, imbued with the spirit of his hidden Himalayan guru, it is the medicalisation of yoga that is promoted under the auspices of the Krishnamacharya Healing and Yoga Foundation (KHYF) today. What it calls Svastha Yoga, 'The Yoga of Health', presents yogic practice as the means to a balanced and healthy lifestyle in a way that Swami Vivekananda would certainly have approved of. The Indian government likes it too; a department within the Ministry of Health and Family Welfare has adopted it, explaining:

> Yoga is primarily a way of life propounded by Patanjali in a systematic form…
> it has the potential for improvement of social and personal behavior, improve-
> ment of physical health by encouraging better circulation of oxygenated blood
> in the body… the practice of Yoga prevents psychosomatic disorders/diseases
> and improves individual resistance and ability to endure stressful situations.
> Though yoga is primarily a way of life, nevertheless its promotive, preventative
> and curative interventions are efficacious.[8]

Once again, the Patanjali seal of approval is there, translated into modern terminology, though it does show some ambivalence at presenting yoga purely as a medical therapy.

Yoga Masala

Interest in yoga was not a new departure for the Mysore royal family. The Maharaja's great-grandfather, Mummadi Krishnaraja Wodeyar III (1799–1868) is credited with composing an exquisitely illustrated *hatha yoga* manual in the Kannada language entitled *Shritattvanidhi*, which was discovered by one of the main investigators of the history of modern yoga, Norman Sjoman, while he was examining the Mysore Palace library in the mid-1980s. What is remarkable about this book is the way it combines *hatha yoga asanas* with rope exercises used by Indian wrestlers, and push-ups utilising the wooden sticks and clubs employed in traditional *akhara* gyms that we examined in Chapter 9. Sjoman and another scholar, Mark Singleton, have interviewed many people involved in the Mysore Palace yoga school during its heyday in the 1930s, and both believe that much of modern body-yoga arose from the glittering pages of *Shritattvanidhi*.

Krishnamacharya himself was certainly familiar with this text, for he cited it approvingly in his own writings. But that was not all. To this existing blend of standard *asanas* cross-bred with Indian wrestling and acrobatic routines, he added another ingredient: his own variety of Western gymnastic drills. With Iyer's gymnastics hall down the corridor in the Mysore Palace, well-equipped with all the latest wall-bars, hanging ropes and other props familiar to the Western gym and body-building cultures, the source was right on hand. Sjoman, who has himself studied the gymnastics manual that was available to Krishnamacharya, claims that many of the techniques from it—for example, the 'cross-legged jump-back' and walking the hands down a wall into a back arch—are to be found in the Mysore repertoire. An important component of the new mixture was the dynamic regime developed by the Danish gymnast Neils Bukh which, as we have seen in Chapter 7, had already been incorporated into the Indian YMCA classes run by the Raj to build up the moral fibre of their Indian subjects. The eclectic system ended up including many of today's favourites, such as sun salutations, standing postures and the triangle pose (*trikonasana*), that are nowhere to be found in any ancient yogic text.

In his groundbreaking *Yoga Body: The Origins of Modern Posture Practice*, Singleton analyses Bukh's 1925 publication *Primary Gymnastics* and identifies the clear influence of these gymnastic routines on the legacy of the Mysore Palace: 'at least *twenty eight* of the exercises in the first edition of Bukh's manual are strikingly similar (often identical) to yoga postures occurring in Patabhi Jois' Ashtanga sequence or in Iyengar's *Light on Yoga*'.[9] He concludes that Krishnamacharya is:

> a major player in the modern merging of gymnastic-style *asana* practice and the Patanjali tradition... Krishnamacharya's sublimation of twentieth century gymnastic forms into the Patanjala tradition is less an indication of a historically traceable 'classical' *asana* lineage than of the modern project of grafting

gymnastic or aerobic *asana* practice onto the *Yogasutras*, and the creation of a new tradition.[10]

As a result, the Mysore yoga *masala* was: 'a synthesis of several extant methods of physical training that (prior to this period) would have fallen well outside any definition of yoga. The unique form of yoga practice developed during these years has become a mainstay of postural modern practice'.[11]

When *Yoga Body* was published in 2010, it caused a fair degree of outrage in the global yoga family. Some thought its careful detective work amounted to accusing Krishnamacharya of plagiarism, mimicry or dishonest expropriation, but that was not what Singleton was saying. Leaving aside the master's questionable biography, *Yoga Body* was simply attempting to show that modern postural yoga cannot be considered to be some pristine teaching handed down, inviolate, for 'five thousand years'. Rather, it has grown organically over time to become an amalgam of old and new, East and West. As a more measured response to the book, subsequent scholarly work on the historical evolution of *asanas* in pre-colonial times has thrown doubt on some of Singleton's evidence, but a fruitful collaboration has come out of this. Singleton is currently working with other yoga academics, such as James Mallinson and Jason Birch, to examine this highly nuanced topic.[12] All in all, *Yoga Body* has been a welcome and galvanising influence in the field of yoga studies.

The Continuing Legacy

While Krishnamacharya's son Desikachar went on to teach his own system, Viniyoga, that emphasised the breath and included a strong spiritual component based on the *Yoga Sutra*, his two other star pupils were to teach more physical, and more influential, systems. Both stayed in India for some fifteen years—Iyengar in Pune, Jois in Mysore—before leaving their homeland for the West. Between them they catered to varied tastes. Iyengar's practice— modest, rigorously workmanlike and unglamorous—appealed more to women, whereas Pattabhi Jois' highly athletic, image-conscious Ashtanga form, initially the more popular of the two in America, ran against the grain of general yoga practice by conscripting mainly male interest and male teachers.

The complex and often self-contradictory trajectory of Krishnamacharya's career has been well studied and need not detain us here.[13] But beyond their entertainment value, the anomalies that emerge are also important, in that they strike home yet more nails in the coffin of the theory that today's yoga stems from a coherent and venerable tradition stretching back into the mists of time. Just how important the veracity of lineage might be, is something we shall look at again in Chapter 27. Until then, though, childhood trances, voracious ants and hidden Himalayan masters, make of it what you will…

15

ENTER THE LION KING

Financed by the Mysore Maharaja, one of T. M. Krishnamacharya's projects was to travel around the subcontinent with a bunch of his best pupils giving inspirational yoga demonstrations. These were a great success, recasting yoga's public image in a more uplifting light and encouraging people to take up the practice to improve their health. It was in 1934, on his return from one of these tours, that the yoga master innocently made a decision that was to have very far-reaching consequences. One of his brothers-in-law was a sickly sixteen-year-old whose long-term frailty stemmed from the fact that, while pregnant with him, his mother had contracted influenza in the 1918 epidemic that killed millions worldwide. The eleventh of thirteen children, the lad suffered a succession of illnesses during childhood—malaria, typhoid, tuberculosis—and by his own account was a very sorry specimen. As he was to write many years later:

> My arms were thin, my legs were spindly, and my stomach protruded in an ungainly manner. So frail was I, in fact, that I was not expected to survive. My head used to hang down, and I had to lift it with great effort. My head was disproportionately large to the rest of my body, and my brothers and sisters often teased me.[1]

Seeing that the boy's health was so poor, Krishnamacharya invited him to join the palace yoga gym, recommending: 'a stiff regime of yoga to knock me into shape and strengthen me up to face life's trials and challenges as I approached adulthood'.[2] The boy did so, and not long afterwards, just before a Y.M.C.A. fitness conference at the palace when *asanas* were to be discussed and demonstrated, Krishnamacharya's top pupil ran away, unable to take the severity of training any longer. The master hastily recruited his young relative as a last-minute replacement and set him to learn a series of difficult poses.

The boy did his best to comply, badly injuring himself in the process, but nonetheless managed to impress the audience. As a result, he joined the elite group of students, who, when not on the road, frequently gave demonstrations to the Maharaja and his guests. They provided an entertaining show: 'showing off their ability to stretch and bend their bodies into the most impressive and astonishing postures. I pushed myself to the limits in my practice in order to do my duty to my teacher and guardian and to satisfy his demanding expectations.'[3] And satisfied they were, as before long Krishnamacharya had the lad going out to teach his method in gyms and colleges. The more he did so, the more his strength and agility grew. And the name of this spindly youth who returned from sickly isolation to become an exemplary yogic acrobat? None other than B. K. S. Iyengar, the Lion King of postural yoga.

It would be hard to underestimate the importance of these early experiences in forming the young Iyengar's understanding of yoga as a physical discipline to cure, strengthen and improve the body. Fired by the very personal need to improve his own health, he was from the start driven to experiment and improvise, always pushing himself further to adjust, soften and tweak his master's method in the search to refine the curative power of posture. He knew firsthand what it was to suffer physical inadequacy and ostracisation, and he recognised that yoga had, metaphorically and perhaps even literally, saved his life. A wealth of heartfelt experience informed his trademark axioms, such as: 'Yoga teaches us to cure what need not be endured and to endure what cannot be cured'. And there are many worldwide who would gratefully attest to the extraordinary—some might even say miraculous— curative power of his system. It continues to alleviate serious long-term conditions such as Parkinson's disease, multiple sclerosis and varying degrees of muscular malformation and paralysis.[4]

In his *Light on Life*, published in 2005 when he was eighty-five, the master, rather against his previous grain, emphasises the importance of mind-yoga and the wider spiritual goals of the practice. Indeed, these are now the point of it all, as is shown by the progressive sequence of the chapter titles that conform to classic descriptions of yoga in its totality: 'The Inward Journey'; 'Stability—The Physical Body' (*Asana*); 'Vitality—The Energy Body' (*Prana*); 'Clarity—The Mental Body' (*Manas*); 'Wisdom—The Intellectual Body' (*Vijnana*); 'Bliss—The Divine Body' (*Ananda*); 'Living in Freedom'. Then, eight years later, a year before he died, his *Light on Pranayama* was released. It dealt not only with the full range of *pranayamas* but also some relaxation and meditation exercises as well. The book is generally seen as a mature and twilight rumination, garnering the fruits of a long and distinguished career, but in fact it was a reissue of a work originally published over thirty years earlier. The book begins with an introduction by Yehudi Menuhin, invocations to Hanuman-ji and Patanjali, and a rather gnomic commendation by Krishnamacharya, who explains that what is to follow: 'deals with the subtle functioning of the breath, various techniques of inhalation, retention and exhalation, and of the filtration of the crimson-coloured fluid—the Life Force—with unchecked flow through the network of channels (*nadis*) and subtle energy centres (*chakras*)'. If by 'crimson-coloured fluid' is meant the blood, this is a curious mingling of gross and subtle anatomical models, not least because in traditional *hatha yoga*, the 'life-force' is always the subtle *prana*, and nothing directly to do with the material we call 'blood'.

In its first edition, the book passed virtually unremarked. Neither it, nor the second edition, alerted Iyengar's global community to the fact that yoga practice should aim beyond the physical. This was presumably because such a dimension had been conspicuous by its absence from his mainstream teaching over the previous forty years or more. Likewise, it is missing from what has been taught in the many schools that bear his name worldwide. On the contrary, from its beginning Iyengar's system became synonymous with a squarely physical orientation, a rigorous approach bolstered by an array of props to facilitate stretching and suppleness. These included ropes and straps to help improve and hold certain positions, specially designed chairs, settles and stools of various height, and eventually numbered over fifty different types of appliance. The maestro's original method had stemmed from his own remedial needs; he developed ever more aids, and increased their use, after a scooter accident in adult life left him with a twisted spine.

Throughout his career, Iyengar did allude to the fact that, historically, it was taken for granted that anyone seriously aspiring to yogic knowledge would have practised *asanas* and *pranayama*, and this included all the ancient sages and yogis. *Asana* was the way first to align the body, and eventually to liberate the self. For an expert, when *asana* is practised with the right awareness the mind can begin the inward journey and experience *pratyahara* or withdrawal of the senses. As he once commented: 'When I stretch, I stretch in such a way that my awareness moves, and a gate of awareness finally opens.'[5]

So much for the serious, by which he meant very well-schooled, yogi. But in general, even *pranayama* was something only those proficient in postural practice should attempt. And meditation was certainly a step too far for most moderns. As he said, no doubt recalling his own experience with the tough Krishnamacharya: 'Penetration of our mind is our goal, but in the beginning to set things in motion, there is no substitute for sweat.' For most of his students, sweating through 'the beginning' would have to suffice. There was certainly a lot of sweat, and setting things 'in motion' took many years, with the result that 'penetration of the mind' usually remained only a distant aspiration.[6] The ascetic discipline of holding a particular pose for a prolonged duration has always been very important in Iyengar's system and it certainly gave him a quite remarkably robust physique; despite suffering heart attacks in 1996 and 1998 he still managed to perform the headstand and hold it for up to half-an-hour until he was ninety-five. A year after his death in 2014 a retrospective book that typifies his consistent approach was published: *Yoga for Sports: A Journey Towards Health and Healing*. As the cover explains this: 'shows how yoga can train the mind and body and help sportspeople become more agile, stronger and focused'. The book contains precise discussions on the human anatomy while detailing techniques for performing over 100 *asanas* with modifications, props and specific sequences.

Iyengar was by far the most important early populariser of yoga in Britain. Every year between 1960 and 1974, the master spent a month based in the leafy north London district of Highgate as a guest of the violinist Yehudi Menuhin, who had developed an interest in yoga after finding a book about it in an osteopath's waiting room as he was waiting for treatment to help the constant shoulder pain and consequent insomnia caused by his remorseless playing schedule. He met Iyengar while on a concert tour of India in 1952, and soon became a serious practitioner, following Queen Fabiola of Belgium in being among the first Westerners to take up Iyengar's method. Like his teacher, Menuhin viewed yoga as a remedial miracle. 'Yehudi's Yoga', an article in *Life Magazine* in 1953, talked not only of yoga's healing power, but that it had led to a breakthrough in Menuhin's playing and was now even more important to him than musical practice. He referred to Iyengar as 'my best violin teacher' and the two maestros became firm friends.

Setting the Stage

When in London, the yogi gave the musician private lessons and spent the rest of his time energetically spreading his system to a wider public. Throughout the early '60s he held demonstrations wherever he could and he also taught classes, open to anyone, through the Asian Music Circle, encouraged by Menuhin's own fascination with Indian music.[7] Iyengar's platforms included smart venues in intellectual north London—the large middle-class living rooms of Highgate, the Everyman Theatre in nearby Hampstead—as well as the stage of the BBC television studios and the Quaker Meeting Hall on Euston Road. By 1984, he was able to perform a sell-out demonstration at the Barbican. Many of these venues featured a stage, and throughout his career, Iyengar would enjoy this means of presentation in which yoga became almost a performance. This, after all, had been his introduction to the discipline back in the Mysore Palace days. The use of the stage allowed the master to demonstrate the correct pose as a model to be attempted by his student. It could also incorporate the improvisation that was to become such a hallmark of Iyengar yoga, as the stage itself became a prop to assist specific poses. Working on its edge, he could lean over in backbends, hang down in an inversion or use it as a ledge for leg raises. This demonstrated that not only specialised gymnasium equipment, but household objects and walls, could equally well be used as a prop to improve *asana* performance. Some purists were unimpressed by Iyengar's unashamed displays of physical virtuosity, considering them to be overly gymnastic, even exhibitionist, and uncomfortably reminiscent of the magical contortions that had so entranced Victorian London a century earlier. Such a theatrical presentation silently posed a question which is debated with more volume today: is yoga primarily an internal or an external affair? Is it a physical practice for public presentation and approval, or an inner, private affair for contemplative, and ultimately sacred, ends?

Looking back today, it is easy to forget just how threatening an Indian yogi on the loose could seem in those days. Iyengar himself, though, remembered all too well:

> I set off in yoga seventy years ago when ridicule, rejection and outright condemnation were the lot of a seeker through yoga even in its native land of India. Indeed, if I had become a *sadhu*, a mendicant holy man, wandering the great trunk roads of British India, begging bowl in hand, I would have met with less derision and won more respect.[8]

Iyengar's first visit to London, in 1954, was only a few years after India's independence. The hotel he stayed in would not allow him to eat in the dining room with the other guests, so the master had to take his meals alone in his room. As his accustomed vegetarian food was not available, he lived off lettuce sandwiches and coffee. The memory of such humiliation went deep; in his last recorded interview, he recalls how people laughed at 'the grass eater' and how, as an Indian in London, he felt that he was looked on 'as a slave'. This callous treatment strengthened his already considerable resolve; henceforth he would be 'a slave-driver to these slave-drivers'. He vowed his fierce teaching method would show that his initials B. K. S. stood for 'Beating, Kicking and Shouting'.[9]

171

Iyengar's strong will reflected not only his successful struggle against his own physical difficulties but also his ascetic view of yoga as 'conquering of the world, mind, body, self'. It was his version of the triumphant victory demonstrated by the ancient sages and *rishis* of India and their modern equivalents, such as Sri Aurobindo, Ramana Maharshi and Mahatma Gandhi. Many of his students liked this fierceness. As time went by, the master was to gather many more celebrity pupils and, like all true stars, his appeal crossed boundaries effortlessly—the very English intellectual Aldous Huxley and the very Bollywood actress Kareena Kapoor were his pupils, as were the Indian cricketing deity Sachin Tendulkar and the American fashion designer Donna Karan.

It was the publication of an encyclopedic illustrated catalogue of yoga *asanas*, under the title *Light on Yoga*, in 1966, that really established Iyengar's reputation and influence far beyond his initial circle of London admirers. The next crucial step came in 1969 when the Inner London Educational Authority offered its first yoga classes as part of the physical education department's programme. All the teachers in its jurisdiction had to be approved by Iyengar himself and, most importantly for the future direction of 'official' yoga, the ILEA stipulated that only postures and a light *pranayama* be taught. Meditation, *samadhi* and the spiritual context of the practice were banished. This was a landmark decision, probably due not only to Iyengar's own preference, but also to the Anglican Church's fear that classical yoga might be a Trojan horse seeking to smuggle Hinduism into the fabric of national life. Whatever the maestro might teach back home in India, in the West his message was shorn of any interiority. What was decided for the capital was soon rolled out in the rest of the UK and the pattern continued steadily for a decade or more.

With the arrival of the 1980s, much of the idealism that had welcomed assorted Indian teachers in the previous couple of decades was brusquely pushed aside. As a wave of materialism swept both sides of the Atlantic, ushering in the Reagan-Thatcher doctrine of toughening up to succeed in the demanding material world, the sheer physicality of the Iyengar brand served it well. Many Western students duly made the journey out to study with B. K. S. at his headquarters in Pune, near Bombay. There they encountered a presence of extraordinary vitality. Iyengar was not tall, but had a very powerful upper body, long hair swept back in leonine fashion and an intense gaze under bushy caterpillar eyebrows. For all his novel methods, he could conform to the traditional stereotype of the fierce *hatha yogi* exemplified by his own master Krishnamacharya. Some thrived under his rigorous regime, even though they would remember coming back home 'black and blue' from his discipline. The fainthearted who didn't relish such a punitive approach, turned to his daughter Geeta, an excellent teacher in her own right, and enjoyed her softer approach. For those who made the grade, and not all did, their return signalled the first time that teaching yoga for a living became a viable possibility. This too was a landmark step. It was good news for genuine yoga systems, but also sowed the seeds of what was to become the fatuous commercialisation of much transnational practice. And then, just when interest in body-yoga might have been expected to dip after enjoying a good generational run, a whole new audience was introduced to the Iyengar method. Right on cue for the new millennium, the supermodel Christy Turlington graced the cover of *Time* magazine in 2001 doing one of his poses; the next year she published her *Living Yoga: Creating A Life Practice*. All in all, throughout his career the once-sickly youth turned yogic maestro had proved himself to be unfailingly in tune with the *zeitgeist*.

After his death in 2014, Iyengar's website posted a smiling image alongside a typically assured message: 'I always tell people, "Live happily and die majestically".' By all accounts, he did both. Perhaps the last word on the remarkable master of tough love is best left to one of his longtime pupils: 'He was extraordinary, a genius; there's no doubt about it. But his teaching was not for everyone. Different students need different teachers and different teachers find different students. It's very strange and fascinating.'[10]

FEMALE FITNESS

16

A WOMAN'S WORK

One thing immediately obvious to even the casual observer of the yoga scene is that it is overwhelmingly a female phenomenon. The figures confirm this initial impression. In the UK, for example, the officially recognised governing body, The British Wheel of Yoga, has over 8,000 members, fewer than ten per cent of whom are male. Among its network of 4,000-plus registered teachers, the proportion of men is even lower. Several of the sub-sets within the yoga culture, such as 'Yoga for Pregnancy' and 'Yoga for Menopause', are exclusively for women, while many articles in yoga magazines deal with specifically female issues, such as weight-loss and regaining a good figure after childbirth, pre-and post-natal routines, skin and beauty care, the secrets of the female pelvic floor or advice on recovering from breast cancer. In fact, leading yoga publications can barely be distinguished from any other women's magazine, with articles on fashion, beauty and shopping, and endorsements, usually by glamorous female celebrities, of what today's woman might need or want. In a typical copy of the best-selling US *Yoga Journal* in 2015, chosen at random, the advertisements featured eighty-three pictures of women, compared to nine of men and a couple each of kids, dogs and cats.[1] The gender bias has been there for years. A quick Google search of '*Yoga Journal* covers' over the last couple of decades will yield an avalanche of long blonde hair and yards of gleaming Danskin. It would be easy to conclude that the goal of yoga is to provide the same thinspiration as the familiar beauty-mag message: slenderness, fitness and an independent self-confidence not entirely divorced from the power of a well-toned sex-appeal.

A scan of Amazon.com likewise reveals that most of the easily available books on postural yoga have a woman on the cover and content slanted towards the female image. They sport catchy titles such as: *Slim Calm Sexy Yoga: 210 Proven Yoga Moves for Mind/Body Bliss* (originally subtitled: *The*

15-Minute Yoga Solution for Feeling and Looking Your Best from Head to Toe); *Super Simple Yoga: 20 Simple Yoga Poses to Start Looking Great!*; *Yoga Bitch: One Woman's Quest to Conquer Scepticism, Cynicism, and Cigarettes on the Path to Enlightenment* and the admirably direct: *Get a Flat Belly with Yoga* (originally titled: *How To Lose Belly Fat: Get a Healthy, Toned Body Using Yoga*). Looking good brings self-confidence is the message, and a typical best-seller in this vein is *Yoga Girl: Finding Happiness, Cultivating Balance and Living with Your Heart Wide Open* by Rachel Brathen (2014). The publicity blurb promotes yoga as the modern woman's way to the millennial must-have life: online attention, physical flexibility, exotic travel and the resultant happiness:

> With more than one million followers on Instagram, Brathen shares pieces of her life with the world every day. In *Yoga Girl*, she gives readers an in-depth look at her journey from her self-destructive teenage years to the happy and inspiring life she's built … featuring spectacular photos of Rachel practising yoga in amazing locations, along with step-by-step yoga sequences and simple recipes for a healthy, happy, and fearless lifestyle, *Yoga Girl* is all you need to inspire your own yoga journey.

However, what if you are more interested in mind-yoga than postural work? Searching for spiritual uplift, you might Google the ancient Sanskrit *mantra* 'Om', hoping to find information on the sacred sound, and instead find yourself directed to *OM Workshops for Women*, run by Nicole Daedone, who teaches what she calls: 'Orgasmic Meditation—a simple way for women to practice their orgasms'. Daedone, a former Buddhist trainee nun who must have spent her time spicing up the solitude of traditional practice, bemoans what she calls 'the female pleasure-deficit disorder'. Her network of over 120 'assistants' operating across the States and now in London, is poised ready to administer the ritualised masturbation they call 'the Buddha's touch' which, for a fee, will deliver a woman 'that special sense of cosmic connectedness, every time'. While critics see this as just old-fashioned prostitution dressed up in a New Age chasuble, the organisation's UK website explains its mission is to: 'bring yoga, mindfulness and orgasm together'. It's easy to be cynical, but mindful masturbation may be going mainstream: *Marie Claire* spread it wide over three pages in their July 2015 issue.

Even if, undeterred by such practised sleight of hand, you continue your search for 'meditation', you may well come up with other ways mind-yoga has been harnessed to serve the needs of today's woman. The feminist website *Reductress* promotes meditation as a way a woman can open her 'second vagina', explaining:

That's why we've put together this how-to for opening your second vagina and the additional power held within it. This sort of advanced technique is not for those who are new to meditation, so make sure to get acquainted with your unique meditation process before embarking on this estrogen-driven journey to vaginal enlightenment...

Some may see this as immature self-absorption, others as puissant fourth-wave feminism, 'putting women back in touch with their bodies' as the slogan has it. But whatever you may think of such *yoni-yoga*, shifting the focus of yoga from *purusha* to pelvic floor is nothing if not a reversal of the fact that for the last two thousand years yoga has been presented from the male point of view. So, welcome back the Great Goddess? Well, perhaps...

Mars and Venus?

Yoga in the US attracts a slightly higher percentage of men than in Britain, principally because it is a staple ingredient in the training regimes of many of America's top sports teams. But in the UK, even though now-retired Premier League icons such as Ryan Giggs and Brad Friedel attribute their unusual playing longevity to yoga, the practice has just not caught on with men. Nonetheless, the prevailing culture around body-yoga is more often one of no-nonsense body-building than a spirituality commonly perceived as feminine. Many women clearly like this approach too. Claire Ginty is a regular at Gymbox—a blue-lit, black-walled workout space humming with a night-club soundtrack, located in London's square mile. She is typical in her appreciation of what is taught there, a system called Broga, that bills itself as 'a trademark signature yoga practice designed for a male sensibility'. One of the newer kids on the postural block, it was created for real blokes of either sex who don't want any of that 'mystical fluff'. As she says: 'It's the best bits put together. It's got the hard stuff we like without taking two hours out of the day. You feel like you've had a really good workout every time, even if you're aching like a bitch afterwards.' Aficionados of the male classes here say it sets them free to flex their tight hamstrings without feeling inept being stuck next to a woman who can effortlessly twist herself into a pretzel. Again, each to their own, but on the physical level, one thing is sure: the 'get-up-and-go' chemicals released by a hearty workout at Broga must be the exact opposite of the 'sit-down-and-stay' type generated by the meditative absorption Patanjali and the other traditional yoga masters advocated.

Instayoga

We are all familiar with the commonly projected image of body-yoga—that perfectly sculpted body in a perfectly held pose, radiating perfect health, hair and composure, shot against a perfect background of Balinese beach, Thai forest or Himalayan mountain. For those happy to compare and show off their bodies, a new and fast-growing attraction is Instayoga—the use of social media on the yoga scene. Searching #yogaeverydamnday on Instagram generates more than 4 million posts; a nameless model known only as *nudeyogagirl* recently attracted 80,000 followers in her first month of joining the site, though admittedly, that may have had more to with the 'nude' than the 'yoga'. Very active on the online scene is Yoga Trail, which bills itself as the World's Yoga Network, connecting teachers, practitioners and groups with each other. Not long ago, it sent out a post advertising its Yoga Poses Gallery, a contest where people could share pictures of themselves doing difficult postures and 'get inspired by other yogis from all over the world'. Yoga Trail would reward the most acrobatic selfies by featuring them on Facebook, Instagram and Pinterest, emailing subscribers:

> Reminder: a huge Yoga Poses Contest is ON right now! The prize: an *all inclusive* Teacher Training on the magical island of Koh Samui, Thailand (= Paradise). It's easy to win: enter your asana, then get your people to ♥ your pic. Right now, the #1 pose has just over 300 ♥s—think you can rally your friends to support you? 12 days to go… you got this!

Some criticise such Instayoga as being an unhealthily competitive exhibitionism that, fostered by mirrored studios, mat-envy and a vacuous trendiness, perpetuates the egoic self-absorption mature yoga practice has long sought to transcend. On the other hand, supporters defend it as a way for people to share a passion, motivate others and celebrate whatever triumphs over physical and mental struggles their practice has brought. And anyway, they add, it is empowering to want to look your best, so what's the problem?

All of this is rather strange when viewed from the perspective of traditional mind-yoga, which is relatively unconcerned with externals. In fact, the sages agree that if there is one root cause of human suffering, it is identification with the body. Ramana Maharshi, acknowledged as perhaps the greatest exemplar of yogic enlightenment in recent times, put this radical insight with his customary clarity:

> After the 'I'-thought has arisen, the wrong identification with the body rises. Identifying yourself with the body makes you falsely identify others also with

their bodies. Just as your body was born and grows and will die, so you think the other also was born, grew and died…But if you cease to identify yourself with the body and realise the true Self, this confusion will vanish. You are eternal and others also will be found to be eternal. Until this is realised there will always be grief due to false values which are caused by wrong knowledge and wrong identification.[2]

If this is indeed the case, then much of contemporary yoga is faced with a sobering irony. It could be argued that, when practised solely with the intention to develop a fit, toned and attractive physique, postural work serves to promote what Ramana refers to above as 'wrong knowledge and wrong identification'. In such cases, rather than inculcating 'unity', yoga could be working to increase, rather than diminish, our chronic sense of separateness.

Yoga Benefits

Added to the demands of paid work, for many women, being the one who is customarily expected to attend to the needs of the family, look after elderly parents and in-laws, and generally keep things together no matter what is no easy job. Yoga can offer a woman not only a means of de-stressing that recharges her batteries for a return to office or home or both, but just as importantly, some rare 'me' time to enjoy being herself, freed from having to attend to the demands and expectations of others. The solidarity of a predominantly, and often exclusively, female group is also a big attraction of many yoga classes; they provide a supportive environment of useful networking and sympathetic listening. This last is important. A typical *asana* session may not contain any postures specifically designed for the ear, but that particular organ can often get a good work-out after the class.

Teaching yoga also suits many women. Although it is generally not easy to earn a decent living as an instructor unless you work full-time with large classes, teaching yoga can fit the bill as the flexi- or part-time work that many women undertake. The freedom of self-employment, doing something that is clearly beneficial to others whilst increasing one's own well-being at the same time, is an attractive option for someone seeking a good work-life balance. Demographics also play their part. Even if a regular yoga routine doesn't seem feasible to many cash-strapped teens and those in their twenties—and time-poor thirties and forties—the new-horizon fifties are often ripe for it. For older women, yoga practice can provide an important step in a journey of self-discovery, pointing a new and perhaps more personally directed path for the second half of life. This has increasingly been the case as patterns of family life and women's expectations continue to change.

The Tradition of Female Exercise

When yoga arrived bigtime in the West in the 1950s, it was transplanted into a cultural soil that had already seen, over the previous half century or so, a growing interest in physical improvement of various sorts—team games, body-building, athletics, keep-fit. Many of these movements had been started by women and predominantly involved women. The most important of them began in the UK with the Women's League of Health and Beauty, an organisation founded in 1930 that was to touch the lives of hundreds of thousands of women all over the world. The League's motto was 'Movement is Life', and as part of a hybrid programme that embraced Pilates (a system of remedial exercise itself influenced by yoga), aerobics and dance exercise it promoted 'spiritual stretching and deep breathing'. Set against a vague philosophical background of Christian mysticism, this eclectic mix was sometimes called 'female yoga' to distance it from the more masculine postural routines which, informed by a tougher philosophy of body-building, were simultaneously gaining popularity with men.

The League and its philosophy owed their origins to an Irish woman named Mary (Mollie) Stack. Married to an army officer posted in India, Stack had noted the physical differences between the British *memsahibs* and the native women, all of whom seemed to enjoy better posture and more flexibility than their colonial mistresses in their stiff European outfits. Attributing this difference to the fact they did yoga (which is by no means certain), she studied the practice with a local *pandit* and, once back in London, with time on her hands after the death of her husband, began to teach her yoga-influenced 'Stretch and Swing System' for women. Stack initiated a flowing posture workout ten years or more before the idea would be developed by Krishnamacharya in Mysore, and rolled out worldwide by his pupil Pattabhi Jois as Ashtanga Yoga. Well-structured, and taught by trained physicians, Stack's classes evolved into the Women's League. Its first home was the YMCA premises on London's Regent Street, which brings us nicely back full circle to those Raj body-building classes in steamy downtown Calcutta.

Born out of the austerity of the inter-war years, the League gave a generation of women who had lost fathers, brothers and husbands during the First World War the opportunity to meet and exercise together in classes of varying levels of difficulty. This was a period of relative female emancipation.

Founded just a year after women had voted for the first time, the organisation offered women of all classes a chance to come together separately from men and free of the demands of their domestic lives. A magazine and huge public exercise displays soon followed, galvanising the British woman, finally free of her Edwardian corsets, to get up and really start moving. The year after the League was formed, 500 of its members put on a display of exercises to music in the Royal Albert Hall; five years later, ten times that number performed together at Olympia. It was a time of public health fears all over Europe, where a fitness craze was simultaneously gathering pace. Perhaps the urge to keep moving was the displacement of an unconscious fight-or-flight response, discharging collective anxiety as the threat of another terrible war loomed silently larger. By the same token, it is interesting to speculate how much of our current addiction to 'busyness'—both in the gym and out of it—is also an anxiety displacement in a rapidly changing and increasingly mechanised world we feel powerless to control or even influence.

When Mary Stack died in 1934, her daughter Prunella, who was then only twenty, took over her leadership. With her long legs and incandescent smile, she had been her mother's favourite model of what the League was all about, and she would soon become known as Britain's 'Perfect Girl'. If there is any-one who can claim to be the foremother of today's fitness obsession, it is Prunella Stack. In the first three years under her direction, the League's British membership had expanded to 166,000 and gone international. In 1937, the government harnessed the momentum into a nationwide health campaign, and she was appointed to promote physical exercise as 'a matter of national importance'. Not long afterwards, she was part of the official reception committee at a dinner held in London's prestigious Claridges hotel to honour the UK visit of the impressively named Gertrud Scholtz-Klink, whom Hitler had described as 'the perfect Nazi woman' and appointed the leader of Germany's 'National Socialist Womanhood'. Unlike Niels Bukh, who was an enthusiastic Nazi sympathiser, Prunella was not seduced by ideals of Aryan body perfection. A few months after the dinner, members of her League were being called up, or enthusiastically volunteering, for war service.

The connection between these fitness movements and what we would recognise as yoga was, at this early stage, tenuous. The most popular physical culture magazines during the 1930s were *Health and Strength* and its sister publication, *The Superman*. Among the occasional articles that appeared on yoga in their pages, not one outlined a course of bodily postures one would recognise from a typical class nowadays. On the other hand, these magazines did carry many illustrated pieces describing various exercise routines designed exclusively for women. Based on stretching and relaxing, they were not designated as, nor associated with, yoga, but this was soon to change.

The Land of the Fit

A similar yoking of physical fitness to the national good took place after the Second World War in America, and it was again instigated by a woman. The Cold War was a time of considerable anxiety in that country, already despondent from its humiliating retreat from the battlefields of Korea. To rub salt into the national wound, the Russian bear had trounced the American eagle in the Helsinki Olympic Games of 1952, and again four years later in the Winter Olympics held in Cortina d'Ampezzo. Then, to top it all, in 1957 the Soviets launched Sputnik and the communists looked set to extend their terrestrial domination by conquering space.

This last was a shocking blow to the national psyche. One immediate reaction was to channel money and attention into promoting maths and physics in the education system. The humanities were sidelined; what was needed was to produce scientific technicians who would save America from being vulnerable to foreign tyrants. Another reaction was more atavistic. As the leaders of a troubled nation searched its soul, they became more and more convinced that the problem really lay in its body: Americans were appallingly out of shape. Various government reports on youth fitness were hurriedly convened; all revealed that youthful America was a nation of flabby couch potatoes that fell way behind its counterparts in Europe. Into the dilemma strode Bonnie Prudden, a world-class mountaineer and all-round athlete, who had conducted her own tests on child fitness around the world and come to the same gloomy conclusion that young America's muscles were seriously sagging. Prudden's work came to the attention of President Eisenhower, who made her responsible for overhauling the fitness programmes in schools and colleges countrywide. She did so with gusto. One aspect of her work was to introduce more energetically gymnastic displays into the all-girl cheerleading teams at football, baseball, basketball and ice hockey games.[3] She went on to write dozens of articles and books, host several TV shows and inaugurate various national fitness campaigns, as well as setting up exercise regimes in schools, hospitals, mental institutions, factories and prisons. All in all, few people have equalled her energetic contribution to fitness-consciousness.

Eisenhower's successor, Jack Kennedy, was to pick up the flag of physical fitness and wave it with no less enthusiasm. In a 1960 article, 'The Soft American', the youthful president-in-the-wings wrote:

Our growing softness, our increasing lack of physical fitness, is a menace to our national security. The stamina and strength which the defence of liberty requires are not the product of a few weeks' basic training or a month's conditioning. These only come from bodies which have been conditioned by a lifetime of participation in sports and interest in physical activity. Our struggles against aggressors throughout our history have been won on the playgrounds and corner lots and fields of America.[4]

Kennedy's thinly-veiled reference to the Duke of Wellington's famous observation that 'the battle of Waterloo was won on the playing fields of Eton' made it clear that if a global empire based on America's economic dominance was to thrive, the new imperialists must be physically up to the mark. This was not exactly Muscular Christianity, but certainly a close relative. In fact, Kennedy's rallying call was an update of the 'Manifest Destiny' philosophy—the doctrine advanced by the Puritan settlers that they had an inevitable and God-given right to expand westwards, and forcibly take over territory from the native American populations. This vision of entitlement had fuelled white self-confidence in its attempts to build a nation since the early nineteenth century, and it was to be useful once more, this time in establishing America's financial pre-eminence in the modern world. It still inspires one of Kennedy's enduring legacies, the American programme of space exploration he inaugurated in 1962.

The urge towards a fitter America then received a boost from an unexpected source: the gathering pace of the 'women's movement'. This was aptly named, as, among other things, it initiated a dynamic wave of keep-fit classes started by, and catering for, women. Many of the instigators had been dancers: Jacki Sorensen (Aerobic Dance), Judi Missett (Jazzercise) and Martha Rounds (Slimnastics) were all highly successful innovators and motivators. Without making overt reference to it, they saw clearly that as well as the exercise, sympathetic camaraderie and networking, what really attracted many women to their workouts was the desire to lose weight.

Right on cue, the woman who was to inspire her '70s sisters to get off their backsides materialised: the Hollywood star Jane Fonda. Unknown to anyone, Fonda was a longtime bulimic, bingeing and purging herself to achieve what she imagined to be the perfect body. Somehow, the actress managed to keep her secret from everyone until she was well into her forties. Her career had started in the '60s with memorable performances such as her steamy role in the sci-fi spoof *Barbarella*, in which she titillated many a male fantasy by appearing almost naked in a latex body suit. Dubbed America's answer to Brigitte Bardot, she duly went on to marry the French film star's former husband, the film director Roger Vadim. Then, wanting to overcome a sprained ankle picked up filming *The China Syndrome* and needing to get in shape to wear a bikini in her next film *California Suite*, Fonda turned to the get-fit routines developed and taught by Gilda Marx, another of those successful ex-dance instructors. Marx had opened fashionable aerobics studios in California and New York, and Fonda was so impressed with what she saw there that she immediately hired an instructor called Leni Cazden and began learning aerobics privately. She also found out where to source the appropriate equipment and how best to run a fitness and aerobics studios. Then, the actress devised the now canonical *The Jane Fonda Workout Book*. Fonda's slogan was 'feel the burn', and her aerobic neo-tapas caught on like wildfire, turning out to be a huge commercial success.

After the book had sold 2 million copies in hardback, its publisher Simon and Schuster held a champagne party to celebrate, at which they handed Fonda a royalty cheque for $1.2 million, the highest they have ever paid out. Next came the *Pregnancy, Birth and Recovery Workout Book*, which sold 250,000 copies, even though it was actually written by a birth-coach to the stars called Femmy Delyser. The initial *Jane Fonda Workout* tape was the first non-film video to top the video charts, and it stayed right up there for three years straight. Seventeen million copies later, it is still the biggest-selling home video of all time. Now over eighty, Fonda has kept going as a remarkable role model of the active senior, albeit fortified by plastic surgery, a new knee and hip, and buoyed up by testosterone patches. She doubtless gained another boost by becoming a born-again Christian in 2000, and in her latest book, *Prime Time*, she has adapted her former role of female fitness-guide to that of sex therapist, relationship counsellor and all-round life coach for the older woman.

Whether at home alone or in the communality of the gym, women exercised mainly because they hoped to look as good as she did. Physical self-help continued to grow apace during the next twenty years on both sides of the Atlantic, and much of its energy was marshalled against what had entered the lexicon of the female body-project as the dreaded 'thunder thighs'. The statistics tell it all. In America, Wendy Stehling's 1982 best-seller *Thin Thighs in Thirty Days* sold more than 425,000 copies within seven weeks of its release, while ten years later American women and girls were spending more than $100 million a year on the putative effects of 'cellulite-busting' creams alone. The insatiable hunger for weight loss has continued. In March 2019, *Pinch of Nom: 100 Slimming, Home-style Recipes* by UK authors Catherine Allinson and Kay Featherstone became the fastest selling book of all time, shifting a staggering 210,000 copies in the first week of publication. In the same vein, the global anti-ageing market is predicted to reach $216.52 billion by 2021.[5]

While physical fitness has become a huge social concern, another concept has gained currency in the twenty-first century: that of 'wellness', in which keeping fit is one of the main spokes in the hamster-wheel of self-improvement. This wellness often has a therapeutic component. Colleen Saidman Yee, the American celebrity yoga instructor and owner of the Yoga Shanti studios, summed up this view of yoga: 'I never want to be called a guru. All I want to do is guide women into their own bodies so they can be more content'.[6] All in all, given the pressures and staying power of the female body-image project, it is little wonder that women play such a dominant role in the contemporary world of body-yoga. Indeed, some would argue that the enormous success of postural practice today derives as much from the Stack–Prudden–Fonda lineage of physical fitness as from any ancient Indian spirituality.

17

PIONEERING *YOGINIS*

The time is a Sunday morning in August 1932 and the place is Bombay. Although the heavy rain stopped a couple of hours ago and will not return until the evening, the sky is overcast with dense, silvery clouds that completely hide the sun and the atmosphere is turgid and enervating. The oppressive humidity, as always throughout these monsoon months, seeps into every crack and pore of the sweltering city. Along the majestic sweep of Marine Drive, the city's prime boulevard that fronts the ocean, people are straggling out for a walk, hoping to take whatever fresh air they can find. At its southern end, near the tip of the metropolitan peninsula, lies Fort, the administrative heart of the city, where the grand Indo-Saracenic Revival pile that is the Taj Mahal hotel sits imperiously amidst a small cluster of art deco town houses newly constructed by the wealthy and the fashionable. In one of the large first-floor rooms at the head of its grand floating staircase, a management committee is drawing up plans for the coming gala dinner-dance to celebrate thirty years of trading. These have been highly successful. Nothing like the Taj had ever been seen in India; with its American fans, German steam elevators, Turkish baths and English butlers, the place has rapidly become a favourite watering hole for a glamorous international set composed of film stars, playboys, fashion icons and the more Europeanised of India's great and good.

At the northern end of the drive, sorely deprived of the deep velvet armchairs and cooled air enjoyed by the Taj's elegant clientele, is a gathering of a very different sort. No less than five hundred Hindu holy men have converged on the city's most popular meeting place, the broad expanse of sand known as Chowpatty Beach. Wearing only loincloths, their unkempt hair matted with cow dung and sinewy bodies smeared grey with ash from the funeral pyre, these *sadhus* are here to provide a public demonstration of the ancient art of yoga. Many in the large crowd of spectators are clearly discomfited by the yogis' contortions. Promenading European couples fresh from matins at the nearby All Saints Church or mass at the Cathedral of St. Francis Xavier, are unexpectedly brought face-to-face with the otherness of India. Many recoil into their fears and prejudice, while their wide-eyed children are pulled away from the strange scene by their dark-skinned *ayah*. Smartly-dressed Indians look on, their natural interest jostling with a barely concealed embarrass-ment, for, as one public official sniffs, 'this is no place for respectable people'. He may well be right, but a young Russian watching the show, an aspiring film-actress resting between bit parts, is spellbound by what she sees and she doesn't give a hoot if it compromises her respectability. At just the time Middle America is beginning to shape up under Bonnie Prudden, this is another remarkable woman, on the other side of the world, who is about to emerge as a leader in the global fitness campaign.

Indra Devi, as she had recently taken to calling herself, was born Eugenia Vassilievna Peterson in Riga in 1899, six years after Vivekananda had wowed them at the Chicago convention. The child of a teenage Russian aristocrat and a middle-aged Swedish banker, who separated soon after her birth, little Eugenia was left with her grandparents while her mother scratched a living as an actress. From the start she straddled two very different worlds—establish-ment and bohemia, money and near-poverty—and this flexibility was to remain a defining characteristic throughout her picaresque life. The first World War drove her to St. Petersburg, then on to Moscow, where she trained for the stage. The advent of the Bolsheviks had her fleeing to Weimar Berlin, where she joined the famous Der Blaue Vogel cabaret that entertained the many Russian émigrés lured to the doomed city by the strength of their ruble. By 1927 Eugenia was tired of the stage and headed to India, a country she had been fascinated with ever since reading *Fourteen Lessons in Yogi Philosophy* by Yogi Ramacharaka, whose nebulous presence we glimpsed in Chapter 12. Her rea-son for the trip was to follow the young Jiddu Krishnamurti, proclaimed by the leaders of the Theosophical Society to be the new World Teacher—though in a couple of years he would reject the onerous mission imposed upon him. While in the subcontinent, she married a Czech diplomat in Bombay, but life as a society wife soon resulted in depression. 'Why have I come to India', she wrote despairingly, 'to become a popular hostess and party-goer?' A period of illness drove her to try yoga, and like B. K. S. Iyengar before her, Eugenia's salvation was to be the great teacher Tirumalai Krishnamacharya who presided over the yoga-gymnasium at the court of the Maharaja of Mysore.

The authoritarian master had at first to be persuaded to accept a female pupil, but the tenacity of this one, combined with the urging of the Maharaja, won him over. Impressed by her commitment, the guru began to see her as someone who, like his star pupils Iyengar and Jois, could be useful as a global ambassador to spread the word about the benefits of his system and, tangentially, the glories of Indian culture. She would, he felt, be able to get the female vote of approval, something that had long preoccupied him as the means to stem the haemorrhaging of *brahmin* values that he saw all around. As he wrote in 1938: 'I think that if we do not encourage women, the great Indian traditions will die because the men are not following the Vedic rules and regulations. They are all becoming business people.'

In addition, acting as his representative and renamed Indra Devi, he believed she might be able to overturn the disreputable reputation of yoga in the US that dubious early adopters such as The Great Oom had created. Due to the restrictions of America's 1924 Immigration Act, which prevented many of the genuine teachers from India moving there, such eccentrics had had the yoga stage pretty much to themselves. There was a gap in the market, and she seemed the right shape to fit it. From India, Indra moved first to Shanghai, living there during the Second World War in a bungalow rented from Madame Chiang Kai-Shek and initiating her yoga-teaching career by giving classes to the wives of American diplomats. Once the War came to an end, she was ready to take on the USA.

Indra taught a gentle body-yoga, quite devoid of mysticism, and its emphasis on health, fitness and female well-being ensured her unobtrusive influence continued long after her. Following the example of Blanche DeVries, wife of The Great Oom, she opened a studio in Hollywood and presented yoga as the means to 'end grey hair and allow neither old age or wrinkles to arise'. What could be more California? She was an immediate success, attracting not only silver screen legends such as Greta Garbo, Gloria Swanson and Marilyn Monroe, but also those West Coast intellectuals who, as we have already seen in Chapter 11, were exploring a more philosophical yoga in the context of Vedantic teachings. More productively, though, she reached the women in L.A.'s affluent suburbs and soon cornered the market for those executive wives needing distraction from the gilded prison of the fully automated kitchen. Housewife yoga had arrived.

More Travels

In the turbulent mid-1960s, Indra's idealism took her to Vietnam on an eccentric peace mission in the mould of 'Hanoi Jane' Fonda. It likewise failed, and she returned to India, where she temporarily became a devotee of Satya Sai

Baba, the miracle-working *avatar*. When, in 1970, John Lennon and Yoko Ono breezed up unannounced at the guru's Puttaparthi ashram near Bangalore, he delegated Indra to show them around. Famously, Lennon had already studied mind-yoga in Rishikesh with Maharishi Mahesh Yogi four years earlier. He had become disillusioned there and spread malicious rumours about his former guru, but, despite his disappointment, was still seeking answers to life's profound questions. Because she was so out of touch with popular culture (or perhaps wittily referring to his acerbic manner) Indra kept referring to the leading Beatle as 'Mr Lemon'. Correctly addressed or not, the couple did not much like what they saw. As the stars of their anti-war 'Bed-Ins for Peace', held the previous year in Amsterdam and Montreal, they particularly resented the fact they were expected to conform to sacred tradition and sit separately in the male and female sections of the prayer-hall. The guru paid them no particular attention and they soon left.

Before long, the peripatetic *yogini* would follow them out of the Baba's ashram, and she ended her days in Argentina, where she died at the age of 102. Her last years were spent as the spiritual adviser to Manuel Noriega's second-in-command, but for Indra herself it was always health, not holiness, that was yoga's goal. Although her attraction to gurus had her travelling halfway around the world, and at one point led her to abandon her second husband as he lay dying, like so many of today's practitioners, she did not expect anything other than physical benefits. As she once admitted with disarming honesty: 'I don't have a trace of sainthood.'

Perhaps not, but Indra Devi's is a vital contribution to our story. Her books brought many to yoga. The best-selling *Forever Young, Forever Healthy* came out in 1953 and then, a decade later, there was *Yoga for Americans: A Complete Six Weeks Course for Home Practice*, dedicated to Gloria Swanson and introduced by Yehudi Menuhin. Indra was also in at the beginning of a radical new departure for the teaching of yoga that, with the arrival of apps, has since become very much part of the scene: lessons without the physical presence of the teacher. Her long-playing vinyl disc *Yoga for Americans* was released in 1965, inspiring other remote-learning albums from female teachers, such as Maureen Easton's *Hatha Yoga at Home*, Treva Zoellner's *Yoga* and Betty June Alexander's *Balanced Living Yoga*. One way or another, Indra's life and work have immortalised her as one of the great popularisers of posture work in America.[1]

Of the few pioneers who did take to yoga as a spiritual discipline, some gave up their conventional lives for their gurus. Best known of these was Margaret Noble, an Irish social worker who was initiated into *brahmacharya* by Swami Vivekananda in 1898 in Calcutta, thus becoming the first western woman to join an Indian reclusive order. She was given the name Sister Nivedita, was very active in the Ramakrishna Mission, and enjoyed a close friendship with Sarada Devi, the widow of Vivekananda's master, Ramakrishna. Nivedita lived the rest of her life in India and, like the leading Theosophists before her, became an advocate of the Independence movement and a champion of the nobility of Indian life. Another spiritual émigré was Margaret Woodrow Wilson, eldest daughter of the American President. A professional singer, she briefly served as First Lady after her mother died, but left the West for good in 1938 to join the ashram of Sri Aurobindo in Pondicherry. Known there as Sister Nishta, she worked with the scholar Joseph Campbell in editing the 1942 English translation of the classic *The Gospel of Sri Ramakrishna* by Swami Nikhilananda. She died in Pondicherry of a kidney infection, having refused to return to America for treatment.

More often, though, wealthy women acted as yoga sponsors and facilitators. We have seen how the kindness of two such, first Kate Sanborn and then Mrs Hale, helped Vivekananda launch his mission in America. Once it was established, the Swami benefitted greatly from the generosity of another duo, the Bostonians Sara Bull and her friend Sarah Farmer. Farmer, who came from a New England Transcendentalist background, hosted a summer series of lectures at their Green Acre Conferences, where, under the world's first Peace Flag—all of thirty-six feet long—thinkers from around the world met and discussed subjects such as the oneness of humanity, the necessity and inevitability of world peace and the essential unity of the world's religions. Vivekananda made many important contacts there. Not long after this, it was to be the generosity of Mary Dodge, heiress to a copper fortune and a devoted Theosophist, that floated the organisation needed to promote the work of the master of *jnana yoga*, Jiddu Krishnamurti. Miss Dodge not only bought land and property for the Society, but settled substantial allowances on the young messiah and several members of his group. These annuities were lifelong and set a pattern of ample and seemingly effortless patronage that continued, in Krishnamurti's case at least, for well over sixty years.

Another would-be midwife of the emerging new age was Rebekah Harkness, a composer, choreographer and sculptor. Married to the heir of the Standard Oil fortune, she was also one of the wealthiest women in America. Yoga had helped her improve her dancing and she invited B. K. S. Iyengar to America in 1956 for his first visit, when he spent six weeks as her guest in Rhode Island. *Life* magazine ran a lead article entitled 'A New Twist for Society', with photographs of him instructing her family in seated forward bends and shoulder stands, as well as shots of the maestro himself performing various difficult poses. But overall the visit did not go well. When it ended, the yogi commented sourly that Americans cared only for 'the three W's: wealth, wine and women', and he did not return to America for almost twenty years. Given his potential audience there, and the prejudice he initially met in Britain, this was a quite extraordinary decision.

Female Teachers

The tide of yoga flowing westwards had been set in motion and it was unstoppable. When Mary Palmer hosted Iyengar in Ann Arbor for his long-awaited return visit in 1973, a new wave of female teachers broke onto the scene. Among them was Palmer's daughter Mary Dunn, along with other instructors who would prove influential: Patricia Walden, Patricia Sullivan, Rama Jyoti Vernon and Judith Hanson Lasater. A further boost to female participation in body-yoga came ten years later when Pattabhi Jois' Ashtanga method was adapted by Tim Miller in his creation of a freestyle Vinyasa in the mid-1980s. This was less rigorously masculine than Jois' original style, and it opened the floor of yoga to the spirit of dance. Women embraced the flow practice with enthusiasm, just as they had taken to Mollie Stack's exercise system back in the '30s. Among teachers who developed Miller's hybrid form, three stand out, not least because they used their dance-posture work in tandem with a wider social activism. Shiva Rea has been involved in environmental and cross-cultural issues; Sean Corn has taken her yoga to Africa with aid projects and, as Sharon Gannon admits in her best-seller: 'I became a yoga teacher only because I felt it might provide a platform for me to speak out for animal rights.'[2] Innovative though such directions may seem, blending yoga with altruistic concerns was not a million miles from Vivekananda's original mission. Other important yoga groups have also been headed by women. There is Emmy Cleaves' leadership of Bikram Yoga, Gurmukh Kaur Khalsa's work in Kundalini Yoga, Ana Forrest's powerfully athletic Forrest Yoga and Beth Shaw's leadership of the YogaFit training.

Back in the UK

Meanwhile, back in Britain, as the advent of TV brightened up the dowdy post-war 1950s, growing interest in women's fitness saw the gym move into the living room. The market leader here was Eileen Fowler, with her trademark foot-strap leotards and jaunty catchphrase: '*Down* with a bounce; with a bounce, come *up!*' Later, other presenters such as Rosemary Conley would also become household names.

194

Alongside these fitness movements, however, body-yoga was also beginning to make inroads. Its earliest proponent was, again, a woman. Arriving in Birmingham in 1960, at about the same time Iyengar was beginning his annual visits to London, an Anglo-Indian immigrant called Bernadette Cabral soon transformed herself into Yogini Sunita, a rather exotic expert on relaxation and yoga. Before long, sari-clad Sunita was giving media interviews to both the local press and the BBC, and within eighteen months was conducting her first yoga evening classes in the Women's Section of the Birmingham Athletics Institute. Soon she was teaching hundreds. Despite their sporty setting, Sunita's yoga classes were not confined to *asanas*. She included a magical ingredient of her own which she called 'the slip second', a simple mental exercise that involved focusing on, and then releasing, anything that is concerning you. The ensuing relaxation could recharge the batteries profoundly, indeed she claimed it was more reinvigorating than a night's sleep. This practice, and her philosophy that 'a moment of complete peace characterises the essence of yoga' brings Sunita much nearer to Patanjali than the typical 'stretch and relax' format that was later to dominate the UK yoga scene. She was a striking presence and charismatic teacher, and her classes grew in popularity through the 1960s. Her students were primarily women and, working within the adult education system, she instructed about twenty female teachers in her system, which she was now calling 'Pranayama Yoga'. How this may have developed we will never know. In 1970, when still only thirty-eight, Sunita was killed by a car while out walking, and quietly disappeared from the pages of history.

CHANGIN' TIMES

18

LORD SHIVA SHAKES HIS TRIDENT

In Hindu mythology, the archetypal ascetic is Lord Shiva. In his form as *Mahayogi*, 'the Great Yogi', he dwells in the high Himalayan snows where he ceaselessly practises meditation and austerities, enjoying the purest atmosphere on the planet. Coloured blue—not from the freezing temperatures, but because in Indian iconography the reflected hue of the sky and sea is seen as a fitting colour to represent infinity—he has piled up dreadlocks matted with sacred cow dung, three horizontal stripes of sacred *vibhuti* ash on his otherwise unlined forehead and wears only a loin cloth and the heavy *rudraksha* beads round his neck that symbolise and encourage celibacy. Sitting serenely in *padmasana* on a tiger skin, he holds upright his emblematic trident of power—the *trishula* or 'three prongs'—for, like the sea-god Neptune in Roman mythology, Shiva is the regal guardian of humanity's psychic depths, the ever-awake custodian of both their treasures and their terrors. The priceless wisdom that Shiva teaches is least valued in the Age of Kali, our current times of metaphysical dullness and materialistic folly, and not long ago, no longer able to tolerate the dissolute ways of our unregenerate world and its disastrous disregard of spiritual truths, Lord Shiva took up his *trishula* in exasperation and gave the planet earth a firm prod. A new evolutionary energy was released, a huge wave of purification set in motion.

The Three Prongs

The first prong to strike the dozing leviathan of materialism into some sort of wakefulness took the form of Swami Vivekananda's mission that we have already discussed in Chapter 11. The world had been alerted to the universalist message of yoga and its culmination in Vedanta, and it had been changed for good. The second prong of the *trishula* galvanised the work of another

Bengali, Mukunda Lal Ghosh, who would soon become known as Paramahansa Yogananda. Born in 1893 into a traditionally devout Hindu family, Ghosh underwent 'English-medium' education, first at the Scottish Church College, and then at a college affiliated with Calcutta University. At this time the political ferment in the metropolis was mounting, and in 1911 the British Raj, nervous about the future, moved their capital away from the international sophistication of Calcutta to the quieter backwater of inland Delhi. Lord Macaulay's imperial project to create 'brown Englishmen' was having unforeseen consequences: the Bengali English-educated elite were becoming too successful, too demanding and asking too many questions about their rightful place in the future. The young Ghosh, however, was not politically inclined; his interest lay in spiritual matters. In his youth he had sought out many sages and saints, hoping to find an illuminated teacher to guide him in his quest, and then, at the age of seventeen, he met one. This was Sri Yukteshwar Giri, an orthodox and *danda sannyasin* of the monastic order established by the philosopher-saint Adi Shankara. Under his teacher's instruction, Ghosh took formal vows to join the order, becoming Swami Yogananda Saraswati, a name signifying 'the bliss of union'.

Like Vivekananda before him, the young man began by working with youth groups, and set up a school for boys in Bengal that combined modern educational techniques with the inculcation of spiritual ideals. Then, in 1920, again like Vivekananda, he sailed to the United States as India's delegate to an ecumenical religious gathering, though this one was the International Congress of Religious Liberals and was held in Boston rather than Chicago. Once in America, still following in the steps of his predecessor, he soon founded an organisation— the Self Realization Fellowship (SRF)—which was to become the worldwide medium to disseminate his teachings on yoga, philosophy and meditation. He called this package 'The Science of Kriya Yoga', and he attributed it, via his master and his master's teacher in turn, to an immortal yogi named Babaji, who lives alongside Lord Shiva up in the Himalayan vastness. The organisation's title 'Self-Realization' was a translation of the Sanskrit *atma bodhi*, a phrase used by the eighth-century sage Adi Shankara to describe the enlightenment that is the classic goal of mind-yoga.[1]

The SRF began in 1920, though it did not become legally incorporated as a non-profit religious group for another fifteen years; for his first few years in America, Yogananda was concerned with teaching a more physical system. His method, heavily influenced by a combination of European body-building and 'mind over matter' New Thought philosophy, went by the intriguing title of 'Yogoda, the Tissue-Will System of Body and Mind Perfection'. It promoted 'muscle recharging through will power' which would grant the practitioner extraordinary 'feats of strength and endurance'[2] and the publicity material announced that the 'Yogoda system of body perfection' was gadget-free, could be practised anywhere, 'puts on or removes fat' and 'teaches spiritualization of the body'.[3]

The Swami gave public demonstrations in various venues around the States, gaining both curious audiences and considerable publicity.[4] His younger brother was also in on the act. As a renowned body-builder who served as the first, and only, Indian judge in a Mr Universe contest, B. C. Ghosh popularised his own *hatha yoga* that was a blend of *asanas*, physical culture and his brother's muscle-control exercises. To promote this mix, he opened a College of Physical Education in Calcutta in 1923, whose most famous alumnus was one Bikram Choudhury, the inventor of Hot Yoga, who we shall meet in Chapter 21. Ghosh was also an ardent nationalist. His 1930 photographic study, *Muscle Control*, illustrated a weights-free method of body-building that he hoped would inspire the youth of Bengal to shape up for the coming fight. Together, the brothers thus exemplified all the various influences—*hatha yoga*, Western body-building, Indian nationalism and a touch of circus performance—that would coalesce as modern postural yoga.

As time went by, Yogananda dropped his physical routines to focus on *kriya yoga*. This was essentially a programme of mental exercises (*kriyas*) recommended in the classic *Hatha Yoga Pradipika*, tantric routines that manipulated energies in the subtle body to bring the individual into alignment with the cosmic intelligence. As Yogananda himself explained:

> The Kriya Yogi mentally directs his life energy to revolve, upward and downward, around the six spinal centers (medullary, cervical, dorsal, lumbar, sacral, and coccygeal plexuses) which correspond to the twelve astral signs of the zodiac, the symbolic Cosmic Man. One-half minute of revolution of energy around the sensitive spinal cord of man effects subtle progress in his evolution; that half-minute of Kriya equals one year of natural spiritual unfoldment.[5]

In 1925 the international headquarters of the SRF was established in Los Angeles, the city which, when Swami Prabhavananda established his Vedanta Society of Southern California there four years later, would become established as the Mecca for seekers of Indian wisdom. L.A. was a natural choice, a place with no defined centre, a blank canvas free from the heavy European influence of the east coast, looking out optimistically towards the future. From his California base, Yogananda lectured and taught across the country for the next several years. He emphasised the fact that yoga, despite the complex and esoteric terms he used to describe his Kriya system, was above all a scientific discipline that could, and should, be discussed and understood in Western scientific terms. His earliest published work, an amplification of his maiden US speech, was called *The Science of Religion*, a title employing an oxymoron that had intrigued progressive thinkers since the late nineteenth century. In its pages Yogananda summarised the principles and practices needed to attain direct experience of the Divine, applying the same practical approach to the betterment of the individual that his predecessor Vivekananda had advocated for social service to the world. The Western intellectual method was being used to transcend its own limitations, and the marriage of science and spirituality, West and East, was to remain the hallmark of his mission.

Yogananda's other predominant theme was the transcendent unity of all religions. To demonstrate this, he focused on the religion of his audiences, Christianity. Developing his master's syncretic interests, his aim was: 'To reveal the complete harmony and basic oneness of original Christianity as taught by Jesus Christ and original Yoga as taught by Bhagavan Krishna; and to show that these principles of truth are the common scientific foundation of all true religions.'[6] The Semitic and Indian teachings come together on the level of the lived experience of the practitioner because, as he explained when discussing the real meaning of Jesus for us today:

> his reappearance to the masses now is not necessary for the fulfilment of his teachings. What is necessary is for the cosmic wisdom and divine perception of Jesus to speak again through each one's own experience and understanding of the infinite Christ Consciousness that was incarnate in Jesus. That will be his true Second Coming.[7]

This ecumenical theme was also the substance of two of his major literary works: *The Second Coming of Christ: The Resurrection of the Christ Within You* and *God Talks with Arjuna: The Bhagavad Gita*. Both books began as serialisations in the SRF magazine, and both argue that eternal principles are the common, and scientific, foundation of all true religion. His understanding of the *Gita*, though, was markedly more interiorised and mystical than Vivekananda's.

Another book that sold well was *The Law of Success*, a small guide to the practical benefits that attend the spiritual life. Published in 1944, it continued the alliance with New Thought philosophy that characterised his Yogada teaching by advocating a practical mental science based on the power of positive thought. Again, this was not a new idea. Historically, it could perhaps be linked to the *siddhis* attributed to yoga, but it had already been presented in America in a more secular and materialistic context, by best-selling writers such as Napoleon Hill, whose *Laws of Success* had been published 1928, and Dale Carnegie whose landmark *How to Win Friends and Influence People* came out in 1936.[8]

For the next several years, Yogananda lectured and taught around the States; thousands came to hear him and he attracted celebrity followers, including the singer Clara Clemens, the daughter and biographer of Mark Twain. He was the first Hindu teacher of yoga to spend a major portion of his life in America, living there from 1920 to 1952, with only occasional trips to Europe or back to his native India. Alongside the SRF, which still operates today, the Paramahansa's most puissant legacy is his third major book: *The Autobiography of a Yogi*. First published in 1946 and still very much in print, it has sold five million copies to date. A wonderful read that has inspired many, it can justly claim to be the most effective 'yogic' book of all time. Continuing to uplift the digital and millennial generations, it is said to be the only book that Steve Jobs had on his ipad and that he re-read it once a year.

In the Spring of 1952, at a Los Angeles dinner for the visiting Indian Ambassador to the US, Yogananda gave a speech on the topic of India and America and their contributions to world peace and human progress. In words that could have been spoken by Vivekananda, he outlined the future co-operation of these two great countries, expressing his hope for a 'United World' that would combine the best qualities of 'efficient America' and 'spiritual India'. By a terrible irony, these two differing perspectives were dramatically manifested almost before he had finished speaking. At the end of his talk Yogananda collapsed on the floor. His disciples who were present affirm he consciously entered yogic *mahasamadhi* by meditating on the third eye; somewhat more prosaically, the American doctors pronounced that he had suffered a fatal heart attack.[9]

Either way, his passing was extraordinary. As the director of the Forest Lawn Memorial Park Cemetery in Glendale, where Yogananda's body was embalmed, reported in a notarised letter:

> The absence of any visual signs of decay in the dead body of Paramahansa Yogananda offers the most extraordinary case in our experience... No physical disintegration was visible in his body even twenty days after death... No indication of mold was visible on his skin, and no visible drying up took place in the bodily tissues. This state of perfect preservation of a body is, so far as we know from mortuary annals, an unparalleled one... No odour of decay emanated from his body at any time...[10]

The Third Prong

The third prong of Lord Shiva's trident, and the most powerful in its long-term effects, came less than ten years after Yogananda's death, in the form of a diminutive white-robed monk called Maharishi Mahesh Yogi. This was a spiritual teacher the likes of which had not been seen before. Ebullient, mercurial, full of joy and refusing to take anything too seriously—other than his mission to enlighten the world—'The Maharishi', as he was soon dubbed, was a true revolutionary. His message, like the meditation technique he taught, was simple and direct: suffering is unnecessary because life is by nature blissful, and the way to realise this, twenty minutes of his Transcendental Meditation twice a day, is easy, enjoyable and suitable for everybody. The idea that the spiritual life was a struggle or involved self-denial or austerity was emphatically rejected as being a confusion between the different paths suitable for a recluse and a householder. While the former might dedicate his life to long and arduous discipline, all that was needed for the latter was regular meditation and a life of balanced activity. Whereas Vivekananda had framed our higher calling in terms of a manly and ongoing battle to overcome one's own base impulses, and Yogananda emphasised a lengthy and esoteric transformation of the subtle physiology, Maharishi's undemanding message was what many people were more prepared to hear, especially if it came from a laughing man who carried flowers wherever he went.

Transcendental Meditation (TM) spread very quickly. From a publicity point of view, the greatest coup of this seemingly tireless innovator was to teach the Beatles to meditate and have them attend his residential courses: first at Bangor University during the high Summer of Love in 1967 and then, six months later, at a purpose built academy in Rishikesh, a traditional yoga-retreat town on the Ganges, seven hours by road north-east of Delhi. Maharishi's association with the Fab Four was to prove a mixed blessing, and in retrospect, he felt that many of what he called 'serious people in society' were put off trying the practice because of the Beatles' connection. Nevertheless, huge numbers of young and idealistic baby-boomers, as yet unencumbered by family and financial obligations, were available to help in spreading the meditation message, and they did so with great enthusiasm.

Many casual observers may have misjudged Maharishi's left-field ebullience as a lack of gravitas, but behind the smiling image was a resolutely classical teacher who allied himself firmly to the Vedic tradition. His teaching that thoughts in meditation are inevitable, and should be accepted rather than resisted, appeared revolutionary, but it was rooted in the traditional *sahaja*—'effortless; spontaneous'—approach that does not seek to control or strain the mind and can be found in both Hindu and Buddhist contexts. At one stroke, what has often been considered a huge barrier to practice is overcome. His analysis of meditation followed the sequence of Patanjali's *Yoga Sutra*, explaining the necessary purification of mind, the qualities of thought and the gradual removal of deep latent impressions from the unconscious psyche.[11] The result was a thorough understanding of traditional mind-yoga, but one couched afresh in a modern form, easy to understand and apply. Similarly, his assessment of the long-term effects of practice is based squarely on the *Mandukya Upanishad*, which explains *turiya*, the 'fourth' or transcendental consciousness that is prior to three changing modes of mind—waking, dreaming and deep sleep—and is their unchanging witness. Maharishi's skill as an exegetist was made clear by his translation of, and commentary on, the first six chapters of the *Bhagavad Gita*.[12]

Three Prongs, One Prod

Although as a personality Maharishi may have been very different from his two more conventional predecessors Vivekananda and Yogananda, there were definite similarities between the three. All were born into the *kayastha* sub-caste of scribes and book-keepers, a social group that had long been exposed to foreign ways through its clerical and administrative role first under the Muslims, and then the British Raj; Vivekananda was the son of a lawyer, while Yogananda and Maharishi were both the sons of civil servants.[13] This legacy was to serve them well in their interaction with the West. It was also perhaps useful, as each of the three was the favoured disciple of a traditional and highly orthodox teacher and renunciate. These mentors had relinquished the world in time-honoured fashion, but they must have recognised that their young disciples were not only less encumbered by tradition, but had been blessed with a native intelligence, a forceful personality and the potential to adapt ancient wisdom to the coming need of the time. For their part, those pupils had all noted the practicality of Christian missionary work in India and they saw clearly that the modern world, with its esteem of science and its belief in material progress, would be wary of traditional teachings that favoured renunciation, extreme material simplicity and an overly austere attitude to life. What was needed was to bring balance to the world, to fortify the fragile house of materialism by establishing it on the rock of spirituality. Again, like his two predecessors, Maharishi taught the transcendental unity of the great religions, emphasising, as they did, that this unicity was no mere theory, but a liberating realisation brought about by profound inner experience of the ground of all being through the practice of mind-yoga.

As a physics graduate from the University of Allahabad, one of Hinduism's most ancient pilgrimage towns and host to the largest religious fair on earth,[14] he very much appreciated Western science. From the start of his mission in the 1960s, he was keen that the physical correlates of his technique be scientifically examined and its benefits catalogued. Scientific studies on Transcendental Meditation eventually began in the early 1970s, initiating a process that over the last fifty years has resulted in the accumulation of vast amounts of data pertaining to various types of meditation and body-yoga as well.

For the first ten years or more of his public teaching Maharishi used traditional terms drawn from the same vocabulary used by his predecessors. For example, in Hawaii in 1958 he told what must have been one of his first international audiences about what he was then calling Deep Meditation:

Meditation is the most effective form of Prayer to God—Personal or Impersonal. Meditation is the most effective means of getting rid of sins by burning them in the fire of Divine Experience. Meditation is the straight flight of the mind to the Kingdom of Heaven present in the heart of everybody.

But following the publication of the early scientific studies, the terminology began to change. Meditation was presented less as the key to spiritual unfoldment, more as an effective stress-buster. Alongside this, Maharishi began to call his teaching 'The Science of Creative Intelligence'. The new science was discussed in inter-disciplinary symposia held regularly around the world, the overarching aim of which was to highlight the correlation between Western science and Vedic science, which he characterised as 'the objective and the subjective means of knowledge'. Some big names, then at the forefront of scientific thinking, attended these symposia, including three Nobel Laureates—physicists Brian Josephson and Ilya Prigogine and biochemist Melvin Calvin—the futurist and designer Buckminster Fuller; Hans Selye, the endocrinologist who popularised the concept of 'stress' and the subatomic physicist E. C. G. Sudarshan.

Behind his media persona of benign stress-doctor, Maharishi continued to promote the universalism of the Vedas and an in-depth understanding of Indian metaphysical traditions, but *sotto voce* now, for he was well aware how easily materialists could shy away from a world-view that stretched their paradigms too far and too quickly. In truth, however, it was these spiritual themes that were always nearest his heart, and they would return to prominence in the last two decades of his teaching.

And finally, all three of these spiritual ambassadors, deeply rooted in the ancient psychic soil of their motherland, were painfully aware that the popular Western image of India was not a positive one. This was especially the case in America, which was still under the gloomy pall of Kathleen Mayo's *Mother India*. Aware that some would automatically doubt the practicality of his message based on the fact that he was Indian, Maharishi would forcibly make the point that India *per se* was nothing to do with it:

> So, it's not India that is going to inspire the people, it's not Hinduism that is going to inspire the people. It is the knowledge about life which is free from any limitations of time and place, this is a universal truth about life, inner being. Now whether one is an Indian, or South African, or Italian, or what. The reality of inner life, and that is our message. We don't talk to the people in terms of Indian philosophy or Indian religion, or Indian, it's not *Indian*.[15]

We shall examine the difficult marriage of science and spirit later, but for the moment, there can be no doubting that, all in all, the exasperated prod from Lord Shiva's trident had not only left an indelible impression, it had pushed the planet in a whole new direction.

19

LOTUS POSTURES, LOTUS EATERS

The blossoming of Flower Power in the mid '60s initially appeared to be just the thing to encourage people to adopt the lotus posture. Along with vegetarianism, assorted magical belief systems and a concern for ecology, body-yoga was certainly one of the tastier items in the lifestyle smorgasbord being offered the young and open-minded. Then in mid-August 1969, two years after the Summer of Love when the Beatles had sat at Maharishi's feet at Bangor, and at just the time the ILEA was approving Iyengar postural practice in the UK, the peace and love culture hosted its biggest celebration to date: the Woodstock Festival in rural upstate New York. India arrived at the jamboree in style. Swami Satchidananda, a charismatic figure who was to become popular in North America with his system of Integral Yoga, helicoptered onto the stage with long hair and beard flowing, to settle down gracefully into an orange-robed *padmasana* and deliver the opening speech to the rapturous crowd.

The Swami may have descended out of the clouds, but his message was as down to earth as Vivekananda's had been. Echoing his predecessor's opening words in Chicago, Satchidananda began his address with: 'Brothers and Sisters of America', though few, if any, of the half a million present would have recognised his wink at history. Like Vivekananda's before him, the yogi's message was all about how yoga should inform work and work should become a yoga, and that the time had come for materially blessed America to start developing spiritual richness too. Flanked by his US students in yellow or white robes, he soon had the crowd chanting '*Hari Om*' to show the way, and bless not just the festival, but the inauguration of a new era. To continue the Indian soundtrack, the sitar maestro Ravi Shankar played at the festival. This gave his music useful exposure, but he would later remember that the hippies were disrespectful, and often too stoned really to appreciate what he was offering:

'I had to explain them, please try to listen with a pure mind, because I assure you that our music has that power that it can make you feel high. But if you are already gone to—so spacey, you know, what you hear is not the real thing…'[1] Still, even the persistent rain and the squelching mud could not dampen the communal spirit; the country, and indeed the youth scene world-wide, was never quite the same again.[2]

Spacing Out, Spacing In

In fact, the Woodstock generation was generally more into hedonism than health, more drawn to wanderlust than work. The desired look was not focused, fit and muscly, but dreamy, decadent and androgynous: the boys wanted to look like Mick Jagger or Marc Bolan, the girls like Marianne, Twiggy or the Shrimp. Most young people weren't really interested in developing their bodies; the new culture was led by stoners who called themselves 'heads' and wanted to go inwards and upwards to meet The Byrds 'Eight Miles High', 'Fly Translove Airways' with the Jefferson Airplane or join the Stones 'Out of Our Heads'. The goal was not to get earthed into yogic physicality, but to transcend bodily limits in an Apollonian reach for the stars: to seriously space out. The occasional body-yoga buffs and the many hippies may both have spent a fair amount of time on the ground, but while the former were assiduously perfecting their postures, the latter were just too wasted to stand up. Even the popular heroes of straight society were ungrounded: astronauts were floating around weightless as if they didn't even have a body. The must-see movie was *2001: A Space Odyssey* and on Christmas Eve 1968, the planet was spellbound by the most iconic image it had ever seen, the Earthrise photograph of itself, taken by the Apollo 8 mission orbiting the moon. Then, just a month before Woodstock, mankind took a giant leap onto the silvery orb itself, an achievement of huge historical, evolutionary and even cosmic importance.

What the hippie culture was really seeking was an expansion of consciousness, and many baby-boomers were happy to try natural ways to free the mind by diving into inner space. The stage was set for the arrival of mind-yoga, and the experts who could teach it arrived right on time, and in a variety of guises. While Swami Satchidananda taught a traditional and spiritual mix of *hatha yoga* and philosophy, Yogi Bhajan, a Sikh guru who had been a star athlete in his youth, taught his own energetic version of *kundalini yoga*, a method generally kept secret in Indian tradition. He created quite an initial stir with his message that kids could get high, legally and without noxious side-effects, and his 3HO (The Healthy, Happy and Holy Organization) had the added attraction of being considered dangerously esoteric by the Establishment. But behind the headlines, the conformist lifestyle of his movement, where everyone dressed in white costumes adapted from Sikhism, and espoused solid family values and drug-free living, did not attract huge numbers. Bhaktivedanta Swami, the Bengali Vaishnavaite who launched the International Krishna Consciousness movement in the West by arriving penniless in America and preaching in a square in New York's East Village, fell into a similar bracket. Chanting 'Hare Krishna' may have been communal fun, but Bhaktivedanta's system was heavily culture-bound, and as it demanded serious devotion to an Indian deity, the adoption of Indian names and dress, a vegetarian diet and—worst of all—a strictly celibate lifestyle, it proved far too restrictive for most. Other teachers who advocated the less cultic sitting practices of mind-yoga had a wider appeal. Swami Muktananda (shaktipat yoga), the boy Guru Maharaj-ji (Divine Light Mission) and the controversial Chogyam Trungpa Rinpoche (Tibetan 'Crazy Wisdom') were among those who stirred up widespread interest in the heady days of the late '60s and early '70s.[3]

But most successful of all was the man who had introduced meditation to the West ten years earlier, Maharishi Mahesh Yogi. His initial appeal had been to solid middle-class professionals, many of them in middle-age, and not a few followers of the Gurdjieff-Ouspensky system. But when the time came, the psychonaut kids took to him in droves. Indeed, there can be no more representative image of those innocent sunlit days than Paul Saltzman's shot showing the beaming faces of Maharishi and the Beatles, bedecked in flowers and beads, sitting as the centrepiece of a large group at the guru's ashram in Rishikesh. Whether by divine providence or a masterly stroke of PR—probably a mixture of both—the timing was perfect. Transcendental Meditation spread rapidly and the words guru and mantra entered the public vocabulary for good, even if they are still almost always misused.

While the Beatles were not set to continue into the '70s, the mass exploration of inner space they fronted had been successfully launched, and its trajectory would continue. To commemorate its fiftieth birthday in 2008, NASA beamed a song directly into deep space for the first time. It chose the Fab Four's 'Across the Universe', one of almost fifty numbers they had penned during their dreamlike days in the Rishikesh ashram forty years earlier. John Lennon's hypnotic refrain that floated out into the cosmos was the traditional Indian salutation to the spiritual teacher he had learned sitting by the banks of the Ganges: Jai Guru Deva, OM...

Yoga Means Union

Maharishi was very clear that yoga was not just a way to tone the body but a way to culture the mind for enlightenment. And the mind was cultivated not by entertaining lofty philosophical concepts but by going beyond thinking altogether. As Indic *gnosis* from the time of the *Upanishads* onwards had taught, on the far side of thought lies the settled state of awareness known as *samadhi* and it was this that constituted the goal of any genuine yoga practice. He made this clear in a typical early talk, saying meditation:

> brings fulfilment to every system, because in yoga—what is yoga? Union is yoga. When the mind gets united with Being, then it is the state of yoga. Where is the yoga in bending down or standing up or something? There is no yoga, there is no union, in the *asanas*. There is no union in the *pranayama*. If the tongue unites with the nose [*laughter*] it doesn't become yoga... Union is union of the individuality with the cosmic unboundedness. This is union, this is a significant union. There is no union in *asanas*, there is no union brought about in *pranayama* and no union in *pratyahara* or *dharana*. There is no union in *gyana* either. Union is in *samadhi*.[4]

In fact, from the mid-'60s onwards, Maharishi's teaching did include simple sets of *asanas* and a basic *pranayama* that he had had a local *hatha yogi* put together during a course in Rishikesh, but these routines served as much to break up long periods of deep meditation as to encourage a postural discipline to be pursued for its own sake. Almost nonchalantly, Maharishi turned on its head two hundred years of Western understanding based upon the Cartesian dictum, *Cogito ergo sum*—'I think, therefore I am'. 'Oh no!' laughed this new teacher, 'I am, therefore I think'. What was necessary then was to stop doing and stop thinking and simply start *being*. Our problem, according to him, is that we have put Descartes before the source.

A Focused Attention

The sacred texts reiterate that union with the source is bliss, and this was a quality Maharishi certainly exhibited; his lack of solemnity, however, did not indicate that he was not serious. In fact, he was to prove a formidable example of the yogic virtue of *ekagrata*—'one-pointedness of mind'—as he worked relentlessly for over fifty years in his mission to bring meditation to as many people as possible by whatever means necessary. In the early days, when asked why he had left India, he had innocently replied: 'I have come to fill the world with love'. In pursuit of this aim, he was to work twenty hours a day, conduct no less than thirteen world tours, initiate many thousands into meditation himself (including over 25,000 on one short trip to Nepal in 1974) and then teach 40,000 people worldwide to become themselves instructors in his system. His own life exemplified one of his favourite phrases from the *Bhagavad Gita*: 'Yoga is skill in action'.[5]

By his own account, Maharishi's worldwide mission was innocently set in motion when he visited the Great Goddess Temple at Kanyakumari on the southern tip of the subcontinent, just as Vivekananda's had been sixty years or more before. And, as his predecessor would doubtless have done had they been available, Maharishi made every use of modern convenience and technology to speed the spread of his message and ensure its preservation. Lear jets and helicopters, audio tapes and video technology, whatever saved time and energy, and increased efficiency, was utilised. When a devotee once asked him about communicating telepathically, his reply was, 'If I want to contact you, I'll use the phone.'

This was not the homespun, low-tech philosophy advocated by Mahatma Gandhi (of whom Maharishi was critical); this was a cogent remedy for the needs of the time. As he always explained, his work was just a timely revival of the ancient knowledge—taught in the *Vedas* and the *Gita*—that had become corrupted by time and hence lost its effectiveness. While orthodox teachers in India were not infrequently critical of 'the monk who went to the West' and taught meditation to whoever wished to learn, regardless of their motivation or spiritual qualifications, for his part Maharishi was often forthright in his criticisms of how the religious authorities in his country had misunderstood and perverted her ancestral wisdom. This was especially the case with the custodians of the Vedantic wisdom as expounded by its Adi Shankara, from whose lineage he himself came. Due to this misrepresentation, he argued, spirituality had become associated solely with the recluse way of life and its path of rigorous effort, thus depriving normal householders of nourishment. To counteract this misunderstanding, he was offering everyone the means to expand their consciousness.

Between them, then, these teachers catered to all tastes, offering systems of mind-yoga whose philosophical background varied from classical Advaita Vedanta to devotional Vaishnavism and baroque Tantric Buddhism. Boosted by the musical celebrities who came to them, they initially commanded huge numbers. But as time went by, and even the 'forever-young' generation began to age, it became increasingly apparent that the journey to the promised Self-realisation was, after all, a long, and sometimes even an arduous, affair. Inevitably, the popular influence of the meditation gurus began to

wane. Apart from the most dedicated followers, an ardent desire for enlightenment was never going to take root in conventional suburbia, although as
we shall see, something more immediate and tangible—such as relief from
stress—just might.

Postural Practice Goes Public

While mind-yoga was grabbing the headlines, bodywork was making slower
but steady progress on the inside pages. In America, a dedicated and holistic
yoga teacher called Richard Hittleman was quietly ploughing a very fertile
furrow. Born into a conservative Jewish family in the Bronx, Hittleman had
first learned yoga on a family holiday in the Borscht Belt of the Catskill
Mountains, going on to set up his own yoga school in Florida in 1957, then
launching his own television show, *Yoga for Health*, in Los Angeles almost ten
years before Woodstock. By the end of the '60s, it was being syndicated in
over forty TV stations across the US, with repeat after repeat, while in New
York it was screened for more than four-and-a-half years without a break. His
twenty books sold over 8 million copies; Americans, already keen on those
physical activity routines encouraged by the Kennedy administration, signed
up in droves to establish a new and healthy habit. For twenty years Hittleman
brought yoga to huge numbers of ordinary people and established yoga's
niche in contemporary culture.

What differentiated him from so many others in the growing bodywork
subculture was his spiritual interest. He had an abiding interest in Buddhism,
especially its Zen and Tibetan schools, and the influential writer Alan Watts
was among his friends. Most importantly, he claimed to have had personal
contact with the south Indian sage Ramana Maharshi, who he regarded as his
guru. Hittleman introduced his subject in an easy-to-follow fashion to new-
comers, starting with the most elementary postures, then more advanced
ones along with some philosophy. Unlike so many of his contemporaries who
limited yoga to bodywork, Hittleman was a teacher of total yoga in the classical mold of Patanjali, whom he frequently quoted. But whereas the goal of
the *Yoga Sutra* was the Sankhya realisation of *kaivalya*—the unwavering witness
of the ever-restless mind—Hittleman substituted Vedantic non-dualism. In
this, like Vivekananda and translators such as Swami Prabhavananda and
Christopher Isherwood, Hittleman followed the *Upanishads* and the *Bhagavad
Gita*, in teaching that, ultimately, everything is the divine Self (*atman*) and
that: '"Self" is another word for "God". This is the God who is the Absolute,
immutable, without qualities, pure Awareness, without beginning or end.'[6]

Such a lofty message, however inspiring, was probably too abstract for his audience. The quote above comes from his 1962 best-seller *Yoga for Health* and his most popular titles were always those that focused on the physical benefits of what he offered, with titles such as: *Be Young with Yoga* (1942), *The Yoga Way to Figure and Facial Beauty* (1968), *Weight Control Through Yoga* (1971) and *Yoga for Total Fitness* (1983). Rather unfairly, then, Hittleman is remembered as a teacher of body-yoga, but at least he was highly successful. Perhaps too much so, as he spent his last years battling with the IRS over $2 million of unpaid taxes.

Back in the UK, while Jane Fonda's US aerobic routines were selling well and alerting thousands of women to the benefits that deep breathing has on the cardiovascular system, body-yoga proper was making steady, if less spectacular, headway. Lynn Marshall, an actress who had assisted on Hittleman's *Yoga for Health* TV show when it was syndicated in Britain, went on to achieve her own success, promoting fitness yoga with shows and tapes such as *Wake Up to Yoga*. Quite devoid of any spiritual content or context, Marshall's presentations helped to nudge yoga into the market of female fitness. Before very long, every other female TV celebrity would be pushing out her own keep-fit/lose-weight body-yoga video.

The Wheel Starts Rolling

At the same time, what was to prove an enduring yoga culture was surfacing in Adult Education Centres, especially in Birmingham, which had become the preferred destination of immigrants from the Indian subcontinent and had already hosted the successful work of Yogini Sunita. A Sutton Coldfield journalist called Wilfred Clark, who had started yoga while in the army during the First World War, used his networking skills to contact numerous local papers throughout the country, asking for any individuals interested in yoga to write to him. Working with fellow yoga-enthusiast Margaret Ward, he gathered the replies together into regional groups under an umbrella organisation initially known as The Wheel of British Yoga.[7] This began to structure itself as a nationwide body; the first National Congress took place in Birmingham in 1967, and the first teacher training certificate class was run four years later.

Clark always saw yoga from a traditional perspective: as a holistic teaching that included postures, breathing, meditation exercises and spiritual philosophy as a graduated path to union with the Divine. In early Wheel publications he would talk about 'True Yoga', no doubt wary of both the gymnastic yoga then becoming current and, beyond that, the colonial-era image of yogis as anti-social transgressives. But over the years since Clark's wise stewardship,

215

the Wheel has gradually aligned itself ever more exclusively with physical praxis. This preference has been encouraged, or perhaps enforced, by conforming to UK government bureaucratic structures. Since 1995, the Wheel's authority as the national regulatory body for yoga in England has been granted by Sport England and The Sport and Recreation Alliance, which was formerly called the Central Council of Physical Recreation. This secularisation, also observable in the US experience, has gained yoga respectability and an ever-wider acceptance, spawning a billion-dollar industry worldwide. We have come a long way from the colourful parade of pioneers who, in their various ways, first brought yoga to the West. Swami Satchitananda chanting Sanskrit *mantras* with those hirsute Woodstock rebels seems a very long time ago; in fact, it was before most of today's practitioners were born. So, what have been the costs and benefits, the gains and losses involved in yoga's gradual transition into its present near-ubiquity? This is one of the topics we shall examine in the second half of this book.

PART TWO

TODAY

PHYSICAL LIMITS

20

FAKIRS AND FAKERS

Ever since classical times, India has been known as the land of the miraculous and still today reports keep coming in of those popularly known as 'godmen', who possess a blend of divinity and stardom that infers an ability to play fast and loose with the laws of time and space. One such power is an extraordinary depth of meditation, a holy hibernation that puts the body into a deep state of physical and psychic suspension. That such 'living-deaths' are still alive in the popular imagination is borne out by the strange case of His Holiness Shri Ashutosh Maharaj, founder of the wealthy Divya Jyoti religious order in the Punjab. In January 2014, this particular godman died. Or did he? His followers claimed that although the hospital tests showed him to be clinically dead, the flatline was a false reading; in fact, he was really in deepest *samadhi* and would return to the surface only as and when it was appropriate. All attempts to cremate him were blocked as his disciples, spurning fire in favour of ice, placed the body in a commercial freezer until such time as its owner decided to wake up. Just how Ashutosh, who had apparently spent many years meditating in sub-zero temperatures in the Himalayas, would indicate his desire to resurrect from the frozen cabinet was not made clear.

The Punjab police initially confirmed the death, but the state's High Court later dismissed their findings, opining that this was definitely a spiritual matter and that the guru's followers had every right to believe he had temporarily transcended mortality, to return when he deemed fit. The godman's immediate family, however, was not convinced. Suspecting that the disciples were only interested in retaining control over the master's $100 million property empire, freezing their assets as it were, his wife and son demanded the body be released, and the law directed the Punjab government to cremate the body. Several hundred defiant supporters blockaded the ashram in protest; scuffles and a legal appeal followed. Then, almost three years later, the court finally allowed the godman's followers to keep his body in a freezer, although it wisely withheld an opinion on whether he was still alive. And there, for the moment, it remains...

Though Ashutosh got his fair share of headlines, the godman most persistently occupying the front pages in recent years was one Pilot Baba. His story began one day during the 1962 border war with China, when Wing Commander Kapil Singh, as he then was, underwent a spiritual conversion at 20,000 feet. High above the snowy peaks of the sacred Himalayas his aircraft had lost control, contact with the base vanished, and the immediate future looked grim. Suddenly, a meditating figure appeared cruising serenely alongside the plane. It was no less than Goraknath, a famous fifteenth-century guru of the Nath sect of *hatha yogis* we met in Chapter 5. The sage entered the cockpit and promptly guided the plane safely to land. Ten years after this startling aerial intervention, Singh retired from armed service and took up the religious life, reasonably enough taking the name Pilot Baba. He soon established several ashrams in India and Japan. At one time he had the ear of many important politicians and even worked with prime minister Indira Gandhi and her son Sanjay on various rather vague projects for world peace.

As time passed, the Baba began to claim he could control the elements— divert a river, walk on water, dissipate threatening storm clouds, that sort of thing. But his specialisation was to stage spectacular public demonstrations of yogic endurance which allowed him to shut down all bodily functions to the point of clinical death, only to return at a pre-specified time. He would bury himself underground encased in an airtight glass box or submerge himself under water for days, or even weeks, on end. The result of these antics was public awe and monetary donations in about equal measure, but they soon invited controversy. In 1980, the Baba sponsored one of his disciples to be buried underground for ten days in his stead. Hundreds of thousands of rupees were collected from devotees and admirers, and the man was duly lowered into a small pit. When it was opened ten days later, a foul stench announced the bad news. Calculations soon showed that without fresh air being somehow smuggled into the pit, the longest he could have survived there was a mere twenty-four hours. In the middle of the scandal, Pilot Baba dematerialised; so did the cash.

Reappearing in 1992, he was soon on stage again. A huge swimming pool in a Delhi public park was dug, and in front of a crowd of 5,000 paid-up devotees, the Baba clambered down into it, ordered water to be pumped in and disappeared under the flow. When he reappeared after five days however, sceptical investigators discovered the tarpaulin-covered pit contained a concealed cubicle that had enabled the sub-aquatic yogi to enjoy a relatively comfortable five-day sojourn, insulated on dry ground. The same trick was exposed again four years later in a five-day earth-burial. Baba's final performance was less glamorous, when, as one of a number of godmen busted by a well-organised TV sting operation, he was caught on camera volunteering to turn 'black' money into 'white'. The holy man's offer of transubstantiation was not based on magical power, however, just the sluicing of £1,200,000 through his ashram accounts in return for a 30 per cent commission. Exposed, he hastily retired to set up an ashram in the Himalayan foothills that is today much patronised by Russians. As money-laundering scandals are two-a-penny in the new India, the Baba's case is presently just one of many patiently waiting their turn in the bulging in-trays currently blocking up the arteries of the country's sclerotic legal system. No doubt he is hoping it will remain buried far deeper, and for far longer, than he himself ever managed.

Yogic scams and credulous victims are not, of course, confined to India. A notable recent example in the West is a US-based New Age movement called the Breatharians, whose members claim that by practising a special type of *pranayama* they can live off nothing but fresh air and sunlight. Sadly, for those hoping to reduce both waistlines and food bills, the sect's high priestess, an Australian woman who calls herself Jasmuheen, was rather caught out when a crew filming an interview in her apartment discovered a stash of chocolate digestive biscuits hiding in the fridge. Seeking to rescue her reputation, the self-styled 'Ambassador of Peace' accepted an invitation from the television programme *60 Minutes* to go without food and water for ten days under medical supervision. Despite her claims, Jasmuheen lasted only forty-eight hours before the studio doctor noted that she was displaying all the predictable symptoms of dehydration, stress and high blood pressure. The stunt was finally abandoned after four days as her health continued to deteriorate. Astonishingly, such public humiliation does not seem to have derailed the promotion of her Self-Empowerment Academy, nor collapsed the credulousness her followers. By 2012, Jasmuheen's Breatharian teachings had been linked to the death of five of them, though she consistently refuses to accept any responsibility.

In the light of such fiascos, it would be easy to dismiss any reports of extraordinary yogic feats as either self-delusion or wilful deception, and of course, most people do, usually citing science as the main witness for the prosecution. But in fact, there is also credible evidence that the normal limitations of the body can be spectacularly transcended, and it can come from some reputable sources. At the furthest extreme of the self-healing spectrum, there was news in 2014 of a Tibetan *lama* who appears to have used nothing but meditation to cure himself of gangrene. Lama Phakyab Rinpoche migrated to America as a thirty-seven-year-old refugee from Tibet, where he had been imprisoned and brutalised by the Chinese. As a result, he suffered from diabetes and a circulatory deterioration so bad that his right foot and leg had already developed the condition. He was examined by three different US doctors who all shared one opinion: amputation. But the monk's mentor, the Dalai Lama, asked Rinpoche to forego an operation and instead utilise his *Tsa Lung* meditation skills. Practitioners of this particular technique visualise a 'wind', a kind of subtle life energy that is one with the mind, moving down the central energy-channel in their spine, flushing out blockages and impurities before moving on to clear and vitalise ever smaller energy-channels throughout the body. In other words, it uses a Tibetan version of the physiological model well-known to *hatha yoga*: directing *prana* through the *nadis* of the subtle body. So, armed only with special *mantras* given to him by the Dalai Lama, Rinpoche took no medicine, but meditated all day every day, breaking only for meals.

In the early weeks of this regime, the putrid discharge from his leg ran black; a few months later it turned cloudy and bruising started to appear. The swelling increased and became more painful. The odour was sickening, he recalls, but he stoically continued and after nine months, the liquid leaking from his disabled limb began to run clear. The swelling went down. Soon he could put some weight on the leg, and a month later, he could walk again with crutches. A short time later he was down to one crutch, and then, before even a further year had passed, he was walking on his own. The tissue decomposition hadn't simply been halted—his leg was back to full health, as new. And the diabetes was gone as well.

A group of doctors at New York University began studying Rinpoche's brain. Team leader Dr William Bushell, an MIT affiliate and the director of East-West Research for Tibet House in New York, said:

> This is a cognitive-behavioural practice that present East-West science suggests may be more effective that any existing strictly Western medical intervention. It is not entirely clear from a Western perspective what the 'winds' are, but the scientific evidence suggests to me and others that the meditative process of directing imagery to both superficial and deep tissue sites in the body precipitates increased local blood flow, metabolic activity, and oxygenation.

And so?

> Such increases could in principle combat even powerful bacteria such as *staphylococcus aureus*, which not only can be the cause of gangrene but is now often resistant to antibiotics.

Bushell's colleague in the study, one Dr Josipovic added:

What has become evident is that a great variety of meditation techniques and the states of consciousness they engender, pose a considerable challenge for understanding them in terms of the established constructs of Western science.[1]

In other words, it sounds like time for a paradigm change.

The Mysterious Mataji

In Gujarat, there is an eighty-two-year-old *sadhu* called Prahlad Jani, who is apparently able to live happily without food or water. Perhaps not surprisingly, he has no need to answer nature's calls, either. Let's start with the bio-data. According to his own account, Jani left his home in Rajasthan at the tender age of seven and went off to live in the jungle. This renunciation alone was extraordinary, although in India such youthful asceticism is not as unusual a career choice as it might sound to Western ears. When he was eleven, the boy underwent a profound religious experience that turned him into a devotee of a Hindu Mother Goddess called Ambaji. Since then, he has chosen to dress as one of her female devotees, wearing a red *lungi*, jewellery and crimson flowers in his shoulder-length hair. He is commonly known as Mataji—the shorthand name of The Great Mother. According to his own explanation, his devotion to the Goddess is rewarded by her granting him all the nourishment he needs through a liquid that drips down from a hole in his palate. Such supernormal sustenance is known in *hatha yoga* literature as *soma*, or the divine nectar; it can be caused to flow by the *khechari mudra*, a technique of placing the tongue into the nasal cavity.[2] Mataji explains all this matter-of-factly: 'I get the elixir of life from the hole in my palate, which enables me to go without food and water.' He also claims he did not speak for a period of forty-five years and has never experienced any medical problems. Since the 1970s, the abstemious hermit has been living in a cave deep in the rainforest near to Ambaji's main temple in Gujarat, waking at 4 a.m. each day and spending most of his time in meditation. According to witnesses, he frequently enjoys an ecstatic state of *samadhi* far beyond body-consciousness.

As time went by, word got around about Mataji, and he eventually came to the attention of a neuro-physician called Sudir Shah who worked in nearby Ahmedabad, the state capital. In November 2003, after over a year of coaxing, the recluse was finally persuaded to participate in a scientific research study at Shah's hospital, in which a team of twenty-one specialists would observe him over ten days. The yogi was closeted in a sealed room and given only 100 ml of water to use as mouthwash each day. The doctors conducted a battery of tests, noted that he passed no urine or stools during the whole time and reported that he was physically quite normal, except for a small hole in the palate. The tests raised more questions than they answered, but everyone concerned agreed on one thing: whatever else he might turn out to be, Mataji was not some publicity seeker hoping to fake his way to fame and fortune. Initially resistant to being examined, he remained rather bemused throughout the whole procedure, but remained benignly disposed to what was going on around him.

Further and more rigorous tests were carried out in 2010, again by Dr Shah and his team, but this time under the auspices of the government's Defence Institute of Physiology and Allied Science (DIPAS). Mataji was incarcerated in a specially prepared room with a sealed-off lavatory, glass door and continuous video surveillance. Staff members were assigned to stay in the room with him around the clock. He was allowed out of the room every so often, both for tests that needed special equipment—such as MRI, ultrasound and x-ray procedures—and also to have his daily dose of exposure to the sun. All these excursions were filmed. To guard against any possible intake of water, no baths were allowed, but he was again permitted a small measured quantity of water to use as a mouthwash, the liquid being spat back into a beaker and measured to verify that none of it had been swallowed. Among the daily clinical examinations were tests on hormone levels. The doctors were interested in two in particular: ghrelin, which stokes a person's hunger, and leptin, which signals their satiety. Ultrasound techniques showed that a fluctuating amount of urine did in fact accumulate in the subject's bladder but was spontaneously reabsorbed into his system. At the end of fifteen days during which he did not eat, drink or go to the lavatory, not only was his condition quite normal but the research team described him as being in better overall health than someone half his age.

All this was posted on the website of the Defence Research and Development Organisation (DRDO), the agency that sponsored the tests.[3] They conclude that 'Jani enjoys some extreme form of adaptation to starvation and water restriction', though 'enjoy' is perhaps not the word that such deprivation brings to mind. This being the Defence Institute, their interests are solidly pragmatic rather than yogic. As Dr Shah explains on the website:

> Our aim is to determine the metabolic pathways and genetic modifications which allow a person to survive in extreme conditions where food resources are limited. This could tremendously benefit mankind in general, as well as

soldiers, victims of calamities and astronauts, all of whom may have to survive without food or water for long spells.

Predictably enough, the religious devotee turned scientific guinea pig has gathered both followers and detractors. American medics were first into the fray, accusing Shah of not publishing his results in any scientific journal, and of seeming generally unwilling to release specific details to the sceptical world at large. A doctor from Harvard dismissed the observation results as 'impossible', because profoundly malnourished people quickly consume their own body's resources, a process that results in liver failure and heart problems. A spokesman for the American Dietetic Association added that the human body could perhaps survive for 'up to fifteen to twenty days', but only if it drank water, and anyway no one could expect to meet their body's vitamin and mineral requirements without eating. Critics also queried the short length of the experiment, especially as Jani also makes the astonishing claim not to have eaten or drunk substantially since the end of World War II. Nonetheless, good science advances by abandoning even cherished paradigms if they no longer fit the observed facts. Even so, the lack of any published articles subjected to peer review is certainly a major weakness in Shah's case. At the least, it seems to be a sadly wasted opportunity to further our understanding of the limits of human endurance, let alone the chance to shed light on some not uncommon yogic claims.

Mataji Jani is not even Dr Shah's most remarkable subject. In 2000, also in his Ahmedabad clinic, he investigated a pious sixty-four-year-old follower of Jainism called Hira Ratan Manek who was undertaking a fast which lasted no less than 411 days, i.e. almost fourteen months. During this time Manek followed a purification regime practised in his religion, taking only boiled water between 11 a.m. to 4 p.m. each day and no other food or liquids whatsoever. He also underwent some emotional deprivation, being forbidden the customary Indian support of having a friend or relative stay with him in hospital. Again, teams of observers were present throughout and exhaustive tests—including ECGs, ultra-sound, EEG, CT and MRI scans—were taken. At the end of the fast, all of them showed that his physical systems and cognitive abilities were perfectly normal. Manek had lost some weight, about 19 kg in the first three months, but this process then stabilised. When the fast terminated, the only changes found were slight reductions in both pulse rate and blood pressure.

Dramatically, there was more to come. On the 401st day of the marathon, Manek left his hospital room to undertake the famous pilgrimage to the holy citadel of Shatrunjaya, one of Jainism's most sacred sites. This cluster of white marble temples sits perched on the summit of the sacred mountain Palitana, and the pilgrimage route is an arduous climb taking about three hours, usually before sunrise to avoid the blazing heat. So steep is the ascent, that not a few of the plumpier pilgrims are carried up in palanquins. Mr Manek scorned any such contrivance. Unaided, he took only ninety minutes to reach the top, leaving many of the five hundred supporters who accompanied him literally gasping in his wake. Again, an unfortunate lack of rigorous scientific procedure undermined the credibility of this extraordinary case.

Indian Rationalists

For some critics, the mere fact that both Mataji and Manek performed their feats within a religious context was enough to discredit them. Predictably, the loudest complaint came from Sanal Edamaruku, the president of the Indian Rationalist Association. Formed in 1949 with the encouragement of the British philosopher Bertrand Russell, this body is dedicated to the eradication of religious superstition and exploitation throughout the subcontinent. Edamaruku and his 100,000-odd members believe that the gullibility of the poor and uneducated is the greatest single obstacle to India taking her rightful place on the world stage in the unfolding century. His targets are not only well-known godmen like Pilot Baba and Ashutosh, but also the tantric *fakirs* who travel around the country claiming to be able to heal pious but ignorant villagers. Such folk are normally in need of medical treatment that is relatively straightforward, but not infrequently their gullibility costs them their lives.

Edamaruku has criticised various aspects of Dr Shah's *modus operandi*, including the fact that during his spell under observation, Mataji was allowed to gargle and sunbathe. He also claims that he himself was excluded from visiting the Ahmedabad tests by the yogi's 'influential protectors'. His association adds that individuals making similar claims in the past have been exposed as frauds, which may well be true, but is surely irrelevant to these particular cases. Happily, scientists with no axe to grind are now coming forward from several countries to join in further tests on the flower-wearing godman, so we may yet learn more of the truth.

India being India, it turns out that Edamaruku, a jovial and portly Keralite from Calicut, is something of a circus turn himself. In pursuit of his relentless exposure of trickery, he likes to dress up his accomplices as fake godmen and then film them duping villagers before orchestrating a dramatic denouement. In March 2008, he appeared on a primetime show on Indian TV, in which he challenged a so-called tantric *fakir* to demonstrate his powers by casting a spell that would kill him. The station's ratings soared as the *fakir*, Pandit Surendra Sharma, chanted his lethal *mantra*: *Om lingalingalingalinga kilikiliki* while waving his hands around unconvincingly; to the disinterested observer the whole pantomime smacked of a set-up, and a pretty crude one at that. Four years later, Edamaruku was in the news again when he claimed that a weeping statue of Jesus in a Catholic church in Mumbai owed its tears not to divine intervention but a leaking drainpipe. The church authorities filed law-suits against him for 'hurting the religious sentiments of a particular com-munity', which is an offence under Indian law. The latest reports are that to escape these charges he has relocated to Finland, from where he plans to undertake a tour of Europe campaigning for free speech.

Many Indians today must find themselves in a curious position with all this. Heirs of a culture long-nourished on the belief in psychic powers and alterna-tive realities, they are now part of the brave new world of solid scientific materialism and its inherent scepticism. Caught between Edamaruku's Rationalist Association which believes in nothing, and assorted religious groups prepared to believe in just about anything, the average twenty-first-century Indian must feel himself to be not unlike one of those subjects in Dr Shah's laboratory experiments—suspended between two stools and with the eyes of the world expectantly upon him.

21

SOME LIKE IT HOT

One reason that yoga is so cool these days is that it can chill you out. This is quite in conformity with a key tenet of classical practice called *sheetali:* the idea of 'cooling' or 'soothing'. In *sheetali pranayama*, for example, the inhaled breath is moistened by being passed through a curled tongue that the texts liken to a bird's beak or an unfolding leaf. This water-saturated air is said to calm hunger and thirst, reduce fatigue and high blood pressure, and facilitate an appreciation of solitude. According to Ayurveda, the technique works to correct the bodily excess of the *pitta dosha* that leads to impatience and carelessness, and cultivates calmness and a freedom from emotional reactivity.

The Sanskrit for this desirable state of yogic non-attachment is *vairagya*, a word which derives from *vi*, a suffix which implies 'separation from', and *raga* which literally means 'colour' or 'hue', and is used particularly to denote the colour red. From this come the ideas of 'passion' or 'inflammation'. Red, a highly-vibrating colour, is rich in symbolic associations. In Indian art and poetry it often conveys the idea of heat, ardour and passion, ripe fruit and ready lips, while in religious iconography, red is primarily the colour of the Goddess, which alludes not only to traditions of blood-sacrifice, some of which are still practised, but also the maternal earth element and thence the worldly power of material well-being. In contrast, yogic *vairagya* is 'separation-from-red'—Shiva's white to *shakti*'s scarlet—signifying freedom from the engorged attachment to life and desire that colours the mind and obscures the clarity that is our true nature.[1]

In his serene non-attachment, then, the yogi is the living microcosm of the cosmic separation of *purusha* and *prakriti* that, as we saw in Chapter 3, is the true state of things.[2] Rightly understood, however, this dispassion is not a lack of empathy or an uncaring detachment, but a wide-open awareness, an impartial and expansive context in which the movements of the world and the swings of the mind naturally rise and fall. According to Patanjali, non-attachment is not merely one desirable virtue amongst others; it is the essential condition of any practice that leads to real insight or wisdom.[3] Lord Krishna concurs when he speaks of *vairagya* as the key means for bringing control to the restless mind.[4] The idea of coolness is also implicit in other terms, such as the Sanskrit *nirvana* and its Pali equivalent *nibbana*—literally 'the extinguishing of a flame'—that are frequently used in pan-Indian yogic texts to describe the state of enlightenment.

Hot Yoga

In today's febrile yoga scene however, some evidently like it hot, and none more so than those who practise the Hot Yoga invented by Bikram Choudhury. Choudhury began his study of yoga when he was only four, under Bishnu Ghosh, the younger brother of Paramahansa Yogananda, but his first love was gymnastics. He won many athletic competitions in his teens, but when he was seventeen, injured his knee weightlifting and was told by doctors he would never walk again. He turned to yoga as a remedial regime and, by all accounts, after six months of strenuous practice he was as good as new. Like B. K. S. Iyengar, he was inspired to extrapolate his own healing journey into a solidly physical model of praxis, which he took to the United States in the 1970s. His brand, however, had one crucial USP: a gym-like environment, stoked up to excessive heat—typically around 40°C (104°F)—which, so he claimed, emulated the climate of India. Thus was Bikram Hot Yoga born. It comprised a signature ninety-minute sequence of twenty-six poses along with a couple of breathing exercises, a rigorous routine he claimed was more authentic than the faux-spiritual forms of the ancient science that were currently offering a hippie message of peace and love. Bikram opened studios in both California and Hawaii and was soon to roll out his system worldwide.

The Hot Yoga basement studio in Beverley Hills rapidly attracted a celebrity clientele, including Michael Jackson and actors such as Jeff Bridges, Shirley MacLaine, Barbra Streisand and Jamie Lee Curtis. In a social milieu of sycophancy and flattery, Bikram's treatment of Hollywood's aristocracy was uncharacteristically abrasive. Interviewed by a tabloid magazine in 1977, for example, four years after he had arrived in Los Angeles, he pulled no punches about Raquel Welch, who ten years earlier had drawn admiring gasps as, clad in a fur bikini, she lithely dodged sabre-tooth tigers in the the blockbuster movie *One Million Years BC*. In the yoga guru's eyes, however, things had gone seriously south since then. Nowadays, he announced: 'She has a terrible body. She has cottage cheese muscles, fat legs and a stiff body.'

But rather like the restaurateur who guarantees an adoring clientele because of his rudeness, Choudhury drew many of the glitterati: George Clooney, Lady Gaga, Gwyneth Paltrow and Jennifer Aniston among them. Sports stars enjoyed Hot Yoga too; tennis ace Andy Murray relished it as 'tough and ugly', while Serena Williams and David Beckham were also fans. Choudhury's personal flamboyance assured him high visibility. Radiating muscular health and always a snappy dresser who favoured crocodile-skin shoes, gangster fedoras, black Speedos and jewel-encrusted watches, he liked to cruise around in a Royal Daimler (just one of his fleet of forty-three luxury cars) that was once owned by the millionaire Howard Hughes and had a toilet in the back. His other eccentricities included loathing the colour green and banning people from wearing it, and insisting that all his steamy studios be carpeted, hygiene be damned, because, it was said, never having seen a carpet until he arrived in America, he believed it to signify the height of luxury. Soggy floors or not, the business thrived. At its peak around 2010, Choudhury's pony-tailed, waxed-chest image adorned the walls of around 650 licensed Bikram Yoga studios across the world. For many, despite his lack of social graces, he was a life-style mentor as well as the inventor of an exercise class. Hobnobbing with the stars had done him no harm at all. In fact, the eager immigrant from Calcutta had become one of them: 'I'm Bikram, a gangster like Cagney, like DeNiro, like James Caan, like my most favorite, Mr James Caan, Sonny, Sonny, Sonny Boy...'[5]

This trademark *chutzpah* presaged a spectacular fall. Choudhury's success as a global brand really took off from the 1990s, when the money started to roll in from the twice-yearly teacher training sessions, where up to 400 students would pay well over $15,000 to undergo nine weeks of intensive practice to become certified Bikram instructors. The courses centred on two mass Hot Yoga sessions a day, interspersed with anatomy seminars and lectures that included some New Age psychology, and backed up by rote learning of forty-five pages of copyrighted Bikram dialogue. According to several accounts, they could be very tough. The combination of heat and vigorous activity not infrequently caused people to vomit, break down and pass out, or lose bladder control in a room full of their fellow students. The master liked to conduct the evening class from a throne, typically with one female attendant brushing his hair and another massaging his legs. He openly encouraged an attitude of devotion, regularly likening himself to Jesus Christ and Buddha. He was in no doubt as to the superiority of what he was offering, often describing his system as the 'one true yoga', the ancient science, compared to which all the numerous other yoga modalities are simply 'shit'. Most nights, viewing of Hindi Bollywood movies was mandatory, with Bikram giving a running commentary in English and sessions often going on to 3 a.m. A typical course would draw participants, mostly young and female, from over thirty countries and altogether they earned Choudhury a personal fortune estimated at $75 million. They also served to disseminate some 11,000 certified instructors to run Bikram Hot Yoga studios all over the globe, from Alaska to Alabama, Buenos Aires to Bangkok.

Success breeds imitation, and Hot Yoga has already spawned variations popular in the worlds of athletics and fitness training. One type—Hotpod Yoga—was recently added to the training regime of the Harlequins, one of the UK's foremost rugby clubs. Trainers there say it helps to bring the body back into balance from the fight-or-flight alertness that is the default setting in high-contact sports. The heat allows tight muscles to lengthen and relax and the increased blood flow helps to clear away stress chemicals such as lactic acid, a by-product of excessive exercise. Lower-limb injuries in knee and ankle ligaments, as well as hamstring pulls and tears, also benefit from the increased flexibility brought about by the application of heat.

An added attraction in the marketplace is that despite the physical pain a Hot Yoga session can bring, the system can really burn off the pounds—'no pain, no loss' so to say. This seems logical, but recent studies by academics from Texas State University under the leadership of Dr Stacey Hunter, quoted in the journal *Experimental Physiology*, have found that performing Choudhury's set of *asanas* at 40 degrees does not actually yield healthier outcomes than when the poses are performed in normal conditions with no added heat. Turning up the temperature may sound a harmless option, but a conversation with Professor Susan Yeargin, who conducts heatstroke research at Indiana State University, is hardly likely to send one rushing to sign up for a Hot Yoga course. She says: 'When I study heat stroke I put people into a room that is 104° F to purposely stress their bodies. That type of situation can be devastating if the core body temperature rises to a dangerous level, leading to rapid deterioration of organs, coma, even death.'[6]

Hot Yoga presents just one example of how a new offshoot of ancient knowledge can jettison subtle holistic understanding on the way. Many yoga schools advocate early-morning sessions, in part because at that relatively cool time, the body is naturally regulated as to what it can easily perform in the way of stretching and flexing. In addition, traditional body-yoga was practised with a one-to-one focus and in the context of Ayurvedic knowledge concerning the different body-types, each with their different needs and varying strengths and weaknesses. While a rigorous regime in heated conditions might be good for some *kapha* (water element) constitutions, helping to burn off their sluggish inertia and free up energy, it could be less than helpful for the heated *pitta* (fire element) types who already tend to over-excitation and irascibility. And guess what? Most typical Westerners already have an excessive amount of *pitta* in their physiology, so the last thing they need is something that exacerbates it.

On a psychological level, critics point out that the mirrored walls of a typical downtown Hot Yoga studio can easily distract students from having any inner focus in their practice and may turn a yoga session into a gathering of competitive individuals narcissistically striving to outdo each other. Hot Yoga advertises itself as offering 'the most exciting, hard-working and effective yoga classes in the world'. The adjectives 'exciting' and 'hard-working' betray a gymnastic approach shared by other schools that employ fast and vigorous *asana* sequences, such as an extended routine of 'salutation to the sun' (*surya namaskar*) or the various flow-based sequences inspired by Vinyasa Yoga. These have no precedent in the classical Indian corpus of *asanas*, though as we have seen in Chapter 9, wrestlers and bodybuilders in the traditional *akhara* gymnasia may have employed some similar exercises. In fact, today's dynamic sequences are just orientalised exercise programmes, calisthenic routines posing as yoga, and all too often shoe-horned into the cult of 'looking good'. Moving rapidly from one posture to another without any sense of physical anchoring, or dwelling in the posture, let alone enjoying some interiority, is in danger of feeding into the dominant neurosis of constant and unreflective activity, slavishly undertaken to get on to the next thing as soon as possible.

Those who had reservations about Choudhury's methods may have been annoyed by his ostentation but they were considerably more upset in 2011 when he began launching a series of aggressive lawsuits to copyright his poses. He won a case against Raquel Welch, she of the 'cottage cheese muscles', for stealing his sequence for her exercise book *The Raquel Welch Total Beauty and Fitness Program*, enabling him to buy a mansion in Beverly Hills. But the law was not always on his side. Attempts to monopolise his choice of *asanas* were thrown out by a California federal judge in 2012, who ruled that yoga poses cannot be copyrighted. There were other indications that fame and fortune were taking their toll, as his eccentricity began to implode. Benjamin Lorr, whose personal experience of Hot Yoga sparked his exploration of the bizarre world of competitive body-yoga, attended a training course in Las Vegas in 2009 and found himself drawn to Choudhury, despite describing him as 'clearly a buffoon'. By the third evening, Choudhury had told the class that not only had he launched Michael Jackson's career, cured Janet Reno's

Parkinson's disease and Richard Nixon's persistent phlebitis, but he had also been best friends with Elvis. To top it all, he had experienced 'seventy-two hours of marathon sex, where my partner had forty-nine orgasms. I count.'[7] His frenetic self-promotion appeared to know no bounds.

By now, something was clearly going wrong. Choudhury's lessons were punctuated by long conversations into his mobile phone while vindictive personal criticisms of his students became a daily occurrence. An investigative journalist for GQ magazine went to a class only to hear him ranting at students: 'You, Miss Teeny-Weeny Bikini! Spread your legs! You, Mr Masturbation! Until I say "Change," you do not move a muscle!' But his pupils still seemed to love it all; held in thrall by his charisma and self-confidence they shrugged off any weirdness with, 'Oh, that's just Bikram!' The typical attendees at his classes, often numbering more than a hundred, were, according to the GQ article: 'aged twenty-two to thirty-five and presented a lot of really beautiful bodies, all dressed in tight shorts and bikinis. They seemed highly impressionable.'[8]

The beginning of the end came in January 2014 with an article in Vanity Fair that publicised a series of damning claims against him.[9] These included rape, sexual harassment and false imprisonment, as well as general bullying and grossly discriminatory behaviour against gay people, women and racial minorities. The world of American yoga was rocked to the core, and the man his critics had long dubbed 'the Master of McYoga' fell dramatically to earth. There are now six separate lawsuits working their way through the California courts and plaintiffs are queuing up to describe a cult-like atmosphere where members of the teacher's inner circle lived in fear of his blazing temper and consequent banishment from the 'Bikram Family'.

The main complainant is an Indian woman called Minakshi Jafa-Bodden who worked for Bikram for two years as his legal advisor. According to her testimony, as soon as she began the job she realised that Choudhury had a tendency not to settle the hotels bills for his training courses; her first task was to fight Marriott Hotels over an unpaid sum of $1.8m. Choudhury also liked to use the company account as a personal credit card. As did everyone else in the guru's inner circle, she put these oversights, along with his lavish Bollywood lifestyle, down to his eccentricity. But not far down the line, Jafa-Bodden would be summoning seventy witnesses to present a series of strong accusations. On her own behalf, she claimed that not only had she never received her promised salary, but in the course of working for the master, she had lost all sense of independent agency, becoming reliant on him for her work visa, her apartment and her car. Even her mobile phone was connected to his and her every move was monitored. In early 2016 a Los Angeles jury

1. Forest yogis, sandstone panel from Sanchi, first century BC.

2. Yogi with disciples and attendants; Lakshmana Temple, Khajuraho, tenth century.

3. Yoga pose from Achyutaraya temple, Hampi, fifteenth century.

4. Indians performing yoga *asanas* under a Banyan tree in Seurat, 1688.

5. Shiva in eight yogic postures, with his trident, late eighteenth century.

6. A prince and attendants visiting a noble *yogini* at an ashram, India, c. 1765.

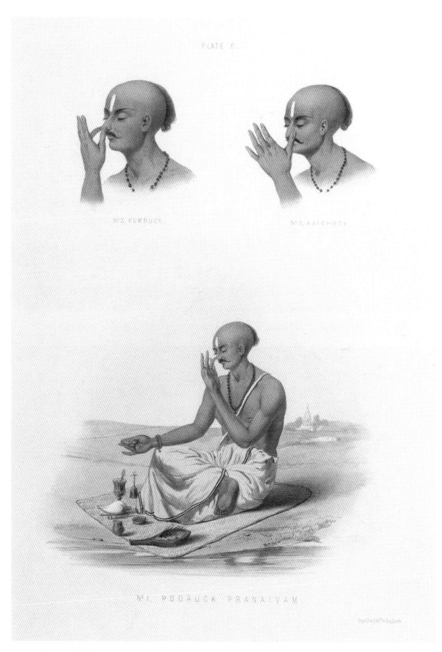

7. Lithograph showing three types of *pranayama*: *puraka*, *kumbhaka* and *rechaka*, 1851.

8. Lord Krishna instructs the warrior Arjuna in the *Bhagavad Gita*, c. 1820.

9. Five *brahmin* priests, five kings and a deity, participate in a *yajna* fire offering to win
   the blessings of the gods.

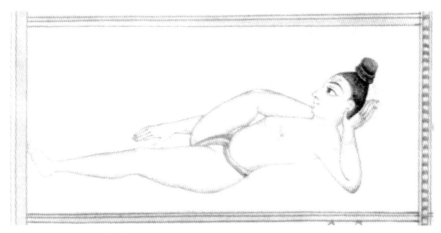

10. An illustration of the *ankushasana*, the 'elephant goad' pose (now usually known as the *bhairavasana*, 'formidable' pose), from the mid-nineteenth-century *Shritattvanidhi*.

11. Raja Ram Mohan Roy, founder of the Brahmo Samaj and leading light of the Hindu Renaissance, in 1868.

12. Swami Vivekananda in September 1893. On the left, written in his own handwriting: 'One infinite pure and holy—beyond thought beyond qualities, I bow down to thee.'

13. The yogi Vishvamitra, one of the most venerated seers of ancient India, being tempted out of his meditation by the nymph Menaka. Late nineteenth-century oleograph.

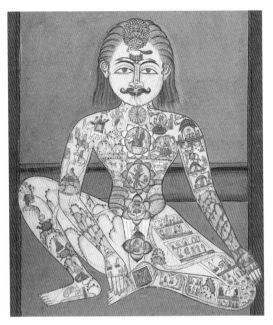

14. Subtle body illustrated in a vernacular yoga text, 1899.

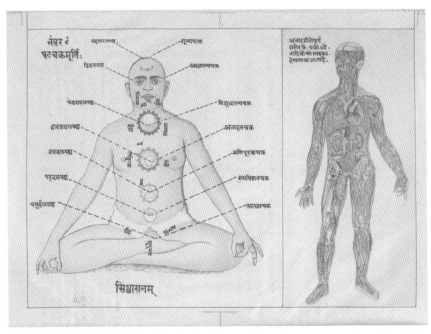

15. Text by Swami Hamsvarupa comparing yogic and Western medical models of the physiology, 1900s.

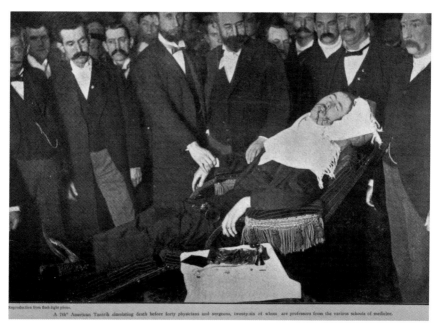

Reproduction from flash-light photo.
A 7th* American Tantrik simulating death before forty physicians and surgeons, twenty-six of whom are professors from the various schools of medicine.

16. Professor Pierre Arnold Bernard demonstrating the Kali Mudra death trance in front of a medical audience, San Francisco, 1898.

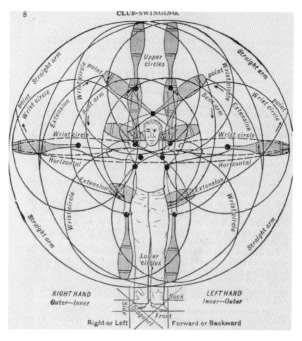

17. Indian club manual's mandala-like illustration, 1901.

18. A *fakir* relaxing on his bed of nails in Varanasi, 1907.

19. A wrestler, possibly Gamma the Great, performing the *dand* push-up.

20. Swami Yogananda teaching yoga at Mt Washington, 1950.

21. Bonnie Prudden, American physical fitness guru, leading a class at her White Plains school, 1956.

22. Swami Satchidananda opens the Woodstock Festival, 15 August 1969.

23. Yogic strongman Sri Chinmoy in the 1970s with Muhammad Ali, three-times heavy-weight champion of the world.

24. and 25. A modern *yogini*.

26. B. K. S. Iyengar, aged ninety-five, receiving the Padma Vibhushan, India's second highest civilian award, in 2014.

27. Prime Minister Narendra Modi wears the Indian flag to lead the first International Yoga Day in New Delhi, 21 June 2015.

awarded Jafa-Bodden nearly $6.8 million in punitive damages, in addition to $924,000 in compensatory damages, after finding she had been subjected to sexual harassment, non-payment of wages, wrongful dismissal and a number of further charges.[10]

In May 2016, the rock star yogi fled to India, where he opened yoga studios in Mumbai and the fashionable health resort of Lonavala, near Pune. Undaunted, he continues to run training camps outside the US; the latest went ahead in Acapulco in the autumn of 2018 at the cost of around $16,600 a head. When cornered by a TV journalist from HBO's Real Sports at one of his teacher training camps near Mumbai in October 2016, Choudhury seemed to have lost all touch with reality. He insulted his interviewer, ranting into the camera that 5,000 women a day would line up to have sex with him: 'Why do I have to harass women? People spend a million dollars for one drop of my sperm. Are you that dumb to believe those trash?' As to the power of his system, he boasted: 'This yoga is worse than cocaine. You can get rid of cocaine, but once you're used to this yoga, you can't stop.'

Given the habitual endorphin rush generated by those strenuous overheated exercises, the devotion of his yogaholic followers and his own manic trajectory, on this last point he may be right.

Two months after this bizarre interview, with Choudhury still refusing to return to the US, the California judge ordered that the income from his studio franchises and his intellectual property be handed over to Jafa-Bodden, so the formerly downtrodden lawyer is now the controller of a substantial global empire. To cap it all, a month later, his wife of thirty-three years, herself a Hot Yoga instructor, finalised divorce proceedings against him. The settlement was all very *Hollywood Wives*: she was awarded their sumptuous mansions in Beverly Hills and Los Angeles, as well as several of his luxury cars (which have somehow all gone missing), while he is allowed to keep only an apartment in Hawaii. In November 2017, the global outreach, Bikram Choudhury Inc., filed for bankruptcy protection, with debts of £11.5 million.

As the errant yogi continues to feel the heat, his followers are in a dilemma. A group has grown up, calling itself 'the Bikram community-in-exile', which is composed of people who used to be at the heart of the movement and say they suffered horrendous abuse in their pursuit of Hot enlightenment. Nevertheless, they still swear by the twenty-six-pose sequence. Typical of these is Francesca Asumah, a fit sixty-five-year-old, half-Ghanaian, half-English teacher who hails from Manchester and is currently one of the most sought-after Hot Yoga instructors in California. Her treatment in the inner circle led her to define it as 'a grossly racist cult', but she still runs classes at the Hot 8 Yoga studio in Beverly Hills. No doubt mindful of the continuing mayhem, she is keen to boost her students' sense of self-worth in a New Age way, bellowing at them in a strong Mancunian accent: 'You must learn to love yourself, guys! If everyone loves themselves, then the whole world will be loved. And beware false gurus!' If only it were that simple.

Meanwhile, there are around thirty yoga studios that carry the founder's name in the UK, and many have removed photographs of Choudhury and distanced themselves from their former teacher. Some are rebranding; in several parts of London, branches of Hot Yoga now operate under the name 'Fierce Grace'. To some observers, 'Fierce Disgrace' might be more appropriate.

To dwell at any more length on these sorry details would be tedious, but they do provide a salutary warning of what can happen when yoga, faced with the relentless twenty-first-century demand for innovation and lucrative commodification, operates well outside the self-regulation inherent in a traditional *parampara* lineage. The story of Hot Yoga poses a wider question we shall examine later: Does the proven fallibility of the messenger necessarily debase the message? This is a difficult topic that other, more conventionally religious, believers are also having to face.

22

RISKS AND REGULATION

In the summer of 2017, there were some sharp intakes of breath among the international yoga community. These were not the result of a mass *pranayama* programme, but a report in the *Journal of Bodywork and Movement Therapies*[1] which claimed that yoga causes more injuries than all other sports combined. The study quoted had shown one in ten participants develop musculoskeletal pain from their practice, particularly in the arms, and a fifth of those with existing conditions have suffered from worsened pain. In a third of cases, the pain was so severe that the person affected was out of action for three months. The study was quite small—350 people from two New York studios—and may tell us more about the downtown Manhattan macho-culture than anything else, but nonetheless, such figures are worrying, not least because they appear to be just the tip of the iceberg. Body-yoga has enjoyed fifty years of astonishing popularity in the West; now the casualties are limping in.

Given what is to follow, it is as well to remember that the vast majority of yoga teachers out there are conscientious and professional people, who look after their students to the best of their ability and are well aware of their responsibility. Their dedicated efforts ensure that millions worldwide gain an enormous amount of benefit from a postural practice that they pursue with moderation and common sense. Compared with the number of people doing body-yoga, the number of cases of reported damage is still generally small. What negative outcomes do occur are caused not so much from the physical posture *per se*, but from the mental attitude behind it, either in the case of plain bad teaching or ill-informed and over-optimistic learning. The best outcome for an injured student would be that, having learned the hard way, if and when she becomes a teacher herself, she passes on the benefit of her experience by being especially sensitive to the necessity not to overstrain the body.[2] We have already heard what Patanjali has to say on *asana*. It is clear and unambiguous, but given the general confusion, bears repeating:

239

The physical postures should be steady and comfortable. They are mastered when all effort is relaxed and the mind is absorbed in the infinite.[3]

Casualties

A detailed and sobering account of what can happen when too much effort is applied is provided by the American journalist and author William J. Broad. As an investigative heavyweight—winner of two Pulitzer Prizes and one Emmy Award—Broad instances the dangers of dilettante yoga in *The Science of Yoga: The Risks and Rewards* (2012). For example: merely sitting too long in one *asana* caused one man to lose all feeling in his legs, resulting in near-paralysis, while a woman doing the seated forward-bend fell asleep and suffered permanent nerve damage. Other unfortunate participants suffered from strokes, seizures and heart attacks. Broad does not just rely on second-hand experience but draws on his own. After doing yoga for years, he was injured in 2007 while coming out of a pose known as the 'extended side angle' (*utthita parsvakonasana*) which, ironically, is a posture recommended as a cure for many diseases. His back gave way and weeks of agony followed before he recovered. It was this unpleasant, but salutary, experience that set him off on a search to find what damage incorrect practice can do.

The Science of Yoga deals with far more serious stuff than Broad had to. His main informant is Glenn Black, one of the US' most renowned and experienced instructors, who often features as a guest tutor at The Omega Institute, a holistic centre in upstate New York which hosts a large and prestigious international yoga conference each year. A few years ago, Black had himself to undergo a five-hour operation to fuse damaged vertebrae together. Four decades of over-zealous backbends and twists—particularly the 'plough' (*halasana*) and the 'shoulder stand' (*jiguasana*)—had left him with spinal stenosis, a serious condition in which the openings between vertebrae begin to narrow, compressing spinal nerves and causing excruciating pain. The surgery was a success, but his range of movement will never be what it was.

Scarred by his own experience, Black shares Broad's determination to do what he can to protect others and now spends much of his time giving cautionary talks on the dangers of yogic over-exertion. His message is clear: *asana* is not a panacea or cure-all. In fact, if you do it with ego or obsession, you'll end up causing problems. Unfortunately, he says, a lot of people don't like to hear this. In an excerpt published in *The New York Times* review of his book, Broad summed up the situation with directness:

> A growing body of medical evidence supports [the] contention that, for many people, a number of commonly taught yoga poses are inherently risky... The

problems ranged from relatively mild injuries to permanent disabilities… Surveys by the Consumer Product Safety Commission showed that the number of emergency-room admissions related to yoga, after years of slow increases, was rising quickly.[4]

Warnings about the potential dangers of postural yoga are not new. Specialists have known for decades about possible injuries resulting from faulty practice, and many have been listed in some of the world's most respected journals, with *Neurology*, *The British Medical Journal* and *The Journal of the American Medical Association* among them. Witnesses lined up for the prosecution include Columbia University's College of Physicians and Surgeons, prominent Oxford neurophysiologist W. Ritchie Russell and Willibald Nagler, a renowned authority on spinal rehabilitation at Cornell University Medical College. They also include members of the yoga community itself, particularly in the US. Timothy McCall, a physician who is the medical editor of the flagship magazine *Yoga Journal* and Roger Cole, an Iyengar teacher who has written extensively for the magazine and advises the American College of Sports Medicine on yoga safety. Both have made sizeable contributions to the debate. A former editor of *Yoga Journal*, Kaitlin Quistgaard, and Carol Krucoff, a yoga instructor who works at the Integrative Medicine Center at Duke University in North Carolina, have both shared cautionary personal tales of injuries they themselves suffered while on the mat. Out in the field, complaints are now so numerous that even the Product Safety Commission has come in on the act, investigating malpractice amongst irresponsible teachers in the US.

Shoulders, knees and necks seem to be most at risk, and sometimes from even what are generally considered basic poses. Even the iconic 'sun-salutation' (*surya namskar*) may not benefit many of those who consider it essential to their practice. That seated spinal twist (*ardha matsyendrasana*) with bent knee placed over the opposite straight leg—which often feels so good for the back—can, in some cases, destabilise lumbar joints and lead to later arthritis or sciatic nerve issues. There are also reports of more dramatic and permanent injuries, such as strokes and other brain conditions. The main culprits here are those poses that involve over-arching or excessive extensions of the neck, such as the wheel or upward bow (*urdhva dhanurasana*), advanced spinal twist (*marichyasana*), the cobra (*bhujangasana*) and both shoulder stand (*salamba sarvangasana*) and headstand (*shirsasana*). Practitioners of body-yoga typically move the neck vertebrae much farther than these bones would naturally go. An intermediate student can easily turn his neck ninety degrees, which is nearly twice the normal rotation and sounds impressive, but can

241

result in damage to the vertebrae and the vertebral arteries that feed the brain. Even sitting too long in *vajrasana*, a posture where one rests on the knees, can deaden a branch of the sciatic nerve that runs behind the knee to branch down into the calf and foot, giving rise to a condition that has become common enough for doctors to have named it 'the yoga foot-drop'.

Back in 1972, William Ritchie Russell, a professor of clinical neurology and elder statesman of the British medical establishment, was already ringing alarm bells. Writing in the *British Medical Journal*, he was specifically critical of the cobra and shoulder stand postures. Almost fifty years on, a recent article in *The Times* reported that health professionals found the penetrating heat of Hot Yoga could raise the risk of overstretching, muscle damage and torn cartilage. One specialist noted that ligaments—the tough bands of fibre that connect bones or cartilage at a joint—failed to regain their shape once stretched out, resulting in a flaccidity that increases the risk of future strains, sprains and dislocations. Many reports are now coming in from long-term practitioners of Ashtanga Yoga, a system which uses energetic vertical jumps, who are complaining of serious arthritis in their toes and knees. There is also the possibility of undiagnosed pre-existing conditions being aggravated by over-enthusiastic bodywork.

In all such cases, a prime danger lies in a 'follow the leader' and 'one size fits all' approach which does not pay enough attention to the variations of the individual students. This danger is increased the larger the class becomes, and the incentive to increase class sizes is always there, because the larger the class, the more lucrative it is for the teacher. Gymnasium-sized classes were never part of genuine yoga, nor will they ever be, because each student is different. Bearing this in mind, from a traditional angle ideally informed by Ayurveda, the yoga teacher should always be cognisant of the nature of the student and their imbalances as well as the nature of the posture. Merely being proficient in the latter is not enough.

Modern Pitfalls

We should perhaps not forget that body-yoga was originally developed for and by Indians, whose daily lives were generally full of physical movement, nourished by simple meals, and who typically squatted and sat cross-legged for hours on end, as many in the subcontinent still do. What the West now practises as *asana* grew out of these commonplace living habits but has been grafted onto an urban lifestyle in which many sit all day hunched over a computer, lifting nothing heavier than a mobile phone, and probably taking very little exercise. Into the bargain, they may well have a history of unhealthy eating and neglect of their physical well-being. To walk blithely off this insouciant street into a yoga studio and start moving quickly through poses that put unaccustomed weight on wrists, spines and knees could be counter-productive. Straining hard to attain ever more difficult poses is not the way of real yoga. Mind you, being Indian is no guarantee of safety. Glenn Black's most gruesome story concerns an event that took place when he was studying at Iyengar's yoga school in Pune, a place then renowned for its toughness. As he recounts, a young local man came into the studio and enthusiastically: 'threw himself into a spinal twist. I watched in disbelief as three of the man's ribs gave way—pop, pop, pop.'

It is not just badly supervised novice students who damage themselves, experienced and celebrated instructors can do so as well. Black cites well-known yoga teachers in the US who have put so much effort into some basic poses that they have permanent damage. One of the most celebrated of these instructors lost all movement in her hip joints because she had strained over many years; the sockets became so degenerated that she had to have hip replacements. Astonishingly, she still teaches. Others have backs so crocked from faulty practice that they must now lie down to teach their students. Black's conclusion is radical indeed. He believes 'the vast majority of people' should give up yoga altogether because it's simply too likely to cause harm. He counsels:

> Instead of doing yoga they need to be doing a specific range of motions for articulation, for organ condition, to strengthen weak parts of the body. Yoga is for people in good physical condition. Or it can be used therapeutically. It's controversial to say, but it really shouldn't be used for a general class. There's such a variety and range of possibilities. Everybody has a different problem... To come to New York and do a class with people who have many problems and say 'Okay, we're going to do this sequence of poses today'—it just doesn't work.[5]

This is controversial advice indeed, not least because many of the founders of modern postural practice made no mention of its risks. Jagannath Gune, (aka Swami Kuvalayananda), the pioneer of the scientific study of *hatha yoga*, whose journal *Yoga Mimansa* and book *Asanas* (1931) were hugely influential in the early years, is silent on any dangers. So is Indra Devi in her best-selling *Forever Young, Forever Healthy* (1953); so indeed is B. K. S. Iyengar, the godfather of modern postural yoga, in his seminal *Light on Yoga* (1966). Reassurances about yoga's safety regularly feature in the do-it-yourself guides of other popular teachers, such as Swami Shivananda, K. Pattabhi Jois and Bikram Choudhury. The energetically peripatetic Swami Gitananda, the 'Lion of

Pondicherry' who made ten world tours and founded ashrams on several continents, proclaimed confidently: 'Real yoga is as safe as mother's milk.'[6] Well, fair enough, but what is the guarantee you are being fed 'real' yoga?

In all of this, body-yoga is a victim of its own success. So rapid has been the explosion of interest that there are now inevitably many studios where teachers lack the training necessary to recognise the early warning signs of injury in their students, or even in themselves. While responsible teachers will always pay attention to the varying ages and conditions of their students, and make sure they allow sufficient warm-up time for any class, this degree of care cannot always be assured. Worryingly, nearly all teachers who get themselves or their students into trouble have in fact been educated up to, or above, the minimum standard that is recognised by those who hire them. So why don't these teachers know how to teach an authentic and safe practice? Part of the problem is that some degree of injury has now been widely accepted as almost inevitable—a mark of comradeship, or even a badge of honour. A couple of years ago an article in *Yoga International* quoted a Facebook post in which a self-described 'yoga teacher/mentor' cheerfully tells her students: 'We've been through so much together, so many changes. I've seen some of you become mothers, others retire, we've ripped hamstrings and blown shoulders…'[7]

Really? Whatever happened to the cardinal yogic virtue of *ahimsa*—do no harm?

Irregular Regulation

Many observers of the scene conclude that the ultimate responsibility lies with the bodies who set and regulate teacher training. In America, since 1999, this has been Yoga Alliance, the world's largest registry of yoga schools and teachers. According to its director Pam Weber, the organisation currently has about 40,000 instructors and 3,000 schools on its books; all are registered as complying with its standards. This considerable number is increasing at a quite extraordinary rate: every day, the organisation receives approximately 1,000 teacher certificate requests and every month, seventy-five school certification requests. Such figures put Yoga Alliance way ahead of any comparable outfit, so to the untrained eye it would surely appear to be the gold standard. Most of the fitness-centre managers who hire yoga teachers don't do yoga themselves, so when they see that a prospective teacher has YA's stamp of approval, they understandably expect that she has been rigorously trained. However, they might be shocked to learn that the YA training involves no stipulated or specific curriculum, nor is there any required assessment of a registered teacher's skill. Once accepted, you are on the register, and no follow-up, monitoring or re-evaluation ever takes place. And there are no plans to change that.

These omissions leave the US yoga world with arbitrary curricula being taught to uninformed prospective teachers. According to the YA website, all that is required is that 200 training hours be spent covering each of five areas of study, which breaks down as: 100 hours of practice, twenty-five hours of teaching methodology, twenty hours of anatomy, thirty hours of philosophy and ethics and ten hours of practice teaching. The actual content of each area of study is left up to the individual school. Instead of creating content standards for its accredited schools, Yoga Alliance has decided to introduce a kind of customer feedback register. As their website explains: 'Past trainees provide social ratings and comments about their training experience, which may be shown on our public directory.' Director Pam Weber adds: 'We are empowering the trainees and schools to want to comply without us having to enforce it. Social credentialing is our solution to gaining more rigor.'

That last sentence is extraordinary. It is, in fact, an abdication of the responsibility incumbent upon anybody seeking to teach a transformative praxis such as yoga. Reliance on customer feedback is, in effect, saying that recently graduated students should determine the future agenda for the teacher! Such an avoidance of pedagogic authority may well be in line with fashionable trends of educational democracy, and conform to the modern idea, ever more observable in higher education, that as students are paying consumers they have a decisive voice in what they are purchasing. But such an attitude is the reverse of yogic traditions of lineage, and whether you can conduct an authentic programme of postural instruction through a glorified Tripadvisor mechanism is highly questionable. Apart from anything else, if taught and practised correctly, yoga is a transformative process, and sometimes profoundly so. As such, it is at heart an initiatory process and to cast aside the principle of authoritative guidance in favour of a Yelp-like feature on a website is no substitute for responsible teaching. Whether we like it or not, tradition has a place in yogic transmission, and tradition includes clear and disinterested instruction in areas the student, by definition, is relatively unfamiliar with. To sacrifice the benefit of experience and the wisdom of forerunners on the altar of commercial or social expediency will not serve yoga well, nor will it benefit those wishing to teach, or learn, it.

Respect for tradition and the status of the teacher does not equate with the sort of unquestioning acceptance that would be anathema to most modern students. On the contrary, there is a long and vibrant history of dialogue and debate within all the various yogic and spiritual traditions of India. Everything proposed can be questioned and the teacher must be able to prove his point by reasoned argument and, most importantly, by example. Some extensive and lively exchanges between teacher and pupil have achieved legendary status. In the *Brihadaranyaka Upanishad* for example, a revered sage called Yajnyavalkya implores Gargi, a wise woman who is particularly persistent in her enquiries, to stop asking so many questions lest her head fall off![8] In practice, the genuine teacher always welcomes questions because there is no more effective means to bring out the deeper levels of what he is attempting to impart. The teacher learns by teaching and this helps ensure his benign motivation.

In fairness to the regulatory bodies, formulating rigorous guidelines is a daunting task, not least because of the wide and ever-growing variety of what is called 'yoga'. Nonetheless, as is the practice in almost all vocational training, what is needed is a clear set of specific objectives that an accreditation course is required to meet. Other US yoga organisations, such as the International Association of Yoga Therapists, have managed to do it, though the narrowness of their remit, i.e. providing only body-yoga and strictly avoiding any philosophy, must help. In 2012 they published their *Educational Standards for the Training of Yoga Therapists*, running to nineteen pages, that covered detailed training requirements for yoga therapy programmes seeking their approval, as well as skills assessments for their licensed practitioners. But even here there is confusion, as their qualification of Registered Yoga Therapist (RYT) uses an acronym that also refers to a Registered Yoga Teacher. Is the student being told that a teacher is the same thing as a therapist?

The British Wheel of Yoga

In the UK the situation is generally more tightly regulated, but no less confused. The government-approved official body, the British Wheel of Yoga (BWY) which has 8,000 members, 4,000 teachers and the power to accredit affiliated organisations' teacher training programmes, is making increasingly strenuous efforts to implement uniform standards. But not all UK yoga is taught under the auspices of the BWY; at most 50 per cent comes under its umbrella. To run classes in gyms and leisure centres, yoga teachers must also join the Register of Exercise Professionals (REPs) in the same way as, for example, aerobics instructors do, but anyone can set up a yoga class privately. Many who do are not always scrupulous in vetting the would-be-teacher's qualifications. Even if they wish to be, as they themselves generally know little or nothing about the subject, they may not fully understand the vast difference between a diploma with BWY that involves up to three years commitment with regular assessment, and a month-long training course on a laid-back summer beach in Ibiza. As a result, there are still too many improperly qualified teachers out there. This is something a growing number of physiotherapists would concur with, for it is they who have to deal with the aftereffects of people wanting to achieve that impossible posture they have seen in all those glamorous Instagram pictures.

Even within the BWY there is growing discord over what constitutes effective accreditation and from whom. The situation is not improved by the fact that the relationships between all the UK sporting and leisure organisations is itself hopelessly muddled. The official BWY website[9] currently states that they have received National Governing Body status from Sport England (formerly called the Sports Council) with no mention of the Sport and Recreation Alliance (SRA) that, under its former name of the Central Council of Physical Recreation (CCPR), formerly recognised them as the governing body. However, the BWY is still a member of SRA but is now located within its 'Movement and Dance' division. Given modern body-yoga's connections with the female exercise movement, this is a significant placing. To add further confusion, the Wheel is also affiliated with SkillsActive, a government quango determined to establish and maintain national training standards. Together they hope to develop a National Occupational Standard for Yoga (NOSY).

At best, these multiple layers of official oversight may serve as a reassurance to the nervous and a bulwark against quacks, frauds and over-enthusiastic amateurs. But the acronym NOSY is all too appropriate for some traditionalists who like their yoga more free-spirited and less claustrophobically regimented. Incumbent on all those having to do with government-approved education in the UK is an ever-increasing burden of bureaucracy, involving copious health and safety norms, child protection measures, equal opportunity outreach, LGBTI sensitivity, ethnic minority inclusivity, background criminal checks and so on and on. Every few months another stipulation seems to appear from on high, another set of forms to fill lands on the hapless administrators' desk.

Buried somewhere underneath this growing mountain of paperwork lies the desire to make a yoga teaching qualification comparable to a university degree or equivalent academic diploma. Since the New Labour government of twenty years ago, the desire to embellish practical skills with an academic gloss has bedeviled much higher education in the UK, devaluing the worth of apprenticeships and technical training in their own right.[10] Many working in yoga would dispute the validity of such gentrification, arguing that empathetic skill in hands-on instruction is something quite different from the typical academic qualification, and cannot be conjured up by the lists of aims and objectives that accompany classroom teaching.[11] In its defence, NOSY emphasises that its concern is solely with the safety of its members, not in regulating individual interpretations of what yoga may, or may not, be. Bearing in mind the failings of some teachers, such scrupulousness may seem fair enough, though it has clearly spawned unintended consequences.[12]

In any regulation, the question of content is central. In tandem with government rules and the desire for scientific respectability, the Wheel's curriculum has progressively been dominated by anatomy and physiology, postures and breathing exercises. The price of official recognition has been the omission of Patanjali's 'heart of yoga', the less quantifiable, and more interior, dimensions of the praxis. This policy has been adopted partly in order to avoid offending both secular and religious sensibilities ever since the London Education Authority adopted Iyengar yoga in the 1960s. Where it does occur, the meditation module seems to be an inchoate affair, sporadically catered for, at best. For some Wheel groups, interiority is virtually non-existent, for others a generalised relaxation such as *yoga nidra* is offered. For the few that do pay the subject any real attention some form of mindfulness is currently the preferred option, because that system has gained respectability in government schemes of health and welfare.

Within the UK yoga community itself, many are unhappy with the way the Wheel is rolling. As far back as 2004, a number of independently-minded teacher trainers got together to form the Independent Yoga Network, an attempt to combat what they saw as the fitness industry's ill-informed attempts to define and regulate what is acceptable. To them, the government-backed initiatives were headed in the wrong direction. One particular spokesperson for those who are fed up with the Wheel's stodgy diet of 'anatomy & physiology' and hungry for more soul food is Swami Ambikananda, a British Hindu renunciate who lives in Berkshire and is the founder of the Traditional Yoga Alliance. An experienced devotee of spiritual yoga and respected author on the subject, she is critical of what is happening in most yoga classes, saying: 'selling yoga back to its teachers is pure neocolonialism', and seriously doubting the government's right to legislate: 'When powerful organisations seek control, they always say it's to "protect the public" and "keep them safe". Are these not the claims put forward by any group seeking to impose its authority and undermine all other groups existing alongside it?'[13]

Her feelings are shared by many who have become alarmed at the Wheel's increasing bias towards the secular and the quantifiable, a narrowing of focus in its effort to become more mainstream and respectable, backed up by adding unnecessary costs in the form of membership fees and dues levied on teachers who have no choice but to belong. Emotions have been running high. In May 2018, the BWY chair, Paul Fox and his deputy Shelagh MacKenzie resigned, claiming members of their National Executive Committee wanted to relax the standards incumbent on teachers. Fox is a passionate advocate of the organisation's highest level of teacher qualification, known as Level 4, which other board members, who had themselves been unable to attain it, criticise as being 'over-regulation'. Fox admitted to feeling 'gutted and quite emotional' and now plans 'to build a grassroots movement' that would 'take back control of our organisation from conservative members who I do not believe represent anything other than the past'.[14]

To the problems of regulation must be added the challenges of running a large organisation requiring multiple types and levels of expertise on a largely voluntary basis. At the BWY, this confusion between *seva* and salary has coincided unhappily with a recent history of financial mismanagement, unhealthily rapid personnel changes at high levels of the organisation and the rise of many other competing UK yoga groups. All in all, in recent years, the Wheel has been looking decidedly rather wobbly.

The Problem of Definition

In the end, most of the trouble around yoga governance boils down to the simple fact that, if there is to be an effective regulatory system in place, you need to know exactly what it is you are regulating. And so we come back to the question that has cropped up in many different contexts throughout this book—what exactly *is* yoga? Which type should be considered authentic? Is it body-work or soul-culture, gymnastic or contemplative, hard and fast, or soft and slow? Some might say it can be all of these, but if so, in what proportion? And if yoga is to be viewed as, at the least, a partly spiritual discipline, things become even more complicated. What should be the guiding philosophy behind the practice? Is it a Sankhya-type dualism as promoted by Patanjali, the early Buddhists and the Jains, a baroque and magical worldview as propounded in the *Hatha Yoga Pradipika*, or a Vedantic non-dualism as espoused by many medieval *hatha* texts and promoted by missionary yogis such as Swamis Vivekananda, Yogananda and Prabhavananda? Should the yoga practitioner have to take seriously the supernormal *siddhi* abilities, as all traditional yoga authorities certainly do?

Given such complexities, it is quite understandable that the easiest practical policy is to avoid philosophy altogether and present yoga as an unreflective physical routine that simply grants better health and well-being. But such a mechanistic approach runs the risk of throwing the spiritual baby out with the superstitious bathwater, and it denies the very real thirst for higher knowledge evinced by many yoga students. As things currently stand, the international jury has retired in some confusion to consider these complex questions. It doesn't look as if it will return with a verdict anytime soon.

23

SCIENCE, SPIRIT AND STRESS RELIEF

It did not take the ambassadors of yoga long to realise that if their spiritual nourishment was to be acceptable to the unsophisticated palate of the West, it was best served up mashed and strained through the sieve of science. Esoteric wisdom from the mountain-peak would never do; yoga had to come down to earth if it was to spread widely. A key figure in this transition was a Gujarati *brahmin* called Manibhai Haribhai Desai, better known as Shri Yogendra. Less flamboyant, and not as articulate as the cosmopolitan Swami Vivekananda, he was in his own way a crucial player in the modernisation of yoga and its move out of the ashram and into the clinic. As he once said: 'It is my satisfaction that instead of passing my life in the jungle, obscure and lonely, by some certain inspiration I have been directed to reveal to the public what I felt is truth about this science.'[1] And science is the key word here, for, whatever he may have meant by it—the term is often used differently on the mat and in the laboratory—it was his application of *asanas* and *pranayama* to the field of remedial medicine that have earned him his largely unsung place in the yoga hall of fame. Yogendra was the first practitioner of what is now known as yoga therapy, and the initiator of the scrupulous focus on anatomy and physiology that characterises the application of posture work as a healthy remedy for our chronically unhealthy times.[2]

The beginnings were unlikely. As a sceptical and rationalist student in Bombay, Desai was highly suspicious of *sadhus* and the whole guru paraphernalia, but while passing through a period of depression was prevailed upon by classmates to visit the ashram of a *yogi* called Paramahansa Sri Madhavadasji Maharaj. We know very little about this teacher, apart from the fact he was a Bengali and devotee of Lord Vishnu who was acknowledged to be a great yoga master. At the age of eighty, after a lifetime of wandering and learning, he finally settled down on the banks of the sacred Narmada river and began to teach the hidden secrets of yoga to a few select disciples. According to his followers, he far surpassed the Vedic ideal of longevity—a hundred autumns—by dying at the ripe old age of a hundred and twenty-three. In a re-run of Vivekananda's fateful meeting with his own guru, as Yogendra remembered in his autobiography, all his sceptical misgivings disappeared as soon as 'as our eyes met'.[2] For his part, the teacher was also struck by the young man's qualities, decided he was to be his successor and apprenticed him immediately. Desai quit college to spend two years studying with his new mentor, where much of his training centred on the 'nature cure' then being administered to patients in the ashram's sick ward. Then, on Christmas Day 1918, in another echo of Vivekananda, the twenty-year-old launched his own mission by founding what is the oldest organised yoga institution in the world.

The Yoga Institute was situated in the grounds of 'The Sands', a splendid beachside estate on the outskirts of Bombay belonging to one of the city's most respected denizens, Dadabhai Naoroji. This was a happy choice of patron in several ways. Naoroji, by then known as the 'Grand Old Man of India', was a Parsi intellectual, author and wealthy cotton magnate, one of that extraordinary community of Zoroastrian refugees from Persia who did so much to lay the civic foundations of Bombay as a great trading metropolis. He was also a social activist committed to the Independence movement and one of the founders of the Indian National Congress. Later he would move to the UK, establish the first Indian company in that country, teach Gujarati at London University while pursuing his business interests and end up as Britain's first Asian MP, representing Finsbury Central for the Liberals. To honour Naoroji's egalitarian ideals, Shri Yogendra's Institute was the first yoga centre to offer courses for free to men, women and children of any caste or creed.

Once the Institute was up and running, Yogendra set sail for America, establishing the Yoga Institute of America in Bear Mountain in upstate New York in 1919. He then toured the world, teaching yoga, treating patients and gathering manuscripts on *hatha yoga* wherever he could. He returned to India in 1924, aiming to go back to the States, but was thwarted by the new immigration restrictions against Indians.[3] Following his marriage, he stayed put in India, but in time there would be branches of his Institute stretching around the world: in Australia, Brazil, Canada, Finland, France, Italy, Japan, South America, Switzerland, Yugoslavia and the UK. The Institute's journal, *Yoga*, was first published in 1933 and is still going strong today, as is the place itself, with a thousand people passing through its gates daily. Indeed, the day that our planet is finally colonised by extra-terrestrials, Shri Yogendra's version of yoga may well be the one interpretation of the ancient doctrine they come across. In 1940, some of his publications were microfilmed and preserved in the Crypt of Civilization, a time capsule held at Oglethorpe University in Atlanta, that is not due to be opened for another 6,000 years.

The Yoga Institute found a permanent base in the Bombay suburb of Santacruz in 1948, and since then has in many ways continued to be the public face of therapeutic yoga in its homeland. In 1951, it was the setting for the government's first documentary film on the subject, and six years later the institution was briefed to conduct a nationwide survey. When it finally gained official recognition the next year, state funding was made available for scholarships for teacher training and placement of yoga instructors in schools across the subcontinent. Yogendra died in 1969; the following year, the Medical Research Unit for research on yoga's application to psychosomatic and psychiatric diseases was launched.

Shri Yogendra was not the only influential disciple of the enigmatic Paramahansa Madhavadasji. Another Gujarati *brahmin*, Jagannatha Ganesha Gune, later known as Swami Kuvalayananda, was also to exert a profound influence on the direction of modern yoga. Gune started his own research in 1920, and published the first scientific journal specifically devoted to the subject, *Yoga Mimamsa*, in 1924, which since then has continued to publish details of scientific experiments on the effects of various yogic techniques. The same year, he set up the Kaivalyadhama Health and Yoga Research Centre in Lonavala, a hill station in the Western Ghats about sixty miles from Bombay, to be a premier centre for medical and scientific study, offering training, therapy and a resource library of ancient texts. He looked to the *Hatha Yoga Pradipika* as scriptural authority, as did Yogendra, but, of course, shorn of its inconveniently purple passages. His yoga was to be a practical system of exercises and regimes to promote good health and physical fitness, nothing more. Kuvalayananda set up several more such institutes before his death in 1966.

By this time, several other groups were active in the West. These included the Shivananda Yoga Vedanta Centres, founded by Swami Vishnudevananda in 1959, which taught a Vedantic yoga under the banner 'Serve, love, give, purify, meditate, realise', and the holistic Bihar School of Yoga, started in 1963 by Swami Satyananda. But systems such as these, which sought to balance physical prowess with interiority, were less successful than the Iyengar-Jois approach which, continuing in Yogendra's approach, presented yoga as a preventative, curative and keep-fit regime.[4]

Transcendental Medication

Mind-yoga was likewise soon to be presented as a quasi-medical therapy, a process best exemplified by Maharishi Mahesh Yogi's simple technique of Transcendental Meditation. When he left India to begin his worldwide teaching mission in the late 1950s, Maharishi couched his message in largely spiritual terms, a traditional vocabulary that included Hindu deities, *kundalini* and *chakras*, reincarnation, God, *karma* and enlightenment. However, such riches were disregarded by some of his pupils in light of their immediate medical needs. Landing in California in 1959, like the earlier generations of Vedantists before him, Maharishi established himself in Los Angeles. Soon after one of his first public talks, he was shocked by an article in a local paper that praised TM as a natural cure for insomnia. As he commented bemusedly: 'I have come to awaken the people and all they want to do is go to sleep! This seems to be a strange country, values are different here...'[5]

In Britain, some journalists were surprised by his irrepressible happiness and dubbed him 'the giggling guru'. Others looked on him as a charming oddity, a monkish idealist, well-meaning but out of touch with modern life, as evinced by the opening words of one of his first talks in London: 'My vision in the world is spiritual regeneration, to regenerate every man, everywhere in the world, into the values of spirit. The values of the spirit are pure consciousness, Absolute bliss'.[6]

The press was unresponsive to such an ambitious mission, but, as in America, did label the meditation a 'non-medicinal tranquiliser'.[7] No doubt disappointed by the media's shallow approach, the yogi will surely have noted what they focused on. By the time of his talk to an audience of heirs to the European Enlightenment in Cambridge later the same year, Maharishi had begun to temper his public presentation:

> We belong to the realistic age of science. Let us be sure that all we strive for and achieve remains realistic. Our age of scientific unfoldment does not give credence to anything shrouded in the garb of mysticism. Let us realize the Absolute Being through a scientific and systematic method of achievement whose every achievement will be supplemented by the personal experience.[8]

In the modern world, then, the nervous system of a meditator was to serve as his own personal laboratory in which to conduct experiments in the expansion of consciousness. That Maharishi was tapping into a widespread need was evident the following Spring when 5,000 members of the public came to hear him speak at the Albert Hall in what was called 'The First World Assembly of the Spiritual Regeneration Movement'. Here, again, the white robed monk, introduced as 'coming from the Valley of the Saints, Himalayas' skilfully walked the tightrope between sacred and secular. Working hard to accumulate evidence of the quantifiable benefits of interiority, he invited 4,000 doctors to come and hear him at a medical presentation in London. Four turned up. Undaunted, during the following decade he continued to push to gather scientific interest and get investigative studies done wherever he could. These would not prove anything about meditation of course, nor even explain how it worked, but they could certainly catalogue bodily correlates of the mental practice. In this way, sensible physical data could perhaps be used to indicate that something interesting lay beyond them. There is a saying in India that an elephant needs two sets of teeth: one to display and one to chew with. In 1967, Maharishi explained his use of this strategy to a teacher training course held in his Rishikesh ashram:

> TM is a very natural and systematic, scientific procedure for the Holy Spirit to dawn on man. When we say Holy Spirit to dawn on man, in the ordinary sense it seems to be an absolutely emotional thing. Nothing to do with any scientific value. But when we say TM opens the awareness to the transcendental, unbounded area of life, it sounds scientific... it is just a matter of expression, the phenomenon is the same... we formulate our expression in the current language. The content is the same. Nothing is new. That proverb, 'Nothing is new under the sun'. The reality is the same, the Holy Spirit is the same...[9]

Scientific Studies

At the beginning of the 1970s the policy paid off when the first results on TM were published, with articles in *The Lancet* and *Scientific American* showing that a twenty-minute sitting practising the technique resulted in a marked drop in breath rate along with some reduction in the rate of metabolism. The results of such deep rest were both pleasurable and beneficial for the practitioner and led to a profound sense of well-being and consequent relief of stress. Many more peer-reviewed scientific studies were to follow, showing subtle but profound changes in brain function and a wide range of benign effects in all areas of life. In the forty-five years since, experiments have continued at an impressive rate. Over 600 papers have been published on the physical, psychological and social effects of this particular type of meditation; a rate of more than one a month. In 2012, one of these showed that regular practice reduced by 48 per cent the risk of heart attack, stroke and death in people with heart disease; Californian research published in the autumn of 2014 showed that AIDS sufferers who meditated were also getting sick less frequently, were less fatigued and more energised, as well as being less stressed, anxious and depressed.[10] TM, along with the Buddhist *vipassana* method, remains the most tested of all the meditation techniques and the results generally appear solid and impressive.[11]

Given the wealth of available data now accumulated, one might wonder why TM has not been more widely adopted by those charged with looking after our medical and psychological welfare; a report issued by the NHS in September 2017, stated that one in every three sick notes issued by doctors cites stress and anxiety. For some in the medico-scientific establishment, however, much of the research on all types of meditation, despite its volume, has remained problematic, even pseudo-scientific. Good science is hard to do; it requires, apart from anything else, asking a clear question of nature and then setting experiments up in such a way as to get a clear answer. The researcher who already has the answer in mind and unconsciously projects their beliefs into the experiment may ignore or side-line data that does not fit their deduction. At their worst, such investigations become what the American physicist Richard Feynman has called 'cargo cult science',[12] i.e. research which has the outward appearance of genuine science but lacks the necessary substance, rigour and critical spirit. From a scientific point of view, which is what government agencies must work on, anecdotal evidence, however abundant, will not suffice. And so, studies on meditation continue to accumulate, and the discussion goes on.[13]

Upsetting the Apple Cart

Just when the scientific establishment was beginning to accept that meditation might be a quantifiable and non-religious wellness strategy, Maharishi upped the ante with the introduction of what he called the 'TM Sidhi Programme', an advanced course that utilised Patanjali's *sutras* to develop supernormal abilities. Stress relief was augmented by psychic abilities, though these were not offered as an end in themselves, but, following Patanjali's teaching, as a means to speed up the progress to enlightenment.[14]

It was a bizarre coupling. Cast your mind back to 1977 when an obscure upstate New York newspaper, the *Press Republican*, carries an advert for a lecture entitled: 'TM and Supernormal Powers' to be held on 15 June in the local town of Plattsburgh (pop. c. 16,000) that, for as long as anyone can remember, has been quietly minding its own business a few miles south of the Canadian border. The venue is archetypally and reassuringly all-American: a Howard Johnson's Hotel. Alongside a beaming picture of Maharishi, the advert states with admirable yogic calm:

Regular practice of the TM technique develops supernormal powers such as:
Levitating the Body at Will; Invisibility; Supernormal Sight and Hearing.

To advance such claims in the conservative heart of small-town America was proof indeed of the TM movement's ability to juggle East and West, and its self-confidence in doing so. The organisation may have been offering the solid citizens of Plattsburgh invisibility, but maximum exposure was clearly what it wanted for itself. A month later, the 6 July edition of their local paper invites the residents of Greenville, South Carolina, a sober Baptist township of perhaps 60,000 souls, to the Sheraton Hotel, with the startling offer: *You are invited to develop powers of a Superman*. And so it went on.

In time, the 'TM Sidhi programme' became central to the movement's global promotion, backed by the argument that it was a potent aid to gaining enlightenment. When practised regularly in sufficiently large groups, it would help bring about world peace as a ripple effect of the orderliness, positivity and bliss felt by the participants. In 1986, to demonstrate the group practice of levitation, the first 'International Yogic Flying Competition' was held before 10,000 people at the Indira Gandhi Sports Arena in New Delhi. Religious dignitaries, including the Shankaracharya of Jyothir Math, Swami Vishnudevanand Saraswati, were in attendance, as was Dr B. D. Triguna, President of the All-Indian Ayurveda Congress, India's largest association of Ayurvedic physicians. The whole show was introduced by a cherubically youthful Deepak Chopra. The Delhi competition was followed the next sum-mer by a demonstration of the 'world champion yogic flyers' in Washington, D. C., attended by 110 journalists and thirty-two TV crews.[15] A month later came another demonstration of 'yogic flying' in approximately one thousand cities around the world on the same weekend, organised by local practitioners of the technique. However well-co-ordinated, such displays were not to everybody's taste; for many, they were simply unpalatable. The British tabloids dubbed them 'Maharishi's Flying Circus' and treated them with predictable contempt. Such displays certainly combined various aspects of yoga's histori-cal trajectory by mixing meditation, psychic abilities, stress-relief and public performance, but yogic flying was simply way over most people's heads.

Undeterred, the TM movement has continued to juggle ancient and mod-ern. Its chief researcher into the physiology of consciousness is an MIT-educated neuroscientist called Tony Nader. According to a 1998 press release, for his scientific discovery that the Veda resides in the human body, the Maharishi Vedic University of Holland rewarded him with his weight in gold.[16] Two years later, Nader was crowned Maharaja Adhiraj Rajaraam, the leader of the 'Global Country of World Peace' and appointed by Maharishi as his successor. In 2005, twenty-two subsidiary *rajas* were made the national and regional leaders of the organisation, each entitled to wear ceremonial attire of white silk robes, gold medallion and golden crown.[17] Their training course took about two months and each participant was advised to contribute $1,000,000 to the Maharishi World Peace Fund.[18]

Not surprisingly, none of this has helped the TM cause gain wider, let alone scientific, credibility. Sixty years after Indian meditation teachers arrived in numbers to the West, many people are now drawn to practices they perceive to be more secular and less culture-bound. Mindfulness is the prime example, as we shall see in Chapter 25. Such techniques of applied psychology may not reach the same profound depths of interiority, but they are no doubt less challenging to current paradigms than promises of levitation or neo-Vedic kings in glistering headgear.

The David Lynch Foundation

Today, the most vibrant propagation of TM is to be found in the activities of the David Lynch Foundation, a charitable organisation set up by the art-house film director. Lynch could be a character from his own cult hit *Twin Peaks*, a mix of down-home America and far-out surrealism that results in something of a Jimmy Stewart from Mars. As such, he seems a suitably eccentric ambassador for scientific-supernormal meditation and is himself a long-term practitioner who enthusiastically attributes his prodigious creativity to the technique. His eponymous foundation offers relief from stress, and to the most stressed-out people in society what's more: war veterans suffering PTSD, severely disadvantaged inner-city kids, drug addicts, displaced refugees and assorted overburdened 'first-responders' (ambulance staff, fire-fighters, riot police and the like). Recently, the foundation taught meditation to the inmates of the notorious high-security jail on Rikers Island, an institution that counts among its alumni the Reverend Al Sharpton, the dapper Mafioso John Gotti (known as the Teflon Don), and former Hollywood bad guy James Cagney. TM may finally have laid some troubled ghosts to rest.

Suffering and Stress

Lynch's organisation operates out of a smart central Manhattan office devoid of any obvious reference to its inspirational Indian sage. It is a noble campaign doing very valuable work, no doubt, and if meditation can help deal with the current pandemic of stress, then, like Arjuna, it must enter wholeheartedly into the battle, preferably with government backing. But the philosophically inclined might be hesitant about such medicalisation. After all, to promote meditation solely as a stress-relief technique devoid of any greater context is to advance an historical oxymoron, adapting an ancient teaching to a syndrome that did not emerge until towards the end of the twentieth century. The great sages of earlier times—Mahavira, the Buddha, Shankara—were not concerned with 'stress' in the sense that we moderns use the word; for them, the concept did not exist. Of course, suffering was everywhere, the perennial problems of 'sickness, old age and death' that the Buddha identified as 'the three marks of impermanence', but that was, and for far too many on the planet still is, in a different league from what we now call stress. Unlike suffering, stress is not written indelibly into the human script, but is largely the consequence of our own lifestyle choices; we are run ragged by our chosen preoccupations—frantically updating social media profiles, worrying about the next mortgage payment or juggling the demands of childcare with earning as much money as we can. Of course, intense or chronic stress can turn into suffering, but in the sages' clear-eyed view, meditation was not a remedy for a lifestyle skewed out of balance. It operated on another level altogether, being the key to self-knowledge, a process of physical and psychic purification that gradually transmuted your born condition of suffering into wisdom and, with a good karmic wind behind you, might one day yield enlightenment.

Stress was first identified in the scientific community by the Swedish endocrinologist Hans Selye in his 1956 work *The Stress of Life*, and the concept took almost twenty years to enter the collective consciousness. Selye's next book, *Stress without Distress*, was published in 1974, coinciding nicely with the first scientific research on meditation, and he was one of the headline contributors to Maharishi's 'Science of Creative Intelligence' symposia at the time. It should be noted that Selye's use of the term was more sophisticated than the popular understanding. He argued that experience can be 'stressful' whether the impulse is judged positive or negative, as all experience leaves its mark on the mind-body complex. Selye termed negative stress 'distress', and positive stress 'eustress', with the former being more problematic. As a disease of adaption, stress manifests especially in mental, cardiovascular, gastrointestinal and hypersensitivity ailments which are caused by inappropriate responses to the inputs of everyday life.

The system whereby the body copes with stress, the hypothalamic-pituitary-adrenal axis (HPA axis) system, was also first described by Selye, who pointed to three stages in the body's adaptation to strong input: an 'alarm state', a 'resistance state' and an 'exhaustion state'. The effects of the last

259

stage persist in modified form. This understanding conforms to yogic psychology's concept of *samskaras*, the name given to residual impressions that lodge deep in the mind and function as subliminal activators of future desire and action. Much the same mechanism has been identified by western theories of the unconscious since Freud. Whichever model one prefers, there is no doubt that the mind-body has a long memory and stress may be occasioned by events we take for granted. Thus, it now seems that the distress of circumcision for six-month-old baby boys can resurface as post-traumatic stress disorder in their middle-age.[19] Looking further, recent research in the new science of epigenetics suggests that deeply stressful circumstances can affect the behaviour of genes not only during the present life but even into future generations.[20]

Meditation was historically associated with a simple life of rural tranquillity, whereas in general, the people who use it as a medical remedy are relatively privileged urbanised first-worlders. Stress breeds stress, each generation adding to the list of syndromes, and with each increment a new wellness therapy pops up to deal with the problem. We now have a stress disorder called *orthorexia nervosa* caused by an unhealthy obsession with eating healthily; then there is *nomophobia*, the smartphone separation anxiety recently identified among Generation Z. Initiated by the success of *The Mindfulness Colouring Book: Anti-Stress Art Therapy for Busy People*, stress-relieving 'adult' colouring books regularly top the sales charts and the market is worth millions per year. A British regional train service recently introduced a pilot scheme of combining colouring books with on-board yoga as a stress-busting regime aimed at its commuting 'phone zombies'.

The Trojan Horse of Stress Relief

Stress management may sometimes reach banal levels, but it may also conceal a deeper purpose. The principle of disguising a challenging spiritual truth in easily acceptable terms is an ancient one, made necessary because of the inevitable gulf of understanding between the teacher and the student. It is the job of the former to bridge it as skilfully as they can. This skill, known as *upaya* in Buddhist traditions, may involve a degree of benign expediency. In one of his influential commentaries, Adi Shankara, the South Indian sage who established the non-dual tradition from which Maharishi came, refers to the situation with disarming frankness: 'First let me set them on the right path, then in time I will gradually be able to bring them round to the final Truth.'[21]

Many ambassadors of mind-yoga came to the same conclusion. How could they best present their teaching in terms that their unschooled audience could understand and relate to? If students are so mired in metaphysical ignorance that they need to be tricked into enlightenment, the means to do this is to address that ignorance on its own terms. Pragmatism must trump theory, and if relief from stress is the pressing need, so be it. Those motivated to dive more deeply into meditation (and perhaps read judiciously between the lines a bit) may in time discover those realms of psychic possibility that lie patiently hidden within their remedial routine. Until then, needs must.

GOING WITHIN

24

FOUR TYPES OF MIND-YOGA

Despite its ubiquity, the word 'meditation' is notoriously imprecise. Meaning different things to different people, the term is used to cover almost anything in addition to a formal sitting practice: walking the dog, pottering in the garden or enjoying a quiet day's fishing can all qualify. Benign and restorative such activities may well be, but that is just the point, they are still *activities*, whereas 'real' meditation, deep mind-yoga, is the gradual lessening of all activity and a commensurate entry into silence.

Even within the orthodox repertoire of sitting practices, we find numerous schools, approaches and philosophies. As well as the venerable contemplative traditions of Judaism, Christianity and Islamic Sufism, India alone has produced many different types of meditative practice. Some of these are detailed in early texts such as the *Shvetashvatara Upanishad*; the best known is the use of the *mantra* OM that Patanjali recommends. Then come Jainism and early, or Theravadin, Buddhism, that champions the calming and centring practices of *samatha* ('settledness'; meditation which steadies the mind and brings about a state of 'calm abiding') and *vipassana* ('insight'; a contemplative exercise enabling one to discern the conditioned nature of phenomena), and the cultivation of compassion, or loving-kindness, through the technique of *metta bhavana* (an affective focus that generates compassion for all living beings). From around the end of the first millennium, Hindu Tantric and Mahayana Buddhist schools (especially the Tibetan Vajrayana), advocate the use of *mantras* and visualisation. A more emotive approach emerges in medieval times, with the culture of surrender to divine love through the means of theistic worship (*puja*), devotional chanting and singing (*bhajan*, *kirtan*) or dedicated service (*seva*) to a deity, such as Krishna, Rama or the Divine Mother in one of her many forms. Within all these systems there are further distinguishing factors, such as the different uses of sound, whether the eyes are open or closed (and the way this changes the meditative experience), and the distinction between a method employing awareness of the breath, or other physiological functions, as opposed to a purely mental focus that is detached from bodily grounding.

Nevertheless, whatever the practice, meditators themselves have always known that it has definite subjective effects, which is presumably why they bother to continue. Scientists, on the other hand, the high priests of our secular age, are slower in the uptake, generally beginning to take interest in a phenomenon only when it becomes noticeable as an economic and cultural factor in society. This tipping point has now been reached with yoga and meditation, whose success over many decades indicates that they are no mere passing fad, but reflect deeper needs, ways of thinking and changes in society at large. Realising that an examination of yoga can tell them something about how people live under the taxing conditions of modernity, researchers have been exploring the territory over the past forty years or more, and continue to do so with enthusiasm.[1]

Featuring prominently among the data accumulated so far are the physical changes accompanying meditation, or what we can call the bodily imprint of mind-yoga. The general state of the meditating body can be measured by its breathing rate and volume, and its level of rest as shown by these, the metabolic rate and galvanic skin response, as well as various chemical and hormonal changes in the system. More excitingly, concomitant changes in brain-activity are monitored by examining the electroencephalogram (EEG) readings of the brainwaves, which show the electrical activity of millions of neurons as they rise and fall at different frequencies, depending on our state of consciousness and what we are doing. Two American reseachers, Fred J. Travis and Jonathan Shear, have recently proposed a useful model which identifies three basic types of meditation, each with its own characteristic physical and mental parameters.[2]

1) Focused Attention

This first type of meditation involves focusing the attention on some object or perception, by concentrating on a single point and disallowing the mind from wandering off it. The object of such a focus could be virtually anything: a candle flame, a geometric *yantra* diagram, or a regular bodily rhythm are all methods typically employed in such a system. The aim is to train the attention to hold steady in one place and thereby to frustrate its natural habit of jumping from one thing to another. The shorthand term 'monkey-mind' is used in many teachings, likening our chronic mental restlessness to the movements of a monkey that leaps from branch to branch, chattering incessantly. Such instability, so the argument goes, can only be overcome by forcibly centring the attention so that it remains undistracted on the present point of focus. EEG imaging techniques have identified the various areas of the brain associated with mental meandering, as well as those associated with registering distraction, re-orienting awareness and holding a sustained focus. These show that in this Focused Attention meditation, the EEG movement is rapid, rising and falling twenty to thirty times a second to produce what is called '*beta* wave EEG'. It can be even faster, in the range of thirty to fifty times per second which is known as '*gamma* wave EEG'. Studies cited in *Scientific American* suggested that, as one might predict, practising this type of meditation improves the mind's ability to focus.[3] However, high frequency EEG is not a restful, calm or expanded state but a relatively active, even tensed, one, consistent with concentrating in a focused, and exclusive, manner.

2) Open Monitoring

Another general category of meditation is Open Monitoring. This employs a volitional control of the mind, in order to change how it reacts to stressful information. The practitioner of this type of technique observes their thoughts, experiences and emotional reactions as they appear and disappear, and tries to maintain a non-judgemental attitude towards them. Continuously cultivating a neutral response to whatever sensations arise and pass away in the mind, and remaining free of reactivity to them, develops the strategic habit of separating the experiencer, the 'I', from his mental impressions. This separation works to correct, redirect or even inhibit, his spontaneous reactions. With sufficient practice, this habit persists outside of meditation as well. So, for example, if patients suffering from depression school themselves to monitor the memories, and observe the feelings, they find problematic, they will become better able to manage sadness, anxiety and so on, in everyday life. When and if such feelings do arise, they will carry less force and be less dominant.

Neuro-imaging studies confirm that Open Monitoring reduces activity in those areas of the brain involved in anxiety and the technique has been shown to help people deal with symptoms of depression and anxiety. One dramatic example is that of war veterans suffering post-traumatic stress disorder. Open Monitoring also decreases disturbed sleep patterns. This type of meditation is characterised by a slower EEG wave pattern, called *theta*, which oscillates only five to eight times a second. *Theta* EEG occurs naturally when someone is preoccupied—for example, while reading a book—and is no longer aware of outside stimuli, such as surrounding noise or other sensory input from the environment. This lack of attention to ambient information is due to changes in the functioning of the thalamus, that part of the brain responsible for processing incoming sensory data. While Open Monitoring can be seen to correspond to what Patanjali calls *pratyahara*—the withdrawal of the sensory focus in an inward direction as the attention settles down—it still requires continuous focus and thus some degree of mental effort is involved. This effort is less than that required in the Focused Attention method, and may not be experienced as onerous, but it still works to engage the awareness in a focus which is limiting and exclusive. Because of this, the mind is still confined to a relatively surface level of thinking and perceiving.

3) Self-transcending

The third type of meditation corresponds to the process that Patanjali advocates in his classic text, which is to say, a progressive interiority that culminates in the settled state of the mind known as *samadhi* ('coming together' or 'coherence'). What is crucial about this process, and what distinguishes it from its two predecessors, is the fact that it is non-volitional and proceeds automatically. In other words, the awareness easily and effortlessly settles inwards of its own accord. The subjective experience is one of thought becoming increasingly quieter and less defined, rather as if the volume of the radio were gradually being turned down until it becomes silent. This progressive renunciation of experience is felt as a growing peacefulness and quiet enjoyment.[4] The surrender of experience culminates in a state free of sensory perceptions, thoughts or emotions, whatever their content or character. Mind-yoga teachings call this 'pure consciousness'—the word 'pure' meaning free of all admixture—describing it as a state of undisturbed being, free of all mental input. With the cessation of its activity, the limited sense of self as volitional agent is gradually transcended.

During 'self-transcending', a middle frequency EEG wave pattern typically occurs, at seven to nine cycles per second. This is called *alpha-1* and is characteristic of reduced mental activity and increased relaxation. We can imagine these coherent *alpha* waves as functioning something like the conductor of an orchestra, working to bring all the different instruments into a harmonious whole. This orderly activity in frontal *alpha* waves was first discovered in practitioners' self-transcending meditation over forty years ago. More recently, a meta-analysis published in the American Psychological Association's

Psychological Bulletin in 2006 cited seven studies showing that in self-transcending meditation *alpha* EEG coherence increases between the left and right sides of the frontal brain and continues spreading until the whole brain becomes synchronised and coherent.

Such synchrony appears to enliven a coherent state of consciousness that has beneficial effects for both mind and body. When the mind settles, the level of biochemical and physiological stress decreases significantly. This reverses our ancient biological inheritance, the 'fight-or-flight' response, that is marked by an increase in heartbeat, respiration rate and the production of powerful stress hormones, such as adrenalin and cortisol, as well as stress-related compounds such as lactic acid. This stress-reflex is still hard-wired in the human animal because our early ancestors were stationed squarely in the middle of the food chain, eating smaller creatures but in constant danger of being eaten themselves. Our high-alert setting continued until relatively recently in evolutionary terms, and such ancient and intrinsic biological mechanisms cannot just be wished away by conscious intention. However, when mental activity settles down naturally, without any coercion and of its own free will, the direct opposite to the 'fight-or-flight' response seems to occur in the body. 'Self-transcending' techniques bring about a 'stay-and-play' physiological response, marked by a reduction in stress chemicals and a generally benign blood chemistry.

It seems the repeated restfulness of this state allows for not only the spontaneous dissolution of accumulated physical fatigue and tension but, over time, the neutralising of those deep-rooted psychological and emotional impressions that, as we saw in the last chapter, Hans Selye identified as the persisting effects of 'distress'. One clue as to how this self-healing—or to use a yogic phrase 'purification'—happens may lie in its analogy with dreamless sleep. Self-transcending techniques mimic sleep, but practitioners do not lose consciousness and they also register different types of physiological changes from those brought on by sleeping. Studies published between 2012 and 2015 show that in sleep, the brain switches on an internal detox-system that uses the cerebrospinal fluid moving between the brain and spinal cord to wash out cellular waste from the central nervous system.[5] This so-called glymphatic system uses the cell's batteries—the mitochondria—to flush out up to three pounds of waste proteins a year, in much the same way as the lymph system in other organs removes waste to the kidney and liver. If this cleansing and re-vitalising process is, in fact, activated by the restful nature of dreamless sleep, it may well be replicated and augmented by the deep rest of regular meditation.[6]

Subjectively, the relief of being free from the burden of any sort of thinking, whether directed or not, is immense. From a yogic point of view, this process is a gentle withdrawal of awareness from the habitual outward pull of the senses (*pratyahara*), followed by the gradual settling of the waves of thought and feeling (*chitta-vrittis*) as their content is purified and released. Eventually there comes a falling back into what Patanjali calls our 'true nature' (*sva-rupa*). In this way, self-transcending meditation allows the practitioner eventually to become consciously familiar with the core of their being, an area that lies beyond all mental activity, which yoga teachings identify as *purusha*, 'the Person', that is to say, our irreducible essence.[7]

Yoga Nidra

Any discussion of meditation in the context of yoga must also consider 'yogic sleep', or *yoga nidra*. Over the years this has become something of an umbrella term to describe systems of progressive relaxation or 'guided meditation'. The *yoga nidra* method usually proceeds by consciously directing the attention to different parts of the body and relaxing them. Typically, this begins with the right hand and proceeds, stage by stage, through the entire body. As this procedure is guided by the teacher, from the point of view of Patanjali's Eight Limb progression, the practitioner of *yoga nidra* remains in a state of light withdrawal of the senses (*pratyahara*) with four senses more or less internalised, but the sense of hearing still functioning externally to act as a connection to the spoken instructions.

The system was promoted in the mid-twentieth century by Swami Satyananda Saraswati of Rishikesh, a *sannyasin*, yoga teacher and guru, active in both his native India and the West. Coming from the lineage of Swami Shivananda Saraswati, the founder of the Divine Life Society, he founded the Bihar School of Yoga, esteemed as a traditional and holistic spiritual path, in 1963. Satyananda, who was also an astonishingly prolific writer of over eighty books, claimed that the *yoga nidra* technique was very ancient, though following a pattern we have already seen with several other relatively modern teachings, when examined, the substantiating textual references to it seem vague at best.[8]

Conscious Sleep

While Satyananda's meditation system comprises an imaginative journey through eight stages, including awareness of body and breath, relaxation and the input of creative intentions, and visualisation, other teachers have defined *yoga nidra* more abstractly as being the state of conscious sleep. In this paradoxical state, the body sleeps (or dreams), but there remains a spontaneous and effortlessly maintained inward awareness throughout.[9] In the terminology of Sankhya, the philosophical framework of all classical yoga, this inner lucidity results from the enlivening of the 'witness' (*sakshi*), a mode of awareness attributed to a deeply interior level of the mind known as *buddhi*. The word literally means 'wakefulness' but is usually translated as 'intellect', by which is meant not only the process of conceptualising but, most importantly, the faculty of discrimination. Sufficiently refined and purified, the *buddhi* is able to discern absolute reality, and reflect the infinite consciousness that exists prior to the mind and its perceptions. In this, the *buddhi* of yoga is comparable to the 'intellect' as described in the writings of the Apostolic Fathers and St. Augustine, which, as it happens, were more or less contemporary with the *Yoga Sutra*. Just as these Christian thinkers saw the intellectual faculty to be the link between the limited human mind and the limitless being of God, so the individual *buddhi* serves to reflect the universal 'Person' or spirit, the *purusha* that is unbounded consciousness.[10] For the advanced yogi, this consciousness is an unbroken experience, whether his body-mind is waking, sleeping or dreaming.[11]

Experiments conducted on *yoga nidra* at the Menninger Foundation in Kansas in 1971 were among the first to test brain activity in yoga. The subject was Swami Rama, the author of an influential autobiography, *Living with Himalayan Masters* and founder of the Himalayan Institute of Yoga Science and Philosophy. Rama's brainwave activity, recorded while he progressively relaxed, passed from prolonged *alpha* waves, achieved simply by his imagining an empty blue sky with drifting clouds, into a state of dreaming sleep characterised by prolonged and slower activity of *theta* waves. Finally, the Swami entered the state of deep sleep with characteristic slow rhythm *delta* waves. However, he remained inwardly perfectly aware throughout and was later able accurately to recall the various events which had occurred in the laboratory while his body lay snoring. In another experiment, he caused two areas a couple of inches apart on his right hand to change temperature in opposite directions. The difference was 5°C; one part of his palm turned red from the heat, and the other blue from the cold. He also raised his heart rate by an effort of will, from seventy to 300 beats per minute, and could stop his heartbeat for seventeen seconds.

Scientific studies, laboratories, questionnaires and statistics all seem necessary tactics to smuggle spiritual truths into a profoundly materialistic culture

271

such as ours. Behind this quantifying project lies the utopian vision of human perfectibility that has underpinned modern science from the days of Francis Bacon onwards. Time will tell whether meditation techniques shorn of their spiritual provenance will continue to be popular simply to relieve stress, granting pragmatic benefits to practitioners who remain unmotivated to investigate the deeper transformative possibilities of what they are doing. From a yogic perspective, the hope would be that regular meditation will elicit a transformation from deep within, and eventually provide access to greater self-knowledge and superior orders of reality. In this light, the entry-point of stress relief, and the painstaking and piecemeal approval of scientific validation, will be seen to have served a valuable purpose, but to count for little in the end. After all, when you are in love, does it really matter to you what chemicals are whizzing around your system or what your brain waves are doing?

25

MINDFULNESS À LA MODE

And so we come to Mindfulness, by far the most successful of the Open Monitoring techniques described in the previous chapter, and very much the current flavour of the month. Invigorated by the oxygen of publicity and a slew of scientific evidence in recent years, not since TM swept the board in the '70s has there been such a widespread interest in a meditation method. The extraordinary popularity of Mindfulness is more mainstream than its predecessors: government departments, conventional businesses, health, education and psychiatric professionals, hip young entrepreneurs, stressed-out politicians—you name it, everyone seems to be doing it these days. Or at least talking about it. Among the system's many attractions is its perceived freedom from cultural baggage and its 'instagrammability'. For the highly focused millennial, who typically checks their phone a hundred times a day, even the presence of a teacher is dispensed with, as there are apps you can download, and off you go. The look-down generation is learning to look inwards, and they like it.

First, some context. What we call mindfulness today began its current incarnation in Burma as an early twentieth-century revival of the ancient entry-level Buddhist meditation called *vipassana*, a simple technique to centre the wavering attention through directing awareness to the body and breath so as to view the mind's activity dispassionately. Practised since the time of the Buddha, this well-trodden path was seen by the Burmese people to be a potent way to reconnect with their Buddhist roots and regain their cultural and national integrity in the face of British colonialism and the accompanying spread of Christianity. This process clearly parallels the rediscovery of yoga in nineteenth-century India that we examined in Chapters 7 and 8. Then, in the 1960s, some young Americans, mainly soldiers on R'n'R from the war in Vietnam, discovered this *vipassana* in Burma and particularly in neighbouring

Thailand, which shares the same Theravadin form of early Buddhism. After partying in Bangkok, hungover G.I.s would head up to forest monasteries in Isaan, the rural northeast of the country, to chill out, detox and meditate. Several Thai Buddhist teachers there, the most renowned of whom was Ajahn Chah, took on Western students who so enjoyed their *vipassana* practice that they brought it back home to America. Once there, the insight meditation technique—pioneered by Jon Kabat-Zinn, a professor at the University of Massachusetts Medical School who had already had experience of Zen meditation—became established as a remedial therapy in 1979 with the introduction of an eight-week course he called 'Mindfulness-based Stress Reduction'. In setting up the programme, which was principally for cancer patients, Kabat-Zinn made the crucial decision to extract the technique from its Buddhist context, conforming to a trajectory we are by now familiar with: as wisdom moves from East to West, a sacred teaching is transformed into a secular healing remedy, preferring to align itself more with science than spirit. Kabat-Zinn went on to pen several popular books on mindfulness.

Buddhism Lite?

Forty years on, there is no doubt that the technique is proving very useful for many people. A good number of them were probably previously suspicious of mind-yoga or what they felt lay behind it, and most of those who take up mindfulness are either unaware of the deeper Buddhist implications of the practice or uninterested in them. If it works, it works, and that's enough. By the same token, most teachers of the technique feel no need to mention the *vipassana* connection, presenting the system as a simple form of applied psychology, free of any religious or mystical baggage, and untainted by problematic guru-structures or alien cultural contexts. This secular presentation has proved just what the doctor ordered at a time when the general public is more sceptical of charismatic teachers than they were in the naïve 1960s, yet at the same time increasingly stressed and desirous of non-chemical treatment.

On the other hand, many Buddhist purists would claim that the popularisation of mindfulness has traduced it. The original insight technique has many levels of deeper application beyond the initial focus on the body or breath to wean the attention off irksome or troubling thoughts. Correctly understood and progressively applied, Buddhist mindfulness involves nothing less than a graduated deconstruction of our identity as an independent 'self', and a radical revisioning of the behaviour that stems from such a habitual selfhood. This transformative agenda distinguishes traditional practice sharply from what we can call psychotherapeutic mindfulness, which is a tool to fix a conventional sense of self that, for whatever reasons, is temporarily malfunctioning. A Buddhist might challenge this approach by asking if you can ever really become well by adapting to the norms of a society that is itself chronically sick. So, while the goal of therapy is restoring the self to what is considered normative 'mental health', Buddhist endeavour aims at selfless enlightenment (*nibbana*), which is quite a different matter. These two approaches are grounded in two distinct understandings of the nature, scope and cause of human suffering.

In practice, therapy aims at the alleviation of symptoms that are experienced as extrinsic, peripheral or temporarily damaging to the patient's core sense of identity, and its role is to heal such a damaged self in order to allow it to return to normal functioning as soon as possible. Buddhism, on the other hand, sees human suffering to be intrinsic to, and inseparable from, that conventional sense of the ego-self as an independent agent, separated out from the rest of the world and defined by its capacity to think and act autonomously. Whereas psychotherapeutic mindfulness seeks to restore the impaired structure of self-as-agent and ensure its robust continuance, Buddhist meditative practice engages in a sustained and methodical dismantling of all self-centred functioning, whether it be judged admirable or aberrant by conventional standards.

This difference is mirrored in the application of the technique itself. In much therapeutic mindfulness (and there are already several variant schools), the open monitoring of mental experience—which, as we have already seen, is a non-judgemental observing of mental and emotional states as they arise unbidden—is only employed in the initial stage of the regimen. Having achieved adequate distance from disturbing thoughts and urges, the patient is then encouraged to move seamlessly from simply observing to actively judging them as undesirable, and finally to consciously choosing a healthier or more 'normal' way of thinking. In this way the troubled self is gradually returned to a less disturbed state, and this return is deemed a healing process. In classic Buddhist mindful practice there is no such judgement, intervention or wilful re-construction because *all* mental states are viewed as being equally empty or illusory, precisely because they are the manifestations of a self-identity that is itself falsely imagined in the first place. In its traditional monastic context, mindfulness is not used as a spiritualised form of psychotherapy or a device for restoring egoic competence; much less is it a strategy for achieving the invulnerable self-sufficiency that, since 1970s California, has become the goal of so much ego-therapy. Buddhism is not concerned with fashioning a more successful—and no doubt higher-earning—individual, but with cultivating morality and offering eventual liberation from that very sense of being an individual ego that is the habitual clench of selfhood.

Behind this uncompromising perspective, and all too easily ignored, lies the fact that, from the start, the Buddha's instruction was primarily directed to monastics: men and women who had chosen a lifestyle dedicated to the undermining of normal householder patterns of desire, activity and accumulation. Those who find secular mindfulness has advanced their career or improved their golf-handicap might be surprised by the more radical detachment counselled in many of the Buddhist scriptures. An early Theravadin scripture integral to Thai and Burmese discipline replicates the instructions the Buddha himself gave in the *Satipatthana Sutta*. It advocates the practice of 'reflecting on the repulsiveness of the body' (*patikulamanasikara*), explaining:

> Here a monk, in regard to his own body which—from the sole of the feet upwards and from the hair of the head downwards—is bounded by the skin and filled with manifold impurities, reflects thus:
>
> 'There are in this body hairs of the head, body hairs, nails, teeth, skin, flesh, sinews, bones, bone-marrow, kidneys, heart, liver, pleura, spleen, lungs, intestines, mesentery, undigested food, excrement, bile, phlegm, pus, blood, sweat, fat, tears, grease, spit, mucus, synovial fluid and urine.'[1]

Contemplation of these thirty-two bodily impurities is a standard procedure. As the basic depth-practice associated with body awareness, it demonstrates yet another dissonance between traditional practice and modern understanding.

The separation of householder and monastic life is paralleled in Buddhist teaching by the distinction it draws between conventional truth (*sammuti-sacca*), which governs day-to-day, practical affairs, where appearances are taken seriously, and ultimate or absolute truth (*paramattha-sacca*), which reveals the illusory nature of these self-same appearances. To Buddhist critics of popular mindfulness, these levels have become hopelessly conflated. What was originally a revolutionary tool to deconstruct egotism, desire and suffering, has been glibly marketed as a strategy to paper over the functional cracks of the twenty-first century. A potent critique to shape a new world has been diluted to a social emollient. Many agree with a recent trenchant criticism of modern mindfulness as: 'Buddhism sliced up, commodified and drained of all reference to the transcendent.'[2]

Mechanically Mindful

None of the above undermines the perceived benefits that secular mindfulness can bring, of course. Traduced or not, the practice is here to stay. It has even become digitalised. Building on late 1960s studies pioneered by the American cardiologist Herbert Benson—who was among the first to test TM subjects and went on to invent his own Relaxation Response method—the ever-inventive Apple launched its app 'Breathe' in the autumn of 2016. The makers claim it will improve your health in only sixty seconds, so even the busiest of twenty-first century achievers should be able to squeeze in the odd session. The app encourages one to breathe slowly in and out for a minute—you can alter the time if you wish—and just in case you lose track of this basic activity, a gentle pulse will tap your wrist and display your heart rate—assuming you have an Apple watch, of course.

A rather un-Buddhist competitiveness has also been factored into mindfulness, to encourage its practice. Apps such as Headspace and Calm, Apple's 'App of the year, 2017' which has been downloaded more than 27 million times, allow users to track how often they meditate and for how long, logging each session into a running total. On the Headspace app, a coloured rosette flashes up after your first session. Another rosette is earned if you practise for three days in a row and then another at the ten-, fifteen-, and thirty-day marks. From here, the goals become further apart, with awards offered to those who sit mindfully for ninety and 180 consecutive days and then for a full year, at which point a golden trophy flashes up on screen surrounded by confetti. The bliss such an award gives may hope to simulate *nibbana*, but if you go a single day without sitting, your winning streak is broken and the count returns to zero. The word on the street is that many mindful meditators are getting stressed at the prospect of missing a de-stressing session and hence losing their points.

Indeed, in the world of self-improvement there seems to be no end to our adolescent fascination with getting electronic gadgets to help us to do what we could perfectly well do naturally. The New Age guru Deepak Chopra is never far from the forefront of the latest craze. Maharishi's former student is the author of numerous books selling in their millions that, with titles such as *The Seven Spiritual Laws of Success*, have brought Dale Carnegie's positive thinking into the twenty-first century. Now the man some wittily call 'Deep Pockets' Chopra has invented a new twist on mind-yoga: his Virtual Reality Meditation app was unveiled in Los Angeles a couple of months before Apple's 'Breathe'. Chopra narrates the simulation and hopes to sell the experience at $10 a pop at booths in airports, hospitals and other populous locations, as well as via phones and laptops enabled with VR platforms. He was not backward in coming forward when recently describing the benefits of his brainchild to *The Guardian* newspaper: 'In twenty minutes you get a journey to enlightenment. The goal is to feel grounded and understand yourself a little better.' A journey to enlightenment? Well, the viewer does get trippy graphics heavy on 1960s pink and purple, with otherworldly sound effects laid over statements which, depending on your perspective, are either insightful, gnomic or nonsensical. Sceptics may raise an eyebrow, but Hollywood's ebullient guru is unlikely to be deterred. There is no paradox in finding your true self via virtual reality, he explains, because everything we experience is itself a simulation. The app, called 'Finding your true self', aims to shortcut the tedious investment of time, effort and discipline which has always been considered necessary for self-knowledge but frustrates many time-poor twenty-first-century seekers. Unerringly in tune with the times, Chopra offers a simulation which mixes 'insights, contemplation and entertainment'. What's not to like?[3]

Whichever way yoga develops, it looks as though technology will be a part of it. One of the medieval *siddha*'s main objectives, longevity stretching even to immortality, is now being touted as a biomedical possibility in Silicon Valley. On a less ambitious level, there is the Muse headband for monitoring your own brainwaves in order to bring about meditative states. And if you're feeling unsure of your mat moves, for $250 Amazon will search through its three billion items and speedily dispense a drone bearing some Nadi X: stylish mesh yoga pants that connect with an iPhone app to vibrate and guide your body through a particular posture. Cyborg yoga, here we come...

Quantifying Benefits

Slick marketing aside, other advocates of therapeutic mindfulness are working hard to prove its relevance by amassing scientific evidence. In the first UK conference of its kind, held in November 2013, researchers from around the world met with mental health experts and yoga teachers to discuss the effects of body-yoga, especially on the brain. A whole range of conditions was shown to respond well to postural work: post-traumatic and anxiety disorders, depression, alcoholism, ADHD, epilepsy and eating disorders. One cause is the coherence established between the sympathetic ('fight-or-flight') and the parasympathetic ('stay-and-play') nervous systems. However, not unsurprisingly, the submitted evidence made no mention of the second, or 'aerial' nervous system, the subtle body that, as we saw in Chapter 5, is integral to the classical yogic world-view. Nor were any supernormal powers discussed. To date, discounting such fringe research tools as Kirlian energy-photography, which peaked in the seventies and has since faded from view, science simply does not have the capability to measure such refined levels of quasi-physiological functioning. We are left with a partial picture of what yoga is actually doing because our attention is confined to the relatively gross anatomy and its sensible activities. Not being in the business of speculation, science has little or no idea of where the full range of yogic practices might lead.

The conference also heard evidence on mind-yoga in the form of mindfulness. Research from Harvard Medical School was cited, which suggests that just eight weeks' practice can promote brain growth. Thicker grey matter was found in the left hippocampus—a small horseshoe-shaped structure in the central brain involved in memory, learning and emotional regulation—as well as the posterior cingulate cortex, which is involved in memory and emotion. Similar growth was found in the temporoparietal junction (TPJ), an area that is responsible for collecting and processing a vast amount of external information, as well as playing a crucial role in self/other distinctions.

The study only involved sixteen participants, but hinted at future possibilities by showing that the effects of being mindful constitute more than just a generalised mood of peacefulness and relaxation. Specific cognitive and psychological changes occur during the practice that persist throughout the day, and they are based not just on mood swings but on deep-seated changes in the brain's structure and functioning. Some of these changes may be long-term. One of the most recent studies, conducted by researchers working in Wisconsin, Spain and France, shows that the practice can even have genetic effects, limiting the expression of those genes associated with chronic inflammatory conditions in the body. Other, more wide-ranging, studies corroborate this.[4]

Similar data has long been known from previous studies on other meditation techniques, but the novelty of mindfulness ensured the results created a bit of a stir. One outcome was that in 2015, under the Mindfulness Initiative, an all-party parliamentary group was set up in the UK with the remit to investigate the evidence and applicability of the technique in many aspects of national life. This resulted in the Mindful Nation UK report being published in October 2015, and the Initiative is now working with government ministers, opinion-formers and employers to raise awareness of the report's findings and recommendations. A specific area of focus is education, where huge potential is envisaged and many schools have already implemented programmes. The Myriad Project—an acronym for My Resilience in Adolescence—is a study being run by Oxford University to see how applicable therapeutic mindfulness could be to everyone involved in education: pupils, teachers and parents alike. The biggest trial of its kind ever attempted, the Project involves 25,000 pupils spread over eighty schools and five years, and aims to report its findings in 2022. According to an article in *The Guardian* in October 2017, 145 MPs have so far taken the hybrid course in 'mindful-ness-based cognitive therapy' to increase their ability to come up with better policies. The long-suffering UK electorate, deeply disenchanted with the performance of their elected representatives throughout the Brexit fiasco, will no doubt be sincerely hoping it works.

However, not everyone is optimistic about the benefits of mindfulness. Scepticism centres on the fact that therapies, phone apps and other interven-tions are being rushed to market without sufficient rigorous testing and appropriately staggered implementation. More generally, the scientific com-munity is by nature dubious of anything to do with consciousness alteration, arguing that, if a psychological technique is powerful enough to bring about beneficial effects, it could well create harmful changes too. This caution has been justified in the case of other therapies, Cognitive Behavioural Therapy for example, and some experts warn that a combination of skilled marketing, genuine eagerness to do the best by their pupils and a reliance on only anec-dotal evidence may lead unwary educators to adopt the technique before it has accumulated a respectable track-record.

Such sceptics point to worrying results released from a study at the University of California in the autumn of 2015. These show that mindfulness can disrupt the brain's ability to discriminate between different scenarios. Simply put, it can stop people differentiating between what is real and what is imagined, thereby inducing a solipsism that is already observable in many New Age teachings and the narcissism of our celebrity culture. Participants who engaged in a fifteen-minute session were less able to distinguish between words they had seen written down and those they had only thought about, leading to the possibility that the technique might hamper the cognitive pro-cesses that contribute to accurately identifying the source of a memory and thus, rather than lead to greater mental clarity, work to facilitate a confusion of realities. The study, published in *Psychological Science*, a journal of the Association for Psychological Science, concludes: 'As a result, the same aspects of mindfulness that create countless benefits can also have the unin-tended negative consequence of increasing false-memory susceptibility'.[5]

Another recent study from economists at the universities of Edinburgh and Gothenburg came to the distinctly downbeat conclusion that watching re-runs of the TV documentary *Ancient Worlds* is about as good for your health as doing mindfulness. Researchers took a sample of 140 students, putting half of them on a six-week course of the practice. They found that these were no more likely to eat healthily, exercise or give up smoking and alcohol than the other half of the sample who had spent half a dozen hours as dedicated couch potatoes watching programmes about Mesopotamia. The biochemical stress responses to being quizzed under time pressure were also similar for both groups, although the students who had been on the mindfulness course did say they felt less stressed. Placebo meditation? The study added to what is a generally confused picture, but some researchers are in no doubt, and downright critical. Miguel Farias is one. A reader in cognitive and biological psychology at Coventry University, he has found that the practice can induce mania, depression or psychosis, echoing a charge that has been levelled at other meditation techniques over the years.[6]

Whatever the system, there are always two sides to the meditation coin: the technique itself and the person who is using it. This, of course, is precisely the reason that any genuine practice must be learned directly and on a one-to-one basis from a suitably qualified teacher, who can monitor the student's progress and make whatever adjustments may be necessary along the way. Real teaching is always a human interaction, a psychic osmosis, even, and although educational technology has begun to dispense with the vital person-to-person encounter, virtual gurus are just not the same thing at all. The Headspace app, with its ten-minute guided meditations, has more than three million users worldwide and is currently worth over £25 million. However popular, the teaching of mind-altering techniques remotely, without the feedback loop of personal monitoring, can be a risky business, as Farias has found. There is mounting evidence that even an unsupervised three-day session on Headspace could be a very risky business for vulnerable people.[7] Nonetheless, the propagation of digital instruction continues apace; even the respected Buddhist magazine *Tricycle* recently ran an online Mindfulness course.

A more speculative query has also been raised that is interesting in the light of the pronounced gender imbalance in body-yoga. Research published at the beginning of 2017 suggested that while mindfully directing their attention to present feelings and sensations has a significant impact in helping women overcome a down mood, it has the reverse effect on men. A team from Brown University that followed a mixed group through a forty-hour programme found that the women benefitted, but the men felt worse. One suggested explanation is that women typically like to deal with a problem by going over the issue repeatedly, often talking it through with female friends until they find a solution. Men on the other hand avoid such rumination and prefer to distract themselves to gain some distance. For them to suddenly confront a problem head-on with little wriggle-room may have an adverse effect. In this particular study, the men spent on average seven hours longer doing the practice than the women, but even with this additional time, their outlook showed no signs of improvement and in some cases, deterioration.[8]

CONTEMPORARY CAUTIONS

26

YOGA SHMOGA

'Yoga' has become an extremely elastic term these days. Indeed, 'stretch and relax', the slogan of many a postural class, now seems to apply to the word itself, which has become as saggy as any unworked midriff. 'Yoga' now means just about whatever you want it to; reduced to a commercial suffix it can be added onto any type of new exercise routine to make it appear contemporary and cool. There seems to be no end of those eager to jump on the yoga *bandha*wagon, and while new and hybrid forms are constantly being created, even among the well-established ones there is a huge variety.

The briefest overview of the current set menu would have to include:

Anusara Yoga (spiritually oriented)
Ashtanga Yoga (spandex body-building)
Bihar School Yoga (traditional, spiritual and integrative)
Bikram 'Hot' Yoga (Hollywood heat)
Dru Yoga (done in a *tai chi* style of breathing and movement)
Hatha Yoga (traditionally a rigorous purification, nowadays a general physical
    approach)
Iyengar Yoga (rigorous precision, often using supports)
Kripalu Yoga (individualised regimes and lengthy holding of postures)
Kundalini Yoga (subtle body energiser)
Power Yoga (gym-style calisthenics)
Scaravelli Yoga (therapeutic spinal alignment)
Shivananda Yoga (motto: 'simple living, high thinking')
Vini Yoga—aka the Association of Yogic Studies (tailored to each individual)
Vinyasa Yoga (posture-flow synchronised with breathing)

The above list is composed of well-established systems with clear identities and, in most cases, authentic lineages, but just below this tip of the iceberg is a heaving mountain of neo-yogas—vacuous innovations, brand-exercises and near-spoofs—that is growing weekly. Classical yoga was never a homogenous body of teaching (one of the leading yoga academics has identified no fewer than forty different aspects of traditional practice),[1] but what *is* new is the rate, and type, of innovation. Yoga buffs may be used to a lot of hot air coming from *pavanmuktasana*, the knees-to-head 'wind-releasing posture', but the time has evidently come to gain proficiency in a brand-new pose: the 'tongue placed firmly in the cheek'. For those interested in Sanskrit terminology, this would be something like the *auparodhikasthiti asana*.

Thanks to social media, neo-yogas can spread with astonishing speed. An example: one day in February 2017, Scottish teacher Finlay Wilson uploaded his 'Kilted Yoga' sequence on YouTube before beginning a teaching session. The video stars Wilson as a bare-chested Braveheart, doing acrobatic yoga poses against a background of rugged Scottish scenery. The climax of the show, predictably enough, is his headstand, which answers for a new generation the age-old question of what a Scotsman wears under his kilt. By the time Wilson emerged from his class a couple of hours later, the video had collected a million views; by the time he went to bed that night, it had racked up 17 million. Soon afterwards, the kilted star had appeared on NBC's *Today* show in the US, marched in New York's annual Tartan Day Parade, and talked men's health with the Health Secretary of the UN. The video has now been viewed 67 million times on Facebook and countless fans await his book, *Kilted Yoga: Yoga Laid Bare*, with bated breath.

If upturned kilts are not your thing, you can practise Flow Yoga, Yin Yoga, Rocket Yoga, Jivamukti Yoga, or Dharma Yoga. Some of these use music, others don't. Then there is Acroyoga, which combines yoga acrobatics and healing for two, or Yogalates (not to be confused with the trademarked Yogilates), which may sound like a new Starbucks line but is in fact a mellow, some might say frothy, blend of yoga and Pilates. Billed as being 'for those who can't decide which path to follow', it is becoming popular in many health clubs and studios across America. On the other side of the world, Kalaripayattu Yoga is gaining wide acceptance down under in Australia. This system mixes yoga *asanas* with the ancient martial arts regime from Kerala that, according to legend, Buddhist monks took to China and Japan to seed the fighting disciplines there. A recent offshoot, Shadow Yoga, emphasises three dynamic exercises to prepare the body for general *asana* practice; they build strength in the legs and core and increase flexibility in the hips and spine.

Back in the UK, people currently seem to prefer another, less manly, new blend called Nine Lives, which teaches what it calls Unity Yoga. This is not, as the name might imply, an aspiration for closeness to the Divine, but, rather more prosaically, a system for those who don't want to feel lonely on the mat. As their website explains: 'you work together with your partner's support to try out new things. We use each others' bodies to deepen your breath, your strength and flexibility, improve body awareness, increase alertness and improve connection in working together.' Nine Lives also combines *hatha* and *vinyasa* from the traditional list above: 'to explore poses you could not master alone, as well as find deeper release with the help of others.' The more the merrier it seems; the blurb adds: 'We cater for flash mobs to yoga hen parties and yoga jams to bespoke team-building.'

If you don't feel drawn to bonding with your mates, why not get closer to your favourite animal? Someone in India has just broken the world record for the longest time spent performing yoga on horseback (ten hours, as it happens), while Doga, which is yoga with dogs, began in California (of course) and is gaining increasing popularity in the UK too. (Doga is not to be confused with Broga, however, which is gym-yoga for real blokes who don't want any of the girlie mystical fluff.) While the dogs do not really get a workout themselves, they certainly play a cuddly part in some of the poses. However, an outfit called the Dogs Trust is getting concerned. A spokesman says: 'It is important to remember that dogs can't tell us when they have had enough. Doga, and any variation of it, should always be carried out under the watchful eye of trained professionals.'

Well, dogs are not that passive, surely, and anyway, professional 'whats?' one might ask. We all know about the 'downward dog', but Doga? Barking.

There seems no end to mix 'n' match brands. Some of those currently making waves in the US can be found from a randomly selected issue of the country's market-leading *Yoga Journal*: there's dancer Jocelyn Gordon with her 'let it all hang out' Bhakti Boogie Yoga; Mark Divine, a retired Navy SEAL commander with his macho-militarised Warrior Yoga, and Christian evangelist Brooke Boon with her Holy Yoga.[2] Such exercise routines calling themselves yoga don't even need a tutor to be physically present. With over a million YouTube tutorials to choose from, sessions can be carried out anywhere, anytime.

If this plethora of choice is beginning to depress you, you can always cheer yourself up with a bit of Laughing Yoga. Started by Indian doctor Madan Kataria in 1995, this combines gentle *pranayama* breathing exercises and stretching, with simulated laughter. The idea is that deliberately practised jollity in a group setting soon becomes genuine and turns into a hilarious aerobic workout. The immune system, heart and diaphragm all benefit, as do the abdominal, intercostal and facial muscles, while the endorphin rush gives you a sense of well-being and aids bonding. With more than 400 clubs across the US and 6,000 groups worldwide, a lot of people are taking laughter yoga seriously. If Laughing Yoga doesn't save the world from excessive gravity, Aerial Yoga certainly will. Carried out whilst suspended upside down in a cotton sack that swings off the ground like a hammock, this system is marketed as 'a playful and fun way to practise yoga'. Mick Jagger reputedly uses it to keep fit for his sixth decade of gruelling live performances, but the mandatory celebrity endorsement is provided by Gwyneth Paltrow, who, by the way, has recommended several different types of yoga, all with equal enthusiasm. As the *Daily Mail* gushed, commenting on a photoshoot that showed her draped revealingly over a sportscar flashing Bulgari bling: 'The athletic actress has written a rave review of the practice on her blog and, if her svelte figure is anything to go by, it is working a treat!'[3]

If such celebritisation has you seeing red, you had better sign up for a course of Rage Yoga. Lindsay Istace started her classes in Calgary, Canada and they were a roaring success; now they are available online too. As her website says: 'Want to better your strength, flexibility and become zen as f#ck? Enjoy the occasional f-bomb or innuendo? You've come to the right place.' The combative twenty-four-year-old has concocted a brand where the most important *mudra* is giving the finger to the stereotype of yogic tranquillity, and she uses a heavy metal soundtrack to help. One devotee explains why she finds Rage Yoga so beneficial: 'I love that in the middle of a tough pose, it's OK to giggle or swear if you stumble. So it's a bit of a double benefit—the stretch and calm of yoga and the de-stressing you feel after a beer with your friends afterwards.' Interesting that the 'de-stressing' seems to be due to the beer rather than the yoga. But wait a minute, those who like drinking don't have to wait until after their yoga session to indulge in a few pints. The website of Beer Yoga, a group that started in Germany and is popular in Australia and parts of Asia too, tells us: 'We take the philosophies of yoga and pair it with the pleasure of beer-drinking to reach your highest level of consciousness.'

Why stop with beer? The coolest hit on the yogalternative scene is currently the Cannabliss Yoga offered by London's trendy Gymbox chain. Before getting into their yoga poses, customers are given a patch infused with cannabidiol, known as CBD, which is derived from cannabis plant but does not make you high because it contains only tiny levels of the plant's psychoactive element. Instructor Firas Iskandarani told the *Daily Mail* that: 'The breathing and the CBD patch catalyse everything and make the relaxation exercises work more effectively.' Presumably, Cannabliss Yoga is especially good for the joints. And while all this may seem a long way from the ethos of classical yoga, let's not forget that the master Patanjali did mention the use of herbs (*oshadhi*) as one way of gaining those *siddhis*.[4]

Lubricating your *asanas* with draughts of the amber liquid, or soothing them with CBD patches, may still not achieve the promised sleb body, avocado-rich skin or serene smile of the ultimate yogasm. If so, it may be time to graduate to a more ascetic discipline. Why not try Boxing Yoga? Matt Garcia, the proprietor of the Total Boxing Club in north London, realised that yogic stretching could help fighters release muscles made tight by hours of crouching, twisting, ducking and weaving around the ring. He wasn't the first to make the connection; professional sluggers such as Darren 'Dazzling' Barker and Floyd 'Money' Mayweather had already added yoga to their routines. Boxing Yoga is fast, focused and distinctly unfluffy; sit-ups, stretches, back bends, chest and shoulder openers and spinal twists, are all performed in speedy sequences. A few boxing postures are thrown in: jabs, crosses and the odd defensive tucking of fists under the chin. And best of all for those who, like so many moderns, feel uncomfortable with silence—it is all done to a loud music soundtrack.

Perhaps the secret of the perfect yoga session really lies not in its sequences but its setting. Fancy combining your downward dog with a few big cats? Then African Yoga Safari is the style for you. A Bali-trained teacher called Polly Mason leads retreats in South Africa's Makalali Game Reserve on which, according to her advertising: 'each day includes a different yoga session and a distinct *mantra*, *chakra* and theme, from "empowering" to "letting go"'. This may sound a tad traditional, but swimming, big-game viewing drives, aromatherapy and massage are also part of the package, with 'savannah facing outdoor tubs' and 'a four-poster bed sleep-out experience' as optional extras. All in all: 'The beautiful vistas, musical animal calls and exotic scents all create a perfect back-drop for yoga.' Sights, sounds and smells—this Makalali malarkey does outshine that draughty village hall, and it exemplifies a growing trend to include a yoga component in far-flung travel and exotic life-experience packages.

The self-help industry's constant need to come up with eclectic innovations extends to mind-yoga too. The latest brand is Sophrology. Just when everyone had finally got their head around mindfulness, this new quick-fix stress-buster claims to be a mixture of yoga, Tibetan Buddhism, Japanese Zen, hypnosis, psychology and neurology. This meditation mongrel has in fact been around since the early 1960s, when it was devised by Alfonso Caycedo, a Colombian doctor working in Spain, but its recent adoption by the French rugby team and media-magnate-turned-well-being-guru Ariana Huffington have propelled it into the limelight. Sophrology mixes seated and standing tension-releasing exercises, such as pumping the shoulders, head rotations or windmilling bent arms, with walking meditation, positive affirmations and visualisations. Proceeding through twelve progressive levels, it is aimed at those too twitchy to sit still and meditate, or even slide smoothly into a set of conventional *asanas. So yoga nervosa?*

Must-Have Gear

To be seriously cool, whatever it comprises and wherever it takes place, each new yoga style should be accompanied by must-have accessories: special clothes, bags, blocks, blankets, mats, cushions, joss-sticks, chimes, bells, singing bowls, posters, notebooks, greeting cards, memos, books, CDs, DVDs, apps and so on. Even yoga's ascetic backstory can be mined for the latest USP. This can produce some mixed messages. Consider this advert for a to-die-for yoga mat: 'Deepen your *Shavasana* with a thousand-year-old technique. Inspired by ancient gurus, Swedish designed Bed of Nails® acupressure mat takes you into a higher state of *Shavasana* while providing inner health and relief from pain.' A bed of nails to relieve pain? Interesting idea...

A good indicator of the current scene is the OM Yoga Show, an annual event that bills itself as the largest gathering of its kind in Europe and will next take place in Manchester in April 2020. This offers classes at all levels, and, according to its website:

> in addition, the showcase of over 250 exhibitors are on hand to offer a shopping experience like no other. Whatever you need for your ultimate yogic lifestyle can be found at the OM Yoga Show. Yoga mats, yoga clothing, superfoods, equipment—you can even book exotic retreats or sign up for teacher training. You'll find it all at the OM Yoga Show.[5]

OMG yoga looks to be the next stop.

Of course, most serious yoga practitioners deplore this culture of commercialism, but even reputable organisations can succumb to the temptations of business. Yoga Trail, who we met in Chapter 16, recently offered its readers a magical *mala* necklace it claimed would help them materialise their desires: 'DYI Mala Kits: Your Intention—Your Wardrobe! Order your Mala Kit before Nov 25 and receive a free matching stretch bracelet. All orders include Free International Shipping. Check out Andrea Kelly's gorgeous collection!' And if you Google 'lineage in yoga' you will most likely come up with a company selling: 'women's handcrafted lightweight spandex printed leggings for *yoga*, running, fashion, studio to street fitness.'

Spoiling for the Spoils

As so often when lots of money is involved, bitchy backbiting may be close behind. An early example of such spats came in 2011, when Shiva Rea, a Californian *kundalini yoga* teacher who claimed the ultimate celebrity scalp of having taught Madonna, came under social media attack for teaching in low-cut trousers and sound-tracking her lessons with trendy dance music. Then there was the infighting amongst Ashtanga devotees over attempts by Sonia Jones, the wife of New York hedge-fund billionaire Paul Tudor Jones, to market the brand very expensively to well-off Manhattanites. She joined up with Pattabhi Jois' daughter and grandson to launch a line of yoga clothes in 2012, which left so many complaining of rampant commercialism that in March of that year *Vanity Fair* ran a 5,000-word article on the furore under the headline 'Whose Yoga Is It Anyway?' Whatever the criticisms, inventive packaging has paid off handsomely, with the yoga market now worth a staggering $16 billion annually in the US and, according to business analysts Ibis, almost £800 million a year in the UK. Just how conditioned we fast-food guzzlers have become by the constant expansion of Shmoga Yoga was demonstrated by a survey conducted during the 'Love British Food Fortnight' in September 2016. One in ten people polled on the streets of London thought that a kipper was a new type of yoga.

That there can sometimes be a positive edge to modern marketing techniques would be claimed by UK-based Green Yoga, an organisation that allows you to preserve your eco-credentials while doing your practice. A company called Asquith London is selling yoga clothes made from bamboo. Somehow, the plant with a greater tensile strength than steel has miraculously yielded a material which its founder, Alice Asquith, tells the *Ecologist*, is 'soft, silky, drapey and tactile'. And what is more, right on hand there is a squad of perfect saleswomen to push the product. As she says:

> I think the key thing for me is its yoga capacity—yoga teachers wearing it in front of groups of students—because they model it very well, love it and they're very open about how much they love it. They're great walking, talking people and I think for me word of mouth has been fantastic.[6]

Again, this conflation of stretching and selling may sound harmless enough, an astute marketing exercise that benefits all concerned, but it can turn more sinister. Witness the Lululemon phenomenon. This posh apparel company was run by its hard-headed founder Chip Wilson, an ex-snowboarder who made a fortune from convincing affluent white suburban women that if they just wore his pricey workout clothes, they'd soon be in *nirvana*. Wilson seemed to have found the perfect way into the yoga market by selling athletic clothes wrapped in New Age feel-good messages: 'celebrate the beauty of friendship', 'walk your truth', 'live mindfully', that sort of thing. Realising the key to success was a committed sales force, Wilson wanted only yoga people to sell his stuff. Early on, he employed people doing mind-yoga but found that they weren't really motivated to move his merchandise fast enough, so he switched to recruiting a staff of competitive Type-A personalities committed to energetic body-yoga. Employees had an added incentive to sell, as they owned 20 per cent of the firm's lucrative stock. In addition, affiliated yoga start-ups could tap into the store's customer-base to obtain a ready-made clientele for their studios, and with his store customers also getting a discount to attend those classes, a very profitable circle was completed. With profits for 2011 posted at around $250 million, the future of Lululemon looked rosy. But that year, a staff-member in Washington, D.C. went berserk and murdered a colleague, stabbing her victim more than three hundred times over the course of twenty grisly minutes. Critics of the company had long warned that its high-pressure, cult-like atmosphere was a time-bomb waiting to go off. What part, if any, Lululemon's aggressive ethos played in the tragedy is, of course, debatable, but whatever the facts, the public image of Fashion Yoga had suffered a very uncool body-blow.

To avoid the pitfalls of Lululemonisation, you may be drawn to Naked Yoga (also known as Nagna Yoga), which is offered by such UK groups as YogaNu and Altogether Yoga. Designer shorts won't help you here, even if they are made of bamboo or sport the trendiest logo; matching her nail colour to her mat is the nearest a practitioner will get to a fashion statement in this group. Naked Yoga, which sees itself as a critique of consumerism, reminds us in its publicity blurbs that when we strip down, 'we are all the same'. Well, er… not exactly, but we can see what they are getting at. Doria Gani, who offers four-week courses for Naked Yoga London, explains: 'Naked yoga is about being comfortable in your own skin and the amazing confidence that comes with it. It's about knowing, accepting and loving yourself at your core.' Yoga in the buff is gaining ground, especially among women who have problems with their weight, shape and other body issues.

And if all this is beginning to drive you to such distraction that you feel like leaving the planet altogether, you still won't be able to escape the grasping limbs of the ubiquitous yogoctopus. Scientists have found that what they are calling Weightless Yoga may be the cure for the muscle weakness caused by the lack of gravity in space. Back pain and lack of mobility are common problems among International Space Station crews, who spend long periods of time in orbit. An article in the Autumn 2016 issue of the medical journal *Spine* claimed that yoga could be just the thing for crocked astronauts, whose MRI scans show shrinkage in the paraspinal muscles that causes painful displacement of vertebrae discs. So, who will be the first to perform *surya namaskar* on Mars and tweet the ultimate yoga selfie back to planet earth? Watch this space...

A Reminder

From the sylvan retreats of ancient India to the interplanetary space stations of the twenty-first century, from deep inner to far outer space, yoga has certainly travelled a long way on its increasingly bizarre trajectory. Without wanting to spoil the party, perhaps it is time to take a deep breath and come back down to earth for a moment to remind ourselves of some priorities. A good way to do this might be to remember the words of a *yogini* who was deeply grounded in her own tradition yet ever-illumined by a universal perspective. Here the Bengali sage Anandamayi Ma speaks about *hatha yoga*, the general term for postural practice in the Indian tradition:

> Question: Can you explain the benefits to be derived from *hatha yoga*—and what are its drawbacks?
>
> Answer: What does *hatha* mean? To do something by force. 'Being' is one thing and 'doing' quite another. When there is 'being', there will be the manifestation of what is due to be manifested, owing to the *prana* functioning in a particular centre [of the body]. But if *hatha yoga* is done merely as an exercise in physical gymnastics, the mind will not be transformed in the very least. By physical exercise bodily fitness is enhanced. One hears quite often of cases where the leaving-off of the practice of yogic postures (*asanas*) has resulted in physical disorders. Just as the body grows weak from lack of adequate nourishment, so the mind has need of suitable food. When the mind receives proper sustenance, man moves Godward; whereas by catering to the body he only increases his worldliness. Mere gymnastics is nutrition for the body. When the physical fitness resulting from *hatha yoga* is used as an aid to spiritual endeavour, it is not wasted. Otherwise, it is not *yoga*. Unless *hatha yoga* aims at the Eternal, it is nothing more than gymnastics.[7]

27

TROUBLE IN PARADISE

On his Twitter page, Gurmeet Yogi Ram Rahim Singh modestly described himself as a 'spiritual saint and philanthropist', 'versatile singer, film star and film-maker' and, just for good measure, an 'all-round sportsperson'. Such multi-tasking was worthy of a many-armed Hindu deity, but it did not impress the judge presiding over Singh's trial, who augmented the yogi's impressive CV with the rather more downbeat attribute of being 'a wild beast who had projected himself as a godman and taken undue advantage of his position and authority'. The verdict of guilty on several charges of rape and harassment was reached after what was a marathon process, running for fifteen years and over 200 court hearings and carrying a weighty sentence of twenty years hard labour and a £50,000 fine. The conviction unleashed waves of violence from followers, said to total 60 million, and across northern India at least forty people were killed and 300 injured, while government buildings were attacked and official vehicles, trains and the odd bus station wrecked and set on fire. There was more in store for Singh, as in January 2019 he was awarded a life sentence for the murder of a journalist. More ghoulishly, there are pending charges of ordering castration for some 400 of his disciples to ensure their *brahmacharya*. The net worth of his sprawling empire is yet to be properly assessed.

This case, which began in the summer of 2017, was unusually lurid, but the turbulent marriage of yoga and notoriety is nothing new, as we have already seen. When the practice first arrived in the West almost a century ago, it was controversial, particularly in the United States, where it often clashed with xenophobic and conservative undertones in American culture. Determined efforts to promote postural work as a secular system of physical health and fitness gradually overcame such prejudices, and, shorn of its baroque baggage, yoga smoothed its way into the respectable mainstream.

Nine years ago, an article in the *The Wall Street Journal* suggested we had reached 'peak yoga' levels. Blaming 'shareholders, American materialism, craven gurus, cynical marketers', the writer, who has authored a book on yoga herself, argued there is now nothing left to exploit: 'Like Star Wars or Matisse, the merchandising, advertising, and profiteering of yoga has run the full gamut, from action figures to deluxe vacations to how-to-books that apply yoga to almost every human endeavour.'[1] She was wrong. Since her article, the expansion has continued. The Yoga in America Study shows that by 2016 the number of practitioners had increased to more than 36 million, up from 20.4 million in 2012, while the worth of the associated consumer industry had risen to $16 billion, up from $10 billion over the previous four years. According to the survey, 34 per cent of Americans, or 80 million people, said they were likely to try yoga for the first time in the following twelve months.[2]

On the crest of this buoyant tide of popularity, however, a messy debris of scandal is rising. It usually swirls around a powerful male guru, and over the years has engulfed some of the best-known personalities on the yoga scene. Way back in 1991, protesters waving placards reading 'Stop the Abuse' and 'End the Cover Up' demonstrated outside a Virginia hotel where Swami Satchidananda, the monk who blessed the historic Woodstock Festival, was addressing a symposium. Numerous female followers stated that he had used his role as their spiritual mentor to exploit them sexually, but he denied everything and was never charged. Claims of sexual abuse are rife, and even a glance at the list of those involved makes for a very sobering read. Swami Muktananda, founder of Siddha Yoga was also accused of sleeping with his followers, but there were no court cases.[3] In 1994, Amrit Desai, the married founder of the Massachusetts-based Kripalu Center for Yoga and Health, confessed to having affairs with three of his students, and was forced to resign as spiritual director of his own ashram. Three years later, Swami Rama, founder of the Pennsylvania-based Himalayan Institute of Yoga Science and Philosophy and one of the first yogis to be studied by Western scientists, was also one of the first to be convicted of unlawful sex with a devotee.[4] Then there was Kausthub Desikachar, son of T.K.V. Desikachar and grandson of T. Krishnamacharya, who resigned from teaching after allegations were made by students that he had 'emotionally, sexually and spiritually harassed them'.[5] We have already considered the case of Bikram Choudhury. In the 1980s, the free-love yogi Bhagavan Shree Rajneesh's organisation was accused by the American authorities of a long list of abuses including: arson, assault, visa and immigration fraud, organised prostitution, murder, rape, drug-smuggling, illegal arms possession, enforced sterilisation of women, money-laundering, poisoning

local residents, attempted assassination of law officers and government officials, grievous bodily harm, massive tax evasion and sex with minors.
Convicted, fined and expelled from the US, Rajneesh was denied entry by
twenty-one countries, and shortly before his death in 1990 back in India,
rebranded himself as Osho. This attempt to whitewash his reputation seems to
have worked; the organisation continues to function under its new name, and
its founder's books still sell well.[6] In Australia, a 2014 Royal Commission
charged the founder (now dead) of the Satyananda Yoga Ashram, the oldest
yoga organisation in the country, with numerous cases of 'horrific' physical and
sexual abuse, going back thirty years or more.

It is not only Indians who have been in the dock. One of the most shocking of the American yoga scandals involved John Friend, the founder of
Anusara Yoga. In March 2012, an article in the *Washington Post* exposed
stories of drugs and sexploitation that had long been in circulation. Almost
thirty years before Friend sullied yoga's reputation, the first American
teacher to be exposed was Richard Baker, the country's leading Zen monk
and abbot of the San Francisco Zen Centre. Baker was forced to resign in
1984 for multiple improprieties with his female students.

Twenty years later, Eido Tai Shimano Roshi, who had introduced Zen to
America in the 1950s and '60s, had to step down under charges of sexual
misbehaviour that had been whispered around his community for well over
thirty years. Then, in August 2017, Sogyal Rinpoche, another longtime leading teacher of Tibetan Buddhism and author of the best-selling *The Tibetan
Book of Living and Dying*, was toppled from his position as head of the Rigpa
community by an internal revolt over his serious physical and psychological
abuse of students, sexual coercions and unreasonably luxurious lifestyle, said
to have continued unchecked for decades. Following this, the Shambhala
International Buddhist community, which has over 200 sub-groups worldwide, announced in February 2018 that the organisation was to conduct an
investigation into past 'abhorrent sexual behaviour'.[7]

How has a holistic regime for health, fitness and self-discovery turned into
this debacle?

Back in 2012, William Broad, an award-winning journalist and author of a
respected book on yoga had his own explanation:

> Yoga teachers and how-to books seldom mention that the discipline began as
> a sex cult—an omission that leaves many practitioners open to libidinal sur-
> prise... Since the baby boomers discovered yoga, the arousal, sweating, heavy
> breathing and states of undress that characterize yoga classes have led to pre-
> dictable results. In 1995, sex between students and teachers became so preva-

lent that the California Yoga Teachers Association deplored it as immoral and called for high standards...[8]

Leaving aside what happened in Californian body-yoga, and even those purple passages further back in yoga's history, to claim that the practice 'began as a sex-cult' is too crude an estimation of yoga's tantric influences to take seriously, let alone employ as an explanation for the problems that have tarnished too much of yoga's reputation.

Yoga and Therapy

In grappling with the problem of teacher-student abuse, an instructive comparison might be the therapeutic setting, not least because to many students, the yoga teacher acts as a type of therapist. In therapy, the question of boundaries is generally clear, if only because in the consulting room, dysfunction is a given—that is why the client is there in the first place. The professional analyst should be well versed in the dynamics of transference and countertransference; such unconscious projections will have been carefully addressed during their training. Moreover, they will regularly report back to their own mentor for discussion of their own reactions to what may have arisen during the analytic sessions. Since the 1980s there has been an influential school of psychotherapy known as Relational Psychoanalysis, that emphasises the mutual affective engagement between therapist and client. This addresses what it sees as the melding—one might even say interactive alchemy—of the conscious and unconscious psyches involved in the analytic process.

With yoga, on the other hand, the student can walk in off the street and enter unreflectively into what may transpire to be a highly charged and transformative relationship with a teacher who has generally had only physical training. An immature student may find themselves in the grip of a number of projections, seeing their yoga teacher as a parent, healer, priest, wise counsellor or potential lover. A charismatic teacher may embody some, or even all, of these archetypal figures, and if that teacher is correspondingly in thrall to uninspected or narcissistic motives, making them unable or unwilling to recognise such projections for what they are, abuse may well occur.

The Question of Surrender

There is another complicating factor at work here: the traditional idea that the path to wisdom involves surrender to a guru. This condition is generally more emphasised in mind-yoga, and there are, of course, different degrees of surrender. At one level, it may only involve carrying out instructions that one cannot see the immediate point of, or agreeing to undertake some action that appears at the time to have no rhyme or reason. Such apparently trivial tests of flexibility can be effective strategies to expand the student's perspective, and bring about some level of self-transcendence, jolting them out of limiting habits of mind. Willingness to follow the teacher wholeheartedly is a vital part of Indian pedagogy in general, and is found in all sorts of disciplines, be they music, art or wrestling. Obedience, it is believed, fosters receptivity, allowing a creative osmosis to occur between teacher and student.

Innocent compliance is deemed especially important in the spiritual apprenticeship. Open any yogic biography, and sooner or later it becomes clear that the effective fast track to transcend the limited ego is unswerving devotion to an enlightened master. But note well the word 'enlightened'. If the teacher himself has unresolved and narcissistic ego issues, then his follow-ers' devotion may be subverted to satisfy his own childish need to have every whim indulged without question, every urge for approval gratified. And if the student is uncritically dependent, we have the ideal conditions for cultic co-dependence between abusive leader and slavish follower.

An aberrant teacher typically insists that the disciple's recalcitrant ego must be destroyed before enlightenment can blossom. In such cases, a vicious circularity arises: the teacher imposes some impossible or demeaning demand on the student, ostensibly to conquer their egoic obstructions, while any natural or psychologically healthy resistance on the part of the student is taken as proof of the very egotism which must be destroyed. Such demands often feature sex and money because, so the inflated teacher will claim, stu-dents must be tested in just those evolutionary inferior, or 'lower *chakra*', areas in which they display the most tenacious egoic attachment. Teachers may justify their demands for surrender by quoting historical precedents, of which there are many, especially those belonging to the so-called 'Crazy Wisdom' traditions. These adepts operated well beyond the confines of conventional social propriety; their eccentricities tolerated, or even celebrated, because they were believed to be the expressions of a being operating from a higher plane of reality. Some of these 'crazy' gurus were lone mavericks, outside any known lineage, others belonged to established schools that had typically developed in feudal or monarchic societies in which there was relatively little freedom of individual expression, and where authority figures, whether lay or religious, comprised a largely unaccountable aristocracy.[9] Behind all this lies the understanding, axiomatic in sapiential traditions, that there exists a hierarchy of modes of being, and in consequence, a hierarchy of levels of understanding. As a result, so the argument goes, we cannot judge a superior level of consciousness by the criteria of an inferior one. Simply put, and however unacceptable it may be to modern ways of thinking, the metaphysically ignorant are in no position to judge the enlightened.

One classic example of devotion in the face of unreasonable demands is the story of Milarepa, the great eleventh-century Tibetan *siddha*, who was tasked by his guru Marpa to build him a towered house. This he did with his own hands, with great effort and care. When the job was eventually completed, Marpa came to inspect the result. He admired the structure and praised his disciple's painstaking work, but then casually asked if he could just move the building some distance up the hill. The devoted Milarepa complied without a word, dismantling the building and reassembling it again with more weeks of backbreaking labour. Again, the master came to inspect, again he praised the house, but now he asked if it could possibly be moved across the valley. Eventually, after building, dismantling and reassembling the structure several times, Milarepa's selfless obedience opened him fully to the ego-free liberation of enlightenment. But had a time-travelling twenty-first-century psychologist landed in Tibet, and interrupted Marpa halfway through his unanaesthetised open-ego surgery, the full force of the law would surely have been summoned to put an end to such a grievous abuse of human rights.

Such teaching stories, which are particularly numerous in those schools centred on guru devotion, can be understood in different ways. But for most people, who are not suited, either by *karma* or temperament, to undergo the path of surrender to a guru, the point is surely not to imitate the outward behaviour of a Milarepa, but to emulate his heartfelt inner commitment to the path. Remaining true to one's deepest values is the important consideration here, for, as Patanjali makes clear: 'The practice of yoga is the commitment to become established in the state of freedom.'[10]

The Distrust of Authority

For us moderns, what place, if any, does surrender play in spiritual development? Again, this is a complex question. In our increasingly atomised society, most individuals' prime devotion is to their own autonomy, and they would like to claim an inalienable right to pursue their own personal agenda for fulfilment. This process often entails rejection of inherited structures and authorities, especially religious ones. Such individualism is curiously inconsistent, though. While we are happy enough to accept specialised expertise for practical matters—such as the proper functioning of our car, computer or even our own body—we resist such authority when it concerns intellectual and, particularly, spiritual matters. It is as if respect for the sophistication of specialised knowledge is confined to material fields alone; elsewhere, our default setting is one of scepticism.

In matters of spirituality, the dominant paradigm is one of a dogged individualism, a reliance on personal experience, free of intervention. One of the early investigators of consciousness, the American psychologist William James, put his finger on this doubting Thomas syndrome when, in a speech given to an audience at Edinburgh University, he characterised modern religious or spiritual experience as consisting of: 'the feelings, acts, and experiences of individual men in their solitude, so far as they apprehend themselves to stand in relation to whatever they may consider the divine.'[11]

James' America had been shaped by Protestant rejection of received ecclesiastical authority, and the same dissenting attitude is a prominent feature of the New Age, that follows such nineteenth-century precursors as Transcendentalism and the New Thought philosophy, in the advocacy of a self-authenticating spirituality. What is important in these belief systems is an optimistic and sometimes uncritical faith in an 'inner voice' that rejects outer authority, especially in the form of established religion.

Our modern mentality, then, is very different from that of the cultures in which the ideal of self-transcending service to an enlightened being developed and flowered. Contemporary suspicions of authority increase simply because they have so often been proved fully justified. The fact that a tradition has centuries behind it in no way guarantees its worth; consider female genital mutilation, for example. But the problem with such scepticism is that it can all too easily shade into the belief that no received opinion is worth listening to, even if that opinion is informed with historical or linguistic knowledge the doubter himself does not possess. The negative flipside of considering each person to be equally entitled to his or her opinion, is the assumption that all opinions, all views of reality, are basically equal. This relativism further compounds a distrust of expertise that can then lead to a nihilistic denial of any absolute principles, a rejection of precisely those enduring values that form the bedrock of religious tradition and spiritual understanding.

To distrust interpretive expertise when dealing with an ancient wisdom system imported from another culture is to invite misunderstanding. Doing so may lead to misinterpretations, which are at best sentimental and overly romantic, at worst, downright deceitful.[12] Relying only on the inner guru of personal experience can foster the sort of anti-intellectualism that is prominent in the world of commercialised yoga, and is an orientation quite at odds

301

with the culture from which yoga originated. To judge from the surviving texts, at least, practitioners in India considered deeply what they were doing and why they were doing it; an important part of their journey was an appreciation of the levels of reality that were revealed by the experiences they were having. To them, spiritual practice combined two complementary and mutually nourishing elements: direct personal experience and tutored intellectual understanding. As the old saying goes: 'A bird needs two wings to fly'.

The Role of Confidentiality

Modern suspicions are often aroused by the apparent secrecy involved in many initiatory structures, as we can see from the generally hostile reaction to the Masonic orders, for example. We forget that in early Christianity, the Greek word for secret rite or doctrine—*mysterion*—came to mean 'sacrament', signifying the mysterious truth of orders of reality that lie beyond our normal capacity to understand. In this context, privacy need not always connote a dubious control mechanism enforced to bolster the exploitative power of insiders. It is arguably a necessary form of social organisation, a sapiential human rite, that protects and facilitates legitimate participation in higher truths that surpass conventional understanding. From this perspective, spiritual knowledge is a form of specialisation, and to participate in any field of specialised knowledge requires the relevant qualifications. These are often effectively exclusive, if only because of the time and dedicated effort taken to acquire them. Just because metaphysical knowledge is anchored in the transcendent does not mean it is immune to being debased in the world.

The Alchemy of Service

Surrender expresses itself in service, whether to a master, an institution or an ideal. Again, this goes against the grain of much modern thinking, which tends to conflate service with servitude, though they are not the same thing at all. Confusing the two blinds us to the enduring principle, recognised by all the wisdom teachings, that we all have a born duty to serve. Like it or not, we are called to render service, both to those who appear to stand above us in the scheme of things, and to those below. The natural patterns of human living have always recognised this law: parents serve their children, who, with luck, return the service much later in life; the host serves the guest; the well serve the sick. And the living serve the dying. This last is a reciprocal opportunity, as it initiates the one who serves into the process that is the ultimate, and unavoidable, surrender. Such self-transcending activity is the natural expression of human empathy and it has great value on the unitive path, because it cultivates both the finer levels of feeling and the skill of disinterested activity.

Those who choose to engage in a transformative praxis such as true yoga will find this cosmic principle quickened in their own case, unbidden. Service necessitates a still and open mind—the relinquishing of judgement and the granting of space to what is, rather than always trying to shape things as we would like them to be. Without this generosity, there is little room for real change, either of the seer or the seen. From a yogic point of view, a life that ignores the evolutionary imperative of service and is merely self-serving, is a life of wasted opportunity. The true yogi will look back on their life and see its greatest satisfaction as having been able to give a large part of themselves to others.

The Responsibility of the Teacher

Psychosynthesis, the psychology system developed by Robert Assoglioli in the mid-1960s, speaks about what it calls the 'Icarus complex': the ego-inflation that occurs when someone pursues mystical transcendence while avoiding their unresolved and unconscious personality problems. In conventional teaching situations concerned with the transference of information, the teacher's lack of self-knowledge may not matter much. But in yoga, true 'knowledge' is not only what you dispense, it's what you are. Charisma, looks, the ability to speak fluently and write convincingly can all combine to make a flawed teacher appear plausible, at least in the short term, before they are tripped up by their own hubris, and brought down by the inconsistencies between what they teach and how they act. Great damage can be wreaked in the lives of undiscriminating followers before this happens.

One advantage of a *bona fide* spiritual lineage is that, if functioning correctly, it provides a corrective to the possible self-aggrandisement of the teacher. A lineage also allows the student to investigate the provenance and qualities of a teaching before receiving initiation or committing to the school. When this regulatory process goes wrong, however, or there is no genuine tradition behind a charismatic individual, the result can open the ashram gates to a toxic mix of human folly, error and corruption. A genuine teacher is not interested in encouraging infantile dependency or uncritical hero-worship. He or she will want to set their disciples free to sail the boat of their own lives with wisdom, skill and verve, so that they will in time come to realise that the spiritual path is not a matter of self-absorption, or even self-fulfilment, but progressive self-transcendence.[13]

The Responsibility of the Student

If the culpability of an exploitative guru is clear, what is the responsibility of the disciple? The desire to expand and grow under a teacher is natural and commendable, but it can often be tainted by all sorts of uninspected motivations. These may include the need to be loved and considered special, the desire to belong to a supportive 'family', the hope of avoiding adult responsibility with all its attendant challenges, or the drive to please authority figures or fill a chronic internal emptiness. Such needs may be exacerbated by the contemporary fragmentation of family, the atomisation of society at large and the confused search for an authentic identity.

There is an important distinction between the recognition that one has found the right path, teacher or community for oneself (for the time being, at least) and the conviction that you have found 'The One', to whose following it is your duty to convert everyone you meet. This is a phase that most people grow out of sooner or later; it is a learning process that any wise teacher, who would rather be surrounded by equals than dependents, will themselves encourage and hasten.

After fifty years of exposure to imported teachings, it is up to the new generation of students, women and men alike, not only to bring errant teachers to account, but also to do all they can to ensure their own behaviour is above reproach and beyond uninspected complicity. As a teacher is someone who, by definition, has students, it is the continued participation of those students in the relationship that grants him his authority. By the same token, they can also remove it. With this power comes responsibility. Whilst those subject to abuse may have faced challenges in speaking out, in the yoga world, as much as anywhere else, silence about abuse has only served to perpetuate it.

If the yoga community wants to put its house back in order, the need of the time is to reflect, and re-commit to sound ethical principles governing responsible guidelines for the relationship between teacher and student. Such a mutual re-visioning would include: use of language, the creation of expectations, favouritism, touching, dress codes and financial dealings. Top-down regulatory work is already underway, but in the end, the future depends on the self-awareness and maturity of each and every individual involved.[14]

CONTEMPORARY CAUTIONS

The Responsibility of the Organisation

Someone once said that as soon as God had revealed the Truth, the Devil popped up and offered to organise it for him. This pattern is everywhere apparent in the history and operation of spiritual movements, which are no more exempt from human follies than any other ostensibly worldlier organisation. Some would argue such groups are in fact more vulnerable, because they are blinded from self-inspection by what they see as the overriding worthiness of their cause. 'Cult' is a word that should be used with caution, but an organisation doesn't have to be a cult *per se* for a cultic mentality to flourish amongst some of its members. Many a group that is by and large in reasonable psychological health will contain people who would like it to be more authoritarian, more betrothed to a simplistic black-and-white view of the world. Consciously or not, they will be surreptitiously working towards that end.

Ashram 'group-think' can contain many elements of co-dependency, with subtle and often unconscious agreements being struck between group members regarding the correct ways to think, talk, behave or dress. In this, it is no different from equivalents in the secular world—a political cadre or corporate team for example—but, in the ashram, these agreements will also be reinforced daily with stories and anecdotes about *guruji*: his or her life, saintliness, psychic powers, ambitious outreach projects and so on. Outsiders who do not conform to the collective mentality, or insiders who start asking awkward questions, may be censored, rejected or demonised in some way. Some insiders will enjoy feeling that they belong to a group more advanced than the unregenerate outside world, a danger that is greatest among people who join at a young age, before their personalities have been seasoned by rubbing up against the day-to-day realities of life. Successful leaders are entrepreneurs of identity who, intuitively or deliberately, cater to the desired self-image and aspirations of their followers. And, as aspirations go, the perfect body or the illumined mind are hard to beat.

A group's solidarity is often enhanced by its opposition to supposed enemies. No matter what rationale may be developed to support such an attitude, this is a primitive evolutionary position, not unique to *homo sapiens*. All social animals divide themselves into an 'us' and 'them', with the former constituting the safe group immediately around, and the latter, everyone else. Such tribalism is at root an atavistic defence of territory, and in the fervent quest for salvation, this partiality can be just as deadly within faith groups as between them. In 1572, in their disagreement over the nature of Christ's love for humanity, French Catholics killed up to 10,000 Protestants over twenty-four hours, in what became known as the St. Bartholomew's Day Massacre. The Pope was delighted. Special prayers were said all over Rome to thank God for the victory, and it was commemorated in a sumptuous fresco in the Vatican, painted by the maestro Giorgio Vasari. Being cognisant of the dangers of divisive mindsets, even if sanctioned by an autocratic leader, those on the path of yoga might do well to remember Patanjali's method of overcoming negative attitudes by cultivating life-affirming ones,[15] while keeping in mind the Upanishadic aphorism that 'the world is one family'.[16]

Once established, the bond of co-dependence forged between a narcissistic teacher and his followers can be extraordinarily hard to break. Just how hard is shown by the fact that cults persist in contemporary advanced societies long after their abusive nature should, to an impartial observer at least, have caused them to implode and collapse. The hidden fault lines in a group will, however, generally come to the surface with the death of the powerful leader, which allows hitherto repressed factional acrimonies to emerge. Enforced exclusions and splits into sub-groups follow, and then comes the inevitable recourse to lawsuits over legitimate succession, copyright exclusivity and the division of the spoils.

Leaving such melodramas aside, it is well to remember that the teaching and the organisation that conveys it are never synonymous. Speaking on this subject, Swami Shantanand Saraswati, a great sage in the tradition of Advaita Vedanta, has commented:

> The essential teaching as described applies everywhere. Wherever there is an opportunity for spiritual discourse and discipline there will necessarily evolve an organisation; and with every organisation, physical elements and a hierarchy will come to fulfil the needs for the real work of search for truth. The moment importance is switched to the organisational work of the institution, the real work of truth will be compromised. Organisation is necessary and those who help to do that are equally necessary. But they should never be allowed to dominate the real work. In fact, it is so common for this to happen. Therefore, great care must always be taken that spiritual work remains paramount and all material and organisational work remains secondary.[17]

Treading the Path

Many disappointed by their experience in transformative group structures have rejected outright the idea of authoritative guidance. They may champion the 'inner guru', which has the seductive appeal of never being brought up against its own limitations, write the 'bliss and tell' memoir or seek consolation in the ranks of those who reject all initiatory wisdom and locate human perfectibility solely in the application of science and reason.[18] Emotional recoil into such a disillusioned position is not generally helpful however, not least because, as Patanjali tells us, 'aversion is clinging to pain'. When naïvety and unrealistic expectation have finally run their course, what is needed is not a rejection of our yogic purpose to develop and progress, but a new maturity. In the redefinition of the path and goal, we can move away from idealising unchallengeable states of superhuman perfection and embrace a humbler and more applicable paradigm, one that sees liberation not as deification, but as the state of fully-blossomed humanity. This more realistic vision will make it harder for licence to masquerade as freedom, or fantasy to seduce rationality. The true sage is one who operates legitimately within all the necessary confines and boundaries of an embodied social existence, but in so doing is simultaneously released into a state of continuous and conscious self-transcendence.

In the end, no matter how charismatic they may be, all teachers are sitting by the river selling water. Any system, no matter how enlightened its source, is first and foremost a model, a map charting what is currently unknown territory. A map is needed, of course, but we should not hold onto it too rigidly, no matter what its provenance, for signposts are not destinations. Right at the dawn of Indian history, humankind's oldest scripture likens the guru to a person familiar with a certain terrain, who undertakes to guide a foreign traveller: 'The stranger asks the way of him who knows it: taught by the skilful guide he travels onward. This is, in truth, the blessing of instruction: he finds the path that leads directly forward.'[19]

The lived experience of walking our path, enjoying the sights, smelling the flowers and negotiating the potholes and obstacles along the way, will be a unique and personal one. And if we are following a true path, it will not be divorced from simple, day-to-day living; there is no need to lose our humanity in the aspiration for divinity. In old English slang, there was the verb 'to coddiwomple', meaning to travel purposefully towards an as yet unknown destination. For yogic coddiwomplers, then, the melodrama of being 'the spiritual seeker' becomes unnecessary; heartfelt human values are enough. In fact, the more glamorous the path appears, the more suspect it probably is. And as we begin to live the map in our own terms, there may be many surprises in store. Who knows? Perhaps those who travel together must eventually arrive alone, while those whose journey is solitary may end up arriving together...

LOOKING AHEAD

28

YOGA TO THE RESCUE?

The growth of secularised yoga exemplifies a general principle: as the power of belief wanes, the authority of medicine increases. What were formerly considered moral failings—overeating, addiction, hypersexuality—are now classified as diseases, and as more and more of our life becomes medicalised, wellness has replaced goodness as the answer to many of our ills. Yoga has always been remedial, but the sickness traditional practice sought to cure was the metaphysical ignorance that, according to the sages, is the root of human suffering. With the growth of *hatha yoga* in medieval India, our born mortality and a deficit of supernormal powers were seen as ills to be remedied. But in *Kali Yuga*, these ambitious goals have shrunk somewhat. As stress and poor health proliferate, yoga has graduated from being a minority lifestyle choice to a medical option. For many people nowadays, yoga connotes not so much Patanjali and *purusha*, as pregnancy and panic attacks.

Awareness of bodily well-being, or the lack of it, is rising fast. By 2015, one in three Americans was wearing some kind of health-monitoring device, and there are now estimated to be 186,000 health clubs in the world. Working out has become a form of conspicuous consumption, embraced by affluent urbanites and avoided by the poor. The result is a curious regime that blends physical labour with office work, as treadmilling, weight-lifting and muscle-pumping are monitored, diligently recorded on clipboards and electronic machines, and turned into statistics and action plans. Welcome to middle-class asceticism in the age of peak 'stuff'.

We examined yoga's relevance to the current stress pandemic in Chapter 23, but looking ahead, postural work may also be advanced as an aid to deal with the burgeoning problem of globesity. Excess body-fat now costs the planet as much each year in medical and remedial services as all its armed conflicts.[1] Over 2 billion, a third of the world's population, are now considered to be overweight and in 2015, those excess kilos caused four million deaths, along with widespread related illnesses. When the World Health Organization recently announced obesity to be 'the new norm' throughout Europe, the UK's dismal statistics seated her solidly at the head of the groaning table of twenty-two European nations. Today, 70 per cent of British men and 59 per cent of women are officially classed as overweight or obese (i.e. a body-mass-index [BMI] of more than 25), with the figure predicted to expand to 75 per cent and 66 per cent respectively, by 2030. One effect is the prevalence of type 2 diabetes, which already claims 120 amputations a week, and at the present rates of growth, one in ten adults could have the condition by 2035. This, according to the gloomiest estimates, would cost some £39.8 billion, a sixth of the total NHS budget.[2] Part of the problem is inertia. In August 2017, Public Health England (PHE) announced that 41 per cent of adults aged between forty and sixty walk less than ten minutes at a brisk pace each month, a torpor that has severely negative effects on their health. Sadly, being made aware of such statistics may itself be a source of stress as, contradicting their reputation for resolute *sangfroid*, over 60 per cent of Brits now have high blood pressure.

The problem of size starts young. In Bradford, for example, where cheap fast-food is available almost everywhere, 45 per cent of children are either overweight or obese by the time they leave primary school. Globally, childhood obesity rates have soared tenfold in the last forty years. According to a recent study published by the Royal College of Paediatricians and Child Health, one in three children in the UK are obese by age nine, leading to more cases of type 2 diabetes, asthma and high blood pressure and threatening non-alcoholic liver degeneration, while one in four has dieted for weight-loss by the time she reaches her seventh birthday.[3]

Mental Illness

Unfit bodies and unwell minds are often found together. The WHO estimates that 450 million people worldwide suffer poor mental health, and this is not accounting for the millions, technically judged to be mentally healthy, who habitually behave in aberrant ways, harming both themselves and others. While the effects of over-consumption of alcohol cost the UK government £21 billion a year, prescriptions for anti-depressants are at an all-time high, soaring from 64.7 million in 2017 to over 70 million—almost 195,000 a day—in 2018. This costs the NHS more than £250 million a year and marks a rise of over 100 per cent in a decade.[4] Our working life suffers, as a third of all sick leave is currently the result of mental health problems, and one in four of us can expect to experience a period of mental illness in our lifetime. Even politicians are becoming aware of the situation. For the first time in history, the 2015 General Election manifestos of the six main parties devoted considerable space to the question of mental health. Three of them spoke of the necessity for fast and widespread access to various talking therapies, citing counselling, 'managing emotional resilience' and mindfulness as remedies that should be government-funded and widely available.

Health crises apart, we human beings seem generally to be faced with a dwindling of our cognitive powers. In 2015, a Canadian study by the Consumer Insights team of Microsoft Canada, who surveyed 2,000 Canadians found that the attention span of the average adult had shrunk from twelve seconds in 2003 to eight seconds today.[5] Attention deficit disorder, and associated hyperactivity, have become the most common paediatric diagnoses after asthma. Whatever the cure, it will surely include a reversal of the current epidemic of unnatural lifestyles, and perhaps even a review of how we relate to technology. A report published by King's College, London, in early 2015, showed that half of Europeans between the age of twenty-five and twenty-nine now suffer from myopia, brought about by excessive computer use. The meta-analysis of findings from fifteen studies by the European Eye Epidemiology Consortium confirmed that, against the usual disease/education pattern, this disability is twice as high among university-educated students as those without further education. Hours spent on a smartphone are apparently as bad for a child's health as is watching TV. A recent study of 25,000 children conducted by Harvard University links too much screen-gazing directly with obesity, due both to the lack of mobility and the unhealthy snacking that accompanies it.[6] The look-down generation spends an average of four hours a day online, with 75 per cent of teens having an online profile and more than half visiting social networking sites every day, many of them several times. While the former president of Facebook, Sean Parker, recently admitted that the site was deliberately designed to bring about habitual use among its users, as the experience of China shows, the spectre of screen addiction is not just a dystopian fantasy, it is already here.[7] Its global arrival was officially acknowledged in January 2018, when the WHO classified internet gaming addiction as a mental disorder. Even the industry is worried. In June 2018, Apple launched a new app that allows people to instigate a voluntary digital detox by curbing their time spent on the screen. While we may applaud such a move, the irony cannot be overlooked. In needing an electronic reminder to tell us when to extract ourself from the grip of electronic reality, this scheme perpetuates the abdication of human will-power that was the problem in the first place.

Staring down at a screen often extends well into the hours of darkness. The consequent exposure to 'blue light' is putting our body-clocks out of synch, thereby thwarting the body's natural and restorative circadian rhythms. Sleep deprivation results, which can lead to increased illness; cancer, diabetes and heart problems have been cited. The hormone melatonin, central to our feelings of well-being and happiness, seems crucial here. By breaking down the body's active and energetic hormones, it slows brain activity and aids sleep, but it is also believed that its antioxidant properties could help reduce the severity of Alzheimer's and Parkinson's disease. The hormone is made by the pineal gland, but it can only be produced in darkness. Interestingly, the practice of mind-yoga increases its production, perhaps partly because deep meditation is done with closed eyes.[8]

Stress also inhibits sleep, and so stressed is the UK that it hovers near the top of a world table of sleep deprivation. Lack of sleep causes over 200,000 working days to be lost each year, as people take time off from work or perform worse whilst there. This costs the economy about £40 billion annually, which is over 2 per cent of GDP.[9] In the US, the loss rises to 1.2 million working days worth $330 billion, i.e. 2.28 per cent of GDP. It is hard to assess how much of this chronic stress and sleeplessness is due to excessive online activity, but given that the UK is in world terms something of a digital desert, with worse mobile internet coverage than Romania, Albania and Peru, the health prospects for when the country does eventually get better connectivity don't look that great.

The Power of Attention

While the goal of mind-yoga has always been to clear the screen of the mind, it may well be that in the future one of its main benefits will be to clear the mind of screens. Digital technology has given us such an abundance of information that in the competition for interest, a scarcity of attention has been created. In a world where millennials typically look at their phones more than a hundred and fifty times a day, social observers are talking about the 'attention economy'. To the extent that our awareness is constantly being demanded, often by various sorts of advertising, our ability to hold a focus is weakened and our will-power is sapped. Electronic demands are especially hard to resist because they tend to cater to emotional impulse rather than conscious intention, and the digital weapon of mass distraction always there at our finger-tips. Little wonder attention deficit is rampant.

Mind-yoga has always put great emphasis on the importance of developing discernment (*viveka*). Many meditation techniques act by withdrawing the attention from the chronic activity of random thoughts and relocating it to a more stabilising focus, such as a *mantra*, the breath or a specific part of the body. This act of choice is one of the attributes of an inherent faculty, technically known in Sanskrit as *buddhi*, which we have already discussed in Chapter 24. *Buddhi* is the power of discrimination, the muscle, as it were, of choosing, and like any muscle, it becomes stronger the more it is used. In the brave new world of algorithmic intrusions tugging insistently at our awareness, discernment is becoming ever more important. In the end, attention is the most precious of human gifts, and yoga counsels us to grant it wisely, not least because when we focus our attention on something we give it more life, more prominence.

With the advancement of technology, it has, however, become harder to be fully in control of the process of discrimination. The self is becoming ever more a machine-readable set of data points, hungrily devoured by advertisers. This new direction was clearly signalled in October 2017. A huge billboard, about the size of three tennis courts, was switched on in Piccadilly Circus, the heart of London's West End. The screen, immediately nicknamed Big Brother, uses recognition technology to target viewers with hidden cameras that track the make, model and colour of passing vehicles, as well as the age, gender and even the moods, of pedestrians. Brands can pre-programme triggers, so that specific adverts play when certain cars, or people, pass. If yoga practice can help us to regain our conscious autonomy in such an increasingly manipulated environment, that alone is a reason to take it seriously.

The Problem of Body Image

According to research by the American Academy of Facial Plastic and Reconstructive Surgeons, 56 per cent of surgeons surveyed in 2017 reported an increase in clients under the age of thirty.[10] Body-image concern is now being registered by children as young as three; the latest estimates have a third of teenage girls now suffering anxiety or depression,[11] much of which is caused by the demands of maintaining an enhanced and 'likeable' screen presence on social media. This is not hard to do, thanks to image-enhancement apps such as Snapseed, VSCO, Afterlight 2, Enlight and the rest. Millennials will take about 25,000 selfies in their lifetimes and in the American survey quoted above, more than half of plastic surgeons saw patients who wanted procedures to help them look better in selfies. While schools are being urged to start lessons in 'body confidence', according to the work of a mid-2015 survey done by researchers from the University of York and released by the Children's Society, England now rates as the world's second worst nation for child happiness, beaten only by South Korea.[12] This misery stems mainly from bullying and a lack of self-confidence, both of which are very often to do with perceived appearance and the possible ignominy of being swiped left. In a world of airbrushed online celebrities and tanned and toned reality TV icons, the pressure on those aspiring to impress their playground peers is unrelenting.

Yogassistance

If postural yoga can help with both physical fitness and boosting self-confidence, its relevance to the above is clear, and is, in fact, becoming well documented. Overall, the practice is acknowledged to improve general fitness, body-tone and mental balance, but more specific medical endorsement is growing. A recent example comes from researchers at John Hopkins Hospital in the US who report that eight weeks of yoga classes improved the physical and mental well-being of people with two common forms of arthritis: osteoarthritis of the knee and the more generalised rheumatoid arthritis. This is believed to be the largest randomised trial so far to examine the effect of yoga on physical and psychological health.[13] In speaking to the press, Susan J. Bartlett, Ph.D., an adjunct associate professor of medicine at Johns Hopkins University and associate professor at McGill University added: 'There's a real surge of interest in yoga as a complementary therapy, with one in ten people in the US now practising yoga to improve their health and fitness.'

A recent study conducted by the Perelman School of Medicine at the University of Pennsylvania, and published in the November 2016 *Journal of Clinical Psychiatry*, found that *pranayama* helped patients with their health problems, specifically those with severe depression who did not respond well to antidepressant treatments. The technique studied was *sudarshan kriya*, a form of yogic breathing popularised by the Art of Living Foundation of Sri Sri Ravi Shankar that comprises a series of *pranayamas*—slow and calm breaths alternated with fast and stimulating ones—to bring people into a restful and meditative state. The study involved twenty-five patients who suffered with depression despite more than eight weeks on medication. They were randomly allotted to either the *pranayama* group or a control group, for eight weeks. During the first week, participants completed a six-session programme of *sudarshan kriya*, yoga postures, sitting meditation and stress education. After two months, the yoga group cut by several points its mean score on the Hamilton Depression Rating Scale (HAM-D), the most widely used clinician-administered depression assessment, while the control group showed no improvements. Although it is unclear which parts of the routine caused the benefit, the Pennsylvania results are being greeted with considerable interest, not least because more than half of the 41 million Americans who take antidepressants daily—among them one out of every four women in their forties—do not fully respond to them. Existing add-on therapies typically offer only limited additional benefits, or even have side effects that end up prolonging the depressive episode.

Brain Health

In the summer of 2017, it was announced that scientists in Brazil had imaged the brains of elderly female yoga practitioners, and found they had greater cortical thickness in the left prefrontal cortex, i.e. in areas associated with cognitive functions like attention and memory. Such results suggest that postural yoga could be a way to protect against cognitive decline in old age.[14] This followed research published by UCLA in the spring of 2015 that suggested meditation can work in this direction too. As early as our mid-to-late twenties, the brain's volume and weight begin to decrease, along with some of its functional abilities. Therefore although people are in general living longer, the years they gain often come with increased risk of mental illness and assorted neurodegenerative diseases, of which Alzheimer's is just the best known. The Californian study concluded that meditation appeared to help preserve the brain's grey matter. Using high-resolution magnetic resonance imaging (MRI), the team found that among those who meditated, the volume of cerebral tissue did not decline as much as it did with those who didn't. The number of participants was small: each group was made up of only twenty-eight men and twenty-two women ranging in age from twenty-four to seventy-seven; those who meditated had been doing so for four to forty-six years, with an average of twenty years. As always with such experiments, other factors—lifestyle choices, personality traits, genetic differences—may come into play, but nevertheless, this is an important building block in the growing evidence on the benefits of various forms of yoga. Another interesting area of study is the telomere, the tiny protective cap at the end of a human chromosome. While science is only just beginning to understand the relationship between life-experiences and the health of the 50 trillion cells in the human body, reduced telomere length has been linked to chronic stress exposure and depression. Recent studies on meditation show that the technique increases the length of telomeres; in other words, mind-yoga slows cellular aging.[15]

Office Yoga

Looking ahead, exercise will surely become more a part of everyday life. We now know that even a twenty-minute daily walk increases the size of the hippocampus, the brain's memory hub, which is one of the first areas to be destroyed by Alzheimer's. Other forms of simple activity revitalise the synaptic link between cells, and also increase neural connections in the cortex, a change that is linked to increased higher cognitive faculties such as enhanced vocabulary, memory and life-satisfaction. As the brain's plasticity continues into late adulthood, so changes in exercise routines seem able to bring beneficial and lasting physiological changes even well into old age. The world is waking up to this: according to the IHRSA (International Health, Racquet & Sportsclub Association), the $30 billion health and fitness industry in the US has been growing by at least 3–4 per cent annually for the last ten years and shows no signs of slowing down anytime soon while in the UK, with one in every seven people belonging to a gym, the total gym membership has broken the 10 million mark, and the industry, spread over 7,000 facilities, is now worth more than £5 billion for the first time.[16] Some gyms now offer live music and light shows, blurring the boundary between a rigorous arena of self-improvement and a relaxing place to meet and socialise.

Exercise breaks will surely become factored into the work routine too, as they improve worker well-being and team bonding and increase rates of attendance and productivity. It is reckoned that at any one time, one in five workers are actively disengaged from the task at hand, and when they are happier, creativity rises by 30 per cent and absenteeism drops by 9 per cent. Companies are now employing CHOs—chief happiness officers—and many of them recognise yoga can play a part in creating a fitter, more cheerful workforce. This trend will continue as the workplace is made more user-friendly. We are already seeing Silicon Valley corporations where, for the ambitious young professional, the office has become a substitute for family and community, a wraparound environment offering all sorts of activities and diversions that are away from the desk, yet subtly serve to increase attachment to it. The goal, of course, is always greater productivity, and such changes constitute a strategy to relax the staff and get them back to work, rather than any altruistic concern for the well-being of the people involved.[17] In the age of 'peak stuff', leisure-time and holidays are also becoming more of an activity project, with the focus on doing and participating and not just passive accumulation or sedentary enjoyment. Both at work and at home, then, body-yoga seems set to become ever more part of the middle-class lifestyle.

Nonetheless, this adaption of a yoga shorn of its historical context can throw up bizarre anomalies. The latest recruit to anti-stress therapy is *kundalini yoga*, which, as we saw in Chapter 5, first entered the yoga lexicon in the middle ages, with the brotherhoods of Nath adepts. In its original form, this system has been long known in India as a fast-track, and potentially dangerous, path to enlightenment, and was generally viewed with a respect that bordered on fear. Tantric and other texts mention the risks of this praxis, emphasising that the practitioner requires proven mental stability and good physical health, and should always be under the guidance of an accomplished guru.

In 2016, two studies lauded the effects of a 'Kundalini Yoga' programme for what must be considered highly vulnerable groups.[18] The first group were troubled children who had been brought up in institutions, devoid of the stability of parents or foster carers, the second were adult sufferers of Alzheimer's. After a twenty-week yoga programme conducted by a team from the University of Nottingham's Institute of Mental Health, the children enjoyed greater bonding both amongst themselves and with their carers. Improved health and psychological outcomes were also noted, both for the children and for those looking after them.[19] With the dementia patients, twenty-five volunteers over the age of fifty-five were involved, and they displayed decreased depression and anxiety, and improved verbal memory.[20] As a result, the research team recommended that *kundalini yoga* be included in future prevention programmes. Given that a typical session of this therapy ends with half an hour's group singing of the refrain 'I am bountiful, I am blissful, I am beautiful,' it may all sound more like harmless happy-clappy New Age affirmation than esoteric yoga, but what if that unpredictable goddess *kundalini* really were to start rising? Would practitioners totally ignorant of the deeper psycho-physical forces unleashed by the practice be able to deal with the consequences? The caution traditionally granted genuine *kundalini yoga* is not mere superstition.[21]

Yoga in the Boardroom

Mind-yoga has infiltrated some unlikely places. Inspired by books such as George Kinder's *The Seven Stages of Money Maturity*, a new breed of financial entrepreneur is offering investment planning variously based on Hindu spirituality, yoga or meditation. A beaming example is Jeff Bogart. As well as selling a standard wealth management service, he also runs Yogic Investing, which promises 'to move your yoga practice off the mat and into your savings account'. In what is but the latest update of the 'Think and Grow Rich' message of Napoleon Hill, other money men are finding that reduced stress equals increased cash. One of the world's most successful hedge fund managers attributes his success to a daily meditation regimen. Ray Dalio, the financial guru behind Bridgewater Associates and its roughly $160 billion assets, is in no doubt: 'I've been doing TM for forty-four years, twice a day for twenty minutes. It's such a great investment, more than any other factor in my success. It opens up the two sides of the brain, brings a creativity and open-mindedness.' He adds, 'It allows you to clear your head and bring an equanimity to everything.'[22]

Dalio's meditation routine has inspired other Wall Street whizz-kids, including the hedge-fund manager Daniel Loeb, Michael Desmarais, head of global recruiting for Goldman Sachs in New York and *The New York Times* financial columnist Andrew Ross Sorkin. Another firm seeks to 'channel the life force' into profits. This is Abacus Wealth Partners, which has devised a breathing exercise called 'the money breath' to help clients remain calm in the face of the various shocks and crises that are inescapably part of a volatile market. You get inner peace, everyone gets bigger profits. What's not to like?

Strange though it may sound in the present regime, the possibility of America's political leaders meditating together seems increasingly likely. United States Ohio Representative Tim Ryan has organised weekly meditation sessions for Congress for the past three years. In a report in the *New York Post* he says: 'There is a value in having some quiet time before votes—it can help anyone make better decisions.' A Thursday session for staff, and a Monday one for members of Congress, are known as the 'Quiet Time Caucus'. Those who were around at the time may remember that back in the turbulent '60s, the mystical poet Allen Ginsberg led a mass chanting of OM outside the White House. That was a little different though, as his aim was to exorcise the demons he felt had taken the place over.

Yoga on the Streets

At a more grassroots level, away from the boardrooms and political cabals, are groups of younger and humbler folk who see meditation as contributing to the welfare of society at large, and not just their own bank balances. Many are using crowd power to create peace. One such is Meditationflashmob UK, which, since its debut in Trafalgar Square in June 2011, has been attempting a quiet revolution on the streets of cities such as Aberdeen, Brighton and London. Large numbers of people, gathered via social media and online forums such as *Meetup.com* and the *Wake Up London* newsletter, are assembling to meditate for world peace for an hour in a public location. The idea is spreading further afield too, with international groups such as MedMob mobilising synchronised meditation flash-mobs in cities all around the world. Particularly on significant days such as International Day of Peace, World Water Day, World Earth Day, and the winter and summer solstices, they gather together in silence, to do nothing but just be.

This is a new expression of a very old aspiration: channelling the power of collective consciousness to purify the unregenerate world at large. The early Christian contemplatives in their desert communities, and their successors in the monasteries of the Middle Ages, would perfectly have understood MedMob's aim, for they were attempting the same thing for their times. In the heart of London, the proximity of Westminster's Palace and its Abbey still serves a similar purpose, hoping to infuse the temporal concerns of parliament with the spiritual energy of the daily Matins, Eucharist and Evensong. Clearly, the internet will be crucial in the future spread of such coalitions.

Prison Yoga

At the far end of the remedial spectrum is 'Yoga Behind Bars'. Way back in 1988, an innovative UK charity called the Phoenix Trust was founded with the purpose of bringing yoga and meditation into cells that were not monastic. Today it operates in about eighty prisons, either running classes or sending inmates books and CDs. Funded exclusively by donations, the Trust operates independently of the government and zealous Home Office chaplains who for decades have blocked non-Christian rehabilitation programmes such as yoga being conducted in Her Majesty's corrective establishments. In socially progressive Sweden, by contrast, yoga has become integral to the prison system. They have a national yoga co-ordinator, whose job, among other things, is to train prison guards to be teachers. In the US, the Prison Yoga Project has trained 2,300 teachers since 2010 and runs many programmes around the country.

Altogether, yoga of both body and mind are smoothing things out behind bars all over the world and often in the roughest of places: Mexico, India, Kenya, Alabama, South Africa, Myanmar. The West African country of Senegal had a particularly rough prison system until it took to mind-yoga. Since 1987 the TM technique has been taught to more than 11,000 prisoners and 900 staff throughout thirty-one prisons there. The prisoners reported improvements in their daily life that included better sleep, less irritability and aggression, and higher self-esteem. More confidence in themselves and the future, a marked decrease in theft and drug taking and improvements in health were also registered. The staff benefitted too, showing more self-control and concern for prisoners, better health, less absenteeism and lateness, and a markedly greater overall conscientiousness. Sadly, projects such as these tend to rise and fall, as they are vulnerable to changes of personnel in charge of funding bodies or running the institution concerned. Nonetheless, given that prisons are filled with captive audiences with plenty of time on their hands, they would seem the ideal places to launch mass yogic rehabilitation on the Swedish or Senegalese model.

Colombia, a country which, up until a decade ago, was riven with violence, has taken to body-yoga in a big way. Left wing guerrillas battled right wing paramilitary defence units, with cocaine barons, crime syndicates and dissident army factions all in the mix. As a result, more than 5.7 million people were displaced and over a quarter of a million slaughtered. But nowadays, war lingers on only in remote corners of the land, and a countrywide mass yoga programme for both ex-combatants and civilians is making a substantial contribution to the change. Under the auspices of an organisation called Dunna: Creative Alternatives for Peace, former adversaries are taking to the mat to attempt to build a more harmonious coexistence.

In 2013, Oxford University's Department of Experimental Psychology and Psychiatry published its findings from studying yoga in seven prisons, where it measured prisoners' mood, stress, impulsivity and mental well-being. Inmates were divided into two groups: one attended a ten-week course in yoga and meditation, the other simply carried out a conventional exercise routine. Though this study, like others, did not differentiate very clearly between the physical and the mental practices, prisoners in the yoga group clearly demonstrated improved attention spans and considerably less impulsivity.

Academic research and mountainous statistics are all very well, but they only come alive in human stories. Take the rehabilitation of Nick, a former international cocaine trafficker. He spent six years in Villa Devoto, Argentina's most notorious jail, where the open wings had no beds, and up to four hundred people were crammed sleeping on the floor like battery hens. The place was a hellhole of violence and brutality, with murders a weekly occurrence. Luckily, Nick somehow got hold of a book on yoga, started doing *asanas* and went from strength to strength. Not only did his practice keep him sane but, he reckons, it literally saved his life. As he recently told a BBC interviewer:

> At one point I actually became grateful for being in prison because I could feel this massive evolution, this change that was happening within me through

yoga. So I almost became like a grateful convict, happy to be where I was, paying the time for my crime and rehabilitating myself.[23]

Nick now runs an unostentatious yoga studio above a pub in West London. Gone is the millionaire lifestyle, with its silk suits, yachts and wild parties. Gone too are the flashy cars. Today the former coke baron may only ride a modest scooter, but he wears a regal smile.

29

FIFTY SHADES OF SAFFRON

On the highly auspicious day of the 2015 Summer Solstice, an extraordinary scene took place in the heart of New Delhi. Some 35,000 people gathered along Rajpath, the capital's imperial Champs Elysees, and got down on their mats for the world's largest-ever yoga session. Backed by the United Nations, the demo lasted thirty-five minutes, cost some £3 million to organise and was headed by no less a figure than the prime minister, Narendra Modi, a long-time vegetarian and yoga buff. To practitioners around the world, this first International Yoga Day must have seemed convincing proof that yoga has once more resumed its rightful place in the land of its birth. And the fact that the event took place in the middle of the grand ceremonial complex laid out by the Raj's prime architect, Edwin Lutyens, surely gave many Indians a satisfying sense of history's having come full circle.

But there were dissenting voices. Critics of Modi see his vociferous promotion of yoga as part of a suspiciously nationalist attempt to implement cultural conformity. To such sceptics, and there are many of them, the 21 June demonstration was just a publicity stunt to promote the government's policy of *Hindutva*—'Hindu-ness'—and a rather inept one, at that. A huge crowd with little knowledge or experience of yoga, some of whom were coerced to attend by local colleges and political operatives, went rather sloppily through a few postural yoga sequences popularised by Westerners, on mats made in China, and in the monsoon drizzle, too. The disenchanted found the whole pageant faintly absurd: a revamped Veda Vyasa meets a bedraggled Busby Berkeley. Nonetheless, despite the wet blankets, the demonstration showed how far things had come from that other public display in Bombay, eighty-three years almost to the day earlier, that we heard about in Chapter 17. Yoga is now government policy in India.

For his part, the Modi-yogi is very clear on the relevance of the values he is spearheading. When proposing his annual International Yoga Day to the UN

325

in New York, he introduced it into a speech largely devoted to climate change and the environment:

> Yoga is an invaluable gift of India's ancient tradition. It embodies unity of mind and body; thought and action; restraint and fulfilment; harmony between man and nature; a holistic approach to health and well-being. It is not about exercise but to discover the sense of oneness with yourself, the world and nature.[1]

Once back home, the prime minister soon announced a strategy to provide daily yoga lessons to three million Indian civil servants and their families, though as with the Delhi demonstration, it is rumoured that some pressure may be exerted to attend. Next came a government upgrade in which he appointed a new ministerial portfolio with responsibility for promoting 'India's traditional healing arts' under the acronym of AYUSH: Ayurveda, Yoga, the naturopathic Unani (traditional Muslim medicine), Siddha (the South Indian version of Ayurveda) and Homeopathy. Leaving aside the inconvenient facts that Unani came from Greece via the Arabs, and Homeopathy originated in Germany in the 1790s, history seems to be repeating itself here. Ayurveda and yoga were scorned by the Westernised Indian elite until, partly due to European scholarly interest towards the end of the nineteenth century, they were adopted by the nationalist movement as ingredients of an authentic Indian identity. Now, as India moves to the centre of the world stage, assorted Hindu revivalist movements within the Modi government are again promoting the narrative of India's glorious past.

This espousal of tradition has led to some curious anomalies. In 2014, Modi opened a new hospital in Mumbai that was full of state-of-the-art medical equipment. In his speech, he digressed into a eulogy about the skills of traditional medical knowledge, as evinced by episodes in India's past. As an example, he cited the technology that allowed Lord Shiva to remove an elephant's head and graft it onto a human body when creating the much-loved deity Lord Ganesha. Referring to this incident as narrated in the mythistorical *Puranas*, he said, without a trace of irony: 'There must have been some plastic surgeon at that time who got an elephant's head on the body of a human being.'[2]

Talking of medicine, the third-year Batchelor of Ayurveda Medicine and Surgery degree offered by Maharashtra University repeats advice on how to conceive a male child—an extremely sensitive subject in today's India—by quoting the second-century text *Charaka Samhita* to take:

> two undamaged leaf-buds from the east-facing or north-facing branches of a banyan tree grown in a common place and grinding them in curd, along with

two excellent black gram or white mustard seeds, it should be given to the woman to drink at the time of *pushya nakshatra* (a phase of the moon).[3]

This is an example of *pumsavana karma*, procedures to influence the sex of the foetus. Usually performed between the eighth and eleventh week of pregnancy, they are well known in classical Ayurveda.

To strengthen its yoga policy, in mid-2015 the government moved to register exclusive patents on over 1,500 *asanas* and began the process of videotaping them as part of the ongoing Traditional Knowledge Digital Library (TKDL), a newly formed unit of the Council for Scientific and Industrial Research (CSIR) of the Ministry of Science and Technology. The original impetus behind the project was to forestall foreign interference, such as the attempts by multinational corporations to patent medicinal plants and herbs that have been freely grown and used in the subcontinent for millennia. India has already won a case against a US bid to patent *neem*, a tree with several medical uses. Just how indigenous many of the *asanas* being videotaped for the TKDL really are has already been discussed in preceding chapters, but in the downward dog-eat-dog world of commercial yoga, this copyright initiative is perhaps understandable. In January 2019, a debate raged on Twitter after *Scientific American* tweeted a picture of a man doing the alternate-nostril breathing *pranayama* exercise known as *nadi shodhana* alongside the caption: 'Cardiac coherence breathing exercises can stabilize the heartbeat and have a powerful ability to dampen anxiety.' Many Indians online felt this was yet another appropriation of yoga, that would soon be packaged, rebranded and sold back to the public. Shashi Tharoor, the veteran politician and fierce critic of the West's historical role in India was more gracious, tweeting: 'It's taking the West a few millennia to learn what our ancients taught us millennia ago, but hey, you're welcome...'

Alongside such attempts at taking back, giving out—the ethic of service—has become an almost ubiquitous part of contemporary yoga activities in India. Following the model of the Ramakrishna Mission established by Vivekananda, many contemporary yoga organisations are busily providing food, health and educational resources to the needy. This is a laudable effort, no doubt, but it has also created some confusion by mixing what is usually considered the responsibility of government agencies with what has traditionally been considered a private, quasi-religious activity. Once again, secular critics are uneasy about the yoking of yoga and state, though it must be said that their reservations would bear more weight if governmental provision of welfare services was always efficient and incorruptible.

Yoga in Education

Oil—or perhaps it was *ghee*—was cast on the fire at the beginning of February 2015. The government of Rajasthan, following the lead of neighbouring Madhya Pradesh, decreed that each of the state's 48,000 schools, over half of which are government-run, must hold a daily twenty minute assembly which includes *surya namaskar* sequences plus some meditation and chanting of *mantras*. The idea was to evoke a healthy sense of nationalism by promoting ancient Indian values, but it didn't go down well with Muslim and Christian communities, both of whom object that the plan is not unifying, but divisive. They also dislike government attempts to make Sanskrit part of the school curricula, which they see as being another ploy to inculcate a mythistorical version of India's glorious, and unitedly Hindu, past. Then, in late 2016, the Supreme Court was petitioned by a pro-yoga group to make the practice a compulsory part of the syllabus on health grounds. The judges were uncomfortable with the idea as in India, a secular democracy, state schools must be religion-free. Minority groups and assorted educational experts were canvassed and the upshot may well be that India decides against official yoga. But knowing the speed of its legal process, this case could be a long, drawn-out affair, a 'stretch and relax' exercise that would make the typical *asana* sequence look frenetic.

Independent India's first leaders often expressed interest in promoting yoga for the national good, along with other indigenous means to health and well-being. The father of the nation, Mahatma Gandhi, was one of them; to this day, his most read book is not on political philosophy or non-violent revolution, but *A Guide to Health*, which is heavily influenced by Ayurvedic theories. The country's first prime minister, Jawaharlal Nehru, may have been a Cambridge-educated Fabian socialist, but he was reported to practise body-yoga surreptitiously. His daughter, Indira Gandhi, was less circumspect in expressing her spiritual interests. She visited saints to get their blessings, and in the 1970s was closely associated with a Rasputin-like figure called Dhirendra Brahmachari, India's first tele-yogi. His weekly broadcast on Doordarshan, then the sole, and state-owned, television network, promoted the health benefits of postural work, which he introduced to many state-owned schools in the Delhi area. He was also one of the prominent speakers at the World Conference on Scientific Yoga held in New Delhi in December 1970, which attracted a list of high-profile attendees, including Stanislav Grof, a pioneer of using psychedelics in psychotherapy, body-yoga maestros B. K. S. Iyengar and K. Pattabhi Jois and the archetypal *jnana yogi*, Jiddhu

Krishnamurti, as well as the subject of some of the earliest physiological studies on yoga, Swami Rama. Embarrassingly though, Dhirendra also conformed to the disreputable image of the yogi as *bhogi*, 'a lover of pleasures', and he became notorious for his eccentric and lavish ashram and assorted questionable business deals. He also, or so it was rumoured on Delhi's loquacious cocktail-party circuit, enjoyed a rather un-*brahmachari* relationship with Madame herself.

Political Yoga

Modi has his own right-hand *asana wallah*, a charismatic *hatha yogi* and Hindu firebrand called Baba Ramdev. This most conspicuous of the leaders of the national yoga revival took up the practice, as did his predecessors B. K. S. Iyengar, Pattabhi Jois and Bikram Choudhury, to overcome physical infirmity. In his case, a series of childhood illnesses and accidents culminated in paralysis of the left side of his face and a squint. The butt of other children's cruelty, Ramdev read about yoga in a book and began to practise. Leaving home as a teenager to study at a traditional *gurukul*, he became a monk in 1995.

Ramdev's first appearance in public was humble enough: handing out leaflets on the health benefits of yoga and Ayurveda in the streets of the holy pilgrimage city Haridwar. But he then went into partnership with the owner of a TV channel which, a few years later, was hosting the ten most popular religious programmes in the country. The top three featured Ramdev himself, and today over 80 million watch his daily yoga show. He also holds mass camps that draw thousands of participants, though his stage demonstrations there often look more like circus-strongman routines than anything a classical yogi would recognise. His organisation claims to run 50,000 free classes every day in all parts of the subcontinent.

Ramdev's considerable energy is not limited to his *asanas*. He is also a hugely successful retail entrepreneur, operating under the resonant brand-name 'Patanjali'. Initially specialising in nutritional and ayurvedic health products, the company has expanded by promoting *swadeshi* goods as an alternative to imports. The term *swadeshi* means 'one's own country' and is highly charged, as it was first used as a slogan by nineteenth-century nationalists such as Dadabhai Naoroji, Shri Yogendra's Bombay patron, who we met in Chapter 23, and then honed into an anti-imperial economic weapon by Mahatma Gandhi, who called the concept 'the soul of home rule'. Patanjali undercuts multinational corporations with an expanding catalogue of Indian-produced goods: foods, beauty products, health pills and potions, and even

329

blue jeans. The baba's sales pitch is an outspoken critique of globalisation; he once urged his followers to buy Coca Cola because 'it is the best thing to clean your toilet with'. A recent *swadeshi* advertisement warned: 'As East India Company plundered our country for 200 years these multinationals are exploiting our country by selling their harmful chemical products. Beware!'

Patanjali generated £1.2 billion in sales in 2018 and Ramdev's stated aim is to reach £11.5 billion by 2025, some of which will fund research into natural medicines. Such commercial success is certainly impressive, but the company pays its workers keenly rather than generously. All of the firm's employees must forswear meat and alcohol, while a firm management regime and commensurate low staff morale are allegedly the norm in the Baba's varied businesses. Some argue this is benign paternalism. Either way, Baba Ramdev's claim that his policies and enterprises will make India 'a world economic power and a world spiritual power by 2050' testify to the fact that he seems to have created a highly successful blend of patriotism, industry and asceticism, honed by a sharp eye for profit.[4]

So much for the businessman, but what about the yogi? In April 2018, back in Haridwar where he began, Ramdev initiated ninety-two 'scholar ascetics' into *sannyas*, as they sat in their new saffron robes on the banks of the sacred Ganges amidst the chanting of Vedic *mantras*. Renunciates in India are often relatively uneducated, but the group devoting their lives to his yogic national service included former corporate executives, doctors and engineers. Once trained in traditional scriptures and yoga disciplines, they will be part of a 1,000-strong core team that will handle the work currently done by Patanjali. As Ramdev explained: 'The scholar ascetics have resolved to live for goals Patanjali has set before itself and to propagate Indian culture and tradition.'

This aligns the baba nicely with Modi's political agenda, and the Indian media frequently carries pictures of them together. A vociferous advocate of *Hindutva* in general, Ramdev puts yoga at the centre of what it means to be a true Indian. In April 2017, following the landslide victory of the Prime Minister's BJP party, he told the celebrating crowds:

> Yoga has been an inalienable part of our culture. No king or emperor has built India or shaped its destiny. In fact, India has been built by saints, yogis and fakirs. It is a matter of pride for us that the Prime Minister is a yogi, and the Chief Minister of the most populous state is also a yogi… We will do Yoga together and take steps to remove societal illness, diseases, bad habits, intoxication and other negativities. This will make lives peaceful and prosperous.[5]

Ramdev has even initiated government policy. Throughout 2011 he held huge public rallies where he demanded a government crackdown on corruption, black money and withheld tax revenue. Once in power five years later, Modi would dramatically implement just such a reforming programme, declaring overnight that eight out of ten circulating banknotes were no longer legal tender. But the baba can overstep the mark too. His claims that yoga can cure not only cancer and swine flu, but even 'the aberration that is homosexuality', which he has repeatedly condemned as unnatural, have not gone down at all well with some of his compatriots.

Nonetheless, to the many fed up with the nepotistic corruption of the Congress party and the socialist legacy of Jawaharlal Nehru, who had a Western scepticism of India's traditional preferences, the patriotic yogi provides both a nationalist and a religious identity. Thousands assemble at his public meetings and chant the slogan *Bharat mata ki jai*—'Victory to India our Motherland!'—and to them, he is the hero who can stem the tide of Western decadence and return India to the glories of her past. Ramdev is mythistory on the march. Some observers see him as a Hindu version of Billy Graham, the religious showman who galvanised the Christian right and had the ear of several American presidents. Others even make the Donald Trump comparison. Given the yogi's multi-billion-dollar empire, his irrepressible, media-savvy personality and his adroitness at taking every opportunity to market his own brands, one can see why.

An Ecological Hiccup

Those sceptical of the International Day of Yoga were provided with more ammunition in March 2016 when the Ministry of External Affairs promoted the World Culture Festival in Delhi. This was in collaboration with the Art of Living Foundation, the international movement run by Sri Sri Ravi Shankar, former student of Maharishi Mahesh Yogi. Shankar is another guru whose popularity and political influence have surged in recent years. He appeals to a more sophisticated constituency than Ramdev's: a globalised middle-class that is trying to remain connected to its roots. The Delhi bash was held to celebrate the foundation's thirty-five years in operation, and among its three million visitors were the prime minister and many other political big-hitters. This alone was a rare accomplishment; for a private event to gain such official support is highly unusual, even in the patronage-ridden world of Indian politics. Natwar Singh, a former External Affairs Minister, confided waspishly to the *The Hindu* newspaper: 'After all, the diplomatic delegates coming for the conference have led lives that have been far from spirituality.'

The real problem, though, was not the festival's guest list, but its location. The three-day event was held alongside the Yamuna river, historically sacred due to its association with Lord Krishna, but nowadays a polluted stream wending its sluggish way through an area of extreme ecological fragility. Environmental watchdogs had warned against the gathering, but it went ahead, with a stage covering seven acres, pontoon bridges, portable cabins and parking facilities. None of this had official permission. Despite the healthy yoga sessions, sacred rituals and prayers for world peace, the event proved the environmentalists correct, as it resulted in more than £5 million worth of damage reckoned to take ten years to reverse. Shankar was fined over £600,000 as 'environmental compensation' for what the official report called the area's 'loss of waterbodies and wetlands, loss of floodplain vegetation and biodiversity ... and loss of ecosystem functions'. He insisted his organisation had done nothing wrong and that he would go to prison rather than pay up, but settled a year later.

Behind the Scenes

Celebrity performances may be its public face, but nationalist yoga has a soberly erect backbone. This is the Rashtriya Swayamsevak Sangh (RSS), a Hindu-nationalist organisation formed in 1925 to instil discipline and the ethic of selfless service into the coming nation state. Modi is a lifelong member. The RSS is a quasi-military outfit, divided into branches that organise local volunteers in physical fitness drills, first-aid training and various charitable and social activities. In an echo of those Victorian YMCAs, up until recently its cadres dressed in an outfit that recalled the Boy Scout Movement—white shirts, khaki shorts, yellow socks and black shoes. Yoga is a key component of their regime and it is surely no coincidence that 21 June, chosen for International Yoga Day, is the anniversary of the death of Keshav Baliram Hegdewar, the RSS founder.

The promotion of *Hindutva* by the right wing of Modi's government is seen by liberals as a toxic attempt to create an intolerant hegemony that threatens minorities. Fundamentalists are conducting forcible 'reconversions' back to Hinduism, as well as instigating attacks on Christian churches. Supporters of this policy see it as long-overdue revenge for many decades of the Christian conversion of low-caste and tribal groups, who, they say, were bribed with medicines and schools. On the other side, no one has forgotten that it was a former member of the RSS, Nathuram Godse, who assassinated Mahatma Gandhi for being too soft on Muslims. Then there were the 2002 riots in Gujarat when Modi was the Chief Minister of the state, which left over a thousand dead, three quarters of whom were Muslim. Modi and the state government have been accused of complicity in this massive outbreak of violence. Now, even the country's most iconic image has been dragged into the dispute. The RSS wants the Taj Mahal sidelined as a cultural attraction and removed from tourist promotion, because it is not truly Indian, but an alien Islamic import from Persia.

Hindutva *Abroad*

The debate over the ownership of yoga has gone global. A few years ago, the leading Indo-American lobby, the Hindu American Foundation (HAF), started the 'Take Back Yoga' campaign to remind Americans that yoga was made in India by Hindus, and should not be traduced by commercial opportunism, nor used to mop up the consequences of unhealthy Western lifestyles. It campaigns vigorously against what it calls 'the rape of yoga', and many successful members of the Indian diaspora—doctors, engineers, IT specialists—support the project. In their eyes, modern postural yoga is greedily consuming the honey while failing to acknowledge the bees.

One of the HAF's most strident voices is Rajiv Malhotra, an Indian-American author, philanthropist and public speaker. High on his hit list are those liberal American scholars who, through investigations of the history and texts of yoga such as we have seen in the opening chapters of this book, have come to very different conclusions than his. Unabashed, Malhotra puts such Western yoga academics on a par with Marxist guerrillas and Pakistani terrorists, as a malign force undermining Indian unity and endangering her cultural integrity. The author of books with such titles as *Academic Hinduphobia*, his website bemoans the 'powerful counterforce within the American Academy (that) is systematically undermining core icons and ideals of Indic Culture and thought'.[6] He also argues that liberal scholars are obsessed with criticising the caste system, a social phenomenon they consistently misunderstand by automatically equating it with exploitation and prejudice, while 'most well-educated Americans have a blind spot about their own caste system'.[7] Another of Malhotra's targets is *The New York Times*, which, not entirely without justification, he criticises for publishing only negative articles about India, thus perpetuating the 'Mother India' prejudice initiated by Kathleen Mayo almost a century ago. One way or another, as the opposite hemispheres of the planetary brain, America and India seem chronically out of synch.

A book by the widely-respected American academic Wendy Doniger, *The Hindus: An Alternative History*, so offended the *Hindutva* forces that they put pressure on the publishers Penguin to withdraw it from sale. In 2014, the company capitulated and removed it from retail outlets, pulping the remaining copies. This was at the specific behest of the Shiksha Bachao Andolan Samiti (SBAS), or 'Movement to Save Education', an organisation founded and presided over by the longtime RSS activist Dinanath Batra, whose aim is to 'change the face of Indian education', by removing content deemed antinational or hurtful to the feelings and self-image of Hindus. The book did make a return to the marketplace twenty months later, with a different and bolder publisher, but the muscles of *Hindutva* conservatism had been very convinvincingly flexed for all to see.

To complicate matters further, there are some North American scholars who have sympathy with the aims of Malhotra, Batra and the like. The most prominent among these is the prolific author David Frawley, or Vamadeva Shastri as he is known in India, where many have hailed him as a *vedacharya*, or 'teacher of true knowledge'. Along with his colleagues Subhash Kak and N. S. Rajaram, Frawley has marshalled new readings of Sanskrit texts, geophysical research and astronomy in his attempts to show the Vedic texts are far older than has previously been thought, perhaps going back as far as 8,000 BC. In recognition of such efforts, in 2015, he was honoured by the president of India with the Padma Bhushan, the third highest civilian award granted by the government for 'distinguished service of a high order to the nation'. Back home in Western Indology faculties, however, Frawley's affiliations are more loathed than lauded. To these academics, he is engaged in a partisan bid to promote the ahistorical thesis of a unified 'spiritual India' stretching back millennia.[8]

Yogappropriation?

Yoga has also become embroiled in the campaigns to rectify history, and recast language, currently sweeping universities in Canada, America and the UK. In the ideological battle over what constitutes legitimacy in the relationship between erstwhile colonial powers and their former subjects, curricula are being diligently scanned for imperialist and racist bias. Such disputes may be specialised, but their fallout can trickle down to the jobbing yoga teacher. In 2015, at the University of Ottawa, Jennifer Scharf was asked by the student federation to offer remedial body-yoga classes to the Centre for Students with Disabilities. She was then told by woke activists that such a course would be inappropriate, because many of the cultures where yoga originated had 'experienced oppression, cultural genocide and diasporas due to colonialism and Western supremacy'[9] Aseem Shukla, founder of the HAF, congratulated the concerned students for their 'insight and understanding'.

Scharf argued that yoga was a universal discipline and not bound to any one religion or place, but she was overruled by the federation, and her classes terminated for being 'cultural appropriation'. Scharf's defence of yoga, though, is taken further by many Westerners, who claim that yoga is part of nature itself, discovered, not invented. As an aspect of the universal spiritual legacy of humanity, it belongs to the whole planet, and, rather like the laws of physics, is an enduring truth to be utilised for the good of all humankind, not just one nation state. While such arguments may appeal to our inner hippie, they are a tad disingenuous. We cannot overlook, deny or rewrite history just because we feel like it, or because it confronts us with an inconvenient truth. The fact remains that yoga, as we have seen, arose squarely in the context of Indian culture over many centuries, so it cannot be summarily divorced from these roots. To do so completely disregards the diachronic expertise, passed down through generations from master to disciple, that gives the tradition the authority it bequeaths to those who would represent it.

To be sure, the Western (and perhaps especially the American) yoga scene may often be insensitive to the context of Indian culture. There are far too many yoga teachers out there mispronouncing Sanskrit terms, mistranslating sacred verses and incorrectly sounding, or even fabricating, *mantras*. Their comportment, both on and off the mat, may also demonstrate an ignorance of the subtle nuances of what they are purporting to teach. But such failings are generally due more to the lack of a cosmopolitan education than any malign intent. Such insensitivities are not improved by the anti-intellectualism that pervades much of the yoga scene, especially those schools only interested in a keep-fit routine. We have seen that too much of contemporary practice is crass and narcissistic, and in some cases may be actively, even if unwittingly, opposed to the sacred principles on which so much Indian praxis has historically rested. However, none of these shortcomings means that yoga is the monopoly of India, or that Indians should be allowed to copyright its practice or have legal backing to proscribe its format. The influence of Western gymnastics in the Mysore Palace tradition is, on its own, enough evidence to undermine the claim that all postural practice has a hallowed indigenous origin. All in all, accusations that yoga has been stolen from a formerly oppressed country by venal neo-colonials are simply unsustainable. If we study the history impartially, it is much nearer the mark to say that yoga has been a gift from generous Indian teachers who, from Vivekananda onwards, have taken considerable time and trouble to travel westwards to spread their message to as many of us as they could possibly reach.

The Return of the Nath Yogis?

An intriguing aspect of *Hindutva*-yoga is that it has welcomed the Nath broth-erhoods back onto the political stage. Their principal monastery is the Gorakhnath Peeth situated in the Modi heartland of Uttar Pradesh (UP), and two of its recent abbots were very involved in the political scene. One was investigated after Gandhi's assassination because of his frequent criticisms of the Mahatma's accommodation of Muslims. His successor, who served four terms as the local member of parliament, was one of the instigators of the 1992 destruction of a sixteenth-century mosque in Ayodhya and the building of a Hindu temple in its place, an event which sparked some of the country's worst religious conflict since Partition.

In early 2017, the current abbot, Yogi Adityanath, after serving time as an MP and helping to spearhead the BJP's landslide election victory in UP, was rewarded by being appointed the Chief Minister of the state. This is significant not only because of the power of the position itself, but because it is seen as an ideal springboard from which to challenge for the premiership, as it was in Modi's case. An aggressive promoter of *Hindutva* and founder of a militant youth group called the Hindu Yuva Vahini, Adityanath is well-known for advo-cating an extreme policy of saffronisation. His 'anti meat-eaters and cow-killers' policy is clearly a blow aimed at Muslims, as it is they who mainly run the meat industry in North India, and he has called such people 'a crop of two-legged animals that has to be stopped'. In his revisioning of history, the Chief Minister is keen to change Muslim place names to Hindu ones. Most controversial is the reversion of the four hundred and fifty-year-old Mughal name Allahabad, 'the city of Allah', to its previous title of Prayagraj, 'the king of sacrificial sites'. This Hindu name commemorates a key event in mythis-tory: the fire-sacrifice performed there by the four-headed, four-armed Lord Brahma, after he had created the world. The idea is spreading. In neighbouring Haryana, Delhi's gold-rush suburb of Gurgaon, a sprawling building site of shopping malls, call centres and IT start-ups, is now incongruously to be sanctified as Gurugram, 'the village of the guru'.

Tradition and Progress

The world-view that created yoga did not share the optimistic vision of humankind's inexorable progress that is the legacy of the thinkers who articu-lated the European Enlightenment—Rene Descartes, Francis Bacon, Adam Smith, Jean-Jacques Rousseau, Voltaire and the rest. In common with the ancient Greeks, the *rishis* of India considered human life to be in decline from an earlier Golden Age, condemned to a spiralling descent from a time when we lived in harmony with the Natural Law (*dharma*) that upholds life. To the forest sages, then, the word 'enlightenment' had a profounder meaning than the glorification of human reason. For them, enlightenment was the regaining of this lost cosmic harmony, without which, merely rational knowledge and scientific skill will never suffice.

In conformity with the general idea of progress, though, we might expect the younger generation to be keener on change than their parents. So, in the context of yoga, it is interesting to listen to the words of Prashant Iyengar, the son of the master B. K. S., who, together with his sister Gita, runs the Ramamani Iyengar Memorial Yoga Institute in Pune. Now approaching seventy, Prashant has never been fazed by his father's formidable achievements and reputation, though to find his own distinctive voice cannot have been easy. As someone who views yoga as *adhyatma sadhana*—a path to Self-knowledge, squarely based on the teachings of the *Upanishads*, *Bhagavad Gita* and *Yoga Sutra*—his is a different approach from the predominantly physical discipline that B. K. S. taught the West to see as yoga. Indeed, he is clearly not impressed by the extraordinary uptake of postural practice we have been charting in this book:

> The popularity of yoga doesn't fascinate me. Weeds grow when something is popularized; misconceptions spread. People are ignorant and innocent about something not popularized, which is far better than them having misconceptions. My personal opinion, which may not be palatable to everyone, is that misconceptions have spread. I don't feel such a subject has to be popularized. We cannot expect that millions are practising real yoga just because millions of people claim to be doing yoga all over the globe. What has spread all over the world is not yoga. It is not even non-yoga; it is un-yoga.[10]

30

YOGA, RELIGION AND SPIRITUALITY

Science may be warming to yoga, but religion is often distinctly cool. The UK is generally a secular and tolerant place, but many yoga teachers there will have had the experience of being banned from working in premises owned or controlled by the Church. Some dioceses are getting their vicars in a twist, and it's not the yogic sort. A typical snapshot: in February 2015 an Anglican church in Bristol banned a yoga group that had happily been using its hall for nine years. A spokesman explained: 'We are aware that yoga can be practised as either an exercise class or as a spiritual discipline and anywhere in between, however we understand that its roots lie in thinking that it is not compatible with the Christian faith and the Christian faith has not appropriated yoga.' The following week, a Catholic priest in Northern Ireland was more forthright in his condemnation of yoga, lumping it together with the pernicious practice of 'Indian head-massage'. Those who indulge in such things, he said, are taking risks with their spiritual health, opening themselves up to 'Satan and the fallen angels', and they could be on the way to 'the kingdom of darkness' as a result. Explaining further, Father Roland Colhoun told the local *Derry Journal*:

> Pope Francis said 'do not seek spiritual answers in yoga classes'. Yoga is certainly a risk. There's the spiritual health risk. When you take up those practices from other cultures, which are outside our Christian domain, you don't know what you are opening yourself up to. The bad spirit can be communicated in a variety of ways. I'm not saying everyone gets it, or that it happens every time, and people may well be doing yoga harmlessly. But there's always a risk and that's why the Pope mentioned it and that's why we talk about that in terms of the danger of the New Age movement and the danger of the occult today. That's the fear.[1]

A local yoga instructor who described herself as 'a good Catholic' replied to the paper that yoga students can: 'learn good posture and breathing to help them with tension in their bodies and to help calm a busy mind. In all the time I have been teaching, not one person has ever expressed an interest going deeper into the spiritual elements of yoga.' And that, precisely, is the point. Although well-intentioned, her self-defence unwittingly reveals the paucity of so much modern postural teaching, which ostensibly promotes yoga while simultaneously selling it short.

Works of the Devil?

There is no doubt that many church authorities, both Anglican and Catholic, fear that yoga's apparent neutrality conceals a connection with Indian spirituality that could seduce their charges away from the one true faith. The shadow of unalloyed good must always be projected onto something 'other', and in America, some prominent pastors have gone further than Father Colhoun, and denounced yoga as 'demonic'. To them, yoga is nothing less than the latest ploy of the ever-inventive, and now seductively flexible, Satan. They may have taken their cue from Father Gabriele Amorth, for years the Vatican's chief exorcist, who claims yoga is indeed satanic because: 'it leads to a worship of Hinduism and all eastern religions are based on a false belief in reincarnation'.

Such an agile stretch of logic is itself yogic, but whether you agree with it or not, Father Amorth is at least consistent with his faith's historical distrust of the idea of rebirth. The doctrine (along with vegetarianism) was officially declared a heresy at the pivotal Council of Nicea that took place in AD 325. To merit such a ban, both ideas must have been widely prevalent among the disparate groups of spiritual seekers who made up the inchoate Christian community in the first centuries after Jesus' death. The descendants of some of these early groups, such as the Cathars, continued to believe in reincarnation, at least until they were brutally destroyed in the thirteenth century by the Inquisition because of their waywardness.

When it comes to extreme views, Amorth had form. In a speech to an Italian film festival a few years before his death in 2016, he claimed that reading J. K. Rowling's *Harry Potter* books is dangerous, because they encourage children to believe in black magic and wizardry. His animus against yoga was no doubt intended to reinforce previous warnings uttered by the last Pope, Benedict XVI. In 1989, while he was still Cardinal Joseph Ratzinger, the prelate warned Catholics against all 'non-Christian forms of meditation', while challenging the non-dualist teachings of Hindu metaphysics. Lumping together yoga, Zen, Transcendental Meditation and other 'Eastern' practices, he warned they could: 'degenerate into a cult of the body that debases Christian prayer'.

Just how either TM, a purely mental technique, and Zen Buddhism, a fully-fledged religion with an emphasis on prolonged sitting practice, could be construed as 'a cult of the body' is hard to fathom. Perhaps the good cardinal was alluding to the wealth of physiological studies accruing on assorted meditation techniques, and the general interest in this physical data.

In her reply to Father Amorth's attack, Wanda Vanni, the founder of the Mediterranean Yoga Association, assured an Italian news agency that yoga was an unthreatening exercise regime, stating baldly: 'Yoga is not a spiritual practice. It doesn't have even the slightest connection with Satanism or Satanic sects.' While yoga practitioners the world over would doubtless concur heartily with her second statement, many would seriously dispute the first. Both historical theory and modern practice contradict Ms. Vanni's materialistic definition, but one can see how she, like the teacher in Derry, felt backed into a corner when trying to prove she was beyond suspicion. The ghost of the Inquisition has not yet been laid to rest.

Devout Christians have not always disapproved of yoga. In 1921, a Catholic theologian, perhaps aptly named Michel Sage, produced the first French translation of the *Yoga Sutra*. In so doing, he espoused such heresies as reincarnation and the law of *karma*, but somehow remained free of ecclesiastical censure. Then, in the 1950s, Fr. Jean-Marie Déchanet, a Benedictine priest working in the Congo, published two books, *La Voie du Silence* and *Christian Yoga* in which, albeit with great caution, he made the case for how, and why, Christians could benefit from yoga. Ten years later Gaspar Koelman, a Jesuit scholar working in India, produced a meticulous study of Patanjali, *Patanjala Yoga: From Related Ego to Absolute Self*. More recently, no less an authority than Pope John Paul II seemed, tacitly at least, to support what the deeper levels of yoga are all about. On his visit to Ireland in 1979, he told adoring crowds: 'No movement in religious life has any value unless it is also a movement inwards to the still centre of your existence, where Christ is.'

One person who would agree with such open, and inner, mindedness is Rowan Williams, the former Archbishop of Canterbury. He recently disclosed that he spends up to forty minutes a day kneeling and repeating the Eastern Orthodox prayer, and performing breathing exercises, as part of a routine influenced by Buddhism. Now Master of Magdalene College, Cambridge, Williams also spends time pacing slowly and repeatedly prostrating himself, as part of an intense early morning ritual of silent meditation and prayer. He explains that those who perform such contemplative rituals regularly can reach 'advanced states' and become aware of an 'unbroken inner light'. [2]

341

Christian Interiority

How, then, might yoga, and especially mind-yoga, connect with Christian traditions of prayer and contemplation? This is too vast and technical a subject to be tackled in any depth here, but one initial avenue of approach might be to look at the Biblical evidence. While the Hebrew Old Testament has no clear or consistent references to a systematic exploration of consciousness that we can align with yogic models, there are a few tantalising glimpses. The eternal Self as taught by the *Upanishads*, and celebrated by many subsequent seers, seems close to the spirit of these roughly contemporary lines: 'The Lord possessed me in the beginning of his way, before his works of old. I was established from everlasting, from the beginning, or ever the earth was. When he prepared the heavens, I was there: when he set a compass upon the face of the depth.'[3] Then there are better known verses of a more dualistic nature, such as: 'Be still and know that I am God',[4] and 'Be silent before the Lord and wait patiently for Him.'[5]

These point in the direction of a profound inner quietude and receptiveness that Jewish mystics of the time called *bitul*, a state of 'waiting and being'. And while it is true that nowhere in the four orthodox gospels is it mentioned that Jesus taught a specific system of meditation, some of his statements are significant in this context, as they imply that, rather than searching for truth outside oneself, inward contemplation is actually the way. Consider: 'Neither shall they say, Look here! or, Look there! for behold, the Kingdom of God is within you',[6] and, more pithily: 'The Kingdom of God is at hand', or: 'Seek ye first the Kingdom of God, and his righteousness; and all else shall be added unto you.'[7] Other passages have been taken as symbolic references to the contemplative practice of minimising sensory activity and withdrawing the attention from the world as a means to draw closer to God and glorify life: 'But thou, when thou prayest, enter into thy inner chamber, and when thou hast shut thy door, pray to thy Father which is in secret; and thy Father which seeth in secret shall reward thee openly.'[8]

This was certainly how John Cassian, the father of Christian mind-yoga, interpreted it. Quoting his own spiritual mentor, Abbot Isaac, he says:

> We pray within our chamber, when removing our hearts inwardly from the din of all thoughts and anxieties, we disclose our prayers in secret and in closest intercourse to the Lord. We pray with closed doors when with closed lips and complete silence we pray to the searcher not of words but of hearts. We pray in secret when from the heart and fervent mind we disclose our petitions to God alone.[9]

The most numerous references to techniques of introversion are found in the thirteen Gnostic Gospels, discovered at Nag Hammadi in Upper Egypt in 1945, that record teachings of the early Coptic communities. The best known of these is the Gospel of Thomas, which opens with the claim:

> These are the hidden words that the living Jesus spoke. And Didymos Judas Thomas wrote them down. And he said: 'Whoever finds the meaning of these words will not taste death.' Jesus says: 'The one who seeks should not cease seeking until he finds. And when he finds, he will be dismayed. And when he is dismayed, he will be astonished. And he will be king over the All.'

It continues:

> Jesus says: 'If those who lead you say to you: "Look, the kingdom is in the sky!" then the birds of the sky will precede you. If they say to you: "It is in the sea," then the fishes will precede you. Rather, the kingdom is inside of you, and outside of you.'[10]

The idea that this collection might shed light on the esoteric aspect of Jesus' teaching was strengthened in late 2017, when fragments of a third-century text were discovered in Oxford University's library. This was the *First Apocalypse of James*, an original Greek version of an existing Coptic text found at Nag Hammadi. The fact that there were at least two copies of the work signifies its importance. It describes secret teachings, in which Jesus reveals information about the heavenly realms and future events, and the attribution to James, believed to be the brother of Jesus, implies that it was he who would have had the authority to take over as an effective leader of the early communities after Jesus' death. In other words, this Gnostic text may signal a Christian version of the *guruparampara* tradition to pass knowledge on from master to disciple, that characterises all genuine wisdom schools.

Levels of Instruction

While the Orthodox churches have always been sympathetic to the idea of Christianity as a sacred initiatory tradition, the populist Protestant and reformed churches have chosen to present Jesus as a resolutely exoteric teacher. Their saviour, always accessible to even the simplest folk, concentrated on reforming social behaviour, rather than transmitting hidden knowledge and the experience of higher states of consciousness. But, even in the four gospels, there are clear hints that Jesus, like all masters, gave out his teaching at different levels to different followers, according to their capacity. While he mostly taught through simple parables that can be understood in various ways, to a select few he seems to have imparted a higher teaching. At one point he says to them: 'The knowledge of the secrets of the Kingdom of God has been given to you, but to the rest it comes by means of parables.'[11] And he could be scathing of the average person's ability to comprehend deep spiritual truths, saying he would never: 'give to dogs what is holy or cast pearls before swine'.[12] The apostle Mark reiterates that, while parables were the medium of instruction for the general public, Jesus granted his inner circle another form of instruction: 'He spoke the word to them (the crowd) as far as they were able to understand it… but he explained everything to his disciples when they were alone.'[13]

The mystics who followed Jesus and shaped the infant Christian church certainly accepted the hierarchy of sacred understanding and the need to preserve it. St. Dionysius, a Greek judge who was converted by Paul and became the first Bishop of Athens, is very clear on this:

> These things thou must not disclose to any of the uninitiated, by whom I mean those who cling to the objects of human thought, and imagine there is no super-essential reality beyond, and fancy that they know by human under-standing Him that has made Darkness His secret place. And, if the Divine Initiation is beyond such men as these, what can be said of others yet more incapable thereof, who describe the Transcendent Cause of all things by quali-ties drawn from the lowest order of being, while they deny that it is in any way superior to the various ungodly delusions which they fondly invent in igno-rance of this truth?[14]

By 'ungodly delusions' Dionysius meant popular theology, which he saw as crudely anthropomorphic and unrefined by the contemplation needed to penetrate the heart of the divine mysteries. Interiority is a matter of experi-ence, but also right understanding and correct expression. Metaphysics demands its own vocabulary, as the language used to describe the sensible world is often simply inadequate to encompass the higher realms of reality. Indian yogis were always aware of this lacuna too, which is why they invented what was called the 'twilight language' (*sandhya bhashya*) as a kind of code in which to discuss and expound deep spiritual truths, while shielding them from the casual gaze of the uninitiated.

East and West

While most Christians in Europe do not have an overly emotional reaction to yoga's Eastern roots, many may feel a vague distrust of its foreignness. This is a keen irony, considering that their faith derives from a messianic Jewish cult that flourished in the ancient Middle East, surely a foreign world if ever there was one. To those fourth-century Romano-Britons awaiting conversion, the new religion, fresh from victory over rival cults of Isis and Mithras, must have seemed exotic, colourful and decidedly alien. Imported from a far distant land of desert nomads, it had nothing whatsoever to do with Europe and her settled, pastoral landscapes, temperate climate, racial histories and indigenous pagan cultures. The font of the Queen of England's private chapel in Norfolk may hold water from the holy river Jordan, but the faith it represents was originally a very foreign infusion.

In fact, the fledgling Christian communities in Egypt and Syria were themselves highly eclectic. Situated at the western end of the ancient routes to China, such anchorites were very likely influenced by philosophies and practices that, along with the caravans bearing silk and spices, arrived from further east. Their teachings, translated into Latin by the desert monk John Cassian in the fifth century, formed the basis of what was to become known in Christianity as 'ascetic theology': the spiritual discipline of prayer and contemplation. An anonymous practitioner of the time described this path succinctly: 'Every morning put your mind into your heart and stand in the presence of God all day long.'

These first Christian yogis were known as the Desert Fathers. Withdrawal from the world of the senses was practised in, and symbolised by, the desert, itself a metaphysical landscape in which matter has been reduced to almost nothing. The Greek word for 'desert'—*eremia*—literally means 'solitude' or 'abandonment', and is the term from which we derive our word 'hermit'. The spiritual journey, even in community, is always a solitary one; by the same token, those who desert the world are 'monks' who live in 'monasteries', both words coming from the Greek *monos*, meaning 'alone'. Unattractive though they may be to us moderns, for whom loneliness is a surer marker of potential ill-health than smoking, the deprivations of solitude, both outer and inner, have always been understood to purify the pilgrim soul. As an early text says: 'The road of cleansing goes through that desert. It shall be named the way of holiness.'[15]

Plotinus, the third-century Greek philosopher who was a major influence on all subsequent systems of mystical knowledge—pagan, Islamic, Jewish, Christian or Gnostic—described the culmination of the spiritual life as: 'The flight of the alone to the Alone.'[16] The hermits of the ancient Levant were crucial to the development of the new faith that spread so powerfully northwards through Europe, using techniques no doubt influenced by eastern yoga, Jewish Merkabah mysticism and practices going back to Platonic times. These involved bodily positions and breathing exercises, along with the invocation of 'the divine names' that were used in the same way as Hindu *mantras* and what Sufis, following a *hadith* teaching, call 'the beautiful names of Allah'. Such praxis was to become routine for the small groups of monks that lived and meditated on remote islands dotted around the coast of Britain and Ireland. Skellig, Iona and Lindisfarne were soon established as spiritual outposts positioned, literally and metaphorically, on the remote margins of conventional society.

It was not long before this rugged Celtic individualism was superseded by the Rule of St. Benedict, a Roman model of communal organisation that was to shape the future of monastic life in Britain until the upheavals of the Reformation. However, the ascetic pattern set by the original desert hermits continued in the various churches that followed the Eastern Orthodox rite and drew their inspiration from communities such as the one perched on the steep slopes of Mount Athos in northern Greece. Their way was known as Hesychasm, from the Greek word *hesychia*, meaning 'stillness' or 'silence', and the central practice was repetition of the Jesus Prayer. This was not normal prayer, which, deriving from the Latin *prex*—'request'—is either supplicatory, asking for what we need, or intercessionary, asking for what others need. Known as 'infused contemplation' in Catholicism, this was a deeper, *mantra*-like exercise designed to lead the mind to the unstained silence beyond thought. When meditating, Hesychasts adopted an *asana* of bending forward with their head on the chest, a position known in Greek as *omphaloskepsis*, that gained them the nickname of 'navel-gazers'. This introverted posture recurs in the miniature paintings, common in Persia and northern India from the seventeenth century onwards, that depict Sufi and Hindu saints sunk deep in contemplation.

Post-Reformation religion had little time for the contemplative life and the ecclesiastical structures that had facilitated it. After all, it was their indolence and moral decay that the energetic new faith saw itself called to purify. In England, when Henry VIII broke from Rome and set up the Anglican Church, he lost no time in abolishing the monasteries, and with them, traditions they had nurtured for centuries: learning, healing, the arts and education. Another loss was contemplation. However decadent the monasteries may have become, this last was a major blow for English culture. Despite these violent social changes, a few Protestants continued the life of 'ascetic theology', inspired by the teachings of the northern European saints who flourished in the fourteenth and fifteenth centuries. In Britain, the outstanding figures were Julian of Norwich and the anonymous author of the classic manual of the inner life, *The Cloud of Unknowing*. A sixteenth-century Spanish Franciscan,

Francisco de Osuna, left us one of the clearest descriptions of the spiritual journey as a form of mind-yoga, extolling:

> The plenitude of joy and continual consolation felt by those who recollect their mind, for the more you indulge your thoughts, the greater will be your hunger and desire for many things, as the wise man declares. The soul is dissolute and unrestrained when accustomed to let thoughts and mind wander wrongly where they will; when they return, weary and dying of hunger, they contain the seeds of new desires and evil longings.[17]

This could have come from the *Upanishads*.

Christian Yogis

Of those who have worked to reconcile yogic Hinduism and Christianity in practice, the best known is probably the Benedictine monk, Father Bede Griffiths. Introduced to material simplicity inadvertently, when his father was swindled by a business partner and left penniless, Griffiths was drawn to yoga and Indian spirituality as a young man. He went to India as a priest in 1955, with the hopes of living a Christian monastic life married to the Hindu idea of renunciation. His first attempt to build a community in Bangalore was short-lived, but he moved south to Kerala, where Christianity has existed since the visit there of St. Thomas, and lived in an ashram that blended Syrian Christianity and Hindu *sannyasa*. In 1968, by now wearing the ochre robe and known as Swami Dayananda, he finally settled at Sacchinanda, a Benedictine monastic community run on the lines of a Hindu ashram, near Tiruchirapalli in Tamil Nadu.

Under his guidance, the place became widely known as Shantivanam, 'the forest of peace'. This was the time of the momentous Second Vatican Council which encouraged a more tolerant attitude to other faiths, and following Rome's lead, the All India Seminar, an authoritative meeting of the Catholic churches in India, had praised the 'wealth of truth, goodness and beauty in India's religious traditions'. This ecumenical approach continues to be the guiding light of the ashram, whose website states that its aim is: 'to bring into our Christian life the riches of Indian spirituality, to share in that profound experience of God which originated in *Vedas*, was developed in the *Upanishads* and *Bhagavad Gita*, and has come down to us today through a continual succession of sages and holy men and women.'[18]

Shantivanam drew seekers from all over the world, and became an international centre for reconciliation between the two great faiths. Griffiths

wrote a dozen books on the Hindu-Christian dialogue and travelled extensively in the last year of his life, before dying in 1993.

The ashram that Griffiths made famous had been started in 1950 by two
French Catholics, the Benedictine monk Dom Henri le Saux and Abbe Jules
Monchanin. As is clear from their correspondence, both these men had come
to India seeing themselves as ambassadors for what was then called 'Fulfilment
Theology'. This was the idea, popularised by a Scottish educational missionary
called John Nicol Farquhar, that: 'Christ provides the fulfilment of each of the
highest aspirations and aims of Hinduism... In Him is focused every ray of
light that shines in Hinduism. He is the crown of the faith of India'.[19]

Farquhar, an Indologist who knew Bengali and Sanskrit and worked in the
Indian YMCA for twenty years, was convinced that Christ came to fulfil not
only 'the law and the prophets', as the Bible says, but all the world's great
religions as well. Little by little though, Le Saux began to move away from
this surreptitiously colonial theology. A key stage in this transition was his
time with the non-dualist Ramana Maharshi at Arunachala. He spent two
extended periods as a hermit in one of the mountain's many caves, which he
regarded as 'an initiation into Hindu monastic life'. Later, he took the name
Swami Abhishiktananda, and was to acknowledge another Indian holy man,
Sri Gnanananda, as his personal guru.[20] Drawn to an ever more reclusive life
of meditation, Abhishiktananda was happy to pass the running of the
Shantivanam ashram over to Bede Griffiths and in 1968 he headed to the
Himalayas, to experience more of what he would later describe to a disciple
as: 'that constant take-off into the Beyond, the golden Purusha full of glory'.[21]

Towards the end of his life Abhishiktananda increasingly lived the non-dual
realisation of Advaita Vedanta, a transformation that led him to a radical reap-
praisal of Christianity. Like Yogananda before him, he was destined to experience Christ as the living divine essence within, rather than the exemplary
figure of historical legend. Writing in his diary in 1966 he confides: 'Christ is
less real in his temporal history than in the essential mystery of my being'.[22]
Then, three years later, this realisation has developed significantly further:

> Jesus may be useful in awakening the soul—as is the guru—but is never essen-
> tial and, like the guru, he himself must in the end lose all his personal charac-
> teristics. No one really needs him... Whoever, in his personal experience...
> has discovered the Self, has no need of faith in Christ, of prayer, of the com-
> munion of the Church.[23]

This is radical indeed. Echoing the Upanishadic call for an unmediated
vision that transcends all the names and forms (*nama-rupa*) conjured up by the
mind, he is critical of the Church's limiting itself to history and doctrine:

'Christ's *namarupa* necessarily explodes, but the Church wants to keep us virtually at the level of the *namarupa*',[24] stating in a letter written not long before his death: 'The discovery of Christ's I AM is the ruin of any Christian theology, for all notions are burnt within the fire of experience'.[25]

Swami Abhishiktananda died in 1973. His summary of spiritual understanding, published posthumously as *The Further Shore*, has become a spiritual classic.

The Renewal of Christian Mind-Yoga

Spiritual relocation to India would never appeal to many, but the enthusiastic reception of Indian teachers in the 1960s was a wake-up call to the Christian establishment that many of its faithful followers had unfulfilled needs. Shocked by the droves of young people signing up to foreign teachings and techniques, some Christians were galvanised to try to revive their own, largely petrified, traditions of contemplation.

One of the principal attempts at this resuscitation was begun by an Irish priest called John Main, who had learned meditation from a Hindu monk while working as a lawyer in the Diplomatic Service in Malaysia. On his return to Britain, Main joined the Benedictine Order, and some fifteen years later discovered the writings of John Cassian. He was immediately struck by the similarities between his own Hindu-derived practice and Cassian's description of meditation as: 'the repetition of a formula which leads to the interior silence and the permanent presence of Christ in us'. Main went on to establish the worldwide Christian Meditation Movement, in which what yoga sees as the pure consciousness of *purusha* becomes the recognition of Christ within. The meeting of East and West in the technique of using a *mantra*—what Cassian's mentor Abott Isaac had called a 'formula'—is clear in his optimistically titled 'Everything you need to know about how to meditate in 128 words':

> Sit down. Sit still and upright. Close your eyes lightly. Sit relaxed but alert. Silently, interiorly begin to say a single word. We recommend the prayer-phrase *maranatha*. Recite it as four syllables of equal length. Listen to it as you say it, gently but continuously. Do not think or imagine anything—spiritual or otherwise. If thoughts or images come, these are distractions at the time of meditation, so keep returning to simply saying the word. Meditate each morning and evening for between twenty and thirty minutes.[26]

Since Main's death in 1982, his work has been carried on by Laurence Freeman, another Benedictine monk, and the World Community for Christian

Meditation, which seeks to restore the contemplative dimension as essential and central to all Christian spirituality.

Another influential group of open-minded Christian contemplatives is the Center for Action and Contemplation founded by Father Richard Rohr, a Franciscan friar and writer on the perennial wisdom within the great faiths. For many, the public face of the Center is Cynthia Bourgeault, who teaches what she calls 'nondual–Christianity'.[27] Among her many interests is the dialogue of science and spirituality, with particular reference to the vision of the twentieth-century paleontologist and mystic, Pierre Teilhard de Chardin.

The promotion of Christian non-dualism is a revolutionary oxymoron. Over the centuries, mystics from all three Semitic faiths have had to take great care not to overstep the bounds of a theologically acceptable distance from God. To do so could have dire consequences. One of the most luminous apostles of unicity, the fourteenth-century Dominican Meister Eckhart, died on his way to Rome to defend himself against charges of heresy, while poor Mansur al Hallaj, the tenth-century Persian Sufi sage who declared 'I am the Truth' (*ana 'l-haqq*), was rewarded with a prolonged and gruesome execution watched by thousands on the banks of the Tigris river.

From the non-dual perspective, conventional religion does not lead to enlightenment, but serves to console egoity. However benign such consolation may be, it is still what the *Upanishads* call *avidya*, literally: 'not-knowing', by which is meant metaphysical ignorance fuelled by the dualistic presumption of an independent ego-self, ranged against a world that appears separate to it. In the light of non-dualism, it is this very self-possession that blinds us to the true nature of reality. From the conventional viewpoint, not only the world, but the Divine, will always be 'other', whereas the Upanishadic realisation is that the ground of all being is our deepest Self.[28]

Body-Yoga for Christ?

Back down on the mat, some Christians have sought to accommodate body-yoga. In America, where over 20 million now do some sort of postural practice, there is a version called PraiseMoves, an exercise regime that combines Christian worship with yogic stretching exercises. Its founder, Laurette Willis, explains: 'The word yoga is a Sanskrit word that means "union with god" or "yoke". As a Christian, it's a different yoke—Jesus said: "My yoke is easy, my burden is light."'

As someone who is determined to draw people away from Indianised yoga, Willis has a clear idea of the opposition's terrain. Her mother was a yoga teacher, and she herself started postural practice when she was seven, often acting as a demonstration model for the class. She did yoga for twenty-two years, eventually becoming an instructor herself, before seeing the true light. Now she wants 'to win back yoga for God', though just how she rationalises yoga's indisputable connection with ancient India is unclear.

Willis criticises the tranquillity people say they get from normal yoga classes, which to her mind, is not the real peace that only her God can give, but more of what she dismisses as 'a numbness'. Her classes use yogic postures, but rename them, and add an accompanying verse from the Bible. So, the classic Cobra Pose (*bhujangasana*), becomes 'the Vine Posture' and is practised while reciting from John's Gospel: 'I am the vine and you are the branches. If you remain in me and I in you, you will bear much fruit; apart from me you can do nothing.' By the same token, the Bow Pose (*dhanurasana*), becomes 'Peter's Boat Posture', to be done together with St. Luke's words: 'Launch out into the deep and let down your nets for a catch', while the Balancing Stick Pose (*tuladandasana*), is transformed into 'the Angel Posture' and accompanied by the recitation from Psalm 91: 'For He shall give His angels charge over you to keep you in all your ways.'

Rebranding seems to be catching on. In Encinitas in California, children at nine primary schools take part in classes twice a week based on Ashtanga Yoga as part of a 'life skills curriculum' that includes discussions of ethics, nutrition, general wellness and character development. After some parents complained—the US constitution demands schools be secular—the Sanskrit names for the postures were replaced with some child-friendly English ones, such as 'Kangaroo', 'Surfer', and 'Washing machine'. Practitioners of the classic lotus pose might be surprised to learn that it is now to be called 'Crisscross apple sauce'. *Surya namaskar*, imaged by many to be a connection to the source of all light, life and intelligence on our planet, now becomes the stunningly prosaic 'Opening sequence'.

This semantic juggling enables the organisers to insist that they are teaching only a form of physical exercise. However, some unconvinced parents sought the backing the National Center for Law and Policy (NCLP), a group which advocates 'the protection and promotion of religious freedom and traditional marriage and parental rights' and is associated with neo-conservative politics and right-wing Christianity. The case went to law, and in September 2013, the San Diego County Superior Court ruled that although yoga's roots are indeed religious, this modified form of the practice, which has no desire to propagate a faith, does not violate the constitution, and so can be taught in schools. The NCLP appealed the decision but lost the case in 2015.[29]

Yoga and Islam

In the Muslim world, reactions to yoga are mixed. In Iran, where some physical activities, such as roller-blading and walking dogs in public, are already banned, classical yoga has exploded over the last ten years. Classes, magazines and TV shows flourish. Even some 'Yoga shmoga' inventions are doing well; over six months in 2010, 20,000 signed up for Laughter Yoga in Tehran. The government has not yet intervened, but the Iranian Yoga Federation says its teachers are always walking on eggshells, afraid that the tide may turn at any moment. So far, yoga has managed to survive in a country with Sharia law and an Islamist political system by divesting itself of anything that could be construed as blasphemous. The national accrediting body, the Iranian Yoga Federation, always emphasises that yoga has no religious connotations, but is secular relaxation with practical health benefits. Its teachers always refer to 'the sport of yoga', thereby putting *asanas* on a par with tennis or football. As in other sports, competitions are held, and judged by specially invited international yoga teachers. This clandestine policy seems to be working; there is even the odd *mullah* who teaches yoga, and the families of some senior clerics attend classes too.[30]

But the situation remains volatile. In the Spring of 2014, a conference organised in the holy city of Qom by the *basij*—the voluntary militia that enforces social propriety and political loyalty — debated 'The Satanic Plots' threatening to undermine the 'Values and Ideals of The Revolution and Religion'. Yoga figured prominently; delegates were warned against the 'irreversible damage' it can cause. The subtext was the danger of a subversive Westernisation, as these teachers of yoga were not even Iranian, but foreign, and, worst of all, American. Despite the *basij* misgivings, however, an Iranian yoga teacher recently told the BBC that her religious students sometimes report they pray with more concentration after practising yoga: 'They say when we go to Mecca, we feel we are able to make a deeper pilgrimage because of the yoga. Our minds and our bodies move closer to our faith.'

Other teachers point out that the ethical precepts of yoga expressed in the principles of *yama* and *niyama* share many essentials with the Five Pillars of Islam. Even the positions adopted in the *namaz* daily prayer routine could, at a yogic stretch, be considered a type of *asana*, while the Islamic joining of the middle finger and thumb together while praying appears similar to a yogic *mudra*. In Morocco and Saudi Arabia there is great interest in yoga, but in Egypt the Grand Mufti Ali Gomaa, in one of his first pronouncements after being elected to office in 2004, declared it to be a sinful practice. In

LOOKING AHEAD

November 2008, the Malaysian government issued a *fatwa* banning some features of yoga practice, including the chanting of *mantras*, though it was lifted soon afterwards. In the capital Kuala Lumpur, where there is most interest, postures are currently permitted, but chanting and meditation, perceived as Hindu yoga, are forbidden. And in the world's most populous Islamic nation, Indonesia, clerics also declared a *fatwa*, before drawing a similar distinction between body-yoga and mind-yoga, tolerating the former, but condemning the latter.

Yoga and Spirituality

Hindus and Buddhists are in favour of yoga, of course, and for the most part, see it as a spiritual discipline. In fact, as we saw in the last chapter, the Hindu American Foundation ran a campaign a few years ago called 'Take Back Yoga' based on the claim that the West has kidnapped and commercialised their spiritual heritage, reducing it to a crass profit-making exercise. In a debate with a New York yoga teacher called Tara Stiles, Sheetal Shah, a senior director of the organisation, was adamant:

> Christianizing, Judeo-fying or secularizing the Sanskrit terminology, or even cutting out the *Oms* and *Namastes* isn't enough of a twist to cleanse yoga of its guiding principles. Yes, the beauty of yoga is that it can be both flexible and fluid, but without its metaphysical, Hindu bones, yoga falls flat on its face.[31]

Shah also defers from the widely held opinion, first promoted by Swami Vivekananda over a hundred years ago, that deep yogic experience is the experiential heart of all religion. She thinks that someone raised in an 'exclusivist' tradition like Islam or Christianity who goes deeply into yoga, may well eventually experience some conflict with their religious beliefs.

Not all authorities of those exclusive religions would agree. One such is David Rosen, the forward-thinking former Chief Rabbi of Ireland, who says yoga offers 'much blessing and enlightenment' and could help 'recapture Jewish wisdom and practice which may have been lost'. Rosen clearly puts his yoga into action: he is also an outspoken advocate of vegetarianism and a campaigner for ecological awareness. Of the many Jewish teachers on the yoga scene, those who are observant may choose to avoid Sanskrit *mantras* or holding classes over the sabbath. Nonetheless, they still feel yoga can help participants to reach *kavanah*, the meditative mindset considered essential for authentic Jewish prayer and rituals, and the guiding light of genuine Kabbalistic teachings.

Even Communists are getting into yoga. China's rapidly ageing population is one of the most pressing issues facing the ruling party, but the rejuvenating effects of postural practice may help. The government is generally opposed to mysticism and is vicious in its persecution of members of quasi-religious groups such as Falun Gong, who face arrest, enforced ideological conversion, torture and even death. But the central bureaucracy does allow what it calls 'yoga with Chinese characteristics'. This excludes chanting and meditation, and is 'removed from religion, demystified and localized for China', says official policy. Rural villages are taking up the practice enthusiastically.[32]

SBNR Yoga

As we have seen throughout this book, modern yoga is the child of very mixed parentage. Its Indian mother was the wisdom of the *Vedas* and *Upanishads*, medieval magic, the Hindu Renaissance and Indian nationalism, while its Western father was a Christian morality grounded in physical fitness, and the doctrine of the perfectibility of humankind through the application of scientific methodology. As the hybrid grew up, its contemplative heart was removed, and today it is uncomfortably split down the middle along the body-mind divide. While some teachers do include a spiritual component in their body-yoga routines, and a few make spirituality the explicit context, it is also the case that perhaps the majority are ignorant of, or even hostile to, yoga's deeper dimensions.

However, sociologists now identify a large and growing sub-culture of the 'spiritual but not religious' (SBNRs), more concerned with self-development than dogma. Modern life is witnessing a steep rise in frenetic work patterns, taxing material aspirations, breakdown of relationships and communality, and a dogged insistence on individualism. Perhaps for the first time in human history, an individual's social status is judged not by their conspicuous and unproductive leisure, but by their busyness. The historical markers of aristocracy and serfdom have been reversed; these days having no free time signifies we are valued and esteemed and gains us respect. More bizarrely, dysfunction is also a cachet. Celebrities are much more bookable if they have a drama of addiction, divorce, depression and recovery to tell or sell. Perhaps fans feel they can identify with the messy humanness behind the glamorous exterior of wealth and fame; perhaps there is a touch of *schadenfreude* at work. Many recovery packages, following the Twelve-Steps pioneered by Alcoholics Anonymous, have a strong SBNR component, and yoga is often included.

In the context of establishing a positive reorientation, the yoga mat can become an easily transferrable sacred space, even in secular surroundings such as gymnasium, clinic or cluttered living room. As such, it functions not unlike the Muslim prayer mat or a severely minimalist temple, serving as a portable platform providing ascent to another level of being. In a remedial context, where yoga is seen as a process of purification and healing, the limits of the mat can provide a protected and personalised area for this process, even though it may be taking place in public.

The Question of Ishvara

For non-aligned teachers and practitioners, one aspect of the path outlined by Patanjali is often problematic. This is the fifth of the *niyamas* or 'Rules for Living': the concept of *Ishvara-pranidhana*, a compound phrase usually translated as 'Devotion to God'.[33] The question is: Which, or whose, God are we talking about here? Is it an irascible tribal headman, or a loving but chronically absent father, or even a mischievous trickster with an elephant head, pot belly and a love of milky sweets? There are many other options available too.

Derived from the verbal root √*ish*, which means 'to rule, to command, to possess power', the word *ishvara* is perhaps the most neutral word for god used in Indian texts, in that it is devoid of any form, personal characteristics or attendant mythology. *Ishvara* implies, above all, mastery. The other half of the compound, *pranidhana*, connotes devotion in the sense of 'application; endeavour; commitment to, or focusing the attention on, something', rather than the more usual emotional meaning of the word. In the *Yoga Sutra*, the method of relating to *ishvara* is the repetition of his *mahamantra* OM, which, incidentally, is the only practice specifically recommended in the entire text, apart from cultivating positive thoughts to combat negativity.[34] Because this repetition is mechanical, rather than emotive, its effect is not an increase in devotional feeling, but that: 'the mind will turn inward and the obstacles that stand in the way of progress will disappear',[35] with the result that: 'the state of *samadhi* is perfected'.[36] In other words, the surrender brought about by practice of *ishvara pranidhana* is not so much the cultivation of religious sentiment, but the progressive letting go of grosser levels of mental experience, and a corresponding absorption into the depths of *samadhi*, the causal levels of the mind. Given this, the phrase is perhaps better translated as 'surrender to the Lord'.

Prior to Patanjali, the term *ishvara* was not commonly used to refer to a deity, but to a human being of elevated status, such as a king, a lord, or spiritual master. Patanjali's principal commentator, Vyasa, cites the philosopher Kapila, founder of the Sankhya school, as an exemplary *ishvara*. This opens the possibility that the *Yoga Sutra* could be using the word to refer to a master yogi or a guru. This interpretation was followed by Max Mueller, the eminent nineteenth-century Indologist, and it fits nicely with the text when it explains that *ishvara* is: 'a special being untouched by affliction, free from both the cause and effects of action'.[37]

Another way to understand these verses is to see this ultimate yogi as an eternal Self beyond human agency, metaphorically: 'the teacher of even the most ancient tradition of teachers',[38] or perhaps symbolising the finest aspect of relative manifestation (*saguna brahman*), the 'absolute with qualities', as the springboard to the unqualified absolute (*nirguna brahman*). Although various theistic schools of yoga have taken *ishvara* to refer to their chosen deity, in general, yoga was historically a non-sectarian path. Thus the thirteenth-century tantric work *Dattatreyayogashastra*, probably the first text to teach a recognisably systematised *hatha yoga*, tells us: 'Whether a *brahmin*, an ascetic, a Buddhist, a Jain, a *Kapalika* ('Skull-bearer', i.e. tantric follower of Shiva) or a materialist, the wise man who is endowed with faith and constantly devoted to the practice of yoga will attain complete success.'

All in all, then, taking the history of usage into account, there is no need for a modern yoga practitioner to equate *ishvara pranidhana* with 'devotion to God', taking those words in a Christian context. Those who feel at home with Upanishadic terminology could take *ishvara* to signify the impersonal Self, whereas those who think more in terms of the human potential movement might find the more personalised concept of the 'higher Self' conducive. The ecologically concerned might prefer a more pagan idea, such as the almighty power of Mother Nature.

Whatever the focus of inward attention may be, we should not forget that it serves only as a means that has eventually to be left behind, as a boat is left behind when the farther shore is reached. Patanjali's 'perfection of *samadhi*' is *kaivalya*, which means 'aloneness'. In the end, as Swami Abhishiktananda eloquently reminds us, we are talking here about the formless abode of liberation, beyond all name and form.

Yoga in Context

In conclusion, it is worth remembering that traditional cultures are anchored within a religious framework, and that they feed on stability and continuity. The nurturing rhythms and rituals of everyday life, grounded in nature and passed on from generation to generation through people's lived experiences, the songs they sing and the stories that they tell each other, all share the tacit understanding that individualism must never be allowed to compromise the overall coherence of the group. This is a very different context from our prevalent culture of individualism. Today's seekers come and go as they wish, using the gaps in their busy lives to sample the smorgasbord of therapeutic possibilities available. Often, their search is not for higher knowledge or enlightenment, but for an end to whatever problems they are currently carrying around. Many are educated, middle-class and sceptical, and feel some sort of alienation from their own lives. It is this dissatisfaction, rather than any conscious hunger for spiritual truths, that motivates their seeking, though the former may well in time blossom into the latter.

In 1943, the influential American psychologist Abraham Maslow first articulated his hierarchy of human needs, with what he called Self-actualisation at its pinnacle. The idea took off in the 1960s, and, as we have seen in Chapter 10, was conflated with yogic models of the hierarchy of *chakras*. But before long, the lofty aim of self-actualisation dwindled into what occupied the next rung down of Maslow's system: esteem. Catering to this, a global industry sprang up with alacrity; dedicated to the optimisation of a successful 'self' as a highly desirable brand, it is flourishing today. What, if anything, all the effort spent to achieve such an esteemed self has to do with happiness is by no means clear. But for many bent on self-improvement, yoga is one of their prime resources. If ancient methods can bring succour to modern times that is a wonderful thing, but wisdom teachings may well yield their most succulent fruits only when they are planted deep in the soil of a culture that is generally stable and sane and encourages a life that is natural and well-balanced, not neurotic and dysfunctional. Sacred knowledge does not exist to patch up people's lives or remedy their aberrations, nor is it a cure for random human confusion, though happily it may help with all of these. As we have seen in the previous pages, to extract the living kernel of a teaching from its cultural husk is a delicate business. In its attempts to do so, the modern world might do well to heed well-tried pointers as to how spiritual expansion is best grounded in the precious human limitations of day-to-day living. Yoga itself is not a religion, but when practised in the right spirit, it may gradually align the practitioner with those eternal principles on which all true religion rests.

NOTES

INTRODUCTION

1. Figures taken from the 2016 Yoga in America survey, conducted by Ipsos Public Affairs on behalf of *Yoga Journal* and Yoga Alliance.
2. Adapted from Swami Vivekananda, *Raja Yoga*, Volume 1, Chapter 2.
3. The term was coined by Elizabeth de Michelis in her ground-breaking study *A History of Modern Yoga: Patanjali and Western Esotericism* (London: Continuum, 2004).
4. See especially the work of the English academic James Mallinson, e.g. his 'Haṭha Yoga' entry in Volume 3 of *The Brill Encyclopedia of Hinduism* (2011), pp. 770–81.
5. I discuss this topic in Chapter 10. A useful cross-cultural history is Geoffrey Samuel and Jay Johnston (eds), *Religion and the Subtle Body in Asia and the West*, Routledge Studies in Asian Religion and Philosophy, Vol. 8 (London: Routledge, 2013).
6. See Chapter 12 of Georg Feuerstein, *The Deeper Dimension of Yoga* (Boston, MA: Shambhala, 2003). For those interested in the specific histories of *hatha* and *raja yoga*, see the work of Jason Birch, who also contributes to http://theluminescent.blogspot.it/
7. An excellent overall survey of body-yoga is Swami Satyananda Saraswati's, *Asana, Pranayama, Mudra, Bandha* (Bihar: Bihar School of Yoga, 2008 reprint).
8. In his description, Patanjali is very close to many schools of both early Buddhism and its predecessor on the Indian spiritual scene, Jainism.
9. For a discussion of this transplanting as regards Ayurveda, see Frederick M. Smith and Dagmar Wujastyk, *Modern and Global Ayurveda: Pluralism and Paradigms* (New York: University of New York Press, 2008).
10. See James Mallinson and Mark Singleton, *Roots of Yoga* (London: Penguin, 2017) and Karl Baier, Philipp A. Maas, Karin Preisendanz (eds), *Yoga in Transformation: Historical and Contemporary Perspectives*, Vienna Forum for Theology and the Study of Religions 16 (2018).

1. WAY BACK WHEN…?

1. See on this Frances Yates, *The Art of Memory* (London: Routledge, 1966). For a highly readable account of a traditional balladeer in modern India, see Chapter 4 of William Dalrymple, *Nine Lives* (London: Bloomsbury, 2009).
2. The German philosopher Johann Gottfried Herder (1744–1803) was perhaps the first

to put forward the idea that India was the cradle of all civilisation in his influential book, *Ideas on the Philosophy of the History of Mankind*.

3. A popular attempt was R. Gordon Wasson, *Soma: Divine Mushroom of Immortality* (New York: Harcourt Brace Jovanovich, 1968). One of the best surveys of the subject is still *Vedic Mythology* by the German scholar Alfred Hillebrand, first published in 1927.

4. See for example *Rig Veda* 10.135.3; 10.85.8.

5. Cf. Medieval Christianity's description of contemplation as *ars moriendi*: 'the art of dying'.

6. A few scholar-practitioners combine learning with spiritual insight and poetic vision. One example is Georg Feuerstein, author of the magisterial *The Yoga Tradition; Its History, Literature, Philosophy and Practice* (Prescott, AZ: Hohm Press, 2001) and *The Psychology of Yoga* (New York: Shambhala, 2013). Another is Jeanine Miller, who was a student of the Dutch Indologist Jan Gonda and also a Theosophist. The translations of Vedic passages quoted below are hers, taken from *The Vedas* (London: Rider, 1974) and *The Vision of Cosmic Order in the Vedas* (London: Penguin, 1988). See also their collaborative work: *The Essence of Yoga: Essays on the Development of Yogic Philosophy from the Vedas to Modern Times* (Rochester, VT: Inner Traditions, 1998).

7. *Mahabharata*; *Shantiparva* 304.2.

8. See *Bhagavad Gita* 2.31–37.

9. *Yoga Sutra* 3.38.

10. This is his famous debate with Mandana Mishra. See Alistair Shearer, *In the Light of the Self* (Hove: White Crow, 2017).

11. *Yoga Sutra* 4.1.

12. There are many accounts of hippie travels in India, but for the story of their precursors, see Deborah Baker, *A Blue Hand: The Beats in India* (New York: Penguin, 2008). Also, see Chapter 5, note 1 of the present work.

13. *Rig Veda* 10.136.

14. While the *Rig Veda* mentions Vratyas eight or nine times (e.g. 3.26.6; 5.53.11; 5.75.9; 9.14.2) and describes five groups of the Vratyas collectively as the *pancha-vratya* (10.34.12), the *Atharva Veda* (fifteenth *kanda*) devotes an entire hymn titled *Vratya-suktha* to the 'mystical fellowship' of the brotherhood. The *Tandya* and *Jaiminiya Brahmanas* also talk about Vratyas and describe a sacrifice called *vratya-stoma*, which is for all intents and purposes a yogic purification ritual.

15. See *Rig Veda* 1.67.2; 3.26.8.

16. *Rig Veda* 6.9.6.

17. *Rig Veda* 5.40.6.

18. *Rig Veda* 1.164.21.

19. *Rig Veda* 10.47.7.

20. *Rig Veda* 1.16.7.

21. *Yajur Veda* 31.18.

22. *Atharva Veda* 10.

23. *Yajur Veda* 34.3 and 4.

24. For an interesting discussion of the various early uses of the word 'yoga', see David Gordon White, *Sinister Yogis* (Chicago: University of Chicago Press, 2009).

2. THE LEGACY OF THE FOREST SAGES

1. For a summary of the mechanism involved, see *Bhagavad Gita* 3.10–15.
2. *Chandogya Upanishad* 8.1.3.
3. *Maitri Upanishad* 6.25.
4. *Maitri Upanishad* 6.29.
5. *Maitri Upanishad* 6.10.
6. *Taittiriya Upanishad* 2.4.1.
7. E.g. *Taittiriya Upanishad* 2.7.1.
8. *Taittiriya Upanishad* 1.2.1. onwards.
9. *Shvetashvatara Upanishad* 4.6–7. This image is also found in *Mundaka Upanishad*, 3.1.1–2, and in a similar vein at *Katha Upanishad* 1.3.1.
10. *Katha Upanishad* 1.3.13.
11. *Katha Upanishad* 1.3.10. In a Christian context, this journey is known as 'the prayer of quiet' and it forms the heart of what was called 'ascetic theology'.
12. It is given particularly vivid treatment in the sixth book of the *Maitri Upanishad*.
13. *Bhagavad Gita* 5.4–5.
14. *Katha Upanishad* 2.3.10.
15. *Mundaka Upanishad* 1.2.7–9. Translation by Alistair Shearer.
16. Scholars are widely divided on the dating of these heterogenous texts, a situation complicated by the fact that many may have been reworked or added to over time.
17. An example in modern times would be Sri Ramana Maharshi, who, at the age of sixteen, following a spontaneous experience of awakening, travelled to the sacred hill of Arunachala and never left. He died there some fifty-six years later, while his international visitors ranged from Paul Brunton to Cartier Bresson and Somerset Maugham.
18. Compare the tale of Alexander the Great's visit to the philosopher Diogenes, founder of the Cynic philosophy, who was so ascetic he lived happily in a barrel. Diogenes was sunbathing when the all-powerful conqueror arrived. Alexander asked if there was anything he could do for him. 'Yes', the sage replied 'Please could you step aside, you are blocking out the sun.' Alexander was so impressed he declared: 'Ah! If I were not Alexander, then I should wish to be Diogenes!' 'And if I were not Diogenes, I would still wish to be Diogenes', came the reply.

3. THE GREAT PATANJALI PARADOX

1. Such faux-translations are common in New Age spirituality. The most successful are Coleman Barks' renderings of the Persian poetry of the Sufi master Jalaluddin Rumi, which have sold in the millions over the last few years even though Barks neither reads nor speaks Persian. Daniel Ladinsky has published several volumes of poetry that claim to be renderings of another Sufi poet, Hafiz, but they are so wide of the originals that

scholars of Persian can't relate the two versions at all. The most versatile of such interpreters must be Stephen Mitchell. Among what he calls his 'translations and adaptations' are the Chinese *Tao Te Ching*, Sumerian *Gilgamesh*, ancient Greek *Iliad* and *Odyssey*, Aramaic *Gospel According to Jesus* and Sanskrit *Bhagavad Gita*.

2. Swami Vivekananda, *Raja Yoga* (1896).

3. Cover notes to Barbara Stoler Miller, *Yoga: The Discipline of Freedom* (London: Random House, 2009).

4. In the Foreword to B. K. S. Iyengar, *Light on the Yoga Sutras of Patanjali* (London: Thorsons, 1993).

5. David Gordon White, *The Yoga Sutra of Patanjali* (Princeton: Princeton University Press, 2008).

6. *Yoga Sutra* 2.46–48.

7. *Yoga Sutra* 1.2.

8. *Yoga Sutra Bhashya* 1.1.2.

9. The word *vibhuti* also occurs in the *Bhagavad Gita*, where it refers to the divine play (*lila*) of Lord Krishna as he effortlessly manifests, and orchestrates, the world.

10. *Yoga Sutra* 3.38.

11. *Yoga Sutra* 3.43.

12. *Yoga Sutra* 3.37.

13. *Yoga Sutra* 3.51.

14. *Arthashastra* 14.2.42. Patrick Olivelle translation (Oxford: Oxford University Press, 2013).

15. For example, the Charvakas and the followers of the naturalistic system of Vaisheshika. It is often forgotten that no other ancient language can match Sanskrit for its number of atheistic and religiously sceptical writings.

16. These *siddhis* are the abilities to: shrink oneself to the size of an atom (*animan*); expand to a vast size (*mahiman*); levitate (*laghiman*); cover great distances in an instant (*prapti*); enjoy an irresistible will (*prakamya*); control the material elements (*vashitva*); control the subtle levels of life (*ishitritva*); and lastly, fulfil all legitimate desires (*kamavasayitva*).

17. *Yoga Sutra* 3.49–50.

18. *Yoga Sutra* 2.38–3.3.

19. *Yoga Sutra* 3.7.

20. *Yoga Sutra Bhashya* 2.46. Some authorities dispute the attribution of this commentary but see Trevor Leggatt, *Shankara on the Yoga Sutras* (London: Routledge, 1990).

21. The *asanas* Shankara does mention are: the Lotus, Tortoise, Auspicious, Hero, Svastika, Staff, Support, Throne, Curlew, Elephant, Camel, Confirmed and Favourite.

22. In his *Direct Experience of Reality* (verses 116 and 117) Shankara parodies the *Gita's* recommendation (6.13) that the meditator should direct attention to the tip of the nose. The master Advaitin retorts that if the aspirant does this, the nose is all he will be left with! See also his *Brihadaranyaka Upanishad* 2.4.5, and 4.5.6, and commentaries thereon.

23. See Shankara's *Direct Experience of Reality* 102–126 and 143.

24. This error is technically known as the *dehatmavada*. See for example, Shankara's commentary on *Chandogya Upanishad* 8.1.5; his original composition *The Thousand Teachings* 1.64–5 and 10.1–14 and his commentary on the *Brahma Sutra* 3.3.54.

25. *Yoga Sutra* 1.4.

26. *Ibid.* 4.34.

4. *GITA* YOGA

1. Vinobha Bhave, *Talks on the Gita* (Pavnar, Wardha: Paramdham Prakashan (Gram-seva Mandal), 1940).

2. For examples, see especially the final portion of the twelfth book, known as the *Mokshadharma*, 'The Duty of Liberation'.

3. *Gita* 2.50.

4. *Gita* 6.11–15.

5. *Gita* 17.5.

6. The *gunas* (literally 'strands of rope') are: *sattva* (light; purity), *rajas* (motion; activity) and *tamas* (mass; dullness). All levels of material creation (*prakriti*), whether gross, subtle or causal, are due to varied combinations of these qualities.

7. *Gita* 2.46.

8. *Mundaka Upanishad*, trans. Alistair Shearer, 1.2.12. Compare the Buddha's words in the *Dhammapada* 410: 'He who has no craving desires, either for this world or for another world, who free from desires is in infinite freedom—him I call a *brahmin*.'

9. *Gita* 2.45–46.

10. *Gita* 2.48.

11. For a cross-cultural comparison, consider the words used by the great fourteenth-century Dominican seer, Meister Eckhart, to describe this perfect balance between substance and essence: 'You may ask "What is this disinterest, that it is so noble a matter?" Know then that a mind unmoved by any contingent affection or sorrow, or honour, or slander, or vice, is really disinterested—like a broad mountain that is not shaken by a gentle wind. Unmovable disinterest brings a man into his closest resemblance to God.' From Eckhart's 'About Disinterest', in *Meister Eckhart*, trans. Raymond B. Blakney (New York: Harper & Row, 1941).

12. See *Yoga Sutra* 4.34: 'The *gunas*, their purpose fulfilled, return to their original state of harmony and pure unbounded consciousness remains, forever established in its own absolute nature. This is enlightenment'. This radical separation is called *nirvana* in the yoga systems of both Jainism and early Buddhism. Compare the first-century Jain text *Samayasara* ('The Nature of the Self') by Acharya Kundakunda: 'Spirit and non-spirit together constitute the universe. All that is necessary is to discriminate between them.'

13. *Gita* 4.18–22.

14. *Gita* 5.8–9.

15. The image first occurs in *Rig Veda* (1.164.20–22) as: 'Two birds associated together,

and mutual friends, take refuge in the same tree; one of them eats the sweet fig; the other abstaining from food, merely looks on.'

16. *Enneads* 1.3.
17. 'On solitude and the attainment of God' in 'The Talks of Instruction', in *Meister Eckhart*, trans. Raymond B. Blakney (New York: Harper & Row, 1941).
18. See *Gita* 7.24–27.
19. *Gita* 6.29–30.
20. From the introduction to Swami Prabhavananda and Christopher Isherwood's translation of the *Bhagavad Gita* (1956). Huxley played an important editorial role in this influential translation.

5. WILD MEN, DUBIOUS REPUTATIONS

1. For more details see the TV travel documentary *West Meets East* (BBC 4, 2015) which also features Mallinson's pal and fellow old-Etonian, the actor Dominic West.
2. I use the word in its original, rather than its post-Saidian, perjorative sense.
3. The Hatha Yoga Project is a five-year research project funded by the European Research Council. It aims to chart the history of physical yoga practice by means of philological study of texts and ethnographical fieldwork among practitioners. The project team consists of four researchers based at SOAS, one at the École Française d'Extrême Orient, Pondicherry, and one at the Maharaja Man Singh Pustak Prakash, Jodhpur. The project's primary outputs will be critical editions and annotated translations of ten Sanskrit texts on *hatha yoga*, four monographs, and a range of journal articles, book chapters and encyclopedia entries. In September 2016 a workshop for scholars working on critical editions of Sanskrit texts on yoga was held at SOAS, and a second, on yogis, in September 2017. The third, on yoga, was held in September 2019. A free online conference featuring a dozen scholars working in the field was held in February 2018.
4. See the assorted publications of Jason Birch, James Mallinson and Mark Singleton (among others) accessible from hyp.soas.ac.uk/publications. Other technical articles by Mallinson available online include, 'A Response to Mark Singleton's Yoga Body' (2011); '*Shaktism* and *Hathayoga*' (2012); 'Yoga and Religion' (2013); '*Dattatreya's* Discourse on Yoga' (2013) and '*Hathayoga's* philosophies'. A less academic introduction may be found in Mallinson's article 'Yoga & Yogis', *Namarupa* 15: 3 (March 2012).
5. *Chandogya Upanishad* 6.
6. *Mundaka Upanishad* 1.6.
7. This Shrivaishnavism tradition was also the lineage to which T. M. Krishnamacharya, the father of modern body-yoga, owed allegiance (see Chapter 13).
8. See, for example, *Chandogya Upanishad* 6.9.1–6.
9. See, for example, the *Maha Upanishad*: 'One is a relative, the other stranger, say the small-minded. To the big hearted, the entire world is a family. So be detached, be magnanimous, elevate your mind and enjoy the fruit of freedom in *brahman*'. (6.71–75).

10. The means taken can be extreme. To guarantee their vow of celibacy, some *sadhus* will pierce their genitals with swords or lead bars attached to large rings or bind them in iron chains sealed with a padlock.

11. For more details see James Mallinson, 'Yoga and Sex: What Is the Purpose of Vajroli?' in *Yoga* in Karl Baier, Philipp A. Maas and Karin Preisendanz (eds), *Transformation: Historical and Contemporary Perspectives* (2018).

12. *Brihadaranyaka Upanishad* 6.4.10–11.

13. See Michael Witzel, 'Female Rishis and Philosophers in the Veda?', *Journal of South Asia Women Studies*, 11:1 (2009): http://asiatica.org/jsaws/11–1/female-rishis-and-philosophers-veda/

14. On Indian attitudes to semen, see, for example, Morris Carstairs, *The Twice Born: A Study of a High Caste Hindu Community* (Bloomington, IN: Indiana University Press, 1957). An anthropologist who served as President of the World Federation for Mental Health from 1968 to 1972, Carstairs identifies the loss of semen as a major and continuing source of anxiety among Indian men into relatively recent times. The British Raj was imbued with the idea, common in Western medicine during the nineteenth century, that spermatorrhea was a medical disorder with corrupting and devastating effects on the mind and body. For a cross-cultural perspective see Elizabeth Abbott, *The History of Celibacy* (Boston, MA: Da Capo, 1999) and Carl Olson (ed.), *Celibacy and Religious Traditions* (Oxford: Oxford University Press, 2007).

15. 'The Five M's' (*panchamakara*) enjoyed by the taboo-breaking followers of 'left-hand Tantra', which are: *maithuna* (sexual intercourse); *madya* (wine), *mamsa* (meat), *mudra* (parched grain) and *matsya* (fish).

16. *Hatha Yoga Pradipika* 1.33.

17. *Shiva Samhita* 1.1.

18. *Shiva Samhita* 3.84.

19. *HYP* 1.61.

20. *HYP* 3.84.

21. Hans-Ulrich Reiker, *The Yoga of Light, The Hatha Yoga Pradipika* (New York: Herder & Herder, 1971). Swami Vishnudevananda, founder of the International Sivananda Yoga Vedanta Centres also omitted *vajroli* from his 1979 translation.

22. James Mallinson, *Khecarividya of Adinatha* (London: Routledge, 2007).

23. See Carl Olson, *Indian Asceticism: Power, Violence and Play* (Oxford: Oxford University Press, 2015).

24. Abu Zayd al Sirafi, *Two Arabic Travel Books, Accounts of China and India, and Mission to the Volga* (New York: New York University Press, 2014), p. 57.

25. Francois Bernier, *Travels in the Mogul Empire*, trans. I. Brock and A. Constable (Delhi: Asia Educational Services, 2004, reprint), p. 321.

26. *The Travels of Ludovico di Varthema in Egypt, Syria, Arabia Deserta and Arabia Felix, in Persia, India and Ethiopia, AD 1503 to 1508*, trans. George Percy Badger (London: Hakluyt Society, 1863), p. 112.

27. Jean Baptiste Tavernier, *Travels in India (1676)*, Vol. 1, trans. Valentine Ball, William Crooke (ed.) (New Delhi: Asian Educational Services, 2nd edn), p. 67.

28. For more detail on the role *sadhus* played as mercenaries, see William Pinch's *Warrior Ascetics and Indian Empires* (Cambridge: Cambridge University Press, 2012).

29. *Weber: Selections in Translation*, trans. Eric Matthews (Cambridge: Cambridge University Press, 1978), p. 220.

30. *The Kautilyan Arthashastra*, R.P. Kangle (ed. and trans.) (New Delhi: Motilal Banarsidass Publishers, 1986 reprint), p. 307.

31. *Ibid.*, p. 39.

32. In his novel *Kim* (1901), Rudyard Kipling features a spymaster working for the British Secret Services in the Great Game, the battle to defeat Russian influence in South Asia. His name is Lurgan Sahib (code-named E23), and he disguises himself as a yogi in order to move more freely around the country. The character was based upon a rackety jewel merchant and accomplished magician named Alexander Jacob.

33. James Tod, *Annals and Antiquities of Rajasthan; Travels in Western India* (London: Smith, Elder & Co., 1829), p. 612.

34. Their yogic agility was illustrated in the now dilapidated murals of the Nath Mahamandir temple on the outskirts of Jodhpur. Little visited, it remains an atmospheric place. For a contemporary rendering of these murals, see the work of the British artist Katherine Vergilis.

35. For an interesting, if rather overstated, survey of the transgressive side of yoga, see David Gordon White, *Sinister Yogis*.

36. Chandra Vasu, *An Introduction to the Yoga Philosophy* (Allahabad: Panini Office, 1915), p. 2.

6. THE CRESCENT AND THE LOTUS

1. *Qutab Minar & Adjoining Monuments*, Archaeological Survey of India (2002), p. 30. See also Anthony Welch and Howard Crane, 'The Tughluqs: Master Builders of the Delhi Sultanate', *Muqarnas*, 1 (1983), pp. 123–166.

2. See Richard M. Eaton, 'Temple desecration and Indo-Muslim states', *Journal of Islamic Studies* (2000). Shah Jahan's violence was also directed closer to home. To clear his way to becoming 'King of the World', the would-be emperor had to rebel against his father, murder his two elder brothers and their sons, and then, for good measure, two cousins.

3. Abdul Malik Isami, *Shah Nama-i-Hind*, 3 volumes, trans. A. M. Hussian (Asia Publishing House, 1967–77) quoted in William Dalrymple, *City of Djinns* (Penguin USA, 2000), p. 284.

4. Adul Fazl-i-Allami, *Ain-i-Akbari*, Vol. 3, trans. H. S. Jarrett (Royal Asiatic Society of Bengal, 1948), p. 196.

5. *Ibid.*, p. 195.

6. In the view of some orthodox Muslims, divine punishment not infrequently takes the form of being transformed into a lower species than human. See, for example, the works of the influential tenth-century Persian scholar Al Tabari. In the Shi'ite tradition, the murderer of the Prophet's greatly admired grandson Hussein bin 'Ali was punished by being turned into a four-eyed dog.

7. Scholarly work has recently been done on the relationship between Islam, Sufism and Yoga. See, for example, Carl W. Ernst, 'Sufism and Yoga According to Muhammad Ghawth', *Sufi*, 29 (1996), pp. 9–29 and his 'The Psychophysiology of Ecstasy in Sufism and Yoga', *North Carolina Medical Journal*, 59:3 (1998); also Philipp A. Maas and Noémie Verdon, 'On al-Biruni's *Kitab Patangal* and the *Patanjalayogashastra*' in Baier, Maas and Priesendanz (eds), *Yoga in Transformation* (2018). See also: David Gordon White (ed.), *Yoga in Practice* (Princeton: Princeton University Press, 2011).

8. See Ajit Mookerjee, *Yoga Art* (New York: New York Graphic Society, 1975); Mookerjee and Madhu Khanna, *The Tantric Way: Art, Science and Ritual* (New York: New York Graphic Society, 1977) and Philip Rawson, *The Art of Tantra* (London: Thames & Hudson, 1978).

9. As addressed in a *New York Times* article: https://www.nytimes.com/roomforde-bate/2012/01/12/is-yoga-for-narcissists

10. See the beautifully produced catalogue *Yoga: The Art of Transformation* by Debra Diamond, David Gordon White, Tamara Sears, Carl Ernst and Sir James Mallinson (Washington D.C.: Freer Gallery of Art, 2013).

7. AN IMPERIAL YOKE

1. The Dutch East India Company became an exemplar of corporate organisation. By the time it was wound up in 1796, its shareholders in Amsterdam had enjoyed an average annual return of 18 per cent (sometimes rising to 40 per cent) over a period of 200 years.

2. Not to be confused with the Indophile Warren Hastings. As the most popular of all British Governor Generals among his Indian subjects, his seven-year impeachment trial became the first of many public clashes between two opposed visions of empire: one respectful of Indian traditions, the other inspired by self-righteous Eurocentric intervention.

3. Thomas Babington Macaulay, *Education Minute addressed to the Governor General's Council in Calcutta* (2 February 1835). For more, see Zareer Masani, *Macaulay: Britain's Liberal Imperialist* (2013).

4. *The Lady's Newspaper and Pictorial Times*, 21 November 1857.

5. Macaulay's letter to his father, quoted in D. D. Basu, *The Rise of Christian power in India* (Calcutta, 1931), p. 803.

6. See, *The Collected Works of John Stuart Mill, Volume XXX—Writings on India* [1828].

7. In *The New York Herald Tribune* of June 10, 1853, Marx characterised Indian village life as 'undignified, stagnatory and vegetative' and the passive enabler of 'Oriental despotism'.

8. See, for example, *The Serpent Power* (1919); *The Garland of Letters* (1922) and *The World as Power* (1922).

9. See Paul's *Letter to the Corinthians* 9.24–27.

10. 'Great Cities and their Influence for Good and Evil', Lecture delivered in Bristol, 5 October 1857, in *The Works*, Vol. 18 *Sanitary and Social Lectures and Essays* (Hildesheim: Olms, 1969), pp. 199–200.

11. Charles Kingsley, 'Nausicaa in London: or, The Lower Education of Women', *Health and Education* (London: Macmillan and Co., 1887), p. 86.

12. Henry Reeve, 'Popular Education in England', *Edinburgh Review* (July 1861).

13. So, too, did a Frenchman, le Baron de Coubertin. His visit to Rugby School to see the effect of team games inspired him to re-invent the ancient Greek custom of the Olympic Games as an international event for modern times. Acutely aware of the defeat that his country had recently suffered at the hands of the Germans in the Franco-Prussian War, which he attributed to the victors' superior physical fitness, de Coubertin saw the games as a way for France to rebuild both her muscles and her national pride. His idea harked back to the classical idea of sport as a good preparation for war, a culture best exemplified by the city-state of Sparta.

14. Thalassery (now known by its Malayalam name Tellicheri) was the site of India's first cricket club. A decent pitch was laid in the 1890s by a local tea-planter called Cowdrey, a cricket fanatic who named his son in honour of the iconic Marylebone Cricket Club, by giving him the initials M. C. C. Like governor George Harris before him, Michael 'Colin' Cowdrey went on to play for Kent and England, becoming one of the greatest all-round players ever to wear the England colours.

15. Our words 'gymnastics', 'gymnasium', etc. come from the Greek *gymnazo*, meaning to 'train naked'. The Olympic Games were originally contested unclothed.

16. To some it still is. Pope Francis described the Vatican cricket team's 2015 tour of the UK as part of 'the Divine Plan' to unite the various Christian denominations in the Global Freedom Network, a multi-faith initiative to eradicate slavery and people trafficking. Nor has the connection between public school and sporting prowess disappeared. In the 2014 Olympic Games, over half the medals won by Great Britain went to those athletes who had been to a public school, though well under 10 per cent of children in the UK attend one.

17. J. G. Cotton Minchin, *Our Public Schools: Their Influence on English History; Charter House, Eton, Harrow, Merchant Taylors', Rugby, St. Paul's Westminster, Winchester* (London: Swan Sonnenschein & Co., 1901), p. 113.

8. WE WANT TO BE FREE!

1. Swami Dayanand Saraswati, *Satyarth Prakhash* ['The Light of Truth'] (1875).

2. This project was to continue in a more general way after independence. From the 1940s onwards, the Indian government funded documentaries made by the Department of Information and Broadcasting to educate Indians in the value of their own cultural traditions.

9. MARTIAL YOGA

1. *Bhagavad Gita* 2.21.

2. The expert on Indian body-culture is the anthropologist Joseph S. Alter. See: *The Wrestler's Body: Identity and Ideology in North India* (Berkeley, CA: University of California Press, 1992) and 'The Sannyasi and the Indian Wrestler: The Anatomy of a Relationship',

American Ethnologist 19:2 (1992). With regards to the relationship of martial arts to the development of *asanas*, the Los Angles based yoga teacher Rob Zabel, a graduate of the Loyola University yoga studies programme, has a useful article: 'Martial Medical Mystical: The Triple Braid of a Traditional Yoga' in Karl Baier, Philipp Andre Maas, and Karin Preisendanz (eds), *Yoga in Transformation* (Vienna: Vienna University Press, 2018), to which I am indebted for much of what follows.

3. Cf. *Katha Upanishad* 1.3.3–6.

4. *Brihat Sharngadhara Paddhati* 1.5, an eclectic text that also contains an analysis of yoga.

5. See *Shrimad Bhagavatam*, Book 11.

6. Quoted in Edwin F. Bryant, *The Yoga Sutras of Patanjali* (New York: North Point Press, 2009).

7. See D. C. Majumdar (ed.), *Encyclopedia of Indian Physical Culture* (Baroda: Good Companions, 1950).

8. For contemporary wrestling *akharas*, see Cynthia Hulmes and Bradley R. Hertel (eds), *Living Banaras: Religion in Cultural Context* (New Delhi: Manohar, 1998). For a scholarly study on the role of celibacy in Indian martial arts see Joseph S. Alter, *Moral Materialism: Sex and Masculinity in Modern India* (New Delhi: Penguin, 2012).

9. See Zabel, 'Martial Medical Mystical'. There continues to be dispute over the genesis and age of what has become the signature sequence of modern postural practice.

10. Taken from the Foreword to D. C. Mazumdar, *Encyclopedia of Indian Physical Culture* (Baroda: Good Companions, 1950).

11. Attributed to Tilak by Patodi as quoted in Joseph S. Alter, *The Wrestler's Body: Identity and Ideology in North India* (Berkeley: University of California Press, 1992), p. 17.

12. See Alter, *The Wrestler's Body*.

13. Gauripada Chatterjee, *Midnapore, the Forerunner of India's Freedom Struggle* (Delhi: Mittal Publications, 1986).

14. Quoted in Joseph Alter, *Gandhi's Body: Sex, Diet and the Politics of Nationalism* (Oxford: Oxford University Press, 2001), p. 131.

15. Compare the traditional Hippocratic oath, still taken by many aspiring doctors today, who swear 'by Apollo the Healer, by Asclepius, by Hygieia, by Panacea, and all the gods and goddesses to hold my teacher in this art equal to my own parents' and 'to impart precept, oral instruction, and all other instruction to my own sons, the sons of my teacher, and to indentured pupils who have taken the physician's oath'.

16. *The Times*, 27 July 1813.

17. For a delightful account of the British fascination with entertainers from India, see John Zubrzycki, *Empire of Enchantment; The Story of Indian Magic* (London: Hurst, 2018).

10. YOGA THEOSOPHICA

1. Opening words of *The Paradoxes of the Highest Science* by Eliphas Levi, to which Blavatsky was herself a contributor, published by the Theosophical Society in 1883.

2. These included Srisa Chandra Vasu, *Shiva Samhita* (1884); M. N. Dvivedi, *Yoga Sutra* (1890); V. L. Mitra, *The Yoga Vasishta* (1891); Srinivasa Iyangar, *Hatha Yoga Pradipika* (1893) and Srisa Chandra Vasu, *Gheranda Samhita* (1895). The tradition of theosophical yoga scholarship continued through up to the 1960s, with the publication of I. K. Taimini, *The Science of Yoga: The Yoga Sutra of Patanjali* (Chennai: Quest Books, 1961).

3. W. Q. Judge, 'Theosophy in the Press', *Path* (1886).

4. H. P. Blavatsky, *Collected Writings* [Vol. 6, 1881–2] (Wheaton, Ill: Theosophical Publishing House, 1982), p. 160.

5. *Ibid.*, p. 104.

6. Annie Besant, *An Introduction to Yoga* (1907).

7. See: Karl Baier, 'Yoga within Viennese Occultism: Carl Kellner and Co.', in Baier, Maas and Preisendanz (eds) *Yoga in Transformation*. I am much indebted to this article for what follows on the Viennese scene.

8. Sigmund Freud, *Civilisation and its Discontents* (New York: W. W. Norton & Company, 1962 [first edn. 1930]), p. 19.

9. Franz Hartmann, 'Die Bhagavad-Gita der Indier', *Wiener Rundschau*', 15 (15 June 1899), pp. 250–259.

10. Franz Hartmann, 'The Dangers of Experimenting in Occultism', *The Occult Review*, vol. 3 (1906)', pp. 133–35.

11. Carl Kellner, *Yoga: An Introduction to the Psycho-Physiological Aspect of the Ancient Indian Yogic Teaching* (1896).

12. Gustav Meyrink, 'The Transformation of the Blood' in Mike Mitchell (ed.), *The Dedalus Meyrink Reader* (Sawtry: Dedalus, 2010), pp. 120–185.

13. *Ibid.* and Carl Kellner, *Eine Skizze uber den psycho-physiologishcen Teil der alten indischen Yogalehre*, Dem 111, Internationalen Congress fur Psychologie gewidmet. (Munich, Kassner & Lossen, 1896), p.12–13.

14. For a modern, and rational, account of such wanderings, see Robert Monroe, *Journeys out of the Body* (London: Profile Books, 1989).

15. Letter dated 6 May 1934, V. L. Dutko (ed.), *Letters of Helena Roerich*, Vol. 1: 1929–1938 (New York: Agni Yoga Society, 1954), p. 203.

16. Letter dated 8 September 1934, *ibid.*, p. 297.

17. Letter dated 6 May 1934, *ibid.*, p. 203.

18. *Ibid.*

19. *Brihadaranyaka* 4.2.3; *Chandogya* 8.6.1–6.

20. See for example, *Vivekachudamani* 159–213.

21. For an interesting discussion, see the essay 'Are the *chakras* real?' by Ken Wilber in J. White (ed.), *Kundalini, Evolution and Enlightenment* (New York: Doubleday/Anchor, 1979).

22. See *Yoga Sutra* 3.20–43.

23. For the often underestimated importance that psychic openness plays in Indian culture, see Frederick Smith, *The Self Possessed* (New York: Columbia University Press,

2006). Such porosity need not involve otherworldly spirits, of course; we can observe it readily everywhere today in the pathology of ideological possession.

24. H. P. Blavatsky, *Collected Writings* [Vol. 4: 1882–1883], p. 615.
25. See *Yoga Sutra* 3.49–51.
26. Arthur Avalon (Sir John Woodroffe), *The Serpent Power, being the Shat-chakra-nirupana and Paduka-Panchaka* (Madras: Ganesh and Co., 1964), p. 22.
27. See Henry Olcott, *Applied Theosophy and Other Essays* (Chennai: Theosophical Publishing House, 1975).
28. Vasant G. Rele, *The Mysterious Kundalini* (Pomeroy, WA: Health Research Reprint, 1985), p. 86.
29. H. P. Blavatsky, *Collected Writings* [Vol. 4: 1882–1883], p. 619.
30. The full story is very well told in Kurt Leland, *The Rainbow Body: A History of the Western Chakra System from Blavatsky to Brennan* (Newburyport: Nicolas-Hays inc., 2016) to which I am indebted for much of what follows.

11. THE SWAMI'S MISSION

1. From a letter written to Swami Ramakrishnananda on 19 March 1892.
2. Quoted from Gopal Stavig, *Western Admirers of Ramakrishna and his Disciples* (Kolkata: Advaita Ashrama, 2010).
3. *Baltimore News*, 13 October 1894.
4. Quoted in John James Clarke, *Oriental Enlightenment* (London: Routledge, 1997).
5. On the relevance of Vivekananda's message to a post-religious and increasingly individualistic world-view see Elizabeth de Michelis, *A History of Modern Yoga: Patanjali and Western Esotericism* (London: Continuum, 2004).
6. Henry David Thoreau, *A Week on the Concord and Merrimack Rivers* (Boston, MA: James Munroe & Co., 1849), p. 74.
7. Henry David Thoreau, *Walden* (Boston, MA: Ticknor and Fields, 1854), Chapter 2.
8. Whitman developed a personal form of restorative and centring meditation using his own name as a *mantra*, as did his fellow poet and almost exact contemporary, Alfred Lord Tennyson, who enjoyed experiences of meditative transcendence throughout his life. Queen Victoria's Poet Laureate might have been surprised to learn that his sovereign was clandestinely entertaining a yogi from Kerala, one Shivapuri Baba, who claimed to be two hundred years old and gave her Imperial Majesty eighteen lessons on esoteric spirituality. See, *The Long Pilgrimage* by J. G. Bennett (London: Hodder and Stoughton, 1965).
9. Compare on this subject the writings of the Jesuit priest and scientist, Pierre Teilhard de Chardin.
10. 'The path is narrow, the sages warn, sharp as a razor's edge, most difficult to tread.' *Katha Upanishad* 1.3.14.
11. *Bhagavad Gita, The Song of God* (1944); *Shankara's Crest-Jewel of Discrimination* (1947) and *How to Know God: The Yoga Aphorisms of Patanjali* (1953).
12. *Ramakrishna and His Disciples* (1965).

13. See for example: *Vedanta for Modern Man* (1945); *What Vedanta Means to Me* (1951); *An Approach to Vedanta* (1964); *Essentials of Vedanta* (1966) and *My Guru and His Disciple* (1980), as well as the many articles that appeared in the magazine *Vedanta and the West*.

14. Christopher Isherwood, Introduction to *What Religion Is in the words of Swami Vivekananda* (Belur: Advaita Ashram, 1972), p. 4.

15. In this too he was a trailblazer; B. K. S. Iyengar, K. Pattabhi Jois and Bikram Choudhury would all follow him in taking up yoga to overcome their childhood illnesses.

16. Swami Vivekananda, *The Complete Works of Swami Vivekananda*, 8.160 (Belur: Advaita Ashram, 1947).

17. Swami Vivekananda, 'The Work Before Us' in *Lectures from Colombo to Almora* (Madras: Vyjayanti Press, 1897).

18. *Bhagavad Gita*, 2.3.

19. Swami Vivekananda, *Complete Works*, 8.213.

20. From Chapter 8 of Sister Nivedita, *Notes of Some Wanderings with Swami Vivekananda* (Calcutta: Udbodhan Office, 1913).

21. Swami Vivekananda, Journal Notes for July 1898, from Sister Nivedita, *Swamiji and his Message* (Advaita Ashrama, Mayavati, 1980), p. 21.

22. Given his importance in America, it was perhaps fitting that Vivekananda left the body on 4 July, Independence Day. He had correctly predicted the date of his death to the French opera star Emma Calve, whilst in Egypt.

12. ROGUE YOGIS SET THE TREND

1. *Bharat* is the original name for the country we call India.

2. *New York American*, 3 May 1910.

3. *New York World*, 5 May 1910.

4. *Los Angeles Herald*, 8 May 1910.

5. *Los Angeles Times*, 22 October 1911.

6. Blanche de Vries can justly claim to be the first female yoga teacher of significance in America. She continued to teach, first in Hollywood, and then in New York, well into her eighties. Many of her clients were movie stars, so she also initiated the long-term marriage of yoga and celebrity.

7. Published as *The Sufi Message of Hazrat Inayat Khan* in 14 volumes (1927).

8. *The New York World-Telegram*, 15 December 1931.

9. See Joseph Laycock, 'Yoga for the New Woman and the New Man: The Role of Pierre Bernard and Blanche DeVries in the Creation of Modern Postural Yoga', *Religion and American Culture: A Journal of Interpretation*, Vol. 23, No. 1 (Winter 2013).

10. Robert Love, *The Great Oom: The Improbable Birth of Yoga in America* (New York: Viking, 2010), p. 237.

11. For the full and very readable account, see *ibid*.

12. According to Ahmadi belief, Jesus' remains are buried in the Roza Bal shrine in downtown Srinagar, capital of Kashmir, where he is revered under the name Yuz Asaf.

13. STRONGMAN YOGA

1. K. V. Iyer, 'The Beauties of a Symmetrical body', *Vyayam, the Bodybuilder*, Vol. 1, No. 6 (1927), pp. 163–66.

2. Iyer, *Muscle Cult: A Pro-Em to My System* (Bangalore: Hercules Gymnasium and Correspondence School of Physical Culture, 1930), pp. 41–42.

3. Iyer, 'A Message to the Youth of My Country', *Vyayam, the Bodybuilder*, Vol. 1, No. 12 (1927), pp. 245–248.

4. Among various popular offshoots, the most extreme example is probably the Rocket Yoga system developed in 1980s San Francisco by Larry Schultz, one of Jois' long-time students who set up his own shop by rearranging and speeding up his teacher's routines. All such innovations show the influence of modern Western gymnastics.

5. In a letter written to *Yoga Journal* in 1995, Jois denounced Power Yoga as 'ignorant bodybuilding'. The origin of 'power yoga' is probably more correctly attributed to Walt Baptiste; it was developed into a brand by his son Baron Baptiste and Bryan Kest, two yoga teachers who themselves coined the phrase for their type of aerobically vigorous practice.

6. *The Economist*, 4 June 2009.

7. See for example: Mark Singleton and Jean Byrne's introduction in Byrne and Singleton (eds), *Yoga in the Modern World: Contemporary Perspectives* (London: Routledge, 2008); Janni Mikkonen, Palle Pederson and Peter William McCarthy, 'A Survey of Musculoskeletal Injury among Ashtanga Yoga Practitioners', *International Journal of Yoga Therapy*, 18: 1 (2008), pp. 59–64, and William Broad, *The Science of Yoga: The Risks and the Rewards* (New York: Simon and Schuster, 2012).

8. *CounterPunch*, 7 May 2013.

9. See *Elephant Journal*, 22 September 2009 and 4 January 2010 and *YogaDork*, 14 September 2009. Jivamukti markets itself as a highly ethical 'path to enlightenment through compassion' but has had a troubled history. In 2014, a top instructor, Dechen Thurman, the son of Tibetan Buddhist expert Robert Thurman and brother of movie star Uma, admitted to sleeping with many of his pupils. A 41-page report by Columbia media law professor Maria Sliwa detailed Thurman's bouts of crying, violent mood swings, threats of suicide and confessions of sex addiction. Thurman left the organisation. In 2016, another senior instructor, Ruth Lauer-Manenti had $1.6 million sexual harassment lawsuit brought against her by a female student, and left New York when Jivamukti settled out of court.

14. THE MYSORE PALACE MASALA

1. B. K. S. Iyengar, *Astadala Yogamala*, Vol. 1 (New Delhi: Allied Publishers, 2012), pp. 51–52.

2. See *Namarupa, Categories of Indian Thought*, 19 (2014), p. 11.

3. *Yoga Sutra* 3.7.

4. The first scholar to point to this connection was Norman Sjoman, a Canadian yoga student and author of *The Yoga Tradition of the Mysore Palace* (New Delhi: Abhinav

Publications, 1999). Another leading academic commentator who has done ground-breaking work on the role the Mysore gymnasium played in the genesis of postural practice is Mark Singleton, especially in his *Yoga Body: The Origins of Modern Posture Practice* (New York: Oxford University Press, 2010). Singleton sees the Mysore Maharaja as the crucial link in the creation of modern body-yoga. This story is also told, in simpler and less detailed form, in Jan Schmidt-Garre's film *Breath of the Gods*: http://www.yogamatters.com/breath-of-the-gods-a-journey-to-the-origins-of.html.

5. Mark Singleton interview with Anant Rao in *Yoga Body* (2010), p. 194.

6. A. V. Balasubramaniam in the film documentary produced by Gita Desai and Mukesh Desai, *Yoga Unveiled: the Evolution and Essence of a Spiritual Tradition* (2004).

7. To this day it is not uncommon to find *pandits* who recite the Veda, but do not know the meaning of what they are reciting. This may seem strange to us moderns who put such a high premium on literacy, but the job of the oral expert is first and foremost to transmit the sacred sounds impeccably and without variation. The subtle physics of vibration are believed to do the rest; any conceptual meaning is very much a secondary affair.

8. *Asian Medicine: Tradition and Modernity*, 3: 1 (2007), p. 177.

9. Mark Singleton, *Yoga Body*, p. 200.

10. *Ibid.*, p. 186.

11. *Ibid.*, p. 177.

12. See *Roots of Yoga*, a new sourcebook of primary yoga texts from the Indian traditions from c. 500 BC to AD 1750, compiled by Mark Singleton and James Mallinson (London: Penguin, 2017).

13. For one account, see David Gordon White's *The Yoga Sutra of Patanjali: A Biography* (Princeton: Princeton University Press, 2008), Chapter 12.

15. ENTER THE LION KING

1. B. K. S. Iyengar, *Light on Life: The Yoga Journey to Wholeness, Inner Peace and Ultimate Freedom* (Basingstoke: Rodale, 2008), p. xvii.

2. *Ibid.*, p. xix.

3. *Ibid.*

4. For examples, see: https://iynaus.org/research/research.

5. 'India yoga guru BKS Iyengar dies', BBC News, 20 August 2014.

6. Though the perfection of physical practice was always the Iyengar way, the anthology *Iyengar: The Yoga Master*, edited by Kofi Busia (Boston, MA: Shambhala, 2013), contains essays, such as Godfrey Devereux's 'The Secret Gift of the Bandhas' which illustrate the subtle depths such practice can reach. Whilst Iyengar yoga superficially appears always technical and gymnastic, and is often criticised as such by other systems, properly understood and practised it is not as constrained as some of its critics have made out.

7. By the nineteenth century, Indian classical music had, much like yoga, fallen into disrespect amongst the country's Raj-educated intelligentsia. The colonists disliked and discouraged what sounded bizarre and discordant to the unschooled Western ear. Part

of their disapproval stemmed from its social setting, as ever since Mughal times musicians had been associated with the native bazaars where they often performed in sumptuous brothels surrounded by *nautch* girls. It was only with the Hindu Renaissance and the work of cultural reclamation carried out by the likes of Swami Vivekananda that music, like yoga, began to be acknowledged by westernised Indians as part of their ancient and pre-colonial heritage, and therefore something they should pay more serious attention to.

8. Ellen Barry, 'B. K. S. Iyengar, Who Helped Bring Yoga to the West, Dies at 95', *The New York Times*, 20 August 2014.
9. See Iyengar's final interview: https://www.youtube.com/watch?v=QOBdVK9_UO4.
10. Silvia Prescott, 'My guru, the yoga teacher' *The Guardian*, 22 August 2014.

16. A WOMAN'S WORK

1. Weightier options include: *Asana, International Yoga Journal* (general); *The International Journal of Yoga Therapy* (medical); *Sutra Journal* (online, for the serious/academic student); *Namarupa* (Indo-cultural) and *Journal of Yoga Studies*, an open-access academic e-journal. The most comprehensive online forum is: http://www.modernyogaresearch.org/. Other specialist sites include: http://hyp.soas.ac.uk; http://theluminescent.blogspot.it/ and http://www.ayuryog.org
2. Sri Ramana Maharshi, *Talks with Sri Ramana Maharshi 1935–1939* (Tiruvannamalai: Sri Ramanasramam, 1955), p. 21.
3. Originally a male preserve, cheerleading was taken over by women in the 1940s, when collegiate men were being drafted for World War II.
4. Jack Kennedy, 'The Soft American', *Sports Illustrated*, 26 December 1960.
5. As predicted by the leading company Zion Market Research, https://www.globenewswire.com/news-release/2016/10/26/882889/0/en/Anti-Aging-Market-Set-for-Rapid-Growth-to-Reach-216-52-Billion-Globally-by-2021-Zion-Market-Research.html
6. 'The First Lady of Yoga' interview by Alexandra Jacobs in *The New York Times*, 5 April 2013.

17. PIONEERING *YOGINIS*

1. For more on Indra Devi see Michelle Goldberg, *The Goddess Pose* (New York: Vintage, 2015).
2. Sharon Gannon, *Yoga and Vegetarianism: The Diet of Enlightenment* (San Rafael: Mandala Publishing, 2008).

18. LORD SHIVA SHAKES HIS TRIDENT

1. *Atma bodhi* is one of the few original compositions reliably attributed to the great Vedantin.
2. From Yogananda's best-selling *Autobiography of a Yogi* (London: Rider & Co., 1949), pp. 248, 374.

3. Swami Yogananda, *General Principles and Merits of Yogoda or Tissue-Will System of Body and Mind Perfection, Originated and Taught by Swami Yogananda* (Los Angeles: Sat-Sanga & Yogoda Headquarters, 1925).

4. For example, the *Los Angeles Post* of 28 January 1925, tells us that 'concentration was his subject, demonstrated by physical control over the principal muscles'.

5. Yogananda, *Autobiography of a Yogi* (London: Rider & Co., 1949), p. 204.

6. As stated in 'The Aims and Ideals of the Self-Realization Fellowship'. See: http://www.yogananda-srf.org

7. Paramahansa Yogananda, *The Second Coming of Christ: The Resurrection of the Christ Within You* (Vols 1 and 2, 2008), p. xxi. See also *Revelations of Christ* (2010) and *The Yoga of Jesus: Understanding the Hidden Teachings of the Gospels* (2007).

8. The message has reincarnated in many successful New Age teachings and publications, such as Deepak Chopra's *The Seven Laws of Spiritual Success*. An indication of its enduring popularity can be seen by the extraordinary number of self-help books that contain the word 'Power' in their titles. Significantly, both the 1930s and today are times of economic and political uncertainty, accompanied by a feeling of powerlessness in the face of implacable global currents.

9. This is according to an eyewitness, Daya Mata, a close disciple who was to head the Self-Realization Fellowship from 1955–2010. See her article: 'My Spirit Shall Live On: The Final Days of Paramahansa Yogananda', *Self-Realization Magazine* (Spring 2002).

10. Harry T. Rowe, Los Angeles Mortuary Director of the Forest Lawn Memorial Park Cemetery in Glendale, California as reported in *Time Magazine* on 4 August 1952.

11. *Yoga Sutra* 4, particularly *sutras* 8–11 and 27–30.

12. Maharishi Mahesh Yogi, *Maharishi Mahesh Yogi on the Bhagavad Gita: A new translation and commentary with Sanskrit text: Chapters 1–6* (London: Penguin, 1967).

13. This is not to suggest that all *kayasthas* have followed such careers in modern times, of course, any more than all *brahmins* are necessarily priests. Nonetheless, the coincidence is significant; Sri Aurobindo was also a *kayastha*.

14. The Kumbh Mela, which in 2013 drew an estimated 120 million pilgrims over two weeks.

15. From a talk given to an audience of meditators in Hochgurgl, Austria, August 1962. Romy Jacobs Archive, in author's personal collection.

19. LOTUS POSTURES, LOTUS EATERS

1. See *The Telegraph*, 12 December 2012. At the Concert for Bangladesh in 1971, Shankar had to point out to his ingenue audience that they didn't need to applaud his lengthy tuning up of the sitar: 'If you appreciate the tuning so much, I hope you will enjoy the playing more'.

2. So powerful is the mythology surrounding those heady years that it is easy to forget the localised and relatively privileged nature of this 'revolution'. All through the Summer of Love, US Airforce b-52s were dropping 800 tons of bombs a day on North

Vietnam; Mao Tse Tung had his country by the throat in a revolution that was eventually to cost perhaps 40 million lives, and the Igbo people of Biafra were either being massacred or starved to death in the Nigerian Civil War.

3. For more details, see Philip Goldberg, *American Veda* (New York: Doubleday, 2010) and Lola Williamson, *Transcendent in America* (New York: New York University Press, 2010).
4. Talk given to an international meditation course in Livigno, 20 June 1970. Author's personal collection.
5. *Bhagavad Gita* 2.50: *yogah karmasu kaushalam.*
6. Richard Hittleman, *Yoga for Health* (New York: Random House, 2013), p.18.
7. The name changed in 1969 to The Western Yoga Federation, which was registered as a charity in 1973, and then was finalised as the The British Wheel of Yoga the next year.

20. *FAKIRS* AND FAKERS

1. Quoted by Maureen Seaberg in 'Can Meditation Cure Disease?', *The Daily Beast*, 25 December 2010 and in *Huffpost* 6 December 2017.
2. See, for example, James Mallinson, *The Khecarividya of Adinatha* (London: Routledge, 2007).
3. https://www.drdo.gov.in/drdo/labs1/DIPAS/English/indexnew.jsp?pg=about-lab.jsp

21. SOME LIKE IT HOT

1. The phenomenon may be physical as well as symbolic. For an interesting approach to depression as a symptom of inflammation of the nervous system, see Edward Bullmore's *The Inflamed Mind: A Radical New Approach to Depression* (New York: Macmillan, 2018).
2. This essential disjunction is spelled out clearly in Kapila's *Sankya Sutra*, from which Patanjali's teaching derives: 'Nor does the bondage of the soul arise from its being conditioned by its standing among circumstances that clog it by limiting it; because that is the fact in regard not to the soul, but to the body. Because this soul (*purusha*) is unassociated with any conditions or circumstances that could serve to bind it, it is absolute… This so-called bondage of the soul is merely verbal, and not a reality; since it resides in the mind, and not in the soul itself' (1.14–15 and 58).
3. *Yoga Sutra* 1.2–4; 1.12; 1.15–16.
4. *Bhagavad Gita* 6.33–36; 13.8; 18.52.
5. Quoted in Benjamin Lorr, *Hell-Bent: Obsession, Pain, and the Search for Something Like Transcendence in Competitive Yoga* (New York: St Martin's Press, 2014): http://www.benjaminlorr.net/characters/
6. *The Daily Telegraph*, 28 January 2013.
7. Richard Godwin, 'He said he could do what he wanted: the scandal that rocked Bikram Yoga', *The Guardian*, 18 February 2017, quoting Benjamin Lorr, *Hell-Bent.*
8. Clancy Martin, 'The Overheated, Oversexed Cult of Bikram Choudhury', *GQ*, February 2011.

9. Ben Wallace, 'Bikram Feels the Heat', *Vanity Fair*, January 2014.

10. https://www.law360.com/articles/750844/yogi-must-pay-atty-6–4m-punitive-award-in-harassment-case

22. RISKS AND REGULATION

1. Marc Campo, Mariya P. Shiyko, Mary Beth Kean, Lynne Roberts, Evangelos Pappas, 'Musculoskeletal pain associated with recreational yoga participation: A prospective cohort study with 1-year follow-up', *Journal of Bodywork and Movement Therapies*, 22: 2 (April 2018), pp. 418–423.

2. An example of this would be the renowned teacher and author Donna Farhi.

3. *Yoga Sutra* 2.46–47.

4. *The New York Times*, 12 February 2012.

5. *Ibid*.

6. Swami Gitananda Giri, 'Real Yoga is as Safe as Mother's Milk', *Yoga Life*, 28: 12 (December 1997), pp. 3–12.

7. Beth Spindler, *Yoga International* (October 2015).

8. *Brihadaranyaka Upanishad* 3.6.1.

9. https://www.bwy.org.uk/

10. There is a parallel here between yoga and Ayurveda. Although the majority of Indian Ayurvedic practitioners perceive the impact of British colonial rule negatively, they have followed Western methods and frameworks to revive the discipline. Thus Ayurvedic praxis has moved out of the traditional *guru-shishya* apprenticeship and into the formal education system. To its critics, this formalisation has actually created an avenue for Ayurvedic graduates to practise backdoor allopathic medicine, because modern-day *vaidyas* tend to perceive their training from an allopathic perspective. Ayurveda has then been further emasculated by its branding as a cosmetic wellness therapy, rather than its traditional role in establishing a healthy lifestyle to prevent disease occurring, and only as a last resort, to prescribe a remedy if it does. This marketing exercise encourages relatively wealthy consumers to buy an ayurvedic package as a detox strategy or even a 'pampering' regime, without really engaging with the deeper levels of the praxis.

11. This does not mean that yoga cannot be studied as an academic subject, of course. Since 2013, Loyola Marymount University in Los Angeles has been offering a two-year Master's degree in 'Yoga Studies', while the School of Oriental and African Studies in London offers a one-year MA in 'Traditions of Yoga and Meditation' under the supervision of James Mallinson.

12. To follow the argument, see for example: http://www.keepyogafree.co.uk/articles_files/Are-the-british-wheel-of-yoga-qualified.html; http://www.skillsactive.com/faqs

13. Swami Ambikananda Saraswati, 'Selling yoga back to its teachers is pure neo-colonialism', *The Guardian*, 26 October 2016.

14. Francesca Marshall, 'Yoga wars as heads of British ruling body quit in protest of "interfering trustees"', *The Telegraph*, 3 May 2018.

23. SCIENCE, SPIRIT AND STRESS RELIEF

1. See: http://theyogainstitute.org
2. See Shri Yogendra, *Paramahansa ni Prasad* (1917).
3. It was only on his return to India that he took the name Yogendra; previous to that he had been known as Yogananda, but to avoid confusion with Paramahansa Yogananda, who had set up home in America in 1923, he decided to change his name.
4. For some recent research on yoga as treatment for depression, for example, see findings from studies presented at the 125th Annual Convention of the American Psychological Association: https://www.apa.org/news/press/releases/2017/08/yoga-depression
5. Maharishi Mahesh Yogi, *Thirty Years Around the World, Dawn of the Age of Enlightenment*, Vol. 1 (1957–64) (Seelisburg: MVU Press, 1986), p. 242.
6. April 1960 transcript taken from *Maharishi's Message* (Washington D.C.: Age of Enlightenment Publications, 1989), p. 6.
7. An early best-seller on TM was Jhan Robbins, *Tranquility without Pills* (New York: Bantam, 1973).
8. Talk given in Guildhall, Cambridge, 11 July 1960. Maharishi Mahesh Yogi, 'Deep Meditation', World Pacific Records (1962).
9. Lecture given in Shankaracharya Nagar, Rishikesh, February 1967. Romy Jacob Archive in author's personal collection.
10. 'How Meditation May Help People With HIV', *Time Magazine*, 30 October 2014. Also see, Sumedha Chhatre et al., 'Effects of Behavioural Stress Reduction: Transcendental Meditation Intervention in Persons with HIV', *AIDS Care*, 25:10 (2013), pp. 1291–97.
11. See Roger Chalmers, 'Summary of Scientific Research on Maharishi's Transcendental Meditation and TM-Sidhi Programme', 16 April 2014. Retrieved from: https://uk.tm.org/documents/12132/2642888/TM+Research+Summary+-+Chalmers+16+April+2014.pdf/ea9f914b-6a4f-4a26-b754-ef19d1e2e36e
12. Richard P. Feynman, 'Cargo Cult Science', Commencement Address at California Institute of Technology, June 1974. Retrieved from: http://calteches.library.caltech.edu/51/2/CargoCult.pdf
13. For differing perspectives, see for example Thomas A. Forsthoefel and Cynthia Ann Hulmes (eds), *Gurus in America* (Albany: State University of New York Press, 2005), compared with David W. Orme Johnson's research on TM: http://www.truth-abouttm.org/truth/TMResearch/index.cfm. On science and spirituality, see Rupert Sheldrake, *Science and Spiritual Practices: Reconnecting through Direct Experience* (London: Coronet, 2018).
14. See *Yoga Sutra* 3.37 and 3.43.
15. Patanjali does not specifically speak of 'levitation' quite as we would understand the term. In his *Yoga Sutra* he talks of 'moving the body upward, so as to avoid contact with such things as water, mud and thorns' (3.39) and then 'moving through the air at will' (3.42). The latter appears to correspond to 'yogic flying'. The sixth book of

the important Vedantic text *Yoga Vasishtha*, entitled *Nirvana prakaranam*, 'The Exposition of Spiritual Liberation', has many verses that detail the stages of lifting up the body and moving it around through mental intention, and the effects of practising this *siddhi*.

16. This ancient Hindu royal custom, called *tuladhana*, was revived by the Mughal emperor Jahangir. He had it performed twice annually, on the first day of both the solar and lunar years, and the coins would be distributed to the poor and needy.

17. *Knight Ridder Tribune Business News*, 13 November 2005.

18. *Hindustan Times*, 11 and 12 February 2008.

19. 'Psychological Impacts of Male Circumcision', *CIRP*: http://www.cirp.org/library/psych/

20. See Rachel Yehuda, 'Cultural Trauma and Epigenetic Inheritance', *Development and Psychopathy*, 30: 5 (2018), pp. 1763–1777; Weaver et al., 'Epigenetic programming by maternal behaviour', *Nature Neuroscience* 7 (2004), pp. 847–854; and McGowan et al., 'Epigenetic regulation of the glucocorticoid receptor in human brain associates with childhood abuse', *Nature Neuroscience* 12: 3 (2009), pp. 342–348.

21. Commentary on the *Chandogya Upanishad* 8.1.1.

24. FOUR TYPES OF MIND-YOGA

1. For a good discussion on the current scientific research into body-yoga see *Namarupa*, 23 (August 2017).

2. See also the work of David Orme Johnson, based at Maharishi University of Management, Iowa. Some recent research on the physiology of different types of meditation can be seen in the following articles: B. R. Cahn and J. Polich, 'Meditation states and traits: EEG, ERP, and neuroimaging studies', *Psychological Bulletin of the American Psychological Association* (2006); B. R. Cahn, A. Delorme and J. Polich, 'Occipital gamma activation during Vipassana meditation', *Cognitive Processes* (2010); R. Brook et al., 'Beyond medications and diet: alternative approaches to lowering blood pressure', *Hypertension: Journal of the American Heart Association* (2013); D. W. Orme-Johnson and K. Walton, 'All approaches of preventing or reversing effects of stress are not the same', *American Journal of Health Promotion* (1998); M. Richard, A. Lutz and J. R. T. Davidson, 'Mind of the meditator', *Scientific American* (2014); and F. Travis and J. Shear, 'Focused attention, open monitoring, and automatic self-transcending: Categories to organize meditations from Vedic, Buddhist and Chinese traditions', *Consciousness and Cognition* (2010).

3. 'The Neuroscience of Meditation', *Scientific American*, Vol. 311, Issue 5 (November 2014).

4. This is why the opening verse of the *Isha Upanishad* counsels us, paradoxically, to 'enjoy renunciation' (*tena tyaktena bhunjitha*).

5. https://www.ncbi.nlm.nih.gov/pmc/articles/PMC4636982/

6. See H. Beneviste et al., 'The Glymphatic System and Waste Clearance with Brain Aging: A Review', *Gerontology* 65 (2019), pp. 106–119.

7. The full process is summarised by Patanjali's opening verses: *Yoga Sutra* 1.2–4. See also *Yoga Sutra* 3.49 and 3.55.

8. See Swami Satyananda Saraswati, *Yoga Nidra* (Bangalore: Nesma Books, 2003). For research on the psychological effects of *yoga nidra* see, for example, Richard Miller, 'Welcoming All That Is: Yoga Nidra and the Play of Opposites in Psychotherapy' in John J. Prendergast, Peter Fenner and Sheila Krystal (eds), *The Sacred Mirror: Nondual Wisdom & Psychotherapy* (St. Paul, MN: Omega Books, 2003).

9. As mentioned in *Yoga Sutra* 1.38.

10. Compare *Yoga Sutra* 4.17–19 with Augustine's *Confessions*, Book 7, Chapters 10 and 11. For Augustine, the inner light illumined the mind 'when it proclaimed for certain that what was immutable was better than that which was not', and thanks to its illumination, his mind 'had come to know the Immutable itself'. Augustine thus sees the light that casts its rays over his mind as the ground and source of an *a priori* experience of the Divine, as the yogi realises the light of consciousness comes from the universal *purusha*, not the individual mind.

11. This transcendental awareness beyond the trio of waking, dreaming and deep sleep is the 'fourth' (*turiya*) described in the *Mandukya Upanishad* 6–8.

25. MINDFULNESS À LA MODE

1. The Pali scripture *Kayagatasati Sutta*, 'Mindfulness Immersed in the Body'.

2. See Barbara Ehrenreich, *Natural Causes: An Epidemic of Wellness, the Certainty of Dying, and Killing Ourselves to Live* (New York: Hachette, 2018).

3. The reign of quantity is unstoppable. Chopra's latest online venture is the Jiyo wellness app, which he hopes will extend the reach of his ideas to more than a billion customers. Another rising electronic guru is Michael Acton Smith, whose Calm app has nearly a million people paying the $60-a-year subscription for daily guided meditations, delivered via smartphones. The company has just raised $27m (£20.7m) from backers, a cash injection that pushed Calm's value to $250m.

4. A University of Coventry team recently found evidence that a variety of mind-body interventions—including meditation, yoga and tai chi—can affect the DNA. Data from eighteen studies with 846 participants revealed a pattern of molecular changes that benefit both mental and physical health. The key was a gene-regulating stress molecule called nuclear factor kappa B (NF-kB). See, Ivana Buric, Miguel Farias, Jonathan Jong, Christopher Mee and Inti A. Brazil, 'What Is the Molecular Signature of Mind–Body Interventions? A Systematic Review of Gene Expression Changes Induced by Meditation and Related Practices', *Frontiers in Immunology* (2017).

5. See Nicholas T. Van Dam et al., 'Mind the Hype: A Critical Evaluation and Prescriptive Agenda for Research on Mindfulness and Meditation', *Perspectives on Psychological Science*, 13: 1, pp. 36–61; Richard J. Davidson and Cortland J. Dahl, 'Outstanding Challenges in Scientific Research on Mindfulness and Meditation', *Perspectives on Psychological Science*, 13: 1, pp. 62–65; Matthew Abrahams, 'Bad Science', *Tricycle* 28: 2 (Winter 2018).

6. See Miguel Farias and Catherine Wikholm, *The Buddha Pill: Can Meditation Change You?* (London: Watkins Publishing, 2015).
7. Dawn Foster, 'Is Mindfulness Making us Ill?', *The Guardian*, 23 January 2016.
8. See the study published in *Frontiers of Psychology*, January 2017, https://www.brown.edu/news/2017-04-20/meditation and https://www.frontiersin.org/articles/10.3389/fpsyg.2017.00551/full.

26. YOGA SHMOGA

1. For details, see Chapter 12 of Georg Feuerstein, *The Deeper Dimension of Yoga* (Boulder, CO: Shambhala, 2003).
2. *Yoga Journal*, May 2015.
3. As reported in *Daily Mail*, 22 February 2013.
4. *Yoga Sutra* 4.1.
5. See: www.omyogashow.com
6. *Ecologist*, 28 February 2012.
7. Alexander Lipski (ed. Joseph A. Fitzgerald), *The Essential Sri Anandamayi Ma: Life and Teachings of a 20ᵗʰ Century Indian Saint* (Bloomington: World Wisdom, 2007), p. 100.

27. TROUBLE IN PARADISE

1. See Stefanie Syman, 'How Yoga Sold Out', *Wall Street Journal*, 26 September 2010.
2. Survey data collected by Ipsos Public Affairs on behalf of *Yoga Journal* and Yoga Alliance, the main US organising body.
3. The complexities of the situation are addressed by Sarah Caldwell in 'The Heart of the Secret: A Personal and Scholarly Encounter with Shakta Tantrism in Siddha Yoga', *Nova Religio: The Journal of Alternative and Emergent Religions*, Vol. 5, No. 1 (2001), pp. 9–51.
4. '$1.9 Million Awarded In Swami Sexual Case', *The New York Times*, 6 September 1997.
5. Kausthub Desikachar, 10 October 2014: http://kausthub.com/legalclosure. After issuing public apologies and taking a year off 'to look deeply into my patterns and myself', Desikachar returned to teaching in October 2014. In the meantime, the authorities in Austria, where the offences were alleged to have taken place, dropped all the charges against him.
6. See the Netflix documentary *Wild, Wild Country* (2018).
7. Mary Finnigan and Rob Hogendoorn, *Sex and Violence in Tibetan Buddhism: The Rise and Fall of Sogyal Rinpoche* (Portland: Jorvik Press, 2019).
8. See William J. Broad, 'Yoga and Scandals: No Surprise Here', *The New York Times*, 27 February 2012.
9. A good survey of this subject is Georg Feuerstein, *Holy Madness: The Shock Tactics and Radical Teachings of Crazy-Wise Adepts, Holy Fools and Rascal Gurus* (New York: Paragon House, 1991).
10. *Yoga Sutra* 1.13.
11. William James, 'The Gifford Lectures', published as *The Varieties of Religious Experience* (1902) (Oxford: Oxford University Press, 2012), p. 32.

12. This critique applies not only to some current understandings of Hindu or Buddhist yoga, it is also relevant to such debased popularisations as Phillip Berg's 'California Kabbalah'.

13. See American Buddhist Stephen Batchelor's article, 'Why I Quit Guru Yoga', Tricycle (Winter 2017). See also the *Buddhist Project Sunshine* (Phase 3 Final Report), authored by former Shambhala member Andrea Winn and issued on 27 July 2018, for discussions of these issues in one branch of the Western Buddhist community.

14. See the excellent: *Teaching Yoga: Exploring the Teacher-Student Relationship* by Donna Farhi (Berkeley: Rodmell Press, 2006).

15. *Yoga Sutra* 2.33–34.

16. *Vasudhaiva kutumbakam*, see *Maha Upanishad* 6.72 and *Hitopadesha* 1.3.71.

17. See http://maclarenfoundation.net/context/schools/

18. For one such trenchant reassessment of spiritual structures, see Joel Kramer and Diana Alstad, *The Guru Papers: Masks of Authoritarian Power* (Berkeley: North Atlantic Books, 1993).

19. *Rig Veda* 10.32.13–14.

28. YOGA TO THE RESCUE?

1. *New England Journal of Medicine*, 377 (2017), pp. 13–27. Based on data from the most recent 'Global Burden of Disease' study.

2. NHS, 'Diabetes: cases and costs predicted to rise': https://www.nhs.uk/news/diabetes/diabetes-cases-and-costs-predicted-to-rise/

3. RCPCH, 'State of Child Health': https://www.rcpch.ac.uk/state-of-child-health

4. 'NHS prescribed record number of antidepressants last year', *British Medical Journal*, 364 (March 2019): https://www.bmj.com/content/364/bmj.l1508

5. Consumer Insights, Microsoft Canada, 'Microsoft Attention Spans Research Report', 2015: http://www.sparkler.co.uk/microsoftattention/microsoft-attention-report.pdf

6. Harvard School of Public Health, Obesity Prevention Source, 'Television Watching and "Sit Time"', December 2016: https://www.hsph.harvard.edu/obesity-prevention-source/obesity-causes/television-and-sedentary-behavior-and-obesity/

7. James Phillips, '"Electronic heroin": China's bootcamps get tough on internet addicts', *The Guardian*, 29 August 2017.

8. There is no mention of the pineal gland in any classical yogic, or tantric, text. It seems to have been incorporated into understandings of the *chakra* system by the Theosophists in the 1880s. In 1995, researchers at the University of Massachusetts Medical Center's Stress Reduction and Relaxation Program found that meditators had significantly higher melatonin levels than non-meditators.

9. UK Government report, *Why Sleep Matters: Quantifying the Economic Costs of Insufficient Sleep*: https://www.rand.org/randeurope/research/projects/the-value-of-the-sleep-economy.html

10. https://www.plasticsurgery.org/documents/News/Statistics/2017/plastic-sur-gery-statistics-full-report-2017.pdf

11. https://www.theguardian.com/society/2016/aug/22/

12. https://www.theguardian.com/society/2016/feb/16/children-in-england-rank-near-bottom-in-international-happiness-table

13. See Steffany Haaz Moonaz et al., 'Yoga in Sedentary Adults with Arthritis: Effects of a Randomized Controlled Pragmatic Trial', *Journal of Rheumatology*, 42: 7 (2015), pp. 1194–1202. See also: James A. Raub, 'Psychophysiologic Effects of Hatha Yoga on Musculoskeletal and Cardiopulmonary Function: A Literature Review', *The Journal of Alternative and Complementary Medicine* 8: 6 (2003), pp. 797–812.

14. See Rui F. Afonso et al., 'Greater Cortical Thickness in Elderly Female Yoga Practitioners—A Cross-Sectional Study', *Frontiers in Ageing Neuroscience* (June 2017).

15. See, for instance, H. Lavretsky et al., 'A pilot study of yogic meditation for family dementia caregivers with depressive symptoms: effects on mental health, cognition, and telomerase activity', *International Journal of Geriatric Psychiatry*, 28:1 (2013), pp. 57–65.

16. 'State of the UK Fitness Industry Report', 2019: https://www.forbes.com/sites/benmidgley/2018/09/26/the-six-reasons-the-fitness-industry-is-booming/#647d30a1506d

17. See Jeremy Carrette, *Selling Spirituality: The Silent Takeover of Religion* (Abingdon: Routledge, 2005) and Ronald Purser, *McMindfulness* (London: Repeater Books, 2019).

18. The *kundalini yoga* in question was brought to the West by the Sikh guru Yogi Bhajan in the 1960s. The system involves vigorous *asanas* and *pranayamas*, but what it has to do with a genuine tantric practice is unclear. Orthodox Sikhs have consistently distanced themselves from Yogi Bhajan, and there have been many questions about the teacher's probity over the years.

19. See: Elvira Perez et al., 'Kundalini Yoga as Mutual Recovery: a feasibility study including children in care and their carers', *Journal of Children's Services*, 11: 4, pp. 261–282.

20. See Magloria Borras-Boneu et al., 'Mild Cognitive Impairment: the Effect of Kirtan Kriya Meditation on Psychological and Cognitive Status', *The Journal of Alzheimer's Disease* 12: 7 (July 2016), p. 1001–1002.

21. Anyone doubting the wisdom of this caution should read *Kundalini: The Evolutionary Energy in Man* by Gopi Krishna (Boulder, CA: Shambhala, 1967), the autobiography of an unwitting recipient of the goddess' favours.

22. See cnbc.com: 'Hedge fund billionaire Ray Dalio: Meditation is "the single most important reason" for my success', 16 March 2018; 'How billionaire Ray Dalio used "mantra" meditation to come back from financial ruin', 1 July 2019; 'Billionaire Ray Dalio attributes his success to the Beatles and an Indian yogi', 27 August 2019.

23. https://www.bbc.com/news/magazine-24272978

29. FIFTY SHADES OF SAFFRON

1. Speech given at the United Nations General Assembly, 27 September 2014.
2. Maseeh Rahman, 'Indian prime minister claims genetic science existed in ancient times', *The Guardian*, 28 October 2014.
3. Gabriel Van Loon (ed.), *Charaka Samhita Handbook on Ayurveda*, Vol. I, Chapter 6, 'On Fertility' (Varanasi: Chaukambha Orientalia, 2003), p. 497.
4. Robert F. Worth, 'Is billionaire yogi Baba Ramdev India's answer to Donald Trump?' *The Times*, 18 August 2018.
5. 'India has been built by saints, yogis, fakirs: Ramdev', *Economic Times*, 29 March 2017.
6. See: https://infinityfoundation.com
7. Rajiv Malhotra, 'Is there an American caste system?', https://rajivmalhotra.com/library/articles/american-caste-system-2/
8. For an introduction to Frawley's work, see his *Gods, Sages and Kings: Vedic Secrets of Ancient Civilisation* (Delhi: Motilal Banarsidass, 1999).
9. Andrew Duffy, 'University of Ottawa students derided for cancelling yoga classes over fears of cultural appropriation', *National Post*, 22 November 2015.
10. Interview in *Namarupa* magazine, Issue 4, Fall 2005.

30. YOGA, RELIGION AND SPIRITUALITY

1. James Dunn, 'Yoga Leads to Satan Says Northern Ireland Priest', *The Independent*, 21 February 2015.
2. John Bingham, 'Rowan Williams: how Buddhism helps me pray', *Daily Telegraph*, 2 July 2014. For Williams on Christian meditation, see Santha Bhattacharji, Dominic Mattos and Rowan Williams (eds), *Prayer and Thought in Monastic Tradition: Essays in Honour of Benedicta Ward* (London: Bloomsbury, 2015).
3. *Proverbs* 8.
4. *Psalms* 46.10.
5. *Psalms* 37.7.
6. *Luke* 17.21.
7. *Luke* 21.31.
8. *Matthew* 6.6.
9. Taken from *The First Conference of Abbot Isaac on Prayer* (Chapter 35).
10. Stephen J. Patterson and James M. Robinson (trans.), 'The Gospel of Thomas', from the Gnostic Society Library: http://gnosis.org/naghamm/gth_pat_rob.htm
11. *Luke* 8.10.
12. *Matthew* 7.6.
13. *Mark* 4.33–34.
14. Chapter 1 of *The Mystical Theology and the Divine Name* (first century AD), trans. C. E. Rolt, (New York: Dover, 2004), p. 192.
15. *Isaiah* 35.8.
16. *Enneads* 6.9. Significantly, the goal of Patanjali's yoga is the state he calls *kaivalyam*, which means 'aloneness'.

17. Francisco de Osuna, *The Third Spiritual Alphabet*, trans. Mary E. Giles (Mahwah, NJ: Paulist Press, 2016), p. 31.

18. See: https://saccidanandaashramshantivanam.000webhostapp.com/?page_id=5

19. John Nicol Farquhar, *The Crown of Hinduism* (Oxford: Oxford University Press, 1913), p. 457.

20. Swami Abhishiktananda, *Guru and Disciple: an encounter with Sri Gnanananda giri, a contemporary spiritual master* (Delhi: The Abhishiktananda Centre for Interreligious Dialogue, 2014).

21. A letter to Marc Chaduc in James Stuart, *Swami Abhishiktananda: His Life Told through his Letters* (Delhi: ISPCK, 1989).

22. Antony Kalliath, *The Word in the Cave: The Experiential Journey of Swami Abhishiktānanda to the Point of Hindu-Christian Meeting* (New Delhi: Intercultural Publications, 1996), p. 253.

23. Cited in Harry Oldmeadow, *A Christian Pilgrim in India: The Spiritual Journey of Swami Abhishiktananda* (Bloomington, IN: World Wisdom, 2008), p. 142.

24. Diary entry dated 24 April 1972, *ibid.*

25. From a letter to Murray Rogers written in 1973, quoted in Harry Oldmeadow, *A Christian Pilgrim in India*, p.143.

26. See: www.johnmain.org. The Aramaic phrase *maranatha* can be translated as 'Come, O Lord'.

27. See: https://wisdomwayofknowing.org and Cynthia Bourgeault, *The Heart of Centering Prayer* (Boulder, CO: Shambhala, 2016).

28. For example, *Brihadaranyaka Upanishad*, 1.4.10: 'Now if a man worships another deity, thinking the deity is one and he another, he does not know'.

29. *Stephen Sedlock et al. v Timothy Baird et al.*, Court of Appeal Fourth Appellate District Division One State of California (2015).

30. Similarly, the British Wheel of Yoga is affiliated with the UK Sports Council. This is also an attempt to mollify the government—though in the UK, the presiding orthodoxy is secular rather than religious. In both cases, however, the deeper and more spiritual dimensions of yoga are effectively sidelined by state decree.

31. See Sheetal Shah, 'Yoga Is a Hindu Practice', *Huffington Post*, 15 March 2012.

32. Sui-Lee Wee and Elsie Chen, 'In a Chinese Village, Elderly Farmers are now Yogis', *The New York Times*, 24 June 2018.

33. *Yoga Sutra* 2.32.

34. *Yoga Sutra* 2.33.

35. *Yoga Sutra* 1.29.

36. *Yoga Sutra* 2.45.

37. *Yoga Sutra* 1.24.

38. *Yoga Sutra* 1.26.

INDEX

Abacus Wealth Partners, 320
Aberdeen, Scotland, 320
Abhishiktananda, Swami, 348–9, 356
absolute truth (*paramattha-sacca*), 276
Abu Zayd al-Sirafi, 63
Abu'l Fazl, 72
Academic Hinduphobia (Malhotra), 333
Acapulco, Mexico, 237
accomplished *asana* (*siddhasana*), 61
acrobatics, 101
Acroyoga, 286
Addams, Jane, 136
adhyatma sadhana, 337
Adinath, 59
Adishesha, 33
Adityanath Yogi, 336
Adult Education Centres, 215
advaita (non-dualism), 32, 38, 41, 43, 50, 60, 74
Advaita Vedanta, 21, 116, 130, 139, 213, 306, 348
Advanced Course in Yoga Philosophy and Oriental Occultism (Atkinson), 142
advanced spinal twist (*marichyasana*), 241
Adyar, 110, 111
aerial nervous system, 278
Aerial Yoga, 288
Aerobic Dance, 185
African Yoga Safari, 289
Afterlight 2, 315
Age of Kali, 199
Agni Yoga Series (Roerich), 115
Agni, 23
ahimsa, 95, 244
Ahmadis, 149, 372 n.12
Ahmedabad, 225
Aiback, Qutubuddin, 69, 70

AIDS (acquired immune deficiency syndrome), 255–6
Ajanta Caves, Maharashtra, 54
Akbar Nama (Abu'l Fazl), 72, 73
Akbar, Mughal Emperor, 72–3
akharas, 95, 98, 99, 100, 103
Alabama, United States, 234, 321
Albania, 314
Alberuni, 73
alchemy, 62, 91, 111, 112
alcohol, 84, 90, 278, 281, 288, 312, 330
Alcoholics Anonymous, 354
alcoholism, 278, 354
Alexander the Great, 55, 64, 361 n.18
Alexander, Betty June, 192
Ali, Cajzoran, 120
Ali, Muhammad, 154
Alipore, Calcutta, 133
All India Seminar, 347
All Saints Church, Bombay, 190
All-Indian Ayurveda Congress, 257
Allahabad, 73, 206, 336
Allinson, Catherine, 186
aloneness (*kaivalya*), 36, 38, 47, 50, 214, 356
Alter, Joseph, 98
Altogether Yoga, 292
Alzheimer's disease, 314, 317, 318, 319
Amazon, 62, 125, 177, 278
Ambaji, 225
Ambikananda, Swami, 248
ambrosia (*amrit*), 59
American Academy of Asian Studies, San Francisco, 123
American Academy of Facial Plastic and Reconstructive Surgeons, 315
American College of Sports Medicine, 241
American Dietetic Association, 227

387

INDEX

INDEX

asceticism, 22, 25, 45, 55–8, 87, 101, 103
  Akbar and, 72
  akharas, 95
  Bhagavad Gita on, 45
  Christian, 342, 345–6, 349
  hatha yoga, 55–8
  Iyengar and, 161, 170
  Jois and, 161
  Krishnamacharya and, 161
  Manek, 227
  Mataji, 225–7
  mortification of the flesh, 55, 87
  Naths, 59
  Sufis, 71
  tapas, 25, 55–6, 161
ashrams, 109
Ashtanga Yoga, 104, 155–7, 164, 182, 194, 242, 285, 291, 351
Ashtanga Yoga Research Institute, 155
Ashtavakra, 31
Ashutosh Maharaj, Shri, 221, 228
Asian Music Circle, 170
Asquith London, 291
Association of Yogic Studies, 285
Assoglioli, Robert, 303
asthma, 312, 313
astral body, 108, 113–14, 115, 117, 118
astrology, 19, 30, 91, 154
Asumah, Francesca, 237
Atharva Veda, 19, 22, 360 n.14
Atkinson, William Walker, 141–2, 151
Atkinson School of Mental Science, 142
Atlanta, Georgia, 253
Atlas, Charles, 152
attention deficit hyperactivity disorder (ADHD), 278, 313
attention economy, 314
attention span, 313, 314
Augustine, Saint, 271, 381 n.10
Aundh, 98
aural tradition, 15–16
Aurangzeb, Mughal Emperor, 70
Aurobindo Ghose, 123, 133–4, 172, 193, 376 n.13
Australia, 252, 286, 288, 297
Austria, 110–14
authority, 15, 16, 31, 300–301
Autobiography of a Yogi, The (Yogananda), 202

autosexuality, 77
Avalon, Arthur, 84
avidya, 350
Awakening of the Chakras and Emancipation (Motoyama), 125
Ayodhya, Uttar Pradesh, 336
Ayurveda, 5, 97, 231, 242, 257, 326, 327, 328, 378 n.10
AYUSH, 326

Babaji, 200
Babu Surdass, 109
Babur Nama, 73
Babur, Mughal Emperor, 69–70, 73
Bacon, Francis, 272, 336
Bahadur Shah, Mughal Emperor, 70
Bailey, Alice, 119, 122
Baker, Ora Ray, 147
Baker, Richard, 297
Balanced Living Yoga (Alexander), 192
balancing stick *asana* (*tuladandasana*), 351
Balathal, Rajasthan, 19
Baldwin, Alec, 77
Bali, Indonesia, 180, 289
ballet, 100
Baltimore, Maryland, 141
Baltimore News, The, 130, 136
Banaras, *see* Varanasi
Band of Hope, 90
bandhas, 3, 29, 30, 61
Bangalore, 151, 152, 153, 192, 347
Bangor University, 204, 209
Baptiste, Baron, 153, 373 n.5
Baptiste, Magana, 153
Baptiste, Sherri, 153
Baptiste, Walt, 153, 373 n.5
Barbarella, 185
Barbican, London, 171
Bardot, Brigitte, 185
Barker, Darren, 289
Barks, Coleman, 361 n.1
Barnum, Phineas Taylor, 102
Baroda, 133
Bartlett, Susan, 316
basij, 352
basti, 3
Batra, Dinanath, 334
Battle of Waterloo (1815), 185

INDEX

INDEX

body image, 315–16
Bodymind (Dychtwald), 124
Bogart, Jeff, 319
Bolan, Marc, 210
Bollywood, 66, 172, 234, 236
Bolsheviks, 190
Bombay Medical Union, 120, 229
Bombay Telegraph, 82–3
Bombay, 80, 87, 189–90, 251–2, 253, 325
Boon, Brooke, 287
Bordeaux, France, 102
Boston, Massachusetts, 130, 200
Bourgeault, Cynthia, 350
bow *asana* (*dhanurasana*), 351
boxing, 103, 114, 148, 154, 289
Boxing Yoga, 289
Boy Scout Movement, 332
Brahmachari, Dhirendra, 328–9
brahmacharya, 58, 97, 192, 295, 329
brahman, 27, 28
Brahmana, 28
brahmins, 15, 16, 20, 25, 46
Brahmo Samaj, 90, 92
brain, 279, 317–18
Brathen, Rachel, 178
Brazil, 252, 317
Breatharians, 223
Breathe app, 277
breathing exercises, *see* pranayama
Brennan, Barbara, 122
Brexit, 280
Bridges, Jeff, 232
Bridgewater Associates, 320
Brighton, Sussex, 320
Brihadaranyaka Upanishad, 26, 31, 58, 116, 246
Bristol, England, 90, 339
British Broadcasting Corporation (BBC), 171, 195, 322, 352
British East India Company, 64–5, 79–80, 83–4, 87, 101
British India (1612–1947), 15, 16, 64–5, 70, 79–88, 89–93
    Anglo-Maratha War, Second (1803–1805), 65
    body building in, 98–9
    civil disobedience movement (1930), 132
    Civil Service, 108, 133, 205
    Delhi made capital (1911), 200

East India Company, 64–5, 79–80, 83–4, 87, 101, 330
    English Education Act (1835), 81
    Hindu Renaissance, 89–93
    Independence (1947), 97, 171
    Independence Movement, 90, 91, 98, 99, 101, 108, 138, 146, 201, 252, 329
    Kalaripayattu in, 97
    Muscular Christianity in, 84–6
    Mysore, relations with, 159
    Sepoy Mutiny (1857), 70, 82–3, 84, 88, 101
    spermatorrhea in, 365 n.14
    sport in, 86–8, 98–101
    suttee, prohibition of, 90
    wrestling in, 98, 100–101
    YMCA in, 88, 98, 103–4, 152, 167
British Manly Exercises (Walker), 99
British Medical Journal, 241, 242
British Wheel of Yoga, 14, 177, 215–16, 246–9, 377 n.7, 386 n.30
Broad, William, 240, 297–8
Broga, 179, 287
Bronx, New York, 214
Brown University, 281
Bruckner, Anton, 110
Brunton, Paul, 361 n.17
Brussels, Belgium, 102
Budapest, 112
Buddha, 25, 139, 140, 259, 276
buddhi, 271, 315
Buddhism, 17, 29, 273–6
    asceticism, 45
    bindu, 57
    egotism and, 42
    Islamic invasion and, 66
    Mahayana, 265
    mindfulness, 273–6
    Mount Kailash, importance of, 163
    mudras, 55
    nirvana, 232, 275, 277, 363 n.12
    Olcott and, 109
    regal supplicants, 31
    rock-cut shrines, 31, 54
    Sankhya and, 38
    Satipatthana Sutta, 276
    siddhis, 37
    Tantric, 213
    Theravada, 123, 265, 274, 276

INDEX

INDEX

INDEX

INDEX

exorcism, 340
Experimental Physiology, 234
Expressionism, 75
extended side angle *asana* (*utthita parsvakona-sana*), 240
extra-terrestrials, 252

Fabian Society, 328
Fabiola, Queen consort of the Belgians, 170
Facebook, 180, 244, 286, 313
Faithfull, Marianne, 210
fakirs, 71, 101, 102, 228–9
Falun Gong, 354
Farias, Miguel, 281
Farmer, Sarah, 193
Farquhar, John Nicol, 348
Featherstone, Kay, 186
female saints, 58
ferocious *asana* (ugrasana), 61
Feuerstein, Georg, 360 n.6
Feynman, Richard, 256
Fierce Grace, 238
fight-or-flight response, 269, 278
Finland, 184, 229, 252
Finsbury Central, London, 252
fire-sacrifice ritual, 19–20, 25, 76, 95
First Apocalypse of James, 343
Five M's, 365 n.15
Five Pillars of Islam, 352
'Five-fold Footprint of the Guru, The', 119
Flow Yoga, 286
Flower Power, 75, 209
Focused Attention meditation, 266–7
Fonda, Jane, 124, 185–6, 215
Forest Lawn Memorial Park Cemetery, Glendale, 202
Forever Young, Forever Healthy (Devi), 192, 243
Forrest Yoga, 194
Foucault, Paul-Michel, 6
Fourteen Lessons in Yogi Philosophy (Ramacharaka), 190
fourth state of consciousness, 28
Fowler, Eileen, 194
Fox, Paul, 249
France, 63, 107, 121, 133, 252, 289, 305–6, 368 n.13
Francis, Pope, 339, 368 n.16
Franciscan Order, 350

Francisco de Osuna, 347
Franny and Zooey (Salinger), 135
Frawley, David, 334
de Frédy, Charles Pierre, Baron de Coubertin, 368 n.13
Freeman, Laurence, 349
Freemason's Hall, City of London, 79
Freemasonry, 110, 302
Freud, Sigmund, 110–11, 260
Friedel, Brad, 179
Friend, John, 297
Fulfilment Theology, 348
Fuller, Buckminster, 206
Further Shore, The (Griffiths), 349
Futuh-us-Salatin (Isami), 71
Futurism, 75

gada, 98
Gama the Great, 100
gaming addiction, 313
Gandhi, Indira, 222, 328
Gandhi, Mohandas Karamchand, 91, 98, 172, 328
    assassination (1948), 332, 336
    on *Bhagavad Gita*, 43, 44
    civil disobedience movement (1930), 132
    Guide to Health, 328
    Krishnaraja Wodeyar IV, relationship with, 160
    Maharishi's criticism of, 213
    swadeshi movement, 329
    Vivekananda, relationship with, 136
Gandhi, Sanjay, 222
Ganesha, 326
Ganga river, 73, 91
gangrene, 224
Gani, Doria, 292
Gannon, Sharon, 194
Garbo, Greta, 134, 147, 191
Garcia, Matt, 289
Gargi, 246
Garrison, Omar, 123
General Election (2015), 313
Generation Z, 260
Genghis Khan, 69
George V, King of the United Kingdom, 100, 151
Germany, 52, 61, 74, 111, 121, 122, 130

INDEX

INDEX

INDEX

INDEX

INDEX

INDEX

INDEX

INDEX

INDEX

INDEX

Palmer, Mary, 194
Paltrow, Gwyneth, 156, 233, 288
panchamakaras, 59, 365 n.15
Pancharatra yoga, 55
pandits, 72, 84, 182, 374 n.7
Panipati, Nizam al-Din, 74
Paradoxes of the Highest Science, The (Levi), 369
   n.1
Paramahamsa Sri Agamya Guru, 112
Paramahansa Sri Madhavadasji Maharaj, 251–2,
   243
paramattha-sacca, 276
parampara, 238
Parashuram, 96
parasympathetic nervous system, 278
Pariskshit, 31
Parker, Sean, 313
Parkinson's disease, 168, 314
pashu, 18
Pashupati, 18
Passage to India (Whitman), 132
Patanjala Yoga (Koelman), 341
Patanjali, 4, 6, 14, 33–42, 119
   Akbar and, 72
   Alberuni's translation, 73
   on *asanas*, 30, 35, 39, 239–40
   Besant's lectures on, 109
   Colebrooke on, 80
   Desikachar and, 165
   on Eight Limbs, 39, 51, 161, 270
   on freedom, 300
   Hittleman and, 214
   on *Ishvara-pranidhana*, 355–6
   Judge's translation, 109
   on *kaivalya*, 36, 38, 47, 214, 356
   Koelman's study of, 341
   Krishnamacharya and, 161, 162, 163
   Maharishi and, 205, 256
   on meditation, 36, 39, 265, 268, 270
   on negative attitudes, 306
   on non-violence (*ahimsa*), 95
   on 'Om' mantra, 265, 355
   on pain, 307
   on *pratyahara*, 268
   Sage's translation, 341
   on *samadhi*, 39, 40, 268, 355, 356
   on Sankhya, 29, 33, 37–8, 214, 249
   on *sanyama*, 117

   on *siddhis*, 36–7, 39, 256, 288, 379 n.15
   on *sva-rupa*, 270
   on *vairagya*, 232
   Vivekananda and, 34, 35, 131
   Wood's translation, 110
Patanjali (brand), 329, 330
Patiala, 100
Paul, Saint, 85
pavanmuktasana, 286
Peace Flag, 193
peacock (*mayurasana*), 31
peak stuff, 311, 318
Penguin, 333–4
Pennsylvania, United States, 296
Penthouse of the Gods (Bernard), 149
Perelman School of Medicine, 316–17
Perennial Philosophy, 52
Persia; Persian language, 70–74, 81, 90, 252,
   333, 346, 350, 361 n.1, 366 n.6
Peru, 314
Peterson, Eugenia Vassilievna, *see* Indra Devi
Phakyab Rinpoche, 223–5
Phenomenology of the Spirit (Hegel), 130
Philadelphia, Pennsylvania, 143
Philosophical Foundations of India, The (Bernard),
   149
Phoenix Trust, 321
photography, 76
Piccadilly Circus, London, 315
Pierre Health Studios, Manhattan, 149
Pilates, 182, 286
Pilot Baba, 222–3, 228
Pinch of Nom (Allinson and Featherstone), 186
pineal gland, 120, 314, 383 n.8
pingala, 59
Pinterest, 180
pitta, 231, 235
pituitary gland, 120, 259
plastic surgery, 315
Plato, 16, 108, 160
Plattsburgh, New York, 256
Plotinus, 49, 345
plough *asana* (*halasana*), 240
polygamy, 90
Pondicherry, 123, 133, 193, 244, 364 n.3
Portugal, 97
post-traumatic stress disorder (PTSD), 258, 278
postures, *see* asanas

INDEX

INDEX

INDEX

INDEX

INDEX

413

INDEX

INDEX

INDEX

INDEX

INDEX